Social Class and
Democratic Leadership

E. Digby Baltzell

Social Class and Democratic Leadership

Essays in Honor of
E. Digby Baltzell

Edited by Harold J. Bershady

upp

University of Pennsylvania Press
Philadelphia

Copyright © 1989 by the University of Pennsylvania Press
All rights reserved
Printed in the United States of America

Library of Congress Cataloging-in-Publication Data

Social class and democratic leadership : essays in honor of E. Digby
Baltzell / edited by Harold J. Bershady.
    p.   cm.
Includes bibliographies and index.
ISBN 0-8122-8158-6
    1. Social classes—United States.   2. Democracy.   3. Leadership.
4. Elite (Social sciences)—United States.   5. Baltzell, E. Digby
(Edward Digby), 1915–   .   I. Baltzell, E. Digby (Edward Digby),
1915–   .   II. Bershady, Harold J.
HN90.S6S54   1989
305.5′0973—dc20   89-4845
                                                                CIP

This book is presented to
E. DIGBY BALTZELL
by the contributors and the editor
with their affection and respect.

Contents

Preface

E. Digby Baltzell came of intellectual age during the Second World War when he encountered the social and political destruction brought about by totalitarian regimes. Democratic governments believed to be durable, and social freedoms upheld by these governments, were swiftly crushed. The feeble resistance of many nations to their conquerors implied that vanquished and victor alike held no great love for democracy and its freedoms. For Baltzell and others of his generation the experience was shocking. Totalitarianism was an immediate danger that had to be fought. But it was also feared that even after its defeat totalitarianism would remain a potential danger, not merely from foreign sources, but from weaknesses in the western democracies themselves. A chief concern for many of this generation of Americans at the conclusion of the war was to identify and correct these weaknesses.

Issues of discrimination were raised in novels and the mass media; higher education was rapidly expanded; Fulbright scholarships were introduced to educate Americans and Europeans to each other's ways; liberalizing movements in childrearing and education became widespread; civil rights legislation was enacted—these were among the public efforts made in the postwar years to strengthen American society. Research on religious, racial and ethnic prejudice; on the history, politics, sociology, and psychology of totalitarian societies; on demagogic leadership; on revolutionary movements; on "mass" societies; on personality dispositions toward totalitarian appeals, poured forth from universities after the Second World War. This type of research, of which this book is an example, continues to be done, although with different emphases.

Baltzell directed his efforts to understanding the wellsprings of American democracy, particularly democratic leadership. Of what does such leadership consist? What are its origins? How is it fostered? How may it be renewed? Sociology and history, the two disciplines he mastered to pursue these questions, became in his practice of them a unity, a single, many–faceted discipline whose illuminating power is far greater than either of its parts. In this he has followed the example of his famous intellectual forbears, Alexis de Tocqueville and Max Weber. Each of the contributors to this volume shares with Baltzell this multidisciplinary approach.

Another influence, not directly intellectual, has given Baltzell a perhaps unique perspective. He is the only American sociologist of the upper class whose interpretations of American society are informed by the presuppositions of his class. "Only a dead man," he is fond of saying, "is unbiased." Baltzell has been able to stand back from American democracy and be critical of many of its characteristics—its leadership, the quality of its culture, the status insecurities it breeds, and not least, the volatility of its politics. The combination of these several influences has enabled him to make an important contribution to the understanding of American democratic society and leadership.

The essays in this book reflect Baltzell's various interests. However, they also endeavor, in the spirit that animates his work, to rise above merely personal predilections and concentrate on clarifying aspects of one central problem: the nature of American democracy. This is not solely a historical, religious, political, sociological or economic subject. The many approaches taken, and the several aspects investigated by the contributors to this book, are a sign of the subject's complexity. However, this signifies something else about the subject: the pluralism of American society that, insofar as it is safeguarded, serves to protect Americans from the imposition of a single, uniform view. This attitude, in keeping with Baltzell's teachings, has also inspired the undertaking of this book.

The editor is indebted to many persons, not least are the contributors. Special thanks are due to Victor M. Lidz, whose counsel at each phase of this project was invaluable, and to my wife Suzanne who served as a source of intelligence and support throughout. The aid of Samuel Preston, Chairman of the Department of Sociology of the University of Pennsylvania, and Michael Aiken, Provost of the University of Pennsylvania, helped to make this book possible.

Harold J. Bershady

Harold J. Bershady

1. Introduction

Public leaders of integrity and talent have come from all walks of American life; so too have leaders who are corrupt. In these respects there is undeniable social equality in the United States. Yet, if strong democratic leaders are to work for the good of the community and nation, they must be both firm against shortsighted demands and impervious to greed. Huey Long, whose name for many was synonymous with venal leadership, was swept into office on a wave of populist fervor, and no doubt responded to pressing needs of his followers. But he was also self-serving, spent public monies on personal pleasures, secured political power by stifling opposition, and kept office by continually inflaming crude passions among the electorate. His leadership was demagogic rather than democratic. Such leaders crop up in American life; they cannot be prevented from arising. But how can opposition to them be safeguarded? Where are alternative leaders to be found?

These questions go to the heart of American democracy. In somewhat different language they were sharply raised, perhaps for the first time, over 150 years ago by Alexis de Tocqueville, in *Democracy in America*.[1] However, no sociologist other than E. Digby Baltzell has devoted an entire intellectual career to their exploration. Baltzell's contributions to our self-understanding are unique. Moreover, only one other sociologist of his generation, David Riesman, has been as deeply inspired by Tocqueville's views of American society. In *The Lonely Crowd*[2] Riesman examined the isolation and anxiety that had enveloped the "common man" in mid twentieth century. His book portrayed certain extreme consequences of social equality and individuality that Tocqueville had seen already operating in American life early in the nineteenth century. Baltzell drew from another side of Tocqueville's thesis and charted the political effects of equality upon the *uncommon* man, the leaders of society. The two sides are not the same, but they cannot be separated; whatever moves leaders, whether in outlook, integrity, or stability, will affect followers. However, because most of us are "common men and women," Riesman's work seemed to speak to the general American public and became popular.

Baltzell's first book, *Philadelphia Gentlemen*,[3] was published in the late 1950s. This was the first study of its kind, not a compendium of gossip, but a sociological and historical analysis of the origins and rise of the Philadelphia and of the American upper class. Baltzell's concerns in this book were to portray the composition and culture of the upper class and its distinctive contributions to the political life of the nation. He provided a fuller understanding of the actual nature of the American upper class than did the simplistic, often hostile, conceptions then prevalent in American social science. His study also corrected the fawning reportage on the social lives of the very wealthy that had been a genre of popular journalism for many years. Perhaps because the book went against popular sentiment and outlook (but also, surely, because of its title, which gave it a parochial ring), it was read by a limited audience, primarily Philadelphians and academics with related interests.

Baltzell's second book, *The Protestant Establishment*,[4] was published in 1964, a time in our recent history when many things inherent to leadership—authority and hierarchy in particular—were becoming suspect for growing numbers of people. Indeed, it is not exaggerating to say that among many intellectuals, radicals and non-radicals alike, "elite" and "leader" became, by the late 1960s and for several years thereafter, virtually synonymous with evil. Baltzell's book was sometimes taken merely as an expression by an insider of anti-establishment—therefore anti-authority and anti-elite—views. After all, how could the inventor of that derisive term "WASP" be a lover of the establishment? In fact, Baltzell was saying the opposite. He aimed in this book to reinvigorate a desiccated establishment, and the authority that establishment wielded, with new sources of vitality. Whether or not it was for the right reasons this book brought Baltzell moderate national attention. However, the counter-culture that soon flooded the nation and universities including professors as well as students, raised the idea of equality with new urgency, and threatened to swamp many conventional institutions along with their leaders. Against this anti-establishment deluge, Baltzell's investigations into the sources of strong democratic authority were almost lost from view. However, he had the intellectual courage to hold fast, largely single-handedly, to his course.

Although his books were not widely appreciated for many years, Baltzell remained one of the most provocative and esteemed professors for several generations of students at the University of Pennsylvania. Not only did he win teaching awards, but he is the kind of teacher whose influence is remembered and celebrated at class reunions. With the subsiding of the social storms of the 1960s and 1970s, his writings have begun to receive the recognition that has long been their due. His *Puritan Boston and Quaker Philadelphia*,[5] published in 1979 and dedicated in part to David Riesman, won the American Sociological Association's prestigious Sorokin Award for a distinguished contribution to the field. Now that the wind has shifted, we are better able to see the distance Baltzell has traveled. He has clarified not only the far-reaching differences in the ethos of these two cities, but also the contribution that each city has made to our distinctive, American brand of democracy. The forcefulness of his ideas and gracefulness of his style have taken him far into the American territory. He has found many things to show us.

*   *   *

Baltzell's lifelong thesis is that responsible leadership has been drawn disproportionately from the American upper class. In *Philadelphia Gentlemen* he charted the formation of a national upper class in the United States from the period following the Civil War to 1940. This class was made up of families whose members had become economic, political, and social leaders of their local communities. However, many of these prominent persons knew each other not only in professional or business dealings. They were also family men who belonged to the same churches, clubs, and civic organizations, lived in the same areas of town, educated their children in the same way, and vacationed in the same places. Given the frequency of their meetings, many of the children of these families intermarried. The upper class was thus formed over a few generations into a kind of confederation of family alliances, an extended kin group whose members knew one another, shared allegiances and outlook, and occupied high positions in the community.

Class and Culture

As business and political activities grew beyond the borders of local communities, so too did the network of upper class families. By the 1880s national preparatory schools such as Andover, Groton, and St. Paul's for boys, and Westover, Farmington, and St. Timothy's for girls, were established. Dozens of such schools, boarding as well as day, sprang up over the next few decades. However, education did not mean mere instruction in academic subjects. As the names of many of the schools testify, education was also one of Christian, predominantly Episcopalian, outlook. A moral education that emphasized service, propriety, and honesty was taught, and this was by far the most important of all the subjects to be learned. These were but an extension of values held dear in family and church. *The Rector of Justin* by Louis Auchincloss[6] is a fine portrait of this sort of moral education in a New England private school set in the early part of this century.

The growth of the preparatory schools in importance and number transformed them into a kind of "surrogate family," as Baltzell put it, which conferred status upon their members solely for having attended and belonged. In part, this implied a weakening of the families of origin of the upper class, an inability of these families, by means of inheritance of name alone, to impart social identity to their children. Individual achievement and selfhood are prized by Americans over inherited status. American life after the Civil War was also rapidly changing, becoming more centralized— organized into larger institutions. There was little recognition of local upper class families in national affairs. Moreover, the eager adoption of ever greater numbers of technological innovations spurred geographical and social mobility, promoted a wider range of occupational specialties, and carried the individualization of Americans to even further extremes. Thus, the national private preparatory schools not only complemented the local upper class family in preparing youth to acquire upper class status, but also served to extend the network of upper class kin-like relationships. To say that one was an "Andover man," for example, linked one with all other Andover men, wherever their actual families were, and became a badge of social class identity.

Much the same pattern obtained in higher education. Even before 1900, several private colleges and universities were identified with the upper class of their particular region. These institutions continued to promote the education in morals and morality fostered in the preparatory schools. As the nation developed and the upper class grew to national proportions, so did the prestige and prominence of the colleges attended by the children of the upper class. The "Ivy League" schools, along with certain smaller colleges such as Amherst and Williams, became leading national institutions of higher learning. Graduation from one of these schools gave one not only a certain cachet, but access to top business and professional firms, several of whose senior members were likely to have graduated from an Ivy League or similar school.

The Upper Class and Democratic Leadership

Inculcated with a culture of service, many members of the upper class sought stewardship of civic and political organizations in the larger community—city, state, and nation. Their leadership, in Baltzell's view, was significant in several respects for American democracy.

First, because many of the upper class were also rich, those who entered public life were less tempted to line their pockets at public expense. It was not that such leaders were less greedy, perhaps, but that they had less need of material gain.

Second, a leader from the upper class had a valued social identity independent of his position as a leader. He also had prominent family, church, friendship, school, and business or professional ties. There was a place in the society to which he could return when he stepped down from leadership (a more humane situation than the one in Soviet Russia, for example, where former leaders become nonentities and seem to disappear overnight). He thus had less need to cling to leadership as a primary source of recognition and acceptance.

Third, and most important, a leader from the upper class derived prestige from his class affiliation as well as from his position of leadership, however ambivalently he or others may at times have viewed that class background. Bolstered by independent wealth and a class identity that was secure and in the main socially supported, such a person could more freely propose new policies that he believed desirable, or challenge policies that he considered detrimental. Franklin D. Roosevelt is a clear instance of this upper class pattern of breeding and independence. Harvard University has at times showed a similar pattern as an institution. Patrician Harvard took the leading role among private universities in openly challenging Senator Joseph McCarthy and defending academic freedoms. This point is fundamental to Baltzell, for he sees a strong upper class as providing not only leadership, but a bulwark against possible domestic tyrannies.

The French Lesson

Baltzell's perspective is inspired in part by Tocqueville's analysis of the French Revolution.[7] The monarchy that rose to supreme power in France during the seventeenth and eighteenth centuries, Tocqueville observed, was central to the nation, but distant from each locality. Isolated from the people, the monarchy nevertheless placed the greatest burdens in services and taxes upon the poor. This occurred with diminishing opposition. The French aristocrats had formerly served as bastions of protection to each of the localities. Tied to serfs and commoners by duties of patronage, the aristocrats had been an integral part of the localities. But when their powers at court and in the royal administration had been weakened by the growth of the central bureaucracy, they began also to abandon their responsibilities. Over several generations the aristocracy enfeebled itself politically and socially, by exchanging local powers for material comforts and a place in the ceremonial and social life of the central court. Upon this leveling of French political life the monarchy could begin to assert its powers unchecked: it could administer a system of justice and execute laws without heeding local needs (to which it was, in any case, oblivious). Monarchic rule grew ever more arbitrary and despotic, and sowed the seeds of its eventual violent overthrow.

Social and political equality, perhaps not fully achievable, would resemble for Baltzell the condition of leveling that let loose the powers of the French monarchy. That condition would be the antithesis of democratic freedoms. Indeed, any society that attempts to eliminate social and political distinctions and reduce its citizens to a uniform mass becomes fertile ground for the growth of tyrannical rulers or worse. During Hitler's rule Germany was made into such a mass society from which no legitimate opposition to the Nazis could arise. There is no hereditary aristocracy in the United States, but the leadership of upper class men and women of talent and wealth, secure in their status and holding themselves responsible for serving the larger society, has been vital, in Baltzell's view, to sustaining political democracy. This point derives essentially from Tocqueville's argument updated and transplanted to American shores.

The Rise and Decline of the WASPs

However, the American upper class is in danger, Baltzell suggests, of becoming enfeebled. In *The Protestant Establishment* Baltzell described processes that had begun to isolate the upper class, not long after its formation, from the larger society. Cultural decay in the form of snobbishness set in. A love of pomp and material success turned the upper class from leadership of their communities to protection of their advantages, thus compromising their commitment to the values of achievement. The massive eastern and southern European migrations of the late nineteenth and early twentieth centuries were greeted by the upper class with alarmed, even if politely expressed, anti-ethnic and anti-Semitic responses. Entry to upper class ranks—whether through marriage, schools, business, professions, or clubs—became restricted mainly to purebred white, Anglo-Saxon Protestants—WASPs, as Baltzell was the first to call them. Between 1880 and 1940 the American upper class closed ranks and became more of a caste than a class.

In turning in upon itself, Baltzell warned, the American upper class has taken a path which, if continued, would lead to an end similar to that reached by the French aristocracy during the ancien régime: its political and social contributions, too, would diminish and eventually cease. However, the Second World War brought a change. Many of the barriers erected by the Protestant establishment were struck down. Revulsion grew against native prejudice that seemed to echo the foreign doctrines against which American soldiers had fought and died. The GI Bill permitted millions of Americans—for the first time in our history—to become college educated. Merit rather than family and class membership became an increasingly important standard. Many of the precincts of the upper class—the most prestigious schools and colleges, business firms, even clubs—opened their doors to others. Parallel institutions of all kinds rose to prominence. State and city universities graduated men and women of various ethnic backgrounds who achieved national distinction. In businesses such as retail merchandising, investment banking, real estate, the mass media, entertainment, and services, in party politics, in law and medicine, and not least in the sciences, strong, new, non-WASP leaders emerged. The class hierarchies that had dominated local communities for generations gave way. A great many of the men and women who have reached the generally recognized "top" in their fields over the past forty years are the new *elites,* as Baltzell calls them, people of undoubted ambition, energy, and talent who lacked upper class backgrounds.

The Upper Class and the Elites

Most of the new elites have remained distant from the upper class, unassimilated to their circles, often shunned by them. The irony in this is that the American upper class was not only initially composed of elite families, but for several generations renewed itself by bringing fresh talent from the elites into its fold. Through marriage, elite entrants contributed original perspectives as well as new sources of vitality. The children of these elites often continued in their parents' path, but as full-fledged members of the upper class who had become socialized to upper class culture in schools and clubs. The upper class has not, of course, entirely discontinued this practice. Notwithstanding many objections quite recently from upper class quarters, the career of the Kennedy family over the past few generations is an instance of upper class renewal. But such instances, however extraordinary, have been too few to ensure the continued contribution of the upper class to American democracy.

American democracy has not grown evenly. There have been periods of rapid growth in which members of one or more ethnic groups rose quickly to leadership, followed by periods of stagnation in which the ethnic—and gender—composition of leadership remained relatively unchanged. The steady rise of the Irish in politics, and their more recent rise in business, the recent rapid rise of Jews in the professions as well as in certain fields of business, the sudden rise, since the mid 1960s, of blacks in the professions are examples of unevenness in the democratic course. Baltzell has questioned what would happen if the democratic process were to be speeded up and the country became ruled primarily by elite leaders. Would American democracy be endangered without the security, outlook, and judgment that membership in the upper class historically has been able to provide many leaders? A great many instances of corruption—willful violations of law, bribery, swindling, dishonesty—have been uncovered among business, professional, and political leaders at all levels in our national life over the past twenty years. Whether this is extraordinary or merely "normal" has yet to be determined. More serious in consequence, but perhaps more difficult to assess, has been the quality of leadership exercised by figures who rose to high national office without upper class education, for example, Truman, Johnson, Nixon, and Reagan.

The Culture of Leadership

In his more recent study, *Puritan Boston and Quaker Philadelphia*, Baltzell sought to clarify the relationship of class to culture. His chief historical exemplar is Max Weber's study of the effects of Protestantism upon the development of the modern west.[8] It is not the upper class in general, wherever it is found, that has contributed to American leadership, Baltzell has observed, but an upper class of a particular kind. The Philadelphia upper class is Episcopalian in church affiliation, yet deeply affected by the Quaker history and early culture of the region. In stressing equality and opposing authority, Quakers located virtue in the conscience and feeling of the private citizen. This has led to a love of nature and pictorial beauty, to literate expression, to spontaneous charity and openness to strangers. These conceptions have led, on the negative side, to lack of local pride and assertiveness on the part of Proper Philadelphians, for to be openly prideful of one's locality is to value it above others. At the same time, the Philadelphia gentry, clothed in the moral vestments of privacy of conscience, have been content to rest smugly in their status, unresponsive to public concerns. Some Philadelphians have amassed personal fortunes and tended their own gardens, but few have become national leaders of distinction in politics, education, philanthropy, literature, or law. The famed Philadelphia lawyers have been technical virtuosi serving private and corporate clients, not leaders of the republic or innovators in jurisprudence.

The Boston upper class, by comparison, is also Episcopalian in church affiliation, but Puritan in history and background. In stressing responsibility and patriarchal rule, the Puritans located virtue in the honorable actions of the public servant. On the positive side, this has led to dutiful concern with improvement of the city, to love of intellect, learning, and law, and to institutional philanthropy. On the negative side, these virtues have led to arrogance on the part of the Proper Bostonian and, beyond pride, to excessive certainty in his own accomplishments. In equating excellence with moral superiority, the Boston Brahmins have become disdainful of outsiders and their possible achievements, isolated themselves thereby, and developed the finest, but also the vainest, achievement oriented colleges and universities in the world. Graduates of these schools have become national leaders of the first rank—in government, the Supreme Court and judiciary, the learned professions, education, and science.

Baltzell has found much in both Quakerism and Puritanism that is of value, and much that is not. If the once vigorous American upper class is now corruptly self-preoccupied and weakened beyond recovery, a new upper class will eventually take its place. The nature of this class, its make-up and culture, must remain an open question. But whether the positive legacy of service and leadership of the old upper class culture can endure is perhaps all the more pressing.

*   *   *

Each of the essays in this book deals with an issue that is important to Baltzell's work.

The first three chapters chart significant alterations in American family life in this century. Frank F. Furstenberg, Jr. describes changes in the structure of many American families, especially since the Second World War. The enormous growth in divorce and remarriage rates, he observes, has doubled the number of parents and grandparents—and often increased the number of siblings—of a large proportion of American children. One consequence has been a growing confusion as to parental and grandparental responsibility. How should new grandchildren, many of whom are acquired, for example, as teenagers, be treated? How much authority should the mother's new husband, or the father's new wife, exercise over children who are not biologically (or, in a great many instances, legally) his or hers? How should the child's and the parent's loyalties and love be distributed? Indeed, who is a parent, who a son or daughter? These ambiguities of relationship that have recently arisen affect families of the middle and upper middle classes—the elites, in Baltzell's terminology. The extent to which upper and lower class families are similarly affected is not known. By charting redefinitions in meaning of a large sector of American family life, Furstenberg's study allows us to ask more pointedly how the moral and personal integrity of the children of elite families is being shaped. It is from these families that many of tomorrow's leaders will come.

Michael Zuckerman's essay describes a feature of American family life that has existed almost from its beginnings, and grown steadily in this century to gigantic proportions. The colonists of the seventeenth century, Puritans and Quakers alike, desired their children to be morally improved and set about zealously instructing them to this end. But since the early nineteenth century, the goal of moral improvement has shifted, become transformed to improvement in all things. Nurturing of the young has been supplanted by training of children at an increasingly early age in the latest skills—for example, the currently fashionable computer applications accessible even to pre-kindergarteners through computer games. Widely voiced views of child guidance experts and the mass media—which extol such precocious achievements as necessary for, and early indications of, future success—leave no group in our society, high or low, untouched. How many parents do not wish to instill such competencies in their children? Zuckerman's essay, however, raises the question of the morality of these anxious efforts. It is not only that childhood is being sacrificed for a narrow and thus all the more uncertain future, but that our sense of the estimable person is becoming correspondingly constricted to that of the technical expert. Will these meager resources furnish the moral outlook of our future leaders?

Samuel Preston's study suggests that three factors, operating in unison, have contributed to a shift in distribution of mortality rates of American children between the nineteenth and twentieth centuries. One is the rise, in the twentieth century, of national economic productivity and material resources of households. Another is greater knowledge of hygiene and health. The third is mobilization of resources and knowledge by public institutions, particularly in cities, to achieve a more hygienic environment—in sanitation systems, water supplies and other public facilities. Whether this pattern will be repeated in developing nations, Preston cautions, is not clear; lowering of death rates is not brought about simply by increase in economic well-being or general education. However, elites in developing countries today have an advantage not available to American elites in the late nineteenth century: a clearer understanding of the nature of disease. Here is an example of how scientific advances, coupled to political power in an undemocratic context, have enabled elites to strengthen their relative position, an observation that has also been made with respect to the transmission of educational privilege. Preston's study also casts light, from a different angle, on a point made by Zuckerman. The longer life expectancy of their young children has likely prompted American families, poor as well as rich, to invest greater material (and of course emotional) resources in their children's upbringing. This has, in turn, stimulated demand to achieve greater life expectancy and social and economic return on earlier investment for adolescents from each social stratum in the population. These demands cannot be met merely by improving hygiene and public sanitation. To bring the distribution of mortality and the chance for attainments among adolescents more nearly to par requires that social as well as physical environments be improved, that neighborhoods be made safer, better housing provided, and educational and employment opportunities expanded. The extent to which American leadership will continue to further the democratic condition of its younger population cannot, of course, be foretold. Thus, whether the potential pool of elite members from which national leaders emerge will continue to grow in size and variety must remain an open question. But the role of leadership in this, as Preston's study shows, is vital. The direction of national and civic policy affects not only ultimate matters of life and death, but the breadth of the democratic fabric that envelops our everyday lives.

It is not yet possible to grasp the full implications of the social, psychological, moral, and demographic changes affecting American families. The descriptions provided by Furstenberg, Zuckerman, and Preston have permitted raising several questions pertaining to future leadership. But a more general question directed to the core of leadership—as Baltzell has clarified—may also be asked: what happens to the definition of a social class when the family, which is one of its constituents, is itself becoming redefined?

The next chapter examines social and moral shifts in Ivy League universities since the Second World War. This topic is of particular interest to Baltzell because these universities have been a training ground for many of the nation's leaders. Richard Farnum's essay describes changes in composition of several traditional upper class colleges, the Ivy League and others, from 1880 to 1970. From local upper class family to prep school to one of a dozen or so national colleges was a pattern followed with little variation by a large segment of advantaged students up to the end of the Second World War. In this way continuity of class identity and of moral and social outlook was maintained. But the boom in demand for higher education, coupled with new private and governmental sources of funding, shifted selection of students following the war to a more meritocratic basis. Performance in secondary school and scores in aptitude tests became the chief standards for admission. Many students in Ivy League colleges are today drawn from families of the elite—professionals, businessmen, and politicians. Many graduates of these colleges will become national leaders. But in giving themselves over increasingly to achievement standards, will these colleges be able to sustain one of their important traditional functions—to provide students with a moral, not merely a technical, education? Farnum suggests the issue is not yet decided. It is possible that these colleges are continuing to inculcate a "culture of responsible service" to their students at the same time they employ standards based on merit. If this is true, then the major change has been merely one of class composition, not of the moral preparation of students. But what if this is false?

Farnum's study is among the ever growing number of inquiries since the end of the Second World War by educators, historians, and social commentators into unprecedented changes occurring in universities. In the past two decades fear has been expressed that universities, in the Ivy League and elsewhere, have so eroded standards by inflating grades that it is hardly possible, purely on the basis of student records, to discriminate differences in student performance. The reason for this, it is charged, is failure of courage among faculty who should serve as models and leaders, but who have succumbed to the shortsighted, populist demands of anxious students.[9] Moreover, it is widely asserted that the general moral tenor of faculty has altered, that in the age of giant universities faculty have become, as a well-known witticism attributed to Clark Kerr put it, merely self-seeking intellectual entrepreneurs with a common interest in a parking space.[10] This is hardly an attitude that will produce leaders of a "culture of service." Universities, many claim, are now so dependent for support on outside funding, on research grants from government and private business, that scholarly standards guiding internal decisions, such as faculty promotion and courses offered, are being supplanted by considerations of expediency, such as a faculty member's ability to raise money or fund students.[11] Universities are "closing" the American mind, it has been recently alleged, by no longer teaching the intellectual and moral heritage of the western tradition from which students could be guided after they leave school. In this view universities have given way to practical clamorings of the moment, replacing courses in humanities with an array of narrow, but popular, technical offerings—for example, in computer science, the social sciences, or business administration—which leave students intellectually and morally impoverished and, even before interest in the particular technique or subject fades, ill-prepared to be independent, responsible leaders and citizens.[12]

The national attention such inquiries receive is not solely an indication that there is a large and growing university-educated readership. Readers are also parents and citizens, and concerned with the implications of such studies for the welfare of their children and the nation. These and kindred studies have in common an interest in the moral future of the university and the quality of outlook and training the university provides. Farnum shares this interest, but cautions us that although universities are changing in many ways, they may not be changing in all ways. The question of whether such changes will deeply affect the outlook and caliber of our future leaders is, in his view, open. His study serves to counter hasty, anxious declarations of doom, but the questions he raises are no less urgent.

The following two chapters are case studies—one historical, the other ethnographic—of the collapse of moral leadership in a community. James Abbott examines the emergence of the political machine in Chicago. Patrician Protestants—Yankees from New England and Cavaliers from the south—had become political and business leaders in Chicago early in the nineteenth century. In general, they viewed political office as an honor and a duty. Their collective presence, Abbott shows, served to strengthen party competition and restrain those, either within or outside their ranks, who merely aspired to political power. Chicago enjoyed a reputation as one of the least corrupt American cities. But after the Civil War, upper class involvement in city politics diminished as many Yankees retreated into business and private pursuits. Politically ambitious men of the upper class turned to local ward leaders for support. The welding together of ward organizations by these men yielded the first citywide machine. Thereafter, political power grew more centralized, and the creator and head of the machine emerged as the major power in the city. Party politics declined. The Haymarket riots, further removal of the WASP presence from politics, and corruption among the remaining upper class permitted seizure of the already functioning machine by aggressive men from the swelling ranks of ethnics. From 1931 to the present, Chicago has been a city of ethnic machine politics, in which the "boss" rules with little opposition.

Elijah Anderson examines social changes in urban black ghettos over the past twenty years. Black doctors, lawyers, pharmacists, and ministers once lived in the ghetto and were held up by less advantaged parents to their children as tangible models of propriety and success, to be respected and emulated. Older men advised and aided neighborhood boys to find jobs, urging them to be responsible and work hard. But from the mid 1960s on, as opportunities for blacks increased and numbers of middle class blacks grew, there has been a steady departure of the middle class from the ghetto. The once socially complex black ghetto is now composed increasingly of poor inhabitants who feel trapped with few prospects for improvement. They have limited skills and training opportunities, and a meager job outlook. Yet they desire success and their frustration mounts. In this environment a new type of advisor has arisen who promises quick success through illegal means—drugs and theft. His expensive clothes and cars, the large sums of money he carries, and the apparent ease with which his advice can be taken make him more immediately visible than the earlier models who have moved away. The counter-advice of the few older men who remain in the ghetto is dismissed as antiquated. The grip of the new advisors on their protégés soon grows tighter and more arbitrary. Many lives will be lost—socially and literally—unless economic and social alternatives are found that will permit poor young people of the ghetto to extricate themselves from the mire in which they are presently caught.

Abbott's and Anderson's studies explore the negative side of Baltzell's thesis. The domestic despots—the "bosses," who rule Chicago, the tyran-

nical, self aggrandizing drug dealers who prey upon the urban black ghettos—have been made possible by the attrition of strong, independent
leaders and moral exemplars who have left the community, depleting its
defenses against autocratic domination. To the extent any historical thesis
can be confirmed, these studies provide grim support for Baltzell's view.

The remaining chapters challenge, qualify, or extend Baltzell's thesis.
Samuel Klausner contrasts several career paths of Jewish executives who
received MBAs in the past fifteen years. He finds little discrimination in
hiring or promotion practices between Jewish and Gentile firms. Jewish
firms tend to recruit more on merit, Gentile firms are more particularistic,
but the differences between the two are not vast. Greater differences exist
in the sorts of economic activity of the two kinds of firm. Jewish firms develop at the economic frontier, and are more often associated with areas of
economic exchange, such as banking and stock trading. Jewish firms pay
higher salaries, on average, and recruit executives with broader, more cosmopolitan backgrounds. A young executive's career path is often within
the network of firms associated with the first firm into which he or she was
hired. Some Jews are absorbed into the establishment, but not always in
ways Baltzell has envisioned. Some Jewish executives are "apostates" and
become fully assimilated; others remain ethnically and religiously Jews,
but nevertheless share economic power with the establishment. All these
executives are elites, in Baltzell's sense. However, Klausner's study raises
the question of the degree to which an elite group must be assimilated in
order to become part of the American upper class. To what extent does the
American upper class support the democratic ideal of pluralism? How
much ethnic and religious diversity can the upper class tolerate among its
members and yet continue to function as a class?

Jerry A. Jacobs examines economic consequences of two different, yet
related, "ethics" upon landed aristocracies in England and France. The
"ethics" were rules stipulating appropriate practices of consumption and
acquisition. The style of life and status honor of the aristocracies depended
on following these rules. Although demands of one set of rules frequently
frustrated demands of the other, some alterations in either could be made.
The different fates of the English and French aristocracies, Jacobs argues,
were due to differences more in national contexts than in status ethics. The
French monarchy's insistence upon lavish display at court, the ostentation
expected in Parisian salons, high estate taxes, and severe proscriptions on
methods of acquisition impoverished many (over time most) noble French
houses. The English monarchy was less insistent on courtly display, but

aristocratic standards of consumption in other respects were high. Economic perturbations led the English nobility to greater rationalization of estates (through rent and mining of lands) than was achieved by their French counterparts. As agricultural entrepreneurs, the English aristocracy could support itself well into the nineteenth century. But industrial activity was disdained as a method of acquisition, and as this method became dominant the English nobility declined.

Are there constraints analogous to the ones Jacobs has analyzed that affect the position and vigor of the American WASP upper class? Perhaps the considerations Jacobs brings out apply particularly to an earlier, southern upper class that was tied—"ethically," in Jacobs' sense, as well as economically—to an agrarian style of life. Nevertheless, the frequency of non-WASP firms at the "economic frontier," as Klausner observed, suggests a possible analogy today. The issue raised by Jacobs' study remains to be further explored in the American setting.

Harold J. Bershady analyzes cities as representing religious, cultural, and political traditions of their nations. In the United States, virtually all cities with adequate economic resources, even when only fifty miles apart, have many of the same kinds of facilities. This pattern does not hold in comparable cities in Europe. Paris is the premier city in France, superior to others in range and quality of each facility—educational, artistic, scientific, communicational, among others. This reflects its earlier history as site of monarchical power and pomp, the apex of a country united by loyalty to Catholic church and nation. In the United States, England, and Germany, no one city can claim monopoly of excellence of each facility. Citizens of American cities hold themselves entitled to facilities enjoyed by any other city and make strenuous efforts to achieve them. American cities are autonomous associations of their citizens with their own laws, courts, and political institutions. They are considered by their members to have value independent of other national associations. This attitude reflects the American stress on equality, individuality, and freedom of association deeply ingrained in the nation's Protestant traditions. It would not be possible for sports teams of American cities to compete if the cities did not consider themselves in some respects equal or at least formally independent. But American cities are not uniform; there is division of labor among them. Baltzell has shown that Boston has contributed disproportionately to the nation's political and legal leadership and stands as a symbol of such excellence. But New York City stands as perhaps the commercial, entertainment, and artistic center of the nation, Los Angeles, the late twentieth century migratory mecca, Detroit the automobile capital. Philadelphia exemplifies American pluralism; this is a kind of leadership of a vital aspect of American democracy. Although hardly a "peaceable kingdom," the "City of Brotherly Love," fifth largest in the nation, has not been as wracked by race riots as Los Angeles, Washington, Detroit, New York, or Boston. Bershady concludes that, although Baltzell's analysis of Boston and Philadelphia is limited in its conception of democracy and leadership, it has opened the way to analyzing the interactions between cities and their larger national environments.

Fred Block reexamines authority from a radical perspective. Aristocratic authority of the sort Baltzell endorses, Block argues, even when informed by an ideology of service, cannot provide adequate protection against abuses of power. Many of the high officials in the Kennedy and Johnson administrations were from the upper class. It was they, he reminds us, who engineered the nation's involvement in Vietnam. The cohesiveness and self confidence of the upper class makes possible not merely their "collective myopia," but also contempt for democratic opinion. However, another kind of authority, more responsive to democratic standards, nonhierarchical and adaptable has emerged in advanced work settings. Block calls this "post-industrial authority." Those who exercise it are recognized as having capacities to innovate. But to do so requires winning the consent of others through dialogue and persuasion—the chief methods through which the soundness of a proffered innovation can be assessed. To accomplish such innovations, post-industrial authority must also be supplemented by formal lines. Although utopian in appearance, Block observes that this kind of authority is occurring more frequently in many advanced work settings, in universities and colleges, between doctors and patients, and in other professional-client relationships. Post-industrial authority is still confined to the workplace, but Block believes this may be the most suitable kind of political authority for developed democracies in the decades ahead.

Victor Lidz's essay describes the shift from aristocratic political life at the time of the writing of the Constitution to the later more familiar democratic social condition. The founding fathers believed that political parties bore seeds of division and faction. They also believed power should not be widely distributed lest it fall into the hands of an impulsive multitude. Only so-called natural leaders, materially independent and talented, should be at the helm. They were to be drawn from the group of wealthy, politically experienced men who were educated and responsible. "Natural leaders" were thus conceived to be part of a distinct status group, smaller in number and superior to commoners. But they were not often found on the expanding frontiers, for example, or in the towns of the middle states. Many commoners resented the "natural leaders" and desired to take the lead themselves. Through long struggle, culminating in the election of Andrew Jackson to the presidency, popular, party-based politics won out over the politics of "noble leaders and great parties," as Tocqueville described it. Ever since, political parties, not social classes, have put forth candidates and supported their contest for public office. This practice is based on ideals of equality and representivity, essentially middle class in outlook, which stress the ability of candidates over their class membership. Political parties, much more than the upper class, Lidz argues, have created and maintained the American system of political democracy.

Although launched from different perspectives, most of the essays critical of Baltzell's views unearth a tendency on his part to reify the contributions of the upper class to American democracy. A culture of service, of honor and duty in leadership, is vital to the integrity of our public servants. Is the upper class the only repository of this culture? Ethnic and religious diversity and pluralism are integral to American democracy. Does—indeed, *can*—the American upper class support such diversity? Loyal, effective criticism is vital to a democratic polity. Does such criticism stem primarily from the upper class? Indeed, can the upper class respond positively to criticism when directed against its own members? Able leadership, demonstrated in a record of achievement, is necessary to the vitality of our democratic political life. Is membership in the upper class synonymous with achievement and leadership ability? The upper class has been crucial in sustaining political democracy throughout American history. Have political parties, then, taken little part in this? Have upper class attitudes—in the sense characterized by Tocqueville and Baltzell—much affected the outlook of major political parties?

These critical questions, however pointed, are raised with the same concerns that have guided Baltzell's efforts: to understand and strengthen American democratic leadership.

The final chapter, by the Rt. Honorable Judge A. Leon Higginbotham, Jr. and Laura B. Farmelo addresses a substantive issue at the heart of American democracy: the idea of American pluralism, with specific reference to the full inclusion of black Americans into the educational, economic, political, and not least, moral life of the nation. This idea has been sounded in preceding chapters, but in different contexts. Higginbotham and Farmelo set out goals shared by Baltzell and the other contributors. It is not sociology, but historical reportage and moral rhetoric. It is a fitting coda to a celebration of Baltzell's work.

Social Class and Democratic Leadership, in sum, takes up the themes, in consecutive order, of changing definitions of class, education for leadership, local tyrannies, the extent to which elites have risen to leadership positions, conditions of upper class maintenance, the contributions of the nation as well as its cities to democratic culture, the shape of democratic leadership, the role of political parties in fulfilling democratic principles of equality and achievement, and not least, the social—not merely political—meaning of democracy.

Notes

1. Alexis de Tocqueville, *Democracy in America,* 2 vols., ed. Phillips Bradley (New York: Vintage Books, 1954).
2. David Riesman, *The Lonely Crowd* (New Haven, Conn.: Yale University Press, 1950).
3. E. Digby Baltzell, *Philadelphia Gentlemen: The Making of a National Upper Class* (Philadelphia: University of Pennsylvania Press, 1977; original edition New York: Free Press, 1958).
4. E. Digby Baltzell, *The Protestant Establishment: Aristocracy and Caste in America* (New York: Random House, 1964).
5. E. Digby Baltzell, *Puritan Boston and Quaker Philadelphia* (New York: Free Press, 1979).
6. Louis Auchincloss, *The Rector of Justin* (New York: Modern Library, 1967).
7. Alexis de Tocqueville, *The Old Regime and the French Revolution,* trans. Stuart Gilbert (Garden City, N.Y.: Anchor Books, 1955).
8. Max Weber, *The Protestant Ethic and the Spirit of Capitalism,* trans. Talcott Parsons (New York: Charles Scribner and Sons, 1930).
9. Cf. Arvin E. Juola, *Grade Inflation (1960–1973); A Preliminary Report* (East Lansing: Office of Evaluation Services, Michigan State University, 1974).
10. Clark Kerr, *The Uses of the University* (Cambridge, Mass.: Harvard University Press, 1963).
11. Cf. Michael B. Katz, "The Moral Crisis of the University, or the Tension between Marketplace and Community in the Higher Learning," in William A. W. Nielson and Chad Gaffield, eds., *Universities in Crisis: A Medieval Institution in the Twenty-First Century* (Montreal: The Institute for Research on Public Policy, 1986).
12. Cf. Allan Bloom, *The Closing of the American Mind: How Higher Education Has Failed Democracy and Impoverished the Souls of Today's Students* (New York: Simon and Schuster, 1987).

Frank F. Furstenberg, Jr.

2. One Hundred Years of Change in the American Family

Introduction

The United States has always been more accepting of divorce than other countries with advanced economies, even though similar trends in marital disruption have recently occurred in Europe (Roussel and Festy, 1979). Divorce became prevalent in the United States earlier than in Europe or Canada and in wake of the baby boom, United States rates climbed to unparalleled levels, unmatched by any other country in the West (Carter and Glick, 1976). Comparing nations that presumably share a common cultural heritage, divorce is two to four times higher in the United States than in England, Canada, New Zealand, or Australia. The latter nations have recently experienced a sharp rise in divorce, but their rates are still below the levels reached in the United States a generation ago before divorce was considered to be a major social problem.

It is not obvious why divorce took root in America so early or why American marriages are so much more susceptible to dissolution. America has had a tradition of early marriage, which itself may be linked to a high risk of divorce. Although the United States legal system generally refused to sanction divorce until the 1960s, it was more accommodating, particularly in certain states, than in many European countries where resistance to divorce remained strong until quite recently. American public attitudes were perhaps more tolerant of divorce compared to those of other countries. (For historical accounts of social and legal changes in divorce laws, see O'Neill, 1973; Halem, 1980; Weitzman, 1985).

None of these potential explanations is adequate, though each suggests a more fundamental reason for the cross-national differences. The highly individualistic marriage system which evolved in the United States is compatible with both early marriage and easier divorce. As historian Edward Shorter has written, the American family was "born modern." American youth have always been permitted a high degree of discretion in marriage timing because nuptial decisions, like so many other features of the family, were governed largely by personal sentiment. The strong sentimental basis for marriage, which some sociologists have described as the "cultural complex of romantic love," is implicated in the evolution of a conditional commitment to matrimony.

Compared to the custom in most other Western nations, Americans embraced love as a standard for marriage, providing young people with a license to enter matrimony with relatively little parental control. Marriage in America was a contract less between families than between individuals. Emotional considerations therefore weighed heavily in mate selection and as a standard of marital contentment. Both professional and popular literature suggest that Americans have been almost obsessed with the elusive goal of marital happiness (Tufte and Myerhoff, 1979). Gradually, Americans shifted from a marriage system which required individuals to remain married even if they were no longer in love, to a system which virtually required them to dissolve their relationship if they were no longer strongly emotionally involved.

This new standard permitted—practically encouraged—divorce, even though Americans continued to pay lip service to the value of life-long monogamy. Thus, divorce has always been regarded as an anomalous event, violating cherished beliefs about the permanence of marriage. Yet, divorce, in fact, has become an intrinsic part of the American marriage system. Other Western nations appear to be following a similar course, though it is too soon to tell whether the American pattern will be adopted wholesale.

By saying that divorce is intrinsic to the American marriage system, I am referring to the fact that divorce has become institutionalized. New norms are emerging that make divorce acceptable, even imperative, under certain conditions, and new guidelines have been invented for divorced families. Since divorce is usually followed by remarriage, it is perhaps more accurate to say that the shift in the marriage system has taken us from a pattern of permanent monogamy to a pattern of *conjugal succession*.

In the United States, it is estimated that at least half of all marriages contracted in the 1970s and early 1980s will end in divorce (Preston and McDonald, 1979; Weed, 1980; Glick, 1984). It is a rare individual, therefore, who will not encounter divorce and remarriage in his or her family of origin or family of procreation. As Cherlin and I (1986) have written:

It will not be uncommon for children born in the 1980s to follow this sequence of living arrangements: live with both parents for several years, live with their mother after their parents divorce, then live with their stepfather, live alone for a time when in their early twenties, live with someone of the opposite sex without marrying, get married, get divorced, live alone again, get remarried, and end up living alone once more following the death of their spouse.

This pervasive experience with divorce and remarriage is profoundly altering American kinship arrangements. In this essay, I shall briefly summarize some observations about how American kinship has been transformed by the pattern of conjugal succession. These observations are discussed more fully in research reports of studies which a number of my collaborators and I have conducted during the past decade, and in studies conducted by other investigators who have traced the consequences of divorce and remarriage on marriage, parenthood, and extended family relations (Furstenberg, 1979; 1982; 1987; Cherlin and Furstenberg, 1986; Furstenberg and Spanier, 1984).

Marriage

Until the middle of the twentieth century marriage was embedded in a tightly sequenced series of status transitions—the initiation of sexual activity, the inception of parenthood, the departure from the family of origin, and the establishment of an independent residence. Marriage was, in effect, the keystone to the passage to adulthood. Today, marriage is usually a discrete transition removed from other events which make up the process of family and household formation. It is no coincidence that as marriage has been stripped of some of its importance as a ceremonial marker of adulthood, the pattern of conjugal succession has also become more widespread.

As divorce has become more common, the cultural value placed on marriage has eroded. Not only has it become more acceptable to exit from marriage, it is now acceptable *not* to enter marriage. Some demographers have estimated that at present as many as one-fifth of all Americans will never marry—a sharp rise from a generation ago when only about five percent of the population never entered matrimony (Norton, 1986).

These changes do not necessarily imply that Americans have come to expect less of marriage. Indeed, as marriage has become less binding and inviolable, standards of what constitutes a satisfactory marriage have been elevated. The increased value placed on marital happiness ultimately means that individuals judge their relations with a more discerning eye, and are accordingly more willing to dissolve a marriage that is adequate but emotionally unrewarding (Swidler, 1983).

When viewed in this light, divorce can be seen as an intrinsic part of a cultural system that cherishes individual discretion and emotional gratification. Divorce is a social mechanism for promoting conformity to these cultural ideals. In this sense, as some observers have pointed out, divorce is not a sign that marriage is devalued, but an indication of a strong commitment to a marital style that is difficult to maintain. The quest for marital contentment often leads to a conjugal career in which, like an occupational career, individuals attempt to upgrade their situation.

In the course of moving from one marriage to the next, the formerly married encounter a series of culturally uncharted social situations. The process of remarriage ultimately involves "rethinking" marriage, as individuals are forced to deconstruct the marital subworld of their first union, and recreate a new belief system based on their current relationship (see also Vaughan, 1986). A study of this process reveals that second marriages are reinvented in a more contemporary form. Remarried individuals are more wary of failure and pay greater attention to monitoring their emotional well-being. This sensitivity only heightens the value placed on emotional gratification which may contribute to the vulnerability of second marriages.

Typically, divorced individuals attempt to shed the legacy of failure from their initial marriage by distancing themselves as much as possible from their first spouse. In studies of the transition from divorce to remarriage, informants often describe their first marriage as an earlier chapter in their lives, a mistake that they were able to correct through personal growth and development. Divorce is viewed as a process of personal transformation in which an old self as well as a biography of failure is shed. Most divorced persons have as little contact as possible with their former spouses, maintaining what amounts to a ritual taboo. There are, of course, exceptions—ex-partners who remain friendly or even friends—but the majority of formerly married couples have little to do with each other. Repudiating a former spouse helps to build solidarity in a new relationship, thus reducing the potential for jealousy. This disassociation serves to reenforce the new relationship, but also creates special problems for individuals who continue to share parental responsibilities. (Further discussion of the process of divorce and remarriage is presented in Furstenberg and Spanier,

1984. For other accounts, see Goode, 1956; Bernard, 1956; Goetting, 1982; Keshet, 1980; Pasley and Ihinger-Tallman, 1984.)

Parenting Apart

The majority of couples who divorce have young children and are therefore obliged to work out some sort of postmarital childcare arrangement. The social guidelines for doing so, which have never been entirely clear, are currently in flux as custody and child support laws are being revised (Cherlin, 1978; Weitzman, 1985). Now, more than ever before, formerly married couples must devise feasible and collaborative childcare arrangements when they often have not been able to get along in married life. Further complicating this task, most divorced persons, as just noted, have a strong desire to avoid contact with their former partner. Not surprisingly, then, studies of childcare after divorce reveal little active co-parenting.

Close to half of all children in the United States will spend part of their childhood in a single-parent family. Most of these children will have little or no contact with their non-residential parent and most will receive little or no economic support from that parent (Bumpass, 1984). A recent national study of children in maritally disrupted families revealed that about half had not seen their father living outside the home in the preceding twelve months and another one-sixth had seen him only a few times. Fewer than two-fifths of the fathers were providing regular child support according to government statistics (Furstenberg et al., 1983).

Longitudinal research shows that most fathers curtail contact soon after the remarriage occurs, reflecting the desire of formerly married couples to sever their ties. Geographical movement and remarriage further erode parental bonds. The pattern of conjugal succession has the effect of creating a child swapping system, whereby residential or sociological fathers replace biological fathers. Of course the system is not that neat. Many biological parents living outside the home maintain regular contact and strong emotional ties to their child or children. Extended kin, as will be described later, often serve to reinforce these bonds. Moreover stepparents, when they assume parental responsibilities, often find themselves in an anomalous role, exercising neither full rights nor responsibilities over the child (Furstenberg and Nord, 1985).

Several studies have demonstrated that both stepparents and stepchildren have problems according full legitimacy to their relationship

(White and Booth, 1985). Their kinship connection, based on in-law rather than blood relationships, makes the linkage more tenuous. Stepparents often report that their stepchildren do not think of them as "real parents" and, indeed, 31 percent of the children currently living in households with stepparents neglect to mention them as a member of their family (Furstenberg, 1987).

Evidence is mounting that the presence of stepchildren complicates marital ties, straining new marriages over and above the tensions introduced by childrearing in nuclear families. A recent study discovered that a substantial proportion of stepparents wished their stepchildren did not live in the home, suggesting that cross-cutting loyalties divide families that are unable to establish the principle of sociological parenthood (White and Booth, 1985). For relations between stepparents and their children to become "real," they must be accorded legitimacy in the kinship system. Stepparents are granted partial legitimacy, contingent on the development of personal ties and loyalties. This discretionary license resembles the treatment of all in-laws in the American kinship system (Furstenberg, 1987).

Whether the acceptance of stepparents in particular family situations is promoted by an attenuation or relinquishment of relations with the biological parent remains an open question. Preliminary information from one study indicates that children who maintain ties with their biological parents are not any less likely to accord legitimacy to their stepparents (Furstenberg, 1987). In short, children in the United States may be able to engage in a practice unthinkable to many adults—acknowledging multiple fathers or mothers. Foreign as this notion may be, the changing imagery and language of kinship signals the possibility that the pattern of conjugal succession is being integrated into the American kinship system.

In studies of remarried families, language was often a battleground over which parents fought to maintain their position within the family. Terms of address were often contested. Remarried persons, especially those with younger children, often attempted to persuade their children to refer to a new mate as "mom" or "dad." More than a few biological parents vigorously protested when they overheard their children referring to stepparents by these terms of address, feeling that their parental legitimacy was under attack.

Just as parents minimize contact with their former spouses, children with more than two parents learn to segregate the separate spheres of family life. They are constrained not to discuss what goes on inside the home of the biological parent when talking to their stepparents, and parents outside the home and vice versa. In effect, children are the common link between two separate clans.

However, relations across households can be quite variable. In a small fraction of the divorced population, parents maintain a high degree of continuity. In most instances, contact between residential and nonresidential parents is minimal. Despite the considerable attention in the media given to joint custody and co-parenting arrangements, most formerly married parents have little to do with one another, especially if their children are no longer young. Usually, they rely on the children to make arrangements for visitation, communicate messages, and even to discuss important parental decisions.

One study of co-parenting found that two-thirds of all custodial parents of adolescent children reported that they rarely or never discussed matters concerning the child with the noncustodial parent (Furstenberg and Nord, 1985). Even among those whose children had frequent contact with their nonresidential parent, close to half stated that they rarely if ever talked to their former spouse about their children. Indeed, these families were particularly inclined to say that they often or sometimes relied on the child to communicate with their former spouse.

In summary, childcare patterns after divorce are rarely collaborative or jointly coordinated. When the nonresidential father maintains contact at all, which only occurs in a minority of families, he usually does so with minimal contact with his former spouse, the child's mother. Children, or sometimes even stepparents, are called upon to serve as intermediaries, thereby avoiding direct confrontations. This childcare pattern is often described as co-parenting. A more apt term for depicting it, however, is "parallel parenting."

In effect, then, patterns of parenting in the United States have undergone a profound change in the past half century as divorce and remarriage have become a pervasive pattern. American children are likely to experience a variety of childcare systems, and many children will experience more than one system during the course of childhood. Considerable ambiguity exists as to which parents will be the salient figures, the precise nature of parental rights and responsibilities, and the rules for coordinating the activities of various parent figures. Children are likely to play a central part in determining how the childcare system operates, as they are the central link between parental figures who typically operate autonomously and with little reference to one another.

Despite a rash of recent studies, relatively little is known about the consequences of this childcare system for the development and well-being of children or for their prospects in life (Esses and Campbell, 1984; Coleman and Ganong, 1984). I shall make no attempt to describe the complex and contradictory findings of existing studies on the outcome of divorce and remarriage on the socialization process. However, the emerging consensus among both psychologists and sociologists who have explored this topic is that there are no simple or uniform results which apply to all or even most children (Rutter, 1971; Herzog and Sudia, 1973; Hess and Camera, 1979; Hetherington and Camera, 1984; Emery, Hetherington, and Dilalla, 1985; Furstenberg and Seltzer, 1986).

Many investigators believe that children of divorce do not fare as well as children from stably married households, but the general effects of marital disruption are nonetheless rather modest. Existing research has not been able to distinguish the particular effects of conflict in the family prior to dissolution, the separation process, and the economic and psychological aftermath of divorce. Most children react adversely to divorce, but most recover in time. Yet, given the ambiguities of parenting and childcare described above, to which most children are exposed, it seems remarkable that the adverse impact of divorce is not more pervasive and persistent. Little attention has been given to how children manage to operate in a changing family system and what features of that system are detrimental to or supportive of the child's well-being (Furstenberg and Allison, 1985; see also Cherlin, 1981; Thornton and Freedman, 1982; Ross and Sawhill, 1975; Lamb, 1978; and Emery, Hetherington, and Dilalla, 1985).

Remarriage and Extended Family Relations

A growing body of research indicates that one source of support comes from the extended family. Following a divorce, grandparents, particularly on the side of the custodial parent, frequently become more active in childcare and sometimes are called upon to lend economic assistance. Research is more equivocal in the role of the noncustodial parent's extended kin. When the father (or mother, when she is the nonresidential parent) remains involved in childrearing, his (or her) activities parallel the custodial grandparents'. The withdrawal of the father from childcare—which occurs more typically—generally attentuates relations with the noncustodial grandparents.

Evidence from a large-scale study of grandparents indicates the strong possibility of a matrilineal tilt in the American kinship system resulting from rising rates of divorce and a pronounced pattern of paternal absence (Cherlin and Furstenberg, 1986). In a less extreme form, the American kinship system resembles the subcultural pattern of black Americans where matrilinearity has become almost the rule. Fathers and their families are only loosely connected to the child who may claim them as kin, but often do not enjoy the full benefits of their sponsorship and aid (Stack, 1974).

Blacks represent an extreme case because the vast majority of formerly married women never reenter matrimony. This is much less true of whites in the United States whose marriages dissolve (Norton and Glick, 1976; Glick, 1984). Close to three-fourths of white divorced women and four-fifths of white divorced men eventually remarry. Little is known about the operation of stepfamilies beyond the boundaries of the nuclear unit. From scattered small-scale investigations, however, it appears that step-relations are often relatively quickly assimilated, on the principle that in-laws become instant relatives. However, this depends on the age of the children at the time of remarriage.

The parents of remarried children may experience some pressure to treat their children's stepchildren as equivalent to their biological grandchildren in order to preserve and reenforce relations with the middle generation. Newly married parents are quick to pick up differences in the treatment of biological and stepchildren by grandparents, and children also are sensitive to unequal attention. Consequently, children readily adopt primary kinship terms when referring to grandparents, uncles, and aunts. The flexibility of the American kinship system permits a good deal of discretion, allowing individuals to ignore step-distinctions if they wish (Schneider, 1980). It is easier to accept the fact that children have six grandparents than to accept that they have three parents.

Conjugal succession expands the child's kinship network exponentially. The succession of marriages creates a chain of relations which are potential sources of assistance. Adults are loosely linked across this "marriage chain" through former and current marriages. Thus, children may speak of the person who helped them get a summer job—their stepfather's sister's first husband, for instance. How important this chain of kinship will be to the child in life is not yet known, but clearly divorce and remarriage generally enlarges the universe of potential kin (Furstenberg and Spanier, 1984; Spanier and Furstenberg, 1986).

From the perspective of adults, conjugal succession implies greater fluidity and uncertainty in kinship relations. Cultivating family ties may become more important as less can be taken for granted about the obligations of particular kin to one another. It is interesting to note that while formerly married persons may frequently observe a form of ritual isolation from one another, their parents may have reason to maintain ties with their former in-laws, either because of sentiment or, more practically, to preserve ties with their grandchildren. However, they may have limited control in preserving kinship bonds.

One survey discovered that the vast majority of recently divorced individuals did not regard their former in-laws as relatives even though they continued to recognize their rights as the children's grandparents (Furstenberg and Spanier, 1984). This anomalous situation has given rise to legal demands for protecting the rights of grandparents after divorce; a large number of states have enacted statutes ensuring grandparents' visitation privileges. This legislation testifies to the inherent ambiguity in the kinship system, for it is difficult to believe that such guarantees are more than of symbolic importance. If parents do not wish their children to see their grandparents, they will find a means of limiting contact.

On balance, the net effect of conjugal succession is to widen, rather than contract, the boundaries of kinship. This potential will be accentuated as the number of children relative to the number of adults declines. The fertility drop in the face of increasing longevity means that a smaller number of children will be shared by a larger pool of adults. Adults may have to give more resources to children if they wish to maintain their allegiance and obligations in later life.

It will be extraordinarily interesting to see the relative strength of consanguineal and affinal bonds within families whose members have been multiplied by successive marriages. How will grandparents divide their inheritance among biological grandchildren whom they barely know, step-grandchildren acquired early in life, or stepgrandchildren acquired from their own second marriage who have helped to nurse them later in life? Do biological fathers have more obligation to send their biological children, who have been raised by a stepfather, to college or their own stepchildren whom they have raised?

Of course, there are no easy answers to such questions. Conjugal succession is increasing the fluidity of our kinship system which already emphasizes discretion rather than obligation. The voluntaristic basis of family relations is bound to grow as individuals are encouraged to cultivate contacts from what Matilda Riley has called a "matrix of latent relationships." More than ever before, family and kinship will be constructed by individuals, which in turn will promote the highly individualistic nature of the American kinship system.

Will this more voluntary system of kinship weaken the bonds between generations and foster a view that family relations are disposable commodities? The greater substitutability of family members may well reduce family loyalty and commitment to kin. The extension of kinship through marriage may, in effect, cheapen the currency of family. Alternatively, blood relations may become even more salient than they are currently as individuals come to distrust the permanency of certain kinship bonds.

To address these issues more attention must be given to how kinship is enacted in everyday life. Divorce and remarriage have exposed the limitations of our understanding of the workings of our kinship system. Tracing the effects of conjugal succession on marriage, parenthood, and extended family relations historically and cross-culturally provides an unusual vantage point from which to study the process of how different kinship systems react to demographic, social, and economic change.

References

Bernard, J. (1956). *Remarriage: A Study of Marriage*. New York: Dryden Press.

Bohannon, P. (1970). *Divorce and After*. Garden City, N.Y.: Doubleday.

Bumpass, L. (1984). "Children and Marital Disruption: A Replication and Update." *Demography* 21:71–82.

Carter, H. and P. C. Glick (1976). *Marriage and Divorce: A Social and Economic Study*. Cambridge, Mass.: Harvard University Press.

Cherlin, A. J. (1978). "Remarriage as an Incomplete Institution." *American Journal of Sociology* 84:634–50.

——— (1981). *Marriage, Divorce, Remarriage*. Cambridge, Mass.: Harvard University Press.

Cherlin, A. J. and F. F. Furstenberg, Jr. (1986). *The New American Grandparents: A Place in the Family, a Life Apart*. New York: Basic Books.

Coleman, M. and L. H. Ganong (1984). "Effect of Family Structure on Family Attitudes and Expectations." *Family Relations* 33, 3:425–32.

Emery, R. E., E. M. Hetherington, and L. F. Dilalla (1985). "Divorce, Children, and Social Policy." In H. Stevenson and A. Seigel, eds., *Child Development Research and Social Policy*. Chicago: University of Chicago Press.

Esses, L. and R. Campbell (1984). "Challenges in Researching the Remarried." *Family Relations* 33, 3:415–24.

Furstenberg, F. F., Jr. (1979). "Recycling the Family: Perspectives for Researching a Neglected Family Form." *Marriage and Family Review* 2, 1:12–22.

——— (1982). "Conjugal Succession: Reentering Marriage After Divorce." In

P. B. Baltes & O. G. Brim, Jr., eds., *Life-Span Development and Behavior,* IV: 107–46. New York: Academic Press.

——— (1983). "The American Family in the Year 2000." *The Futurist* 17, 3:7–14.

——— (1987). "The New Extended Family: Experiences in Stepfamilies." In K. Pasley and M. Ihinger-Tallman, eds., *Remarriage and Step-Parenting Today.* New York: Guilford Press.

Furstenberg, F. F., Jr. and P. A. Allison (1985). "How Divorce Affects the Children: Variations by Age and Sex." Paper presented at the annual meeting of the Society for Research in Child Development, Toronto.

Furstenberg, F. F., Jr. and C. W. Nord (1985). "Parenting Apart: Patterns of Child-rearing After Divorce." *Journal of Marriage and the Family* 47:893–904.

Furstenberg, F. F., Jr., C. W. Nord, J. L. Peterson, and N. Zill (1983). "The Life Course of Children of Divorce: Marital Disruption and Parental Conflict." *American Sociological Review* 48:656–68.

Furstenberg, F. F., Jr. and J. Seltzer (1986). "Divorce and Child Development." In P. A. Adler and P. Adler, eds., *Sociological Studies of Child Development,* Vol. 1. Greenwich, Conn.: JAI Press.

Furstenberg, F. F., Jr. and G. B. Spanier (1984). *Recycling the Family: Remarriage After Divorce.* Beverly Hills, Ca.: Sage Publications.

Glenn, N. O. (1981). "The Well Being of Persons Remarried After Divorce." *Journal of Family Issues* 2:61–75.

Glick, P. C. (1984). "Marriage, Divorce, and Living Arrangements: Prospective Changes." *Journal of Family Issues* 5, 1:7–26.

Goetting, A. (1982). "The Six Stations of Remarriage: Developmental Tasks of Remarriage After Divorce." *Family Relations* 31:213–22.

Goode, W. J. (1956). *Women in Divorce.* New York: Free Press.

Halem, L. C. (1980). *Divorce Reform: Changing Legal and Social Perspectives.* New York: Free Press.

Hareven, T. K. (1978). *Transitions: The Family and the Life Course in Historical Perspective.* New York: Academic Press.

Herzog, E. and C. E. Sudia (1973). "Children in Fatherless Families." In B. Caldwell & H. Ricciuti, eds., *Review of Child Development Research,* Vol. 3. Chicago: University of Chicago Press.

Hess, R. D. and K. A. Camara (1979). "Post-Divorce Relationships as Mediating Factors in the Consequences of Divorce for Children." *Journal of Social Issues* 35:79–96.

Hetherington, E. M. and K. A. Camara (1984). "Families in Transition: The process of Dissolution and Reconstitution." In R. Parke, ed., *Review of Child Development Research,* Vol. 7. Chicago: University of Chicago Press.

Keshet, J. K. (1980). "From Separation to Stepfamily: A Subsystem Analysis." *Journal of Family Issues* 1, 4:517–32.

Lamb, M. E. (1978). "The Effects of Divorce on Children's Personality Development." *Journal of Divorce* 1, 2:163–74.

Norton, A. J. (1986). "Marriage and Divorce Patterns of U.S. Women in the 1980s." Paper presented at Population Association of America meetings, San Francisco, April.

Norton, A. J. and P. C. Glick (1976). "Marital Instability: Past, Present, and Future." *Journal of Social Issues* 32:5–20.

O'Neill, W. L. (1973). *Divorce in the Progressive Era*. New Haven, Conn.: Yale University Press.

Pasley, K. and M. Ihinger-Tallman, eds. (1984). "Remarriage and Stepparenting." Special issue of *Family Relations* 33, 3.

Preston, S. H. and J. McDonald (1979). "The Incidence of Divorce Within Cohorts of American Marriages Contracted Since the Civil War." *Demography* 16:1–25.

Ross, H. L. and I. V. Sawhill (1975). *Time of Transition: The Growth of Families Headed by Women*. Washington, D.C.: The Urban Institute.

Roussel, L. and P. Festy (1979). "Recent Trends in Attitudes and Behavior Affecting the Family in Council of Europe Member States." *Population Studies*, No. 4. Strasbourg: Council of Europe.

Rutter, M. (1971). "Parent-Child Separation: Psychological Effects on the Children." *Journal of Child Psychology and Psychiatry* 12:233–60.

Schmid, J. (1984). "The Background of Recent Fertility Trends in the Member States of the Council of Europe." *Population Studies*, No. 15. Strasbourg: Council of Europe.

Schneider, David M. (1980). *American Kinship: A Cultural Account*, 2nd edition. Chicago: University of Chicago Press.

Spanier, G. B. and F. F. Furstenberg, Jr. (1986). "Remarriage and Reconstituted Families." In M. B. Sussman and S. K. Steinmetz, eds., *Handbook of Marriage and the Family*. New York: Plenum Press.

Stack, C. (1974). *All Our Kin*. Chicago: Aldine Publishing Co.

Swidler, A. (1983). "Love and Adulthood in American Culture." In A. S. Skolnick and J. H. Skolnick, eds., *Family in Transition*. Boston: Little, Brown.

Thornton, A. and D. Freedman (1982). "Changing Attitudes Toward Marriage and Single Life." *Family Planning Perspectives* 14:297–303.

——— (1983). "The Changing American Family." *Population Bulletin* 38, 4.

Tufte, V. and B. Myerhoff, eds. (1979). *Changing Images of the Family*. New Haven, Conn.: Yale University Press.

Vaughan, D. (1986). *Uncoupling: Turning Points in Intimate Relationships*. New York: Oxford University Press.

Walker, K., J. Rogers, and L. Messinger (1977). "Remarriage After Divorce: A Review." *Social Casework* 58:276–85.

Weed, J. A. (1980). "National Estimates of Marriage Dissolution and Survivorship: United States." *Vital and Health Statistics:* Series 3, Analytic Statistics, No. 19. DHHS Publication No. (PHS)81–1403. Hyattsville, Md.: National Center for Health Statistics, Office of Health Research, Statistics and Technology; Public Health Service, U.S. Department of Health and Human Services.

Weitzman, L. J. (1985). *The Divorce Revolution: The Unexpected Social and Economic Consequences for Women and Children in America*. New York: Free Press.

White, L. K. and A. Booth (1985). "Stepchildren in Remarriages." *American Sociological Review* 50:689–98.

Michael Zuckerman

3. Puritans, Quakers, and Modern America: The High-Tech Child in Historical Perspective

In the beginning, American sociology was little more than a conventicle of preachers without pulpits. But in the century since that brave beginning it has largely forsaken and indeed discredited its moralistic origins. Most sociologists see their work as a profession, not a calling; most scorn the overt ethical emphasis that colored the creation of their discipline.

E. Digby Baltzell is one of a diminishing band who have maintained the faith of the founders. Though his researches require a remarkable empirical ingenuity and technical inventiveness to wring illumination from those desiccated directories of the American establishment, *Who's Who* and the *Social Register,* he has never cultivated methodological virtuosity for its own sake. He has always attempted to touch a broader audience beyond his professional peers, and to entice that public to larger possibilities of life than it was inclined to conceive. From his earliest writing to his most recent, he has tried—as any honest preacher must—to move his countrymen to mend their ways.

In the works which culminated in *The Protestant Establishment,* Baltzell chided his own social elite for its debilitating deficiencies of democracy: its unwillingness to open itself more fully to talent, and its consequent incompetence to constitute itself a ruling class as well as an upper class. In *Puritan Boston and Quaker Philadelphia,* he took all of America to task for its enervating excesses of democracy: its corrosion of class confidence and its attendant indisposition to respect or exert real leadership.

For all their formidable scholarship, Baltzell's books were tracts for their times. The studies of the Philadelphia and the national business aristocracies were full of fascinating information about prestigious men's clubs and boys' boarding schools, but they were also, at bottom, sermons to the smug society of the age of Eisenhower. They flayed the failure of governance that followed from the WASP gentry's reluctance to open its ranks to racial and religious outsiders, and they implored commitments more compatible with the American ethos of opportunity and inclusion. The study of Boston and Philadelphia was rich in intriguing contrasts between the two old capitals of American culture, but it was also, unmistakably, a jeremiad to the self-indulgent society of the seventies. It assailed the refusal to assert or submit to authority that followed from exaggerated infatuation with Philadelphian freedom and egalitarianism, and it begged a bracing reaffirmation of Bostonian command.

Baltzell's dedication of his scholarship to issues and imperatives he has taken to be the most urgent of his time surely represents an honorable—if increasingly idiosyncratic—conception of the study of society. But it just as surely runs risks of dramatizing dichotomy in order to make a moral point. It just as surely compels a heightening of contrasts in order to recall its readers from the ways of wickedness to the paths of righteousness they have forsaken.

Readers recognize that Philadelphia and Boston are more than mere cities in Baltzell's analysis. Each is an emblem of far larger American dispositions, the one to a more tolerant, embracing democracy, the other to a more adamant authority and an insistence on unbending rectitude. Quakerism is a metaphor for anarchic personal empowerment, Puritanism for iron inflexibility and the rule of the better sort. Quakerism conduces to a milling middle class scramble, Puritanism to a more disciplined pursuit of more rarefied public purposes.

No doubt there is something to all this. Baltzell's lamentation over the engorgement of Philadelphian ideals and the abandonment of Bostonian values in contemporary America is not devoid of data. Quakers of the seventeenth century were never so confident of their beliefs as to banish or hang those who differed from them in Christian ecclesiology, as Puritans did in Massachusetts from the first decades of settlement to the last years of the century. Philadelphia was founded as a refuge for men and women of many faiths, Boston as a fortress for those of one true faith. Philadelphia was, as Baltzell would have it, a haven of humility, Boston a sanctuary of *soi-disant* saints.

Nonetheless, such treatment is flagrantly one-sided, and the one-sidedness is necessitated by the esthetic and ethical design that shapes the entire endeavor. The counterposition of competing symbols of contrasting lifeways precludes acknowledgment of anything that Boston Puritans and Philadelphia Quakers shared, in the seventeenth century or since. And in truth they did have more in common than in opposition, especially in comparison with colonists elsewhere in British North America.

In other provinces, settlers celebrated the New World for the effortless ease it afforded. In America as in the ancient garden, "everything seemed to come up by nature." The bounty of a benign providence allowed the earth to bring forth "all things in abundance, as in the first creation, without toil or labor." Crops of every kind grew "as easily as the weeds." Grains were "so grateful to the planter" that they returned him "his entrusted seed" with a treble growth. And herdsman as well as husbandman lived "void of care" on the "benevolent breast" of nature. Domestic stock cost "nothing to keep or feed." Animals grazed freely in winter as in summer, sparing settlers the drudgery of fencing and the tedium of foddering them. Flocks increased astoundingly, "without any charge or trouble to the planter." Almost everywhere, according to the early promotions, men managed "very easily" though they were unwilling to work "above two or three hours a day" or more than "three days in seven." Almost everywhere, in the sales pitches of the settlers, flora and fauna were fruitful and multiplied "to supply the wants or wantonness of man."[1]

In Puritan and Quaker precincts, however, people refused such hedonic ease. Embracing an ascetic ethic which anticipated subsequent American work values of much wider diffusion, they warned prospective inhabitants against expectations of indolent abundance. Puritans deliberately insisted on the arduousness of clearing a frontier or establishing a farm. They held the New World a "howling wilderness," the better to hold its enticements at a distance. They sought to see America in straitened terms, the more effectively to accommodate their image of the continent as "a land preoccupied with toil." Quakers similarly advertised austerity rather than plenty. They affirmed the necessity, in Pennsylvania, of "manly labor," and they hailed such hardship as productive of an "ancient discipline that . . . rewarded virtue and industry." Precisely where other colonists exulted in the amplitude of nature, Puritans and Quakers alike, and almost alone, rejoiced in a wilderness reclaimed and redeemed by labor.[2]

In the settlements strewn elsewhere on the Atlantic littoral, pioneers sought primarily to pursue their own private ends and interests. Merely to contemplate crossing the terrifying ocean, they had had to be more mindful of their own designs, and less considerate of the claims of the community, than the mass of their countrymen in the Old World. Once ensconced in their new milieus, they prized principally the opportunity to "get land." Indeed, they advised their brethren back home not to come if they preferred "the pleasure of society" to solitary economic gratification. They acknowledged that the price of their ambition was the loss of "friends and relations and the satisfaction of their company," but it was a price they were prepared to pay. They were determined to "live much better," as they defined improvement. It was "land only that they came for," or furs, or fish. They meant to "follow [their] own inclination," and more than a few of them meant to do so entirely alone, unconnected "with any person whatsoever." [3]

In congregations of covenanted saints and meetings of faithful Friends, however, authorities insisted on public oversight of private endeavor, and to a degree unparalleled elsewhere, citizens submitted to such intrusions. Puritans had to maintain an unremitting "zeal for the morality of others," in order to uphold the social covenant on which they predicated the temporal prosperity of the community, and in order to be confident of the covenant of grace on which their own eternal destiny depended. True converts were bound to attempt the extirpation of every sin with which they had "occasion to meet and meddle at any time." Quakers also pried into personal lives to repress iniquity and achieve "Holy Community." The group life of Friends was their witness to the world, and their discipline therefore demanded "oversight, care, and compassion, one over another." Quakers in the legislature appointed a committee of "manners, education, and arts, that all wicked and scandalous living may be prevented." Quakers in their meetings imposed elaborate regulations on their members' coming and going, mating and separating, and getting and spending, for the sake of "the reputation of Truth." [4]

In the established churches of the Anglicans, men and women who barely bothered about their neighbors' behavior inquired still less closely into their own. Adherents of the Church of England in America exhibited a casual assurance of their own salvation that exempted them from incentives to introspection. Confident that baptism alone "washed off" the "stain and pollution of sin," they "did not despair of God's mercy" even "to those poor children who die without baptism." Certain of divine providence, they rendered thanks for redemption rather than offering prayers for it. [5]

In Quaker and Puritan purlieus, however, an anxious uncertainty for the spiritual fate of believers and their offspring inspired a relentless reconnaissance of conduct. Members of the meetings and of the congregations examined unceasingly the actions and intentions of their fellows, and especially of themselves. While Anglicans were concerned primarily for outward observance, Friends and Puritans lavished intense attention on their own inward existence. The daily journals of Quakers such as Churchman or Woolman were different, to be sure, from those of Puritans such as Shepard or Mather, but in their separate sorts of interiority they were not nearly so different from each other as from southern Anglicans such as George Washington or William Byrd. Quakers and Congregationalists alike set their adherents on endless rounds of self-monitoring and self-improving, because they attached meaning to minute motions of the psyche as Anglicans of the formative era never did.[6]

In other colonies, to come more explicitly to the concern of this essay, such comparative indifference to the details of psychological development entailed a treatment of children that was fundamentally traditional in Philippe Ariés's delineation of the European tradition. In other colonies, and in established church circles in the Quaker and Puritan provinces as well, children grew up more promiscuously and less protectedly than they did in the new world which Friends, especially, were preparing for the young. Far from being sheltered in the bosom of the narrow nuclear family, they came of age in the rough care of the community. Its corruptions were not concealed from them, its responsibilities not withheld. Children were presumed part of the perenniality of existence. They needed no special nurture because they had no special nature. They could be left largely to their own devices—or, more precisely, to the devices of their peers—because they bore no distinctive burdens and anticipated no distinctive destiny.[7]

In Puritan Boston and Quaker Philadelphia alike, committed communards came in pristine passion for an imminent transformation of humankind. In their enthusiasm, they refused resignation to the frailty of the race. Unlike pioneers in other places, they sought something more than mere material betterment. They were far from oblivious to considerations of commerce or elements of advantage, but they were not ultimately engaged in profane endeavors. They expected their efforts to have sacred significance. They intended to escape the wheel of quotidian history and enter into sacred time. They meant to burst the bounds of the human condition; they aimed at a remodeling of men and women, a regeneration of all mankind.

John Winthrop called his community "a city upon a hill." William Penn proclaimed his proprietary a "holy experiment." Winthrop believed that "the eyes of all people" were upon him and his followers, and that they might be a model for "succeeding plantations." Penn professed his faith that his settlement on the Delaware would be "the seed of a nation" and "an example to" all nations. Winthrop accordingly implored his fellow saints to "entertain each other in brotherly affection." Penn bestowed on his beloved capital the name of the fabled city of seventeenth-century mystics, Philadelphia, the city of brotherly love. The poet Daniel Hoffman catches exactly the eschatological audacity of Penn's vision in his evocation of "a green and country town / where history begins anew."[8]

Men and women who meant to begin anew had to ponder not only the implementation of their vision but also its implantation in those who would come after them. Men and women who burned to attain a secular sainthood, a purging of earthly imperfections, had to consider not only the reconfiguration of their own characters but also the promotion of perfection in their children.

Congregationalists and Quakers both commenced the construction of such purified identity by rearranging radically the circumstances under which their offspring would come of age. Both repudiated the medieval mingling of public and private spheres which their seventeenth-century neighbors still took for granted. Both drew back from the entanglements of the complex community to the seclusion of the simple family. Both sought in such privacy a more auspicious environment for the fostering of new selves.

Puritans were among the first people in the early modern West to attempt this disconnection of father, mother, and children from the wider society. But they did not do so as others who essayed a similar severance did, to preserve the impeccancy of their little ones and shield it from contamination. Puritans never did envision childhood as a sanctuary of innocence and irresponsibility. As Edmund Morgan said, they entertained no notions "of developing the child's personality, of drawing out or nourishing any desirable inherent qualities which he might possess, for no child could by nature possess any desirable qualities." Still, Puritans were driven to create familial cloisters for protective child-rearing by their very insistence on innate depravity. Knowing they could not alter the child's inward corruption, they determined all the more imperiously to manage its manifestations in outward conduct. They determined to crush the youngster's every wayward impulse. They prepared, quite literally, to beat the hell out of him. And they put their plans and purposes into practice by maintaining an unwavering watch over their young from earliest infancy. The depth of their devotion to that regimen of unceasing surveillance and that ambition of unremitting control became apparent when they had to choose, before the seventeenth century was out, between the evangelical logic of their faith and the emotional promptings of their intense investment in their children. Over the course of a protracted crisis concerning admission to membership in the Congregational churches, they effectively gave up the effort to remake the world which had been the essence of the Puritan enterprise, in order to preserve the tribal entitlements of their offspring.[9]

Friends carried devotion to domestic priorities even further, and their familism was far more prefigurative of subsequent American modes than was the Puritan pattern. Quakers founded their families on the voluntary love of spouses to a degree the Puritans never did, and followed strategies of tender child-rearing to a degree the Puritans never dreamed. Quaker parents preferred not to inflict physical punishment on their little ones or otherwise manage them by shame or coercion. They appealed to their children's best instincts instead of mobilizing to suppress their worst. They believed that boys and girls grew in the paths their parents exemplified rather than the ones they exhorted. But for all these differences, Quakers were at one with Puritans—and at odds with almost everyone else in early America—in their focus on the family. More than that, they were at one with the New Englanders in their departure from their initial determination to transform Christendom and their subsequent turn to tribalism. Just as the Puritans made membership in their churches increasingly difficult for all who were not born to members, so the Friends increasingly ceased to seek further Friends beyond the ranks of their own children. Quakers did not set doctrinal tests for admission to their meetings. They accepted as Quakers all who called themselves Quakers and behaved like Quakers. But behaving like a Quaker became a progressively more formidable task. It was best accomplished by a kind of osmosis in a Quaker family, under the subtle influence of the family's gentle monitions. It was predicated on acceptance of the decisive passage from a public to a private ordering of life, in which "the trivia, responsibilities, and relations of private life" became "fascinating, profound, and sacred."[10]

These altered estimations of the gratifications and significances of private life became increasingly normative for affluent and aspiring Americans in succeeding centuries. These abandonments of public priorities for personal ones foreshadowed a shift that would increasingly define the respectable classes of the new nation. And these ideals of companionate marriage, child-centered domesticity, and lovingly surveillant nurturance increasingly set the dilemmas which American youth would confront as they came to maturity.

It is not yet clear how impulses and ideas once confined to a couple of distinctive dissenting religious bodies overspread the country. But a few of the forces that converged to constitute privatization and its attendant pressures on young people as canons of propriety and parental adequacy for masses of Americans can be discerned. A few of the sources of the elaboration and secularization of such values that have eventuated in our own developmental ethic can be delineated.[11]

All of them were emergent by the beginning of the nineteenth century. At least one of them was evident at least half a century earlier: the example of the pioneers themselves. Barry Levy has detailed this development among the Friends and their Anglican neighbors in the Chester County countryside near Philadelphia, where the fond, fostering child-centeredness of the Quakers had unintended economic consequences. While Anglican churchmen pursued traditional investment policies, focusing their expenditures on expensive public sports and games for the sake of sociability, honor, and display, Friends confined their purchases to domestic amenities and sufficient land to allow their offspring a stage for their own familial dramas. Yet Anglicans, "unburdened by concern for delicate nurturance and protecting environments, were actually less economically aggressive and able" than Friends who sought primarily to insulate their children from the world. Quakers cultivating an intimate environment amassed markedly larger outward estates than their more traditional rivals. And their distinctive example, which was at first irritating to the Churchmen, eventually became irresistible. In the early part of the eighteenth century, Anglican missionaries preached virulently against "that fatal weed of Quakerism." By the middle of the century, their auditors were demonstrably adopting the same familial focus.[12]

The rise of new dissenting denominations at the end of the eighteenth century also affected the configuration of private life. By the second quarter of the nineteenth century the preponderant churches in the land were the Methodists and the Baptists, and their evangelicalization of America immensely enlarged the ranks of dissenting Protestants and the affinity for the new domesticity. Baptists and Methodists parted from Puritan and Quaker precepts in many ways, but on the decisive dimensions of disengaging public pursuits and principles from private ones and giving privileged status to the private, the new national denominations were even more adamant than the old provincial ones had been.[13]

The emergence of new notions of separation of sexual spheres also enlarged the insistence on incessant attention to private performance, extending it to women as well as to men, and to other Americans outside the Quaker and Congregational folds. In the years after independence, an ideology of republican motherhood advanced. It affirmed the fundamentality of the mother in the moral growth of the child, the fundamentality of childhood in the formation of adult character, and the fundamentality of character in the preservation of the republic. Under its aegis, women had to canvass their children's conduct as ethical actors and, no less, to monitor methodically their own demeanor as mothers. Their judgment of their own adequacy as mothers, quite as much as the development of their children and the fate of the nation, depended on how effectively they attended to their young.[14]

The steady progress of science and technology also spurred diffusion of the energies, ambitions, and anxieties inherent in the new fixation on the family. Technics expressed a comparable compulsion to control, and science a similar fantasy of transcendence of man's traditional estate. Puritans and Quakers had aspired to make people godlike in their mastery of their own inner natures. The scientists and engineers of the nineteenth century sought to make them equally almighty in their command of external nature.

Many years ago, Max Weber traced in magisterial detail the transmutation of a religious ethic into an economic outlook. On much the same model, a religious project passed by stages into a secular passion in the realm of child-rearing. A sheltering surveillance of the young that served initially as a means to spiritual ends—preparation for salvation for the Puritans, guidance to God's inner light for Friends—became in the course of time an end in itself. An intense oversight of youthful development that was undertaken originally for the sake of souls evolved over generations into an all-too-worldly test of women's willingness to fulfill their maternal function, then into a measure of maternal competence, and then into a telltale of parental character and worth.

As it did, parents bent their efforts increasingly to secure suitable outcomes of such tests, and they came to conceive such outcomes ever more competitively. Consummations that had been, for the Puritans, inscrutable gifts of God or, for the Friends, indwelling potentialities available to all, became in subsequent centuries invidious advantages to be engineered at ever earlier ages by ever more promising ploys. Children would no longer be nurtured; they would be trained. And their training would begin earlier, proceed more encompassingly, and last longer, in more formal institutions, than Quakers or Puritans of the seventeenth century could ever have imagined.

By the end of the nineteenth century, the pattern was set. At least a hundred years ago, the great American psychologist of the day, G. Stanley Hall, could publish an essay entitled "Overpressure in Schools" asserting the "real and grave danger" in which the country stood from the conspiracy of circumstances which "favor[ed] precocity and ma[d]e a simple, quiet, healthful life for children increasingly hard."

Hall attributed the danger to the decay of religion, the decline of the countryside, the rise of the city and its "haste and excitement," and especially the "entirely artificial condition which school life involves," and the "violent opposition" of parents and teachers alike to alleviating that artificiality. The refusal to shorten school hours or alter the emphasis of the educational mills on mental rather than physical exercise and on intellectual rather than ethical development seemed, to Hall, to present a prospect of "alarming invalidism" among American youth, and particularly among talented American youth. For the "overpressure" fell primarily upon "clever children," who were "forced forward" by the stimulus of a competition that Hall, following Ruskin, called "the most entirely and directly diabolic of all the countless stupidities" into which the nation had "of late" been "betrayed" by its "avarice and irreligion."

Hall placed the blame for this forcing of the intellectual faculty almost indifferently upon schools and families, teachers and parents. There were many teachers, he maintained, "'so possessed by the demon of education' and so 'professionally nearsighted,' that they claim the almost exclusive right to the child's time, so that he has no opportunity to pursue privately" his own interests and pleasures and "no chance for independent growth." And there were many parents who aided and abetted such teachers. "Long before a child's capabilities [could] be known, parents with false views of life and of school, and perhaps not without vanity and cupidity, not only allow[ed] but sometimes encourage[d] teachers to overpress their children, and sow seeds of suffering and incapacity."[15]

Hall had abundant contemporary company in his concerns. A few years before his article appeared, Herbert Spencer was honored at a banquet at Delmonico's in New York. This commanding intellectual figure of the Victorian era gave the assembled audience of bankers and businessmen not the paean to progress for which they had come but a "doleful warning against overwork." This apostle of Social Darwinism, himself "broken by years of battling with nervous exhaustion," took the occasion of the gala affair to declare his alarm at "the frequency of suicide and nervous collapse among American businessmen." As he saw the situation, "Americans did not know how to relax; they were bored out of harness, driven within it; they were even passing on their nervousness to their children, through high pressure public schools."[16]

No one was noticeably shocked by Spencer's indictment. One editorialist blandly observed that the celebrated Englishman had merely "added his corroboration to the immense mass of testimony which has, ever since the introduction of railroads and telegraphs, been convicting Americans of taking too little relaxation." Another maintained that it was already "universally admitted" that "something must be done . . . to lessen the strain in modern life."[17]

A forum of leading American educators, convened at about the same time to consider the country's "Educational Needs," came back again and again to fears for "the anxious, nervous, worrying tone so generally seen in the faces" of the nation's "brain-worked" children. Participants in the symposium saw a "sallow languor" in the students, an unmistakable "physical deterioration." Felix Adler spoke for them all when he said, "the public are growing uneasy. It is feared that the brains of our little ones are overworked in the schools."[18]

Each of the educators who contributed to the colloquium concurred in the diagnosis: American children were mentally overdeveloped, physically stunted, and morally malnourished. And they agreed as well on the source of that dismal diagnosis: American children were subject to an unwholesome competitiveness that afflicted home and school alike, creating a climate of "worry, terror, and overwork" for the very young, who seemed to "struggle with their studies as weak swimmers struggle with a stormy sea." A principle that ought to have been axiomatic—that excessive strain should not be imposed on growing children—was instead "utterly and necessarily disregarded" by a "system which engaged children in competitive strife." That system fostered a few of the intellectual faculties at the expense of all other youthful capacities. As Mary Putnam Jacobi put it, "imagination, invention, judgment, reasoning, [and] perception" were "left without systematic training," the "senses" were ignored "altogether," and "ethical education" was "entirely left out of sight."[19]

It is a century since those essays, addresses, and editorials, but they might almost have been composed yesterday. Our terminology might be a bit different from theirs, but the deep structures of understanding seem very nearly identical. We remain anxiety-ridden about the same issues. Are we pushing our children excessively or insufficiently? Are we too competitive or not competitive enough? What is it that will make our youngsters happy anyway? And we share the ambivalences of our ancestors.

The perennial issues remain issues of pressure—the pressure we experience as adults, and the pressure we put on our children—and the recurrent ambivalences remain ambivalences over progress. We are tantalized by the possibility which technology holds forth of relief from present pressures, and at the same time we are terrified by the probability that technology presents of intensifying those very pressures. And every generation among us imagines itself the first ever to address such dilemmas, the first to be forced to come to terms with the pellmell pace of modern life. Every generation among us envies its predecessors their exemption from such stress, discounting or indeed dismissing their dealings with equally dizzying dislocations.

I have many students, in a course I teach on the history of the 1960s, who speak seriously of television as the essential source of the turbulence of that decade. I ask them what they mean, and they answer in all earnestness that the eruption of that mass medium upon the American scene altered consciousness, aroused conscience, and brought Americans to common concerns in ways that had never before been possible. They are, to all appearances, utterly innocent of this nation's history of almost two centuries as the world's first mass culture. They are entirely ignorant of the newspapers and pamphlets which blanketed the country by the end of the eighteenth century, and of the magazines, religious tracts, and dime novels which knit the nation together in the nineteenth. They allow nothing of the unparalleled experiment in democratic diffusion of information that attended the advent and elaboration of the telegraph, the public lecture circuit, the telephone, the news wire services, the phonograph, the radio, and the movies; they forget entirely the railroad and the automobile, which had shattered provincial insularity irreparably decades before Milton Berle or "I Love Lucy" ever did.

Yet virtually every one of these technological innovations was heralded in its own day with the same breathless rhetoric of social renewal that television was in its time, or the computer in ours. Commercial telegraphy was barely a year old in 1847 when it was trumpeted as the harbinger of a new epoch in human history, a means of promoting "harmony among men and nations," an instrument of inconceivable "Moral Progress." Its advocates claimed that it would be as much a "missionary of peace and good will to the world" as "The Church," that it would have a "humanizing influence" of extraordinary proportions, that it would, indeed, alter consciousness to the point of "breaking down the barriers of evil prejudice" and impelling "an end to international hostility."[20]

A generation later, the telegraph was already part of the problem rather than the secret of its solution. Editorialists and educators connected it with the coming of the railroads and the rise of the cities as causes of the overstimulation of the senses and overexcitation of the intellect that they feared flowed too readily into overpressure and nervous exhaustion; but by then others were already envisioning another technological innovation, the telephone, as a source of renovation and regeneration. "The fables and fairy tales of old pale before the facts of the present day," proclaimed one pundit after another. In the days in which G. Stanley Hall and his fellow students of development were fretting over the fruits of earlier inventions, the prestigious *Scientific American* was predicting that the telephone would promote "nothing less than a new organization of society—a state of things in which every individual, however secluded, will have at call every other individual in the community." Alexander Graham Bell's revolutionary device would provide at once a "technique of democratization," an instrument of social control, and a means of minimizing all the "little evils and annoyances" which seemed in 1880 "to make life laborious and unsatisfactory."[21]

By the time it was clear that the telephone might magically enhance the human voice, but that it would not mystically make life satisfactory, the siren songs of other cuckoos were heard in the land. The technological transformation of conduct and consciousness which had not attended the telephone would be wrought by radio, or movies, or television. And today, when it is all too apparent that an entire generation brought up on television has managed to remain as anxious, as self-centered, as career-conscious, and as competitive as any of its predecessors—when it appears, indeed, that the young people who grew up "tied to the tube" cannot read, write, sustain attention, analyze issues, tolerate ambiguity, or even score as well as their parents on aptitude tests—we have new enthusiasts offering extravagant forecasts for the generation coming of age with computers. I would not hold my breath waiting for the superpeople these putative superbabies are supposed to become.

But that is not to say I would not worry as Americans before me have worried about the pressures we put on our children, the exaggerated demands we make of them, and the inflated hopes we invest in them. I worry when I read that the parents of four daughters with IQs over 150 recently held a "Donahue" audience spellbound with helpful hints on teaching babies before they are even born. I worry when I see that, in a survey of the qualities they most desired in their little ones, most parents put intelligence at the top of their lists.[22]

I worry when I hear people praise "Sesame Street," with its interminable emphasis on reading readiness and its abiding indifference to emotions and attitudes, while they disparage the Saturday morning cartoons, which at least acknowledge aggression, conflict, and other issues central to life in contemporary American society. I would worry less if I thought that parents wanted their youngsters to watch shows brought to them by junk cereals and Japanese robots which might teach them to come to terms with debased appetites and desires, than I do when I find that parents prefer that their children watch shows brought to them by the letters of the alphabet, which can teach them only a debased intellectual technicianship. I cannot fathom the fuss over a few IQ points or a few months head start in reading. And I simply cannot credit the sublime supposition that parents can shape their progeny to these over-intellectualized images or, for that matter, to any other images.

Even psychologists are beginning to understand what historians and poets could have told them from the first: the best-laid schemes o' mice an' men gang aft agley. History reveals nothing more forcefully than the fatuousness of our faith in our ability to achieve our ends in any straightforward fashion. History is nothing if not a study in unintended consequences. And developmental psychology, which has been scandalously indifferent as a discipline to long-term development, is finally accumulating enough longitudinal studies to enable its practitioners to come to a comparable skepticism of linear continuity of character.

A recent collection of essays by Jerome Kagan, *The Nature of the Child,* summarizes a substantial complement of these accounts. It concludes that infant attributes commonly fade and that infant experiences generally fail of lifelong impact concordant with any conventional theoretical expectations. Some early attributes and experiences are left behind in the course of maturation; others are undone by subsequent experience. One way and another, the first years of childhood prove to have paltry predictive power even for the later phases of childhood, much less for adulthood. One child capitalizes on initial advantages, another is incapacitated by them. One child is crippled by early adversity, another transcends it. But on the whole, adults are not creatures of their infancy or youngest years. "The factors related to adult satisfaction, behavior and emotional problems are almost invariably other adult experiences, not childhood ones." [23]

Kagan does not claim that parents and other participants and elements in the child's early environment make no difference. Manifestly, they matter a great deal. Kagan only insists—as any orthodox historian would—that parental stimuli elicit no *predictable* response from children. Parents who cherish, or dread, their power to form their sons and daughters in particular patterns are simply mistaken, for parents do not determine as much as they hope, or fear. Our children are not ciphers, nor blank slates on which we inscribe aptitudes according to our abilities as parents. We cannot engineer their intelligence or control their capacities in any mechanistic sense.

Like our Quaker and Puritan predecessors, we still seek the renovation of the race, or at least of our own tribal portion of it. We still aspire to transcend our own limits by training our children in our own images of perfection. But our children bring crucial qualities to their socialization that we as parents are powerless to command. They meet the world according to their own temperaments, and they infuse it with their own interpretations. Events are never, therefore, defined solely by what parents do. They are affected every bit as decisively by the intentions and significances that the child sees in the parents' actions. And as Kagan reminds us, those imputed intentions, those childish definitions of the situation, can be idiosyncratic indeed.

Different children in the same community, even in the same family, can find different significances, and consequently draw different strengths and suffer different debilities, from the very same experiences: a harsh word, a smile, a beating, a trip to the shore. Children from entirely different cultures can find even more disparate meanings in the same overt behaviors. No adult conduct carries its own intrinsic significance, independent of personal and social circumstances, or its own irresistible causal efficacy, apart from the complicity of the child. Character is not forged in accordance with deterministic developmental laws or along inexorable predictive paths. Its evolution is subject to the vagaries of temperament and interpretation, and to the exigencies of the historical and cultural moment. The practices and principles of mothers and fathers in the rearing of children can reveal a great deal about the views and values of adults, but very little about the ultimate fate of their offspring.

One of the best accounts of the persisting anxieties and perplexities of parents across the past few centuries in the West is a book which scarcely speaks of children and their upbringing at all. It is a book about mining pumps and machine tools, steamboats and spinning jennies, windmills and watches, a classic book by Lewis Mumford called *Technics and Civilization*. It is pertinent to our purposes because it traces as well as any analysis ever has the emergence in the modern world of mechanistic conceptions of nature and man.

It is that mechanization of our ideas of our cosmos and ourselves, at least as much as anything else, I think, to which we owe our perennial impasse. It is that mechanization of our apprehension of experience which impels our recurrent readiness to seek technological escapes from technologically induced dilemmas, that mechanization of our very imagination which promotes our presumption that the only way out is forward.

The mechanization of the Western world picture evolved over an extended period, but it was essentially in place by the end of the seventeenth century. It rested upon notions of time and space contrary to the common sense of the middle ages and the common experience of people even to this day, notions of the homogeneity and uniformity of spatial and temporal units such as are epitomized in perspective painting and clock time. Such notions expressed a conception of experience inconceivable to the men and women of the middle ages, who had counted numbers but never supposed that only numbers counted. The mechanistic conception converted tangible commodities into intangible cash values. It changed personal ties of feeling into impersonal relations of regimentation. Under its aegis, abstraction and calculation emerged as the essential modes, and standardization and mass production the ascendant norms, in institutions as different as the army, the workplace, and the school.

Since the seventeenth century, mechanization and the mechanistic mentality have ramified ever more elaborately, reaching far beyond the radical Protestant sectarians, Puritans and Quakers among them, who were the core of their original constituency. By now, vast numbers of us are "more at home with abstractions than . . . with the goods they represent." We buy and sell soybean futures or AT&T shares without the slightest comprehension of soybean cultivation or telephonic technology. We even daydream in abstractions, fantasizing that we might be millionaires without the remotest notion what we would do if we were.[24]

The same sensibility that shapes our ideas of our own worth also shapes our ideas of what our children might amount to. The same rage to rate everything and everyone according to simple quantifiable criteria permits us to reduce our appreciation of the intricacies of childhood intelligence to Intelligence Quotients and of the complexities of adolescent aptitude to Scholastic Aptitude Test scores; indeed, it leads us to take such idiocy seriously, as if we could actually distinguish among our young with any utility from one percentile to the next and should actually spend significant energy in the attempt. The same ardor to understand our own development on the model of the machine allows us to embrace deterministic doctrines such as Freud's and become, by our very complicity, the prisoners of childhood his theories posit.

Such sublime, self-debasing faith in mechanism has been constitutive of modern Western culture for several centuries, and nowhere more than in America. It defines us. It is our destiny, unlovely as it may be. We will be publishing colloquia chafing at our technological dependence, and the strain it entails on our children, a hundred years from now as we were a hundred years ago. And those colloquia too will purport to speak of children but in fact betray a rampant adult unease at our technological drivenness and our inability to stop the machine.

The truth seems to be that we cannot stop the machine, and do not even truly want to. Perhaps we are simply playing out our allotted string, for the perverse satisfaction of seeing, in macabre fascination, where it leads. But I think there is more to it than that. I think we are committed to the machine in more than mere agnostic obstinacy. I think we are, in the end, believers in the machine. It is our god, almost our only god. I only hope that, like the rather more human god of the bible, it spares a few of us for a remnant when it finally explodes in wrath. I only hope that, unlike the biblical divinity, it does not take for such a remnant its most devout and faithful followers.

Notes

1. John Lawson, *A New Voyage to Carolina* (1709), ed. Hugh Lefler (Chapel Hill: University of North Carolina Press, 1967), 69, 115; "Arthur Barlow's Discourse of the First Voyage," in David Quinn, ed., *The Roanoke Voyages, 1584–1590* (London: Hakluyt Society, 1955), I: 108; E. W., *Virginia: More Especially the Southern Part Thereof, Richly and Truly Valued* (1650), in Peter Force, comp., *Tracts and Other Papers Relating Principally to the Origin, Settlement, and Progress of the Colonies in North America* (Washington, D.C., 1836–46), III, no. xi, 12–13; Durand of Dauphiné, *A Huguenot Exile in Virginia*, ed. Gilbert Chinard (New York: The Press of the Pioneers, 1934), 122: Daniel Denton, *A Brief Description of New York* (1670), ed. Victor Paltsits (New York: Columbia University Press, 1937), 18; *Proposals by Mr. Peter Purry* . . . (1731), in B. R. Carroll, ed., *Historical Collections of South Carolina* (New York: Harper, 1836), 127; Lewis Leary, "The Adventures of Captain John Smith as Heroic Legend," in J. A. Leo Lemay, ed., *Essays in Early Virginia Literature Honoring Richard Beale Davis* (New York: Burt Franklin, 1977), 16–17; William Byrd, *The History of the Dividing Line*, in *The Prose Works of William Byrd of Westover: Narrative of a Colonial Virginian*, ed. Louis Wright (Cambridge, Mass.: Harvard University Press, 1966), 290.

2. Daniel Rodgers, *The Work Ethic in Industrial America, 1850–1920* (Chicago: University of Chicago Press, 1978), 4–5; William Penn, "The Benefit of Plantations, or Colonies," in *Select Tracts Relating to Colonies* (London, 1732), 26, 28.

3. Belfast News Letter, no. 2926, September 3–October 22, 1765, 7–8; George Scot, *The Model of the Government of the Province of East-New-Jersey* (1685), in William Whitehead, *East Jersey under the Proprietary Governments* (Newark, N.J.: Dennis, 1875), 462; *The Journal of Nicholas Cresswell, 1774–1777* (New York: Dial Press, 1924), 1–8; Jacquelyn Wolf, "The Proud and the Poor: The Social Organization of Leadership in Proprietary North Carolina, 1663–1729," Ph.D. dissertation, University of Pennsylvania, 1977.

4. Charles and Katherine George, *The Protestant Mind of the English Reformation, 1570–1640* (Princeton, N.J.: Princeton University Press, 1961), 102–03; "The Diary of Michael Wigglesworth," ed. Edmund Morgan, *Publications of the Colonial Society of Massachusetts* 35 (1951): 316–17; Frederick Tolles, *Meeting House and Counting House: The Quaker Merchants of Colonial Philadelphia, 1682–1763* (Chapel Hill: University of North Carolina Press, 1948), 63–84; *Book of Discipline of the Society of Friends in Pennsylvania and New Jersey* (1719), copied for the American Philosophical Society, Philadelphia, 1–2; Richard Bauman, *For the Reputation of Truth: Politics, Religion, and Conflict among the Pennsylvania Quakers, 1750–1800* (Baltimore: Johns Hopkins University Press, 1971). See also J. William Frost, *The Quaker Family in Colonial America: A Portrait of the Society of Friends* (New York: St. Martin's Press, 1973); Sydney James, *A People Among Peoples: Quaker Benevolence in Eighteenth-Century America* (Cambridge, Mass.: Harvard University Press, 1963); Susan Forbes, "'As Many Candles Lighted': The New Garden Monthly Meeting, 1718–1774," Ph.D. dissertation, University of Pennsylvania, 1972.

5. [John Page], *A Deed of Gift to My Dear Son, Captain Matt. Page* (1687: Philadelphia, 1856), 190; private prayers of Eliza Lucas Pinckney, 1742–1758, in St. Julien Ravenel Childs papers, South Carolina Historical Society, Charleston, S.C., December 28, 1742, and passim.

6. John Churchman, *An Account of the Gospel Labors and Christian Experiences of a Faithful Minister of Christ, John Churchman* (Philadelphia, 1781); Phillips Moulton, ed., *The Journal and Major Essays of John Woolman* (New York: Oxford University Press, 1971); Michael McGiffert, ed., *God's Plot: The Paradoxes of Puritan Piety, Being the Autobiography and Journal of Thomas Shepard* (Amherst: University of Massachusetts Press, 1972); *Diary of Cotton Mather*, Massachusetts Historical Society, *Collections*, 7th ser., VIII, pt. ii (Boston, 1911); Donald Jackson and Dorothy Twohig, eds., *The Diaries of George Washington* (6 vols., Charlottesville, Va.: University Press of Virginia, 1976–79); Louis Wright and Marion Tinling, eds., *The Secret Diary of William Byrd of Westover, 1709–1712* (Richmond, Va.: The Dietz Press, 1941); Louis Wright and Marion Tinling, eds., *William Byrd of Virginia: The London Diary (1717–1721) and Other Writings* (New York: Oxford University Press, 1958); Maude Woofin, ed., *Another Secret Diary of William Byrd of Westover 1739–1741, with Letters and Literary Exercises, 1696–1726* (Richmond, Va.: The Dietz Press, 1942).

7. Philippe Ariés, *Centuries of Childhood: A Social History of Family Life* (New

York: Random House, 1962); Philip Greven, *The Protestant Temperament: Patterns of Child-Rearing, Religious Experience, and the Self in Early America* (New York: Knopf, 1977); Michael Zuckerman, "William Byrd's Family," *Perspectives in American History* 12 (1979): 255–311; Michael Zuckerman, "Penmanship Exercises for Saucy Sons: Some Thoughts on the Colonial Southern Family," *South Carolina Historical Magazine* 84 (1983): 152–66; Darrett and Anita Rutman, *A Place in Time: Middlesex County, Virginia, 1650–1750* (New York: Norton, 1984).

8. Perry Miller and Thomas Johnson, eds., *The Puritans* (rev. ed., New York: Harper and Row, 1963), 198–99; Jean Soderlund, ed., *William Penn and the Founding of Pennsylvania 1680–1684: A Documentary History* (Philadelphia: University of Pennsylvania Press, 1983), 54–55, 77; Dietmar Rothermund, *The Layman's Progress: Religion and Political Experience in Colonial Pennsylvania, 1740–1790* (Philadelphia: University of Pennsylvania Press, 1961); Daniel Hoffman, *Brotherly Love* (New York: Random House, 1981), 124.

9. Edmund Morgan, *The Puritan Family: Religion and Domestic Relations in Seventeenth-Century New England* (rev. ed., New York: Harper and Row, 1966), 53.

10. Frost, *The Quaker Family*; Barry Levy, *Quakers and the American Family: British Quakers in the Delaware Valley, 1650–1765* (New York: Oxford University Press, 1988). The quotation is from Barry Levy, "The Birth of the 'Modern Family' in Early America: Quaker and Anglican Families in the Delaware Valley, Pennsylvania, 1681–1750," in Michael Zuckerman, ed., *Friends and Neighbors: Group Life in America's First Plural Society* (Philadelphia: Temple University Press, 1982), 48.

11. On the twentieth-century triumph of the developmental ethic see, e.g. Robert Bellah, *Habits of the Heart: Individualism and Commitment in American Life* (Berkeley and Los Angeles: University of California Press, 1985); Christopher Lasch, *The Culture of Narcissism: American Life in an Age of Diminishing Expectations* (New York: Norton, 1978); Joseph Veroff, Elizabeth Douvan, and Richard Kulka, *The Inner American: A Self-Portrait from 1957 to 1976* (New York: Basic Books, 1981); Daniel Yankelovich, *New Rules: Searching for Self-fulfillment in a World Turned Upside Down* (New York: Random House, 1981).

12. Levy, "The Birth of the 'Modern Family'," 43, 40.

13. See, e.g., Paul C. Johnson, *A Shopkeeper's Millennium: Society and Revivals in Rochester, New York, 1815–1837* (New York: Hill and Wang, 1978); Mary Ryan, *Cradle of the Middle Class: The Family in Oneida County, New York, 1790–1865* (New York: Cambridge University Press, 1981); Anthony Wallace, *Rockdale: The Growth of an American Village in the Early Industrial Revolution* (New York: Knopf, 1978).

14. Nancy Cott, *The Bonds of Womanhood: 'Woman's Sphere' in New England, 1780–1835* (New Haven, Conn.: Yale University Press, 1977); Linda Kerber, *Women of the Republic: Intellect and Ideology in Revolutionary America* (Chapel Hill: University of North Carolina Press, 1980); Ruth Bloch, "American Feminine Ideals in Transition: The Rise of the Moral Mother, 1785–1815," *Feminist Studies* 4 (1978): 101–26.

15. [G. Stanley Hall], "Overpressure in Schools," *The Nation* 41 (October 22, 1885): 338–39.

16. T. J. Jackson Lears, *No Place of Grace: Antimodernism and the Transformation of American Culture 1880–1920* (New York: Pantheon, 1981), 52.

17. "American Overwork," *The Nation* 35 (November 16, 1882): 417; "Editor's Study," *Harper's Monthly* 89 (October, 1894): 799–801.

18. "Educational Needs," *North American Review* 136 (1883): 284–304; quotations from G. Stanley Hall and Felix Adler, pp. 286, 290.

19. "Educational Needs"; quotations from Thomas Hunter and Mary Putnam Jacobi, pp. 295–96, 300–03.

20. Richard Du Boff, "The Telegraph in Nineteenth-Century America: Technology and Monopoly," *Comparative Studies in Society and History* 26 (1984): 571.

21. Carolyn Marvin, "When Old Technologies Were New: Electric Communication in the Late Nineteenth Century," paper presented to the Andrew Mellon Seminar in History and Technology, University of Pennsylvania, 1985, pp. 24, 29, 54.

22. *ERIC/EECE Newsletter* 17, 1 (1984): 1.

23. Jerome Kagan, *The Nature of the Child* (New York: Basic Books, 1984); quotation from Carol Tavris, "New Hope for Freud Sufferers," *The Nation* (November 3, 1984): 455–56.

24. Lewis Mumford, *Technics and Civilization* (New York: Harcourt, Brace, 1934), 24.

Samuel H. Preston

4. Resources, Knowledge, and Child Mortality: A Comparison of the United States in the Late Nineteenth Century and the Developing Countries Today*

The great forces driving mortality levels in the past century are enhanced material resources and improved knowledge of the means to avoid disease and death. These factors operate at both the private and public levels. Improved knowledge of diseases can lead to better personal hygiene as well as to public preventive programs of which most individuals are unaware. Richer countries can afford to mount more complex health programs, just as richer people are likely to arrange to have superior medical care within any given system.

We have argued earlier (Preston, 1975, 1980) that increased availability of resources has not been the dominant force in twentieth-century mortality decline. The evidence for that conclusion is simply that countries at a given level of per capita real national income enjoyed higher life expectancies as the century progressed. The curve relating life expectancy to income shifted upward by eight to ten years between the period around 1935–40 and the period around 1965–70. The shift was ascribed to technical advances, usually embodied in government programs.

In this paper we attempt to clarify the importance of knowledge factors and resource factors by examining microlevel mortality differentials under an unusual range of circumstances. In particular, we compare child mortality differentials in the United States in the late nineteenth century to mortality differentials in certain developed countries today. The scheme that underlies the analysis can be illustrated as in the accompanying diagram.

| | | LEVEL OF TECHNICAL KNOWLEDGE ABOUT HEALTH | |
		Low	High
LEVEL OF ECONOMIC DEVELOPMENT	Low	A Third world countries, nine-teenth century	B Third world countries today
	High	C U.S. late nineteenth century	D Developed countries today

The choice of the United States is based upon its having the only national data available for the nineteenth century on children ever born and children surviving. Because of its size, affluence, and ethnic heterogeneity, it may even be the preferred choice, if only one country were used to represent state C.

Both income and health knowledge are distributed along a continuum rather than dichotomously. But by choosing the two relatively discordant circumstances represented by **B** and **C**, we expect to be able to illuminate the important role of both sets of factors under varying circumstances. That the United States in the late nineteenth century was a relatively rich country is shown by the following data. According to the National Bureau of Economic Research's series of GNP estimates, per capita GNP in the United States in 1929 dollars rose from $415 to $497 per capita between 1890 and 1900 (U.S. Bureau of the Census, 1966 Series A11). Converted into 1982 dollars, the range is from $2148 to $2572. This places the United States 1890–1900 in a range with Hungary, Portugal, Romania, Argentina, and Chile today (World Bank, 1984:219). But while these latter countries have a life expectancy at birth of 70–71 years (ibid.: 219), the United States in 1895–1900 had a life expectancy of 49–50 years (Preston and Haines, 1984:275, 277).

The United States in 1890–1900 was also relatively well educated. From 78 to 79 percent of youths aged five to seventeen were enrolled in school, although the average pupil appears to have attended school only the equivalent of about four months per year (U.S. Census Bureau, 1966: Series B 36–39). In 1910 the median adult had attended school an average of 8.1 years (ibid.: Series B 40), and a prior absence of trend in school enroll-

ment figures suggests that the figure was not much lower twenty years earlier. In the 1900 U.S. Census, 87.8 percent of ever-married women were
literate, as were 89.0 percent of their husbands. Like income, these are also
very high levels relative to most developing countries today.

Why did these high levels of literacy and income not translate into high
levels of life expectancy? Our answer—tautologically correct in view of
universality of goals to improve health—is that the United States in this
period simply did not know how to effect this conversion. The germ theory of disease had been validated only in the 1880s and still met with opposition or indifference in many circles. The following brief illustrations of
the state of knowledge regarding disease may be informative. We refer
mainly to the period of the 1890s; we will use cumulative child mortality data from the United States Census of 1900, which refer on average
to 1895.

1. Frederick Hoffman, chief actuary of the Prudential Life Insurance
Company, wrote a monograph for the American Economic Association in
1896 focused on the social demography of the American black population.
Hoffman attributed the slow natural increase and the excess mortality of
blacks from virtually every cause of death (even including malaria, where
the sickle cell trait clearly affords many blacks protection) to inherent ge-
netic inferiority. The following statement is typical (p. 95): "It is clear now
that we have reached the underlying cause of the excess mortality [of
blacks] from consumption and the enormous waste of child life. It is not in
the conditions of life, but in the race traits and tendencies that we find the
causes of the excessive mortality . . . the effect will be to increase the mortality by hereditary transmission of weak constitutions, and to lower still
further the rate of natural increase, until the births fall below the deaths,
and gradual extinction results." The notion that unhygienic conditions
could cause disease is almost completely missing from Hoffman's account,
whose major message is that the white race is inexorably increasing because of its superior innate powers of vital resistance. Hoffman wrote a
good deal on health during this period and was frequently cited. Irving
Fischer, often described as the greatest American economist, was also a
serious student of mortality, having written a census monograph on the
subject in 1899. A later book on health (Fischer, 1909) is full of fascinating
misinformation about fatigue poisons, eye strain, nervous prostration
from prolonged sitting, and sexual irritability from meat eating (pp. 41, 75,
91, 95 among others).

2. In 1894 a crowd of 3,000 persons armed with clubs, knives, and stones

gathered in front of a house in Milwaukee, where health officials were expected to attempt to take a two-year-old child to the hospital with a suspected case of smallpox. The family had previously lost a child in the hospital, which was a notorious death house. The riots spread and prevented many other potential patients from entering the hospital (Leavitt, 1979).

3. As Vogel (1979) has shown, at the turn of the century hospitals were in the midst of changing from an institution most akin to an almshouse to a technical center. The movement was contentious and costly. In 1908, the superintendent of New York Hospital and president of the American Hospital Association declared, "I am absolutely at a loss for an understanding of the value of a medical library in a hospital." He shut the library and gave away its books (Vogel, 1979:113).

4. One student of the history of American medical practice building on the work of Charles Rosenberg has offered the following characterization of medical knowledge in the nineteenth century (Pellegrino, 1979: 246–47):

> At the beginning of the nineteenth century, therapeutics was fixed in a notion of health and illness held in common by physicians and their patients. On this view, illness was an imbalance in the economy of the whole body, expressed in a disturbance in the relationships of input or output of food, sweat, secretions, urine, phlegm, and the like. Treatment was aimed at restoring harmony and balance between environment and constitution. This was best accomplished not by specific attack on some symptoms of disease, but by inducing a physiological effect—sweating, febrilysis, diuresis, vomiting—which helped the body to recover its internal and external balance. . . . At the close of the nineteenth century, physicians were understandably ambivalent about accepting the new conception of a type of therapeutics specifically tailored to particular disease entities which had slowly emerged during the course of the century. . . . It was difficult, as always, to give up long held theories about the nature of disease and how it should be treated. The burgeoning achievements of pharmaceutical chemistry, anesthesia, and surgery *in the early 20th century,* however, finally compromised the older theories." [emphasis ours]

The holistic imbalance theories still present at the end of the nineteenth century doubtless made it much easier to ascribe the high mortality of blacks from such diseases as malaria to racial traits rather than to mosquitoes.

5. The urban public health movement was at the early stages of development. In 1890, 26 of 96 large cities reported having no sewage systems at

all, and in the remaining 70 cities less than half of the dwellings were connected (Meeker, 1972). Improvements in sanitation were surely occurring, but it is likely that only a small minority of the United States population lived in sanitary conditions appreciably different from those of 1800. By 1900, beyond smallpox vaccination, the only important medical advance was the deployment of diphtheria antitoxin in the 1890s.

The foregoing paints a picture of quite considerable ignorance on the part of the intelligentsia and the medical profession at the turn of the century, and a slow implementation of the new ideas about disease causation. Of course, preposterous statements of health matters could be cited today, but it is not likely that they would have the imprimatur of the American Economic Association or the Committee of One Hundred on National Health of the federal National Conservation Commission, as did the monographs of Hoffman and Fischer. It is equally unlikely that they would gain much credibility among intelligentsia in developing countries today.

If ignorance (by modern standards) was widespread in the United States at the turn of the century, we should observe a different pattern of mortality differentials than the pattern that prevails today in the developing world. In particular, there should be much less payoff for increasing amounts of schooling. Schooling effects should reflect only the accretion of material resources that result from the increased earning opportunities; the additional portion of the effect that would reflect closer connection to good health knowledge and practice among the well educated should be largely inoperative in a situation where education "buys" one little knowledge. Indeed, for similar reasons the size of *all* social class differentials in mortality should be smaller in the United States in 1890–1900.

Table 4.1 compares the size of child mortality differentials in classes arranged by father's occupation in the United States in 1900 and in certain developing countries in the 1970s. The values appearing in the table are based upon identical types of data and procedures. All countries have data on the number of children ever born and children surviving. The number of children ever born for each woman is converted into an expected number of child deaths by reference to her age or duration of marriage (an index of exposure) and to the average level of child mortality in the population as a whole as represented by an appropriate model life table. Deaths and expected deaths are then aggregated for all women in a class. For details, see Preston and Haines (1984) and Mensch, Lentzner, and Preston (1984).

TABLE 4.1. Comparison of relative mortality in different occupational classes, U.S. 1900 and developing countries in the 1970s (ratio, deaths to expected deaths among children ever born; expected deaths are based on the average child mortality level in a particular country)

FATHER'S OCCUPATIONAL CATEGORY	U.S. 1900	MEAN OF ELEVEN DEVELOPING 1970s	GHANA 1971	KENYA 1978	LESOTHO 1977	SOUTHERN NIGERIA 1972	INDONESIA 1971	NEPAL 1976	SOUTH KOREA 1971	SRI LANKA 1975	THAILAND 1975	CHILE 1970	PERU 1978
Professional/ Managerial/ Clerical	.933 (769)	.652	.621 (2948)	.652 (425)	.743 (66)	.726 (536)	.789 (11721)	.784 (187)	.673 (101)	.556 (225)	.606 (132)	.629 (455)	.401 (491)
Sales	.831 (173)	.913	.775 (874)	.887 (388)	1.343 (35)	.933 (252)	1.033 (6850)	.844 (173)	.883 (613)	.868 (242)	.519 (108)	1.128 (196)	.828 (406)
Service	1.001 (165)	.841	.665 (1179)	.665 (1179)	.984 (85)	.910 (111)	1.002 (2402)	.760 (148)	— (—)	.767 (189)	1.061 (72)	.866 (135)	.732 (209)
Agriculture	.890 (3375)	1.206	1.128 (30446)	1.059 (1943)	1.197 (66)	1.195 (10481)	1.000 (43467)	.995 (3884)	.956 (1266)	1.141 (1288)	1.123 (1378)	1.213 (685)	1.304 (2197)
Production Workers	1.150 (2967)	1.007	.802 (5081)	1.051 (1203)	1.006 (1705)	1.052 (421)	1.028 (3965)	1.253 (423)	1.088 (491)	.938 (771)	.881 (278)	1.059 (1444)	.921 (1242)

Source: Tabulations of public use data files performed at the University of Pennsylvania.

Table 4.1 shows that the size of mortality differentials in the United States in 1890–1900 (the period to which the mortality data refer, on average) is much smaller than that observed in developing countries today. In particular, the professional/managerial/clerical classes had mortality levels only 7 percent lower than the national average, compared to the 35 percent advantage that this group enjoys, on average, in developing countries today. None of the eleven developing countries examined shows less than a 21 percent advantage for this group.

The other large discrepancy occurs for farmers and farm laborers. This group has mortality 11 percent below the average in the United States in 1890–1900, but 21 percent above the average in developing countries today. The comparison between professionals and agricultural classes is therefore particularly striking. Agricultural classes have mortality 85 percent *higher* than professional classes in our sample of LDCs, today, but 5 percent *lower* in the United States in 1890–1900.

The explanation of the poor performance of professional classes is not to be found in a peculiar composition of the group in 1900. The subgroup that we can label the intelligentsia shared the unexpectedly high mortality of the professional classes, as shown in Table 4.2. It is particularly illuminating that doctors' children had mortality of only 8 percent below the national average, and higher than that among coal miners or farmers. Likewise, teachers were clearly not moved to a position of advantage by whatever health doctrines were being taught in schools. Only pharmacists enjoy the same advantage as professional classes have in LDCs today, but their mortality level is based on only 14 expected deaths.

Taking the figures in Table 4.1 one step further, we can estimate the absolute (rather than the relative) mortality of children born into the different classes in the United States in 1890–1900 and in a composite of LDCs today. The composite is formed in the following way. The level of life expectancy at birth in LDCs in 1975–80, as estimated by the United Nations (1983), is 54.8 years. This corresponds to level 15.6 in the Coale-Demeny (1983) "West" model life tables. At that level, the probability of dying before age 5 $[q(5)]$ is .137. The mean of relative mortality levels for a particular class in Table 4.1 for our eleven LDCs is then applied to this figure to produce the values in Table 4.3. This procedure assumes that the average of the eleven countries is representative of the average of LDCs. "West" mortality levels are in fact relatively close: an average level of 14.9 for our eleven, versus 15.6 for LDCs as an aggregate. The United States 1900 level is estimated at 13.65 (Preston and Haines, 1984:275), and relative mor-

TABLE 4.2.   Ratio of child deaths to expected deaths in selected occupations in
the United States, 1900

FATHER'S OCCUPATION	CHILD DEATHS/ EXPECTED DEATHS	NUMBER OF EXPECTED DEATHS
Physicians, surgeons, dentists	.927	35.6
Clergymen	.805	32.3
Teachers	.999	26.0
Lawyers	.757	22.4
Pharmacists	.647	13.9
Total, intelligentsia	.853	130.2
Coal miners	.902	118.6
Farmers	.863	3056.0

talities in Table 4.1 are applied to the q(5) of .176 that corresponds to that
level. There is good reason to suppose that this multiplicative property
of q(x) that is implicit in our procedure is valid to a close approximation
(Trussell and Preston, 1982).

Table 4.3 shows that the United States in 1900 had much higher child
mortality than today's developing world in every occupational class except agricultural workers. Its disadvantage is particularly great among
the professional/managerial classes. The United States professional classes
in 1900, in fact, had no better child mortality than agricultural workers in
developing countries today, who are by every account a seriously disadvantaged group. The combination of high national income, high national literacy, and high relative social status in 1900 produced the same mortality
level as is observed in the most disadvantaged social group in the world
today. Clearly, the manner in which material resources are converted into
mortality levels has changed dramatically.

Table 4.4 presents similar comparative data on literacy and urban/rural
residence. The results on literacy are similar to those on social class, but
less dramatic. The child mortality advantage for literate mothers in the
United States was 30 percent, compared to an average of 43–47 percent in
developing countries today. Lacking direct data on literacy in most of the
developing countries, we have presented two series, one assuming that literacy is achieved with 4 years of schooling and the other that it is achieved
after 7 years of schooling. In either series, the difference with the United
States is appreciable. Of the eleven countries examined, only Lesotho and

TABLE 4.3.   Estimated probability of dying by age five in two populations

FATHER'S OCCUPATIONAL CATEGORY	U.S., 1900	COMPOSITE OF DEVELOPING COUNTRIES, 1975–80	RATIO
Professional, managerial, clerical	.165	.089	.539
Sales	.146	.125	.856
Service	.176	.115	.653
Agricultural	.157	.165	1.051
Production workers	.202	.138	.683
All classes	.176	.137	.778

South Korea show a lower payoff to literacy than did the United States in 1900.

Multivariate results are more decisive, although the absence of identical data in the different countries means that exact comparability in specification cannot be achieved. Nevertheless, such standard factors as educational attainment (or literacy) of mother and father, occupation of father, and urban/rural residence are available in all data sets. A well-known result is that mothers' education or literacy tends to retain a powerful effect in developing countries even after all other socioeconomic variables are controlled (e.g., Cochrane, 1980). Such a result is also observed in the developing countries examined here. Mensch, Lentzner, and Preston (1984) have shown that the average coefficient on mother's years of schooling in these countries with all other variables controlled is about .035. If the illiterate have an average of one year of schooling, and the literate an average of eight—reasonable figures in the United States in 1900—it implies that the literate should have about 25 percent lower mortality. But the coefficient on mothers' literacy in the United States in only .06, about one-quarter of the expected effect, and it is statistically insignificant.

Note that this result pertains when we have controlled race, maternal grandmother's place of birth, husband's literacy (also having a coefficient of −.06), paternal grandfather's place of birth, husband's occupation in 10 categories, husband's predicted income, urban/rural residence, ownership of home, husband's age and unemployment status, presence of boarders and servants in the house, division of current residence, predicted state income, and length of time in the United States.

TABLE 4.4.   Comparison of relative mortality levels in developing countries today and United States, 1890–1900

	RATIO, CHILD MORTALITY, LITERATE MOTHERS TO ILLITERATE MOTHERS		RATIO, CHILD MORTALITY, URBAN MOTHERS TO RURAL MOTHERS
	Series 1[a]	Series 2[b]	
U.S., 1900 .697			1.279
Ghana, 1971	.495	.361	.732
Kenya, 1978	.666	.613	.809
Lesotho, 1977	.851	.861	1.055
Southern Nigeria, 1972	.609	.611	.816
Indonesia, 1971	.631	—	.831
Nepal, 1976	.483	.313	.519
South Korea, 1976	—	.714	.873
Sri Lanka, 1975	.634	—	.875
Thailand, 1975	.319	—	.580
Chile, 1970	.699	.583	.782
Peru, 1978	.357	.264	.604
Mean developing countries	.574	.540	.770

[a]Assuming women with 4+ years of education are literate.
[b]Assuming women with 7+ years of education are literate.

Unfortunately, income data are not present in the United States data set. The brilliant Woodbury study of 1911–15 in eight United States cities included income data as well as literacy and many other variables. Literacy was dropped from the final report (Woodbury, 1925), perhaps because preliminary results showed it to be unimportant. But the report on the largest city studied, Baltimore, presented a cross-tabulation of infant mortality by fathers' income and mothers' literacy (Rochester, 1923). It is reproduced here as Table 4.5. Clearly, literacy has little if any explanatory power after income is controlled, contrary to results observed in today's developing world.

Table 4.4 also shows very different relations between mortality and urban/rural residence in the United States in 1900 and in today's developing countries. Urban residents (defined as living in places of 5,000+ residents) had 28 percent *higher* mortality in the United States in 1900, compared to an average of 23 percent *lower* mortality in developing countries today.

TABLE 4.5.   Infant mortality rate (per 1000 births) by literacy of mother and earnings of father in Baltimore, 1915

ANNUAL EARNINGS OF FATHER	LITERATE MOTHERS		ILLITERATE MOTHERS	
	Infant mortality rate	Number of births	Infant mortality rate	Number of births
Under $450	161	1193	143	349
$450–549	120	1206	108	241
$550–649	107	1314	126	174
$650 and over	79	5660	86	233

Source: Rochester (1923:332)

Multivariate results are also quite different for the two populations. In most of the developing countries examined, urban/rural residence loses its significance when other variables are introduced, and often turns around in sign (Mensch, Lentzner, and Preston, 1984). The lower mortality of urban residents shown in Table 4.4 is thus primarily ascribed to their higher social standing. But in the United States in 1900, urban residence gains significance when other variables are introduced (Preston, Haines, and Pamuk, 1981); the higher social status of urban residents was actually serving to mask some of the disadvantages of urban life. In fact, size of place of residence seems to be the single most important variable in accounting for variance in child mortality in the United States in 1900.

Haines (1984) reaches similar conclusions regarding literacy and urbanization in his analysis of United States data. Rather than explaining variance at the individual level, he first groups mortality data into occupational classes and attempts to explain why one occupational group has higher or lower mortality than another. The proportion of literate wives in a group is insignificant; the coefficient of the urban proportions in a group is about 2.4, very large and significant.

To what extent was the United States typical of other now-developed countries at the end of the nineteenth century? It clearly shared with them the pattern of higher urban than rural mortality (United Nations, 1973: 132–36). Much less is known about social class differences in child mortality. The only other study of children ever born/children surviving data for the nineteenth century of which the author is aware is Mattheissen's

(1972) study of the Copenhagen Census of 1880. This study also shows relatively small social class differences. The ratio of $q(5)$ among "officials, professionals, and manufacturers" to that among the "working class" is .747 (.231/.309), the ratio for "teachers and clerks" to the working class is .881 and for "master artisans and shopkeepers," it is .990. The United States ratio of "professional, managerial, clerical" to "production workers" from table 1 is .811, well within the range of the Copenhagen data and much higher than in developing countries today (.647). A disproportionate concentration of the professional/managerial classes in high mortality cities like Copenhagen would probably have further reduced their advantage relative to mortality in Denmark as a whole. A later data set for England and Wales, 1911, however, shows much larger social class differences than in the United States in 1900 (Haines, 1984). Professional classes and farmers had mortality very close to one another, as in the United States in 1900, but blue collar classes had much higher child mortality than either group. It is likely that this difference in the pattern of differentials reflects a faster adoption by the professional classes of hygienic practices between 1900 and 1911; the much higher degree of urbanization in England in 1911 than in the United States in 1900, reducing the relative disadvantage of urban living for the professional classes; and a greater inequality of income in England. The forthcoming availability of a 1910 U.S. Census public use sample will permit the testing of the first of these explanations.

Discussion

There is probably no population in the world, today or in centuries past, in which higher levels of material resources in the household are not associated with lower mortality. More and better food and clothing, more space, more leisure, and better sanitary facilities will produce lower probabilities of dying in any environment. These factors are measurable and their impact ubiquitous. As a result, they tend to be emphasized in many accounts of mortality trends and differentials (e.g., McKeown, 1976; Mosely, 1983).

It is increasingly evident that another powerful set of factors has also been at work, which we have labelled "knowledge/technique." First, the material factors fail to account for a majority of the rapid mortality decline between 1940 and 1970 (Preston, 1975; 1980). Second, child mortality in developing countries tends to be powerfully influenced by mother's schooling and by ethnicity even when differences in levels of resources associated with these factors are controlled (Mensch, Lentzner, and Preston, 1984). Such results imply that there are unmeasured variables reflecting child care practices with which literacy and ethnicity are associated. Third, very privileged groups before the twentieth century, such as the European aristocracy, have levels of mortality that would be shockingly high by contemporary standards (see papers in Glass and Eversley, 1965). We have attempted to give further support to this position by showing that knowledgeable and highly advantaged classes in the United States in 1900—highly advantaged even by today's standards—had been unable to convert that advantage into a reasonable mortality level. Indeed, they fared no better than the poor agricultural classes in the developing world today. We have argued that this failure reflects a substantial ignorance about health matters, which we have attempted to document with several examples.

This ignorance was not necessarily confined to such matters as the germ theory of disease. A good bit of the high mortality of the advantaged classes resulted from their living disproportionately in urban areas, which were clearly unhealthy at the turn of the century. But this unhealthiness was not supernaturally imposed; it reflects the widespread failure of urban residents to activate the political institutions that were capable, then as now, of sharply reducing mortality. So the ignorance to which we refer is some combination of ignorance about personal health and ignorance about what public institutions could accomplish in the area of health. That this ignorance has largely disappeared is vividly suggested by the fact that urban residents in developing countries no longer suffer the excessive mortality that their dense living arrangements would otherwise foster.

The fact that literacy had a much smaller health payoff in the United States in 1900 than it has in developing countries today, particularly in multivariate relations, helps shed light on the mechanisms through which this variable is operating today. It suggests that health knowledge itself (perhaps more of hygienic practices than of disease causality, as Lindenbaum (1983) suggests) is one of the most important routes through which education is operating. When relatively little was known about means for reducing mortality, increased schooling produced relatively little mortality reduction.

The importance of these non-material, knowledge-related, factors underscores the possibilities for continued health advance in developing countries. Material progress occurs slowly and is already the major objective of national policy in most countries. That there may be major, affordable, and unexploited means left for improving health knowledge and technique in developing countries is suggested by the sizeable mortality differences associated with ethnicity and literacy. However, the rate of shift in the curve relating life expectancy to income, literacy, and calories appeared to slow down between 1965–69 and 1975–79. Instead of an exogenous gain of three years per decade estimated for the previous thirty year period, the gain was only about one year in the most recent decade (Preston, 1983). It is possible that the slowdown reflects diminishing returns to the knowledge/technique factors, or simply a weakened ability or will to take advantage of what possibilities remain. But whether or not these factors hold the key to the future, they appear to be critically important in understanding the past.

References

* This paper is an outgrowth of two collaborative projects, one conducted with Michael Haines and the other with Barbara Mensch, Harold Lentzner, and students at the University of Pennsylvania. I am grateful for their assistance. I am also grateful for comments by Etienne van de Walle. The projects are supported by the Ford Foundation and the U.S. National Institute of Child Health and Human Development.

Coale, A. J. and P. Demeny (1983). *Regional Model Life Tables and Stable Populations*. New York: Academic Press.

Cochrane, S. (1980). *The Effects of Education on Health*. Washington, D.C.: World Bank Staff Working Paper No. 405.

Condran, G. A. and E. Crimmins-Gardner (1978). "Public Health Measures and Mortality in U.S. Cities in the Late Nineteenth Century." *Human Ecology* 6(1):27–54.

Fischer, I. (1909). *Report on National Vitality, Its Wastes and Conservation*. Bulletin of the Committee of One Hundred on National Health, prepared for the National Conservation Commission. Washington, D.C.: U.S. Government Printing Office.

Glass, D. V. and D. E. C. Eversley (1965). *Population in History*. London: Edward Arnold.

Haines, M. R. (1984). "Inequality and Childhood Mortality: a Comparison of England and Wales, 1911, and the United States, 1900." *Journal of Economic History*.

Hoffman, F. L. (1896). *Race Traits and Tendencies of the American Negro*. Publication of the American Economic Association, Vol. XI (1, 2, and 3):1–329. New York: The MacMillan Co.

Leavitt, J. W. (1979). "Politics and Public Health: Smallpox in Milwaukee, 1894–95." In S. Reversby and D. Rossner, eds., *Health Care in America: Essays in Social History*, 84–102. Philadelphia: Temple University Press.

Lindenbaum, S. (1983). "The Influence of Maternal Education on Infant and Child Mortality in Bangladesh." Manuscript, International Centre for Diarrhoeal Disease Research, Bangladesh.

Matthiessen, Poul (1972). "Application of the Brass-Sullivan Method of Historical Data." *Population Index* 38(4): 403–08.

McKeown, T. (1976). *The Modern Rise of Population*. New York: Academic Press.

Meeker, E. (1972). "The improving health of the United States, 1850–1915." *Explorations in Economic History* 9: 353–74.

Mensch, B., H. Lentzner, and S. H. Preston (1984). *Socioeconomic Differentials in Child Mortality in Developing Countries*. United Nations Population Study No. 97. New York: United Nations.

Moseley, H. W. (1983). "Will primary health care reduce infant and child mortality? A critique of some current strategies, with special reference to Africa and Asia." Paper presented to the IUSSP Seminar on Social Policy, Health Policy, and Mortality Prospects, Paris, Feb. 28–Mar. 4, 1983.

Pampana, E. J. and P. F. Russell (1955). "Malaria: a World Problem." *Chronicle of the World Health Organization* 9(2–3): 33–100.

Pellegrino, E. D. (1979). "The Sociocultural Impact of Twentieth Century Therapeutics." In M. J. Vogel and C. E. Rosenberg, eds., *The Therapeutic Revolution*, 245–66. Philadelphia: University of Pennsylvania Press.

Preston, S. H. (1975). "The Changing Relation Between Mortality and Level of Economic Development." *Population Studies* 29(2): 231–48.

——— (1980)."Causes and Consequences of Mortality Decline in Less Developed Countries During the Twentieth Century." In R. E. Easterlin, ed., *Population and Economic Change in Developing Countries*, 289–360. Chicago: University of Chicago Press.

——— (1983). "Mortality and Development Revisited." Background paper prepared for World Bank *World Development Report, 1984*.

Preston, S. H. and M. R. Haines (1984). "New Estimation of Child Mortality in the United States at the Turn of the Century." *Journal of the American Statistical Association* 79(386): 272–81.

Preston, S. H., M. R. Haines, and E. Pamuk (1981). "Urbanization, Industrialization, and Mortality in Developed Countries." *International Population Conference* Vol. 2, 233–54. Manila.

Rochester, A. (1923). *Infant Mortality: Results of a Field Study in Baltimore, Maryland, Based on Births in One Year*, U.S. Department of Labor, Children's Bureau, Bureau Publication No. 119. Washington, D.C.: U.S. Government Printing Office.

Trussell, T. J. and S. H. Preston (1982). "Estimating the Covariates of Childhood Mortality from Retrospective Reports of Mothers." *Health Policy and Education* 3: 1–36.

United Nations Population Division (1983). "World population prospects as assessed in 1982." Printout dated November 1983.

U.S. Bureau of the Census (1966). *Long Term Economic Growth, 1869–1965: A Statistical Compendium*, Washington, D.C.: U.S. Government Printing Office.

Vogel, M. J. (1979). "The Transformation of the American Hospital, 1850–1920. In S. Reversly and D. Rossner, eds., *Health Care in America: Essays in Social History,* 105–16. Philadelphia: Temple University Press.

Woodbury, R. M. (1925). "Causal Factors in Infant Mortality." U.S. Department of Labor, Children's Bureau, Bureau Publication No. 142, Washington, D.C.: U.S. Government Printing Office.

Richard Farnum

5. The American Upper Class and Higher Education, 1880–1970

Introduction

This paper is an attempt to develop several issues raised by E. Digby Baltzell's work on higher education and the upper class. While he has been concerned primarily with examining the structures, functions and values of the upper class in American society, in each of his books (1958, 1964, 1979) he has devoted some attention to the relationship between the upper class and institutions of higher education, both the colleges and universities members of the upper class have attended, and the contributions these schools have made to the coherence and maintenance of the upper class. A Philadelphian, he has focused for the most part on the upper class of his native city, though he has supplemented this with both comparative study of Boston and generalizations about the national American upper class at large. This study will systematically extend his work in both time and space by examining patterns of college attendance of the upper classes of Philadelphia, Boston, New York, and Baltimore from 1880 to 1970.

What has been the history of higher educational attendance of the Philadelphia upper class since the late nineteenth century? Baltzell found that upper class Philadelphians for the most part attended the local university, the University of Pennsylvania (Penn), until around 1900, at which time it reached the zenith of its prestige as a Proper Philadelphia institution. But during the twentieth century, and particularly after World War I, local fidelity was eroded and eventually eclipsed as a majority began to go away to Harvard, Yale, and Princeton (hereafter referred to as HYP), the national upper class colleges. The precise timing of this pattern and its development after World War II will be examined.

How does this pattern compare with those of other metropolitan upper classes in the east? Baltzell's work on Boston suggested that Harvard's national eminence is attributable at least in part to the greater support and fidelity evidenced by the Boston upper class toward its local college. Further comparisons are in order. New York is of particular relevance here since it shares with Boston and Philadelphia a local higher educational institution of colonial vintage (Columbia, 1754). Have New Yorkers, for example, demonstrated a greater fidelity to their local college than Philadelphians? Baltzell has observed that the rise of a national upper class began in New York in the 1880s where the first *Social Register* was published in 1888. This may suggest that the New York upper class is more cosmopolitan, demonstrating even less local pride than Philadelphians. Baltimore will also be examined, though it did not acquire a local college of repute until the late nineteenth century (Johns Hopkins, 1876).

How have the patterns of upper class college attendance changed since World War II? Much of Baltzell's work has been confined to the prewar period, though in *The Protestant Establishment* (1964) he briefly extended his analysis into the postwar era. There he charted the rise of the achievement principle as both faculty appointments and student admissions became based increasingly on meritocratic criteria. Whereas during the 1930s and 1940s very few Jews received tenure at HYP, by the 1960s these faculties were ethnically quite heterogeneous. Before World War II "good character and adequate preparation" (read "WASP and boarding school") were sufficient to gain admission, but by the 1960s SAT scores of 625 were average, and public school graduates outnumbered those from private schools. Such changes had inevitable consequences for upper class college attendance and elite college functions.[1]

The answers to the above questions should yield some insight into the different constitutions of various urban upper classes as well as the changing functional significance of higher education for the upper class and society as a whole. Baltzell has described the importance of the socialization and status-ascribing functions of HYP for the maintenance of an authoritative establishment up to 1940. Have such colleges continued to perform these functions in the postwar era? Does the evidence from other cities support the claim that HYP became national upper class institutions as Baltzell has suggested? Are there other colleges that also might qualify in this category? What were the grounds for and timing of their emergence into national prominence, and does such prominence still exist? The answers to such questions bear on the issues of the functions of elite education, the stratificational hierarchy among higher educational institutions, and the articulation of these with the class structure. This study, then, is a comparative inquiry into the educational patterns of America's upper class, the changing functions of elite higher education, and the relative prestige of America's colleges from 1880 to 1970.

The data for this study were collected from the *Social Register* in the cities of Boston, New York, Philadelphia, and Baltimore at decade intervals from the 1880s through the 1960s. Two general types of information will be summarized in tabular form for each city. The first attempts to give some indication of the relative concentration or dispersion of the upper classes among few or many institutions. To be presented here are the number of colleges from which upper class members graduated during a given decade as well as the percent of upper class graduates in each decade who received their degrees from either one of the five most frequently attended colleges ("top-five") or a college not among the five most attended ("other"). Such information should illuminate the following issues raised by Baltzell: (1) the extent to which the upper class of a given city is unified in its conception of desirable institutions of higher education; (2) the extent to which the members of the upper class share a common socialization and status ascribing experience; and (3) the extent to which the particularistic association of an upper class with specific institutions has been disrupted since World War II, thereby "democratizing" the upper class with respect to higher education. Each of these conditions bears on the cohesion and integrity of the relevant upper class. For example, it may be expected that those upper classes which have a high percentage in the "other" category would tend to be less cohesive than those where the reverse obtains.

The second type of information concerns the particular schools most attended by an upper class group from 1880 to 1970. The percent attending each of the top-five colleges will be presented for each decade of the period as well as a comparison of the percent attending HYP taken collectively and the percent attending the preferred local institution. These figures will provide evidence for the degree of localism or cosmopolitanism in an upper class, the extent of the hegemony exerted by HYP, and changes in each of these phenomena over time.

Boston

The Boston data are presented in Tables 5.1–5.4 and Figure 5.1. The figure represents in graphic form the information contained in Table 5.3. Tables

TABLE 5.1.   Boston: Colleges graduating social registrants by decades (N)

1880s	1890s	1900s	1910s	1920s	1930s	1940s	1950s	1960s
6	11	5	6	12	11	18	20	35

5.1 and 5.2 bear on the issue of the extent of concentration and dispersion of the upper class in its college attendance. The first and most obvious measure is simply the number of schools mentioned in the *Social Registers* by decades from which members of the upper class graduated.

The overall trend from 1880 to 1970 was a sixfold increase in the number of schools chosen. The expansion began in the 1920s and progressed in three waves. The first, in the 1920s and 1930s, was roughly a doubling of the relatively constant levels from the 1880s to the 1910s. This was very likely the result of the First World War. As David Levine (1981) has pointed out in his study of higher education during the interwar years, World War I initiated the modern era of increased and more democratized college attendance. Martin Trow (1972) has dubbed this the beginning of the shift from elite to mass higher education. The second expansion, starting in the 1940s and 1950s and accelerating in the 1960s, was the result of the even greater democratization of higher education that followed World War II. It is also likely that this trend was in part a response to the institutionalization of increasingly universalistic or meritocratic standards at elite colleges and universities. Faced with such less directly ascriptive admissions criteria, members of the upper class found themselves less able to enter the prestige colleges of choice and were forced to be more "democratic" in their selection of schools.

The information in Table 5.2 generally corroborates the above findings. The percent of the upper class attending one of the five most often selected schools declined by nearly 50 percent. In the earliest period, from the 1880s to World War I, over 90 percent of the upper class attended one of the top five schools, with the single anomaly of the 1890s when the percentage sank to 84 percent. This exception may be explained as a reaction to the more democratic and professional orientation that President Charles W. Eliot was trying to establish at Harvard at the time, but would require more investigation to interpret. For two decades after World War I, however, the percent attending the top five dropped to 86 percent. After World War II, during the 1940s and 1950s, upper class concentration dropped to

TABLE 5.2.   Boston: Colleges of social registrants by decade of graduation (%)

	1880s	1890s	1900s	1910s	1920s	1930s	1940s	1950s	1960s
Top-five	93	84	96	98	86	86	75	74	51
Other	7	16	4	2	14	14	25	26	49
Total	100	100	100	100	100	100	100	100	100

75 percent, and in the 1960s to 51 percent. The mirror image of these trends is presented by the percent of the Boston upper class graduating from colleges other than the five preferred schools. This group dramatically increased sevenfold from 1880 to 1970, paralleling the periodic declines in the top-five category. After World War I, the percent attending other schools doubled, it doubled again after World War II, and yet again in the 1960s. All of these measures indicate a dramatic increase in the dispersion of the Boston upper class in college attendance over the period considered, reflecting both an educational "democratization" of the upper class and a sociological democratization of the most preferred schools. It should be observed, however, that the fact that as late as 1970 over 50 percent of the upper class attended one of the top-five schools, indicates that the Boston upper class remains disproportionately capable of securing admission to prestige colleges and coherent in its pattern of college attendance.

Table 5.3 and Figure 5.1 present information on changing preferences among the top-five schools over time.

Harvard, Yale, Princeton, Williams, and MIT remain throughout the ninety-year period the five most chosen schools, in that order, based on overall average representation. Together they account for 80 percent of the upper class graduates on average. The most dramatic observation to be made here, however, is how much Harvard dwarfed the other colleges. Of the 80 percent average accounted for by the top five, Harvard had contributed fully 67 percent. It was by far the top choice of the Boston upper class. None of the other four ever accounted for more than 11 percent (Princeton in the 1950s), and, on average, none was above 5 percent. Harvard's attraction was a compound of at least two elements: it was both the first and premier local Boston college, and it was, with Yale and Princeton, one of what have traditionally been regarded as the three most prestigious national undergraduate institutions. Yale and Princeton are among the top five for this latter reason alone. Williams and MIT here represent "local" institutions of high standing. (While Williams is not local to Boston, it is

TABLE 5.3.   Boston: Social registrants graduating from top-five colleges by decade of graduation (%)

	1880s	1890s	1900s	1910s	1920s	1930s	1940s	1950s	1960s	M
Harvard	78	72	92	85	70	78	61	54	38	67
Yale	5	2	0	6	4	8	7	5	4	5
Princeton	0	0	2	2	9	0	1	11	7	4
Williams	3	4	2	3	2	0	4	3	1	2
MIT	7	6	0	2	1	0	2	1	1	2
Total	93	84	96	98	86	86	75	74	51	80

in Massachusetts and has long enjoyed a reputation as perhaps the finest, certainly the oldest, New England liberal arts college.)

The other principal observation to be made on this information is that while the share of the upper class attending Yale, Princeton, MIT, and Williams remained relatively constant over time, Harvard's share, with some fluctuations, declined from a high of 92 percent in the 1900s to a low of 38 percent by 1970. Thus the decline in upper class attendance at top-five schools from 93 percent to 51 percent is largely Harvard's loss. Harvard's share of the upper class began to wane sometime in the 1900s, was arrested and actually increased during the 1930s, but sharply descended again beginning in the 1940s. The latter decline may be attributable to the democratizing trends mentioned above. The earlier decline, however, is more difficult to interpret in this way. It is fairly well known that it was not very difficult to be admitted to any of the Big Three during the 1920s and 1930s (Bloomgarden, 1961). Perhaps a more plausible explanation has to do with the perception held by the Boston upper class that Harvard had become too radically democratized under President Eliot. In concrete terms what this meant to the upper class was that there were too many Jews and other non-WASPs. Eliot had attempted to institutionalize a more rigorously universalistic orientation at Harvard and let the sociological chips fall where they might. This had resulted in a rather naked and invidious system of social stratification within the college. Many members of the upper class reacted to this situation by sending their children away from the city altogether to smaller and more protected liberal arts colleges (Synnott, 1979). The plausibility of this explanation of the Harvard decline is enhanced by its reversal in the late 1920s and early 1930s. Eliot's successor in 1909 was

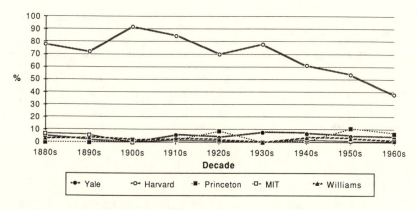

FIGURE 5.1. Boston: Social registrants graduating from top-five colleges by decade of graduation

A. Lawrence Lowell, a man very much attuned to the sociology of the college and of the nation. An active member of the immigrant restriction movement of the 1920s, Lowell in 1922 began a policy of restricting the number of Jews at Harvard by the use of quotas. Insofar as enhancing the attraction of Harvard to the Boston upper class was an objective, his policy apparently succeeded, at least temporarily. As the figures indicate, the percent of the upper class at Harvard increased during his tenure.

It is interesting to observe that Harvard's overall loss of the upper class from 1880 to 1970 was not balanced by increases in the other top five schools. While the share of the other four colleges increased over time, especially Yale and Princeton, most of Harvard's decline must be accounted for by other schools altogether. This is confirmed by Tables 5.1 and 5.2.

Table 5.4 compares the relative shares of the upper class divided between Harvard on the one hand and Yale and Princeton on the other. Harvard's clear supcriority here must be attributed to local fidelity on the part of the Boston upper class. It should also be noted, however, that the share of YP, while small, tended to increase over time. Thus, some of Harvard's losses were to the benefit of Yale and Princeton, especially the latter. During the 1920s Princeton's share of the Boston upper class increased dramatically to close to 10 percent. Princeton is, of course, the smallest, least urban, and, especially during Fitzgerald's era of gin and jazz, the most socially homogeneous of the Big Three. That Princeton would have drawn so many Proper Bostonians in the 1920s lends further support to the idea that they were disturbed by democratization at Harvard.

TABLE 5.4.   Boston: Social registrants graduating from Harvard (H) and Yale–Princeton (YP) by decade of graduation (%)

	1880s	1890s	1900s	1910s	1920s	1930s	1940s	1950s	1960s
H	78	72	92	85	70	78	61	54	38
YP	5	2	2	8	13	8	8	15	11
Total	83	74	94	93	83	86	69	69	49

New York

The New York data are presented in Tables 5.5–5.8 and Figure 5.2. The patterns of concentration and dispersion in college attendance among the New York upper class generally parallel the Boston findings.

The number of schools increased fivefold over the 90-year period. The initial rise, however, began in the 1890s and remained fairly constant until the 1930s and 1940s when a second plateau of minor increase was reached, followed by a nearly 100 percent increase after World War II. The timing of the first major rise, which really extended from the 1890s through the 1940s, may coincide with the influx of southern and eastern European migration to this country in the 1880s. Table 5.6, however, shows different patterns of concentration.

Until the 1920s, the proportion of the New York upper class attending the five most selected schools remained fairly constant, in the 80 percents. The 1930s, 1940s, and 1950s showed a drop of about 10 percent followed by a drop of about 25 percent in the 1960s. The percent attending other colleges than the five most chosen increased nearly threefold. These patterns of dispersion over time, somewhat greater than Boston's, are again indicative of increasing democratization in both higher education and the upper class with regard to higher education.

The data in Table 5.7 on the five most chosen colleges of the New York upper class present both some interesting similarities to and differences from the Boston upper class. For New York as for Boston, Harvard, Yale, and Princeton are three of the five most chosen schools. Columbia, as the local elite institution, occupies a position similar to Harvard's in Boston. Williams, the fifth school, appears for both cities. While local to neither, it is not too far away, and, as mentioned above, had a reputation as a fashionable liberal arts college. For the most part it was the fifth choice and averaged only 2 percent out of the total top-five component of the 73 percent of the upper class. Perhaps the most striking observation to be made here is

TABLE 5.5.   New York: Colleges graduating social registrants by decades (N)

1880s	1890s	1900s	1910s	1920s	1930s	1940s	1950s	1960s
13	22	23	21	24	31	30	58	66

TABLE 5.6.   New York: Colleges of social registrants by decade of graduation (%)

	1880s	1890s	1900s	1910s	1920s	1930s	1940s	1950s	1960s
Top-five	81	82	80	81	89	69	69	70	45
Other	19	18	20	19	11	31	31	30	55
Total	100	100	100	100	100	100	100	100	100

TABLE 5.7.   New York: Social registrants graduating from top-five colleges by decade of graduation (%)

	1880s	1890s	1900s	1910s	1920s	1930s	1940s	1950s	1960s	M
Yale	24	25	26	25	33	34	25	34	20	28
Harvard	15	27	25	32	32	15	20	21	9	22
Princeton	14	13	12	16	19	13	20	12	12	14
Columbia	25	15	16	6	4	3	1	3	3	7
Williams	3	2	1	2	1	4	4	3	0	2
Total	81	82	80	81	89	69	69	70	45	43

that the local prestige college, Columbia, had on average only a 7 percent share of the New York upper class, putting it in fourth place behind Yale (28 percent), Harvard (22 percent), and Princeton (14 percent). Only in the 1880s was Columbia the first choice of New Yorkers and then just barely—25 percent to Yale's 24 percent. By the 1890s Columbia had begun its rather steep descent, arrested only briefly in the early 1900s and insignificantly after World War II. Yale, with the exception of the 1890s and 1910s, when it was marginally surpassed by Harvard, seems to have been the preferred choice of New Yorkers. Harvard and Princeton also began below Columbia, but by the First World War had overtaken it for good. Harvard's proportion increased over 100 percent to its high of 32 percent in the 1910s and 1920s, but then declined to a low of 9 percent in the 1960s. Princeton remained more stable at around 14 percent.

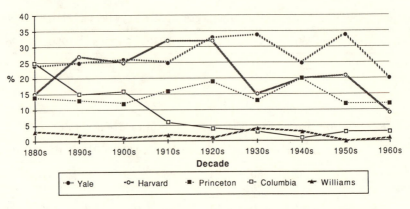

FIGURE 5.2. New York: Social registrants graduating from top-five colleges by decade of graduation

What is particularly interesting here is the timing of the exodus of the New York upper class from the local quality institution beginning in the 1890s. Not unlike the situation in Boston, this may have had something to do with urban heterogeneity and what became known as the "Jewish problem." In the 1920s, under President Nicholas Murray Butler, Columbia, like Harvard, instituted a quota against Jews, who by that time constituted over 40 percent of the student body (Wechsler, 1977). It is just possible that this "democratic" trend occurred first, or at least became more apparent first, in New York, thus prompting the upper class emigration. Whatever the cause, it is clear that Columbia was never able to resist the defection of its local upper class.

From Table 5.8 it is clear that until the 1930s Columbia's loss was HYP's gain. The percentage of the upper class going to these schools actually increased at the same time that Columbia's share declined. Thus, not only did HYP (especially Harvard) take away Columbia's prospects at this time, but they added others as well. It was not until the 1960s that HYP dropped substantially, while Columbia remained at very low levels. This may suggest a greater cosmopolitan on the part of the New York upper class than was true of Boston; it almost certainly suggests less local filiation. At no time did Columbia's share of the upper class exceed that of the Big Three, or any combination of two of them. Harvard, on the other hand, dwarfed all others in Boston, though it was somewhat anomalous in that Harvard was both one of the three national prestige institutions and the premier local college of Boston. Yale and Princeton have no local urban upper class on which to draw.

TABLE 5.8.   New York: Social registrants graduating from Columbia and
Harvard–Yale–Princeton (HYP) by decade of graduation (%)

	1880s	1890s	1900s	1910s	1920s	1930s	1940s	1950s	1960s
Columbia	25	15	16	6	4	3	1	3	3
HYP	52	65	63	73	84	62	65	67	41
Total	78	80	79	79	88	65	66	70	44

Philadelphia

The information for the Philadelphia upper class is presented in Tables
5.9–5.12 and Figure 5.3. The number of colleges attended by Philadelphians
increased threefold from 1880 to 1970—a pattern similar to that for New
York. Unlike New York, however, there seems to be no significant increase
in the number of colleges attended until after World War II. Before the
war the number hovered between 15 and 20. In the 1950s this figure rose to
30, between a 50 percent and 100 percent increase, and then doubled again
in the 1960s. As mentioned above for New York and Boston, upper class
Philadelphians were likely forced away from their most preferred colleges
by the advent of more strictly meritocratic admissions criteria that attended the great increase in college matriculation after the war.

Table 5.10 generally supports the above findings. The percent of the
Philadelphia upper class graduating from one of the five most selected colleges dropped from a high of 89 percent in 1880 to a low of 32 percent by
1970. Correlatively, the percentage attending colleges other than the five
most preferred increased sixfold, from 11 percent to 68 percent. As in Table
5.9, the most radical shift occurred after World War II when the percentage
attending the preferred five colleges dropped by a quarter, from 80 percent
to 60 percent. In the 1960s this was cut nearly in half to 32 percent. The
percent attending the other colleges doubled after the Second World War,
from 22 percent to 40 percent in the 1950s, and nearly doubled again to 68
percent in the 1960s.

Table 5.10, however, reveals that in the 1880s there was something of a
defection of the Philadelphia upper class from the five most preferred
schools, from 89 percent in the 1880s to a level of 68 percent—a drop of
over 20 percent. By the 1900s this figure had again risen to 83 percent, after
which it hovered in the 70 percents until World War II. This temporary
drop is peculiar and difficult to interpret. From Tables 5.11 and 5.12 it can be
seen that some loss was experienced by all of the top-five schools, though

TABLE 5.9.   Philadelphia: Colleges graduating social registrants by decades (N)

1880s	1890s	1900s	1910s	1920s	1930s	1940s	1950s	1960s
20	16	21	16	19	18	19	30	61

TABLE 5.10.   Philadelphia: Colleges of social registrants by decade of graduation (%)

	1880s	1890s	1900s	1910s	1920s	1930s	1940s	1950s	1960s
Top-five	89	68	83	73	74	78	78	60	32
Other	11	32	17	27	26	22	22	40	68
Total	100	100	100	100	100	100	100	100	100

Princeton and Harvard remained relatively constant. In absolute terms, the greatest part of this decline was contributed by the University of Pennsylvania, the local prestige college of Philadelphia, from nearly 50 percent to 40 percent.

One is tempted to argue that the loss of the top five could only be accounted for by a shift to many other schools, but Table 5.9 actually shows that fewer colleges were attended in the 1890s than the 1880s. Without an analysis on the "other" schools that were the beneficiaries of this decline in the top five it is impossible to conjecture on the nature of their attraction.

What can be said, however, is that Penn, in the 1890s, began a policy of admitting local high school graduates without examination if their school was "certified" by Penn. This certification method of admission was adopted in an effort to secure greater numbers of students (Farnum, 1980). From the point of view of the upper class, however, such a policy must have had disconcerting effects, attracting not just greater numbers but a more socially heterogeneous student body from the public high schools. Perhaps this discouraged the Philadelphia upper class from sending its children to Penn. Whatever the explanation, the precipitous drop was temporary and substantially restored to 1880s levels by the 1900s.

Table 5.11 and Figure 5.3 present information on the five most preferred colleges of the Philadelphia upper class. As in Boston and New York, Harvard, Yale, and Princeton, the national prestige institutions, constitute three of the five. The other two are both local, Penn and Haverford. Penn occupies a position formally analogous to Harvard for Boston and Columbia for New York as the local institution of colonial pedigree and greatest

TABLE 5.11. Philadelphia: Social registrants graduating from top-five colleges by decade of graduation (%)

	1880s	1890s	1900s	1910s	1920s	1930s	1940s	1950s	1960s	M
Penn	49	39	51	52	14	23	24	18	14	29
Princeton	16	15	16	11	40	30	35	18	10	21
Yale	8	2	3	7	8	14	14	12	5	8
Harvard	8	7	4	1	7	8	2	6	2	5
Haverford	8	5	8	2	5	3	3	6	1	4
Total	89	68	83	73	74	78	78	60	32	67

TABLE 5.12. Philadelphia: Social registrants graduating from Penn and HYP by decade of graduation (%)

	1880s	1890s	1900s	1910s	1920s	1930s	1940s	1950s	1960s
Penn	49	39	51	52	14	23	24	18	14
HYP	32	24	24	19	55	52	51	36	17
Total	81	63	75	71	69	75	75	54	31

prestige. Haverford is a parallel to Williams,—a small and fashionable local liberal arts college. On average 67 percent of the Philadelphia upper class attended one of these five schools, whose rank order of contribution is Penn, Princeton, Yale, Harvard, Haverford. None of the last three taken individually ever contributed more than 10 percent with the exception of Yale, which rose to 14 percent during the 1930s and 1940s. Pennsylvania and Princeton are the primary choices of Philadelphians, contributing on average 29 percent and 21 percent respectively. This places Philadelphia somewhere between Boston, where the local school, Harvard, dominates the upper class, and New York, where Columbia's contribution quickly fell beneath the levels of each of the Big Three. Philadelphians are apparently neither as cosmopolitan as New Yorkers nor as locally-oriented as Bostonians. This is, as mentioned above, complicated by the fact that Harvard is simultaneously one of the Big Three and the local Boston upper class college.

Penn began with about a 50 percent share of the upper class, and after the hiatus of the 1950s, when this dropped to 40 percent, resumed its earlier high level until the 1920s, at which point it was surpassed by Princeton

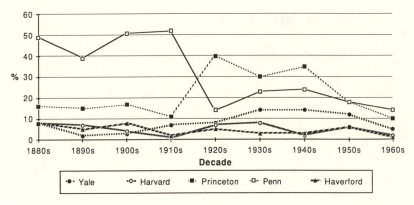

FIGURE 5.3. Philadelphia: Social registrants graduating from top-five colleges by decade of graduation

until after World War II. The most striking aspect of Figure 5.3 was the dramatic drop in Penn's appeal, from 52 percent in the 1910s to 14 percent in the 1920s. Almost all of this decline was mirrored by Princeton's ascent from 11 percent to 40 percent. This is the period in Penn's history when its undergraduate population was characterized as having the "democracy of the streetcar" (Slosson, 1910). Much was made by the upper class alumni and trustees after World War I of the urban setting of the university, a polite euphemism for the increasing admission of Jews and other non-WASPs. A variety of proposals was circulated, largely initiated by disgruntled alumni, to redress what was perceived as an unacceptable and increasing level of heterogeneity. "Education for leadership and character" was hailed as an antidote for mass education and the encroaching power of the state. An unsuccessful effort was made to secure the services of General Leonard Wood, World War I hero and ardent advocate of immigration restriction, as Provost.[2] Perhaps the most ingenious and desperate attempt to rid the college of urban and "un-American" influences was the proposal to move the entire plant wholesale to the pastoral setting of Valley Forge (Cheyney, 1940). Such a move would have had the intended consequence, at least for some, of discouraging those without the means to reside on campus from bothering to attend at all. As this plan fell through, many upper class members deserted the local university for the more socially homogeneous and environmentally congenial setting at Princeton.

While Penn's fortunes rebounded somewhat between the wars from their nadir of the 1920s, its share of its own upper class never again exceeded 25 percent. Only after World War II did Penn again surpass Princeton and reclaim its position as the preferred college of the Philadelphia upper class. Far from a triumph, this seems only to have been the result of the steepness of Princeton's drop after the war, from 35 percent in the 1940s to 18 percent in the 1950s to 10 percent in the 1960s. Penn's decline as less sharp, probably because with the greater clamor for higher education after World War II, it became far harder to gain admission to Princeton than to Penn on a meritocratic basis. The Philadelphia upper class was likely making the best of a difficult situation and attending Penn by default.

Table 5.12 compares the respective shares of the Philadelphia upper class held by Penn and HYP. Until World War I Penn's share exceeded those of the other three combined with around 50 percent, while HYP declined from around 30 percent to 20 percent. The drop in the total is thus accounted for by a moderate shift away from HYP. After the war, however, HYP surged ahead of Penn to levels of 50 percent while Penn declined to around 20 percent. This, as explained above, was primarily the result of defection to Princeton, though Yale, too, experienced substantial relative gains. After World War II both Penn and HYP declined, the latter more sharply, to a low of 17 percent, nearly matched by Penn's 14 percent in the 1960s. Again, this was likely the result of the fact that while it became more difficult after the war to gain admission to any of these schools, the universalistic criteria then being institutionalized were probably more exacting at HYP.

Baltimore

The Baltimore data are presented in Tables 5.13–5.16 and Figure 5.4. As in the other cities, the concentration-dispersion data show an unmistakable trend toward democratization. The number of colleges attended increased threefold, from 17 in the 1880s to 53 in the 1960s, and may be broken into three major periods, bounded by the World Wars. Before World War I the number of schools attended hovered at around 20. During the 1920s–1950s this rose 50 percent to about 30, after which the number nearly doubled to 53 in the 1960s. Table 5.14 demonstrates that the increase in the number of colleges did not substantially alter the concentration of the Baltimorean upper class at preferred schools after World War I. With the single anomaly of the 1890s, when the number rose to 72, 55–60 percent of the upper

TABLE 5.13.   Baltimore: Colleges graduating social registrants by decades (N)

1880s	1890s	1900s	1910s	1920s	1930s	1940s	1950s	1960s
17	20	20	18	26	29	29	30	53

TABLE 5.14.   Baltimore: Colleges of social registrants by decade of graduation (%)

	1880s	1890s	1900s	1910s	1920s	1930s	1940s	1950s	1960s
Top-five	63	72	56	63	57	58	57	49	26
Other	37	28	44	37	43	42	43	51	74
Total	100	100	100	100	100	100	100	100	100

class attended top-five schools. Only after World War II did this percentage drop, to 50 percent in the 1950s and 26 percent in the 1960s. In parallel fashion, the percent attending other than the five most preferred colleges doubled in the ninety years between 1880 and 1970, but the major increases did not occur until after the Second World War. This fact suggests that it was not substantially more difficult to be admitted to preferred elite schools until that time, when the institutionalization of universalism enforced democratization of elite higher education and the educational dispersion of the upper class.

The Baltimore upper class appears closest to Philadelphia in its pattern of concentration and dispersion: 54 percent of Baltimoreans on average have attended preferred schools, compared to 67 percent of Philadelphians. The figures for Boston and New York are both higher. Of the four cities, Baltimore's upper class has been least concentrated in its college attendance.

Table 5.15 and Figure 5.4 present information on patterns among the preferred colleges of the Baltimore upper class. The five schools, in order of relative average preference, are Princeton, Johns Hopkins, University of Virginia, Harvard, and Yale. Thus, once again, we find the influence of both cosmopolitan and local orientations. Princeton, Harvard, and Yale represent cosmopolitan attractions of the national prestige colleges; Johns Hopkins and Virginia embody local filiation. As in the other cities, though perhaps most like Philadelphia, there is an overall two-tier pattern with two schools accounting for the bulk of the graduates and the others at a rather lower level vying among themselves for the remainder.

TABLE 5.15.   Baltimore: Social registrants graduating from top-five colleges by decade of graduation (%)

	1880s	1890s	1900s	1910s	1920s	1930s	1940s	1950s	1960s	M
Princeton	14	21	25	20	26	22	25	20	7	20
Johns Hopkins	37	34	22	24	22	16	10	8	5	18
Virginia	6	7	8	6	5	11	9	11	7	8
Harvard	3	3	0	4	3	7	9	7	5	5
Yale	3	7	1	9	1	2	4	3	2	3
Total	63	72	56	63	57	58	57	49	26	54

This pattern is similar to that for Philadelphia, with Johns Hopkins as the local institution of high prestige analogous to Penn and Princeton as the nearest institution of national prestige. However, whereas in Philadelphia the local school on average held the highest rank, in Baltimore Johns Hopkins (18 percent) is superseded by Princeton (20 percent). That the local school is in this case generally second is perhaps attributable to the fact that unlike Penn, which was established in the eighteenth century and has deeper roots in the local community, Johns Hopkins was not founded until 1876. From the outset, Johns Hopkins established the highest academic standards and tended to focus less on the undergraduate than on the graduate departments, taking as its model the German university rather than the English. If upper class members were selecting colleges less on academic than on social or status grounds, then these two factors would have militated somewhat against the selection of Hopkins over Princeton.

Johns Hopkins began in the 1880s with a high of 37 percent to Princeton's 14 percent. Until the early 1900s Hopkins' descent to around 22 percent was paralleled by Princeton's rise to 25 percent. The two remained fairly stable until the 1930s, when Hopkins began a second steep uninterrupted descent to a low of 5 percent in the 1960s, falling to third position behind Virginia. Princeton's share of the Baltimore upper class remained fairly stable, between 20–25 percent, until the 1960s when it fell to 7 percent. This latter decline was parallel to that which has been observed in all the upper classes subsequent to World War II, when the top-five schools tended to lose much of their share of upper class members in the postwar trend toward democratization.

The University of Virginia seems to occupy a position functionally

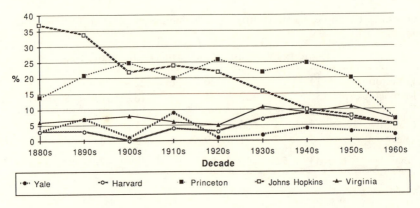

FIGURE 5.4. Baltimore: Social registrants graduating from top-five colleges by decade of graduation

analogous to Williams for Boston and New York and Haverford for Philadelphia. Unlike these two schools, however, Virginia, with the exception of the 1910s when it was marginally surpassed by Yale, stood above both Yale and Harvard. Indeed, by 1970 it even tied Princeton for first rank. This suggests a somewhat more local orientation on the part of Baltimoreans, perhaps owing to a more general southern regional orientation. Harvard and Yale are decidedly New England schools. Princeton, on the other hand, in the middle-Atlantic region, has traditionally drawn a substantial component of its student body from the south. For Baltimoreans the "northernness" of Harvard and Yale may have been sufficient reason to prefer Virginia.

Table 5.16 presents the comparison of the most elite local institution, Johns Hopkins, with Harvard, Yale, and Princeton taken together.

The share of the upper class held by HYP tended to be fairly consistently in the 30 percent range before the 1960s when it fell off to 14 percent. The principal exception (38 percent) occurred in the 1940s. Hopkins exceeded HYP only in the 1880s and 1890s. From the 1900s until the 1930s the percentage of the upper class at Hopkins remained fairly constant, around 23 percent, after which it commenced its long decline to the present 5 percent. One observation to be made here is that Hopkins' losses, at least after World War I, do not appear to have been HYP's gains. This indicates that the loss of the local school is not to the more fashionable schools but to the more democratic process of dispersion to a large number of schools. Thus, the prestige of the Big Three remains fairly constant over time while the

TABLE 5.16. Baltimore: Social registrants graduating from Johns Hopkins in comparison to HYP by decade of graduation (%)

	1880s	1890s	1900s	1910s	1920s	1930s	1940s	1950s	1960s
Johns Hopkins	37	34	22	24	22	16	10	8	5
HYP	20	31	26	33	30	31	38	30	14
Total	57	65	48	57	52	47	48	38	19

democratic process seems to occur at the expense of localism. However, it should be repeated that Hopkins' initial losses in the late nineteenth century were almost entirely to the benefit of Princeton. In that earlier period localism lost not to democracy but to the hegemony of the elite national institutions. This parallels the findings for both Philadelphia and New York where local schools lost out to national ones. Baltimore, however, seems closer to Philadelphia in two respects. Hopkins was never so popular in Baltimore as Penn was in Philadelphia, but, despite its late founding, Hopkins was never so unpopular as Columbia was in New York. Columbia's loss of the upper class occurred both earlier and more dramatically than that for Hopkins and Penn. Second, the Baltimore HYP component (28 percent) was closer to Philadelphia's (34 percent) than New York's (64 percent). New Yorkers have apparently "never" had a local school which could attract a significant portion of the upper class away from HYP.

Summary and Conclusion

The principal findings of this study are generally corroborative of Baltzell's work on the upper class and higher education. First, the upper classes of all four cities examined exhibit a tendency to localism in college attendance. In every case at least one of the five most attended schools was a local college, and in some cases a second was at least proximate. In Baltzell's terms, the local upper class colleges for each of the four cities are as follows: Boston: Harvard, Philadelphia: Penn, Baltimore: Johns Hopkins, New York: Columbia. The second general observation to be made about "localism" is that it tends to decline over time. Averaging the percent attending these four local colleges for each decade it was found that overall "localism" was at its highest in the 1880s (47 percent), the earliest period of this study. Following Baltzell, it is likely that even this figure constitutes a decline from an earlier period, probably prior to the Civil War, after which a national upper class was already developing. Average localism dropped sharply in the 1920s (28 percent), the period when the attraction of the national upper class institutions, Harvard, Yale, and Princeton, was at its zenith, and dropped sharply again in the 1960s to 15 percent. The two World Wars apparently eroded localism considerably.

If the four cities are examined for localism by comparing the average percentage of the relevant upper class attending the premier local upper class college for the entire time period, they rank as follows: Boston (67 percent), Philadelphia (29 percent), Baltimore (18 percent), New York (7 percent). The most striking finding here is the magnitude by which Boston exceeds all the other upper classes in its attachment to its local college. While it is true that Harvard is both a local *and* a national upper class institution, Baltzell would argue that this is no accident. The Puritan fidelity to education and local institutions was precisely the reason for Harvard's accession to national prominence. That New Yorkers demonstrated the least local loyalty is in keeping with the greater cosmopolitanism of the New York upper class, probably the first to shift to the national level. Indeed, as early as the 1890s Columbia had fallen behind Yale and Harvard and was also eclipsed by Princeton in the 1910s and 1920s. In Baltimore Johns Hopkins fell behind Princeton around the First World War, never to recover. It is of some interest to note that Philadelphians were closest to Bostonians in local fidelity (though only in rank order) as, with the single exception of the interwar period when Princeton was their first choice, they have attended Penn in greater numbers than any other college. For all of these cities World War I seems to constitute a watershed in the shift from local to national upper class colleges. Overall, Baltzell's thesis of the loss of local pride and the development of a national upper class is supported. The apparent exception of Boston is only in keeping with the perspective developed in *Puritan Boston and Quaker Philadelphia*.

The second major finding is that the national upper class colleges, Harvard, Yale, Princeton, constitute three of the top-five colleges for all the upper classes studied. The only other higher educational institution to appear in the top-five for more than one city was Williams, attended both by New Yorkers and Bostonians. While somewhat local to both New York and Boston, the fashionability that Williams developed, especially in the 1920s, may suggest that it became something of a national upper class liberal arts college. Its Puritan origins and Massachusetts location would, in Baltzell's terms, only lend credence to this hypothesis. By averaging the percentages attending HYP from all four cities it was found that HYP's influence rose and then fell. From 47 percent in the 1880s, again suggesting that a national upper class was well into the making, attendance at HYP rose to a peak of 63 percent in the 1920s, the "Anglo-Saxon decade," descended slowly to 50 percent in the 1950s, and then dropped sharply to 30 percent in the 1960s. This latter decline supports the argument that increasingly meritocratic standards as well as competition were making it more difficult for members of any upper class to gain admission.

Comparing the four upper classes in overall percent attending HYP gives a rank order different from that for localism, though it is not reversed: Boston (76 percent), New York (64 percent), Philadelphia (34 percent), Baltimore (28 percent). Boston again leads the others primarily because Harvard is both a local and a national upper class school. New York this time is second, a reflection of its exceedingly small local orientation. In a sense, it may even be argued that New York is the most national in its orientation, because unlike Boston it is completely unalloyed with any localism. Philadelphia, while more local than Baltimore, is also more national. Both the local school and the national ones have more influence in Philadelphia than in Baltimore. Again, this may reflect southern regionalism on the part of Baltimore, which deters members of the upper class from being well integrated into a northeastern upper class.

The third major finding of this study is that, over time, in each of the four cities the percentage of the upper class attending the most chosen schools declines and the overall number of colleges attended increases. In other words, there is a general trend from concentration to dispersion in the higher education of each upper class. This trend is especially distinctive of the period following World War II. On average, the total number of colleges attended by all the upper classes rose from a low of 14 in the 1880s to a high of 54 in the 1960s. The average percentage attending the five preferred colleges for all cities correlatively declined from a high of 82 percent in the 1880s to a low of 39 percent by the 1960s. Again, the decline was fairly gradual until after World War II. The average percentage of the upper class for each city graduating from one of the five preferred schools yields the following ranking: Boston (80 percent), New York (73 percent), Philadelphia (67 percent), and Baltimore (53 percent). This, of course, perfectly matches the findings above on both "localism" and "cosmopolitanism." Once again the Boston upper class is found to be the most concentrated in its pattern of educational attendance, thus perhaps having the most "common" socialization experience and the most coherence as a class.

The dispersion of the upper classes throughout greater numbers of colleges and universities may be in major part a result of the upgrading of selection criteria that attended the great surge in college applicants after 1945. From 1945 to 1970 the percentage of the 18–21-year-old age cohort attending college expanded from 15 percent to 50 percent, in real terms from 1.5 million to 6.5 million (Trow, 1972). The system of higher education has responded in a variety of ways to this influx, perhaps especially by expanding, but at the highest levels of the system the principal response has been to restrict entrance by meritocratic selection. This procedure tends to exclude many members of the upper class who were previously admitted on more particularistic grounds. They were thus forced to seek higher education elsewhere. It is clear from the evidence here that the upper class "monopolization" of places in preferred colleges is on the decline. By the 1960s only 51 percent of the Bostonians, 45 percent of the New Yorkers, 32 percent of the Philadelphians, and 26 percent of Baltimoreans graduated from one of the five colleges preferred by their upper classes, all considerable declines.

Each of the above findings, on local upper class colleges, national upper class colleges, and the decline of ascription, is in keeping with Baltzell's work on the upper class and higher education. The findings with respect to the orientations of the different cities also support his views. Boston, the home of Puritanism, hierarchy, and authority, demonstrated the greatest local fidelity as well as the greatest national hegemony among its upper class members. Philadelphia, on the other hand, is inferior in both these regards. The general rank-ordering of the cities on the variables considered suggests that hierarchy, authority, and upper class coherence in educational experience is inversely related to distance from the Puritan Jerusalem. For most of the measures Boston is followed by New York, Philadelphia, and Baltimore respectively. Only in the case of local loyalty are New Yorkers inferior to all others, again reflecting the greater cosmopolitanism and commercial emphasis of that city.

One final piece of evidence that most graphically reflects the value orientation of the four upper classes, especially with respect to education, is the percent of the upper class listed as college graduates in the *Social Registers*. The overall averages for each city are as follows: Boston (55 percent), New York (50 percent), Philadelphia (44 percent), and Baltimore (27 percent). The spread among the four is greatest for the earliest *Social Registers* available for all four cities (1910):[3] Boston (58 percent), New York (43 percent), Philadelphia (33 percent), and Baltimore (16 percent). Thereafter there is a tendency to convergence, especially among the first three. By

1960 Boston, New York, and Philadelphia are all around 50 percent, while Baltimore has risen to only 34 percent. Once again Baltimore seems to be operating by some different standards than the other three. The general convergence, however, probably reflects the fact that education is understood by all today as essential to status attainment and occupational placement. The differential influence of the earlier religious ethics toward education in each city has become both secularized and diluted. As Max Weber observed, once capitalism is in the saddle, it can dispense with the earlier religious ethic that was motivationally required for its institutionalization. In this case the same seems to be true of higher education.

What, finally, is to be made of the socialization and status-ascribing functions that Baltzell found to be essential to the national upper class colleges in sustaining a national upper class, especially in view of the dispersion of all four of the upper classes among a variety of colleges since the Second World War? It is clear that as the upper classes are dispersed among more colleges and universities, none of them is receiving as coherent a socialization experience as was earlier the case. None of the upper class colleges, not even Harvard, Yale, and Princeton, can reach the proportion of the upper class that it has in the past. With the shift to universalistic and meritocratic principles, especially since World War II, these colleges have perhaps ceased to function in the status-ascribing terms observed by Baltzell before the Second World War.

From one perspective such a situation is both deplorable and dangerous. Insofar as the upper class is a repository of responsible values, and insofar as it is unable to sustain its coherence through the common socialization experience at elite colleges and universities, it becomes incapable of exercising its appropriate authoritative and leadership functions in the society, and withdraws to a world of private privilege and social irresponsibility. At the same time it is supplanted by an atomized, egoistic, and acquisitive elite unregulated by the disciplines and unmotivated by the ideals of a moral ethic. In this view elite colleges and universities are performing a "liberal-democratic" but not an "authoritative-aristocratic" function, to borrow the terms of *The Protestant Establishment*. They are assisting in the attainment of individual mobility and equal opportunity without assimilating new elite members into an authoritative communal value orientation. In functional terms they have shifted from status-ascription to status-creation at the same time that they have undermined the structural underpinnings of moral education. Under such circumstances the prospects for a coherent and secure upper class must seem dim.

But from another point of view our judgment may be more sanguine.

Insofar as it is the elite colleges and universities themselves that are the fiduciaries of the moral orientations essential to communal solidarity and authoritative leadership, and insofar as more talented and motivated young adults are being exposed to them as a consequence of meritocratic selection, then in Edward Shils's terms the periphery is being drawn closer to the center, central cultural orientations are being diffused throughout larger segments of society, solidarity is enhanced, and authoritative and responsible leadership will be sustained.

Which side one comes down on hinges greatly on the extent to which elite colleges and universities are sensitive to and responsible in acquitting themselves of this important charge. Having arrogated to themselves the task of selecting and creating the elite of the society, a function once largely discharged through the ascriptive solidarities of family and class, they must also embrace the more diffuse socialization functions performed by those agencies. Whether they are successful in this effort, or can be, is an essential matter for further investigation.

Notes

1. The term "elite" is used here not in Baltzell's sense but rather to suggest those colleges and universities that are most "selective." The criteria for selectivity have of course shifted over time from particularistic to universalistic orientations. In general in this paper I follow Baltzell's usage for the terms "elite" and "upper class," a distinction which has been given insufficient attention in the sociological literature: "The elite concept refers to those individuals in any social system who hold the top positions in their chosen careers, occupations, or professions. . . . An upper class is a sociological and historical, rather than a natural, aristocracy. It is a group of consanguine families whose ancestors were elite members and family founders one or more generations earlier. Whereas elites are formed anew in each generation and according to contemporary criteria, upper classes are always the product of two or more generations." (1979, 24–25).

2. Penn is the only higher educational institution in the country to have had a provost rather than a president as its leader. Not until 1930 did Penn have a president in name, and not until the 1950s did it probably have one in fact. The relative impotence of the provost as against the trustees, symbolized by the anomolous title, is taken by Baltzell as evidence of the traditional distrust of leadership in Philadelphia.

3. The exact dates of the *Social Registers* used for each city are noted in the bibliography. For Boston, New York, and Philadelphia a 10 percent sample was taken, whereas for Baltimore a 25 percent sample was used owing to its relatively much smaller size.

References

Baltzell, E. Digby. *Philadelphia Gentlemen: The Making of a National Upper Class.* Philadelphia: University of Pennsylvania Press, 1977. Original edition New York: Free Press, 1958.

———, *The Protestant Establishment: Aristocracy and Caste in America.* New York: Random House, 1964 .

———, *Puritan Boston and Quaker Philadelphia: Two Protestant Ethics and the Spirit of Class Authority and Leadership.* New York: Free Press, 1979 .

Bloomgarden, Lawrence. "Our Changing Elite Colleges." *Commentary* (February 1960): 150–54.

Cheyney, Edward P. *History of the University of Pennsylvania, 1740–1940.* Philadelphia: University of Pennsylvania Press, 1940 .

Coon, Horace. *Columbia: Colossus on the Hudson.* New York: Dutton, 1947 .

Earnest, Ernest. *Academic Procession: An Informal History of the American College 1636–1953.* New York: Bobbs-Merrill Company, 1953.

Farnum, Richard. "Prestige in the Ivy League: Democratization and Discrimination at Penn and Columbia, 1890–1970." Unpublished paper, Department of Sociology, University of Pennsylvania, 1980.

Goddard, David R. and Linda C. Koons. "A Profile of the University of Pennsylvania." In David Riesman and Verne Stadtman, eds., *Academic Transformation: Seventeen Institutions Under Pressure,* New York: McGraw-Hill, 1973.

Higham, John. *Strangers in the Land: Patterns of American Nativism, 1860–1925.* New York: Atheneum, 1968 .

Jencks, Christopher and David Riesman. *The Academic Revolution.* New York: Doubleday, 1968 .

Karabel, Jerome. "Status-Group Struggle, Organizational Interests, and the Limits of Institutional Autonomy: The Transformation of Harvard, Yale, and Princeton 1918–1940." *Theory and Society* (January 1984): 1–40.

Levine, David. "The Functions of Higher Education in American Society Between World War I and World War II." Ph.D. dissertation, Department of History, Harvard University, 1981 .

Lipset, Seymour Martin and David Riesman. *Education and Politics at Harvard.* New York: McGraw-Hill, 1975 .

Morison, Samuel Eliot. *Three Centuries of Harvard, 1636–1936.* Cambridge, Mass.: Harvard University Press, 1936.

Pierson, George W. *The Education of American Leaders: Comparative Contributions of U.S. Colleges and Universities.* New York: Praeger, 1969 .

Slosson, Edwin E. *Great American Universities.* New York: Macmillan, 1910 .

Social Register. New York: The Social Register Association. Baltimore, 1899, 1912, 1922, 1929, 1940, 1950, 1960, 1974. Boston, 1899, 1910, 1920, 1930, 1940, 1950, 1960, 1975. New York, 1900, 1918, 1930, 1940, 1950, 1960, 1973. Philadelphia, 1910, 1920, 1930, 1941, 1950, 1958, 1965, 1975 .

Steinberg, Stephen. *The Academic Melting Pot: Catholics and Jews in American Higher Education.* New York: McGraw-Hill, 1974 .

Synnott, Marcia Graham. *The Half-Opened Door: Discrimination and Admissions at Harvard, Yale, and Princeton, 1900–1970.* Westport, Conn.: Greenwood Press, 1979 .

Trow, Martin. "The Expansion and Transformation of Higher Education." *International Review of Education.* 18, 1 (1972): 61–84.

———. "The Second Transformation of American Secondary Education." *International Journal of Comparative Sociology* 2 (1961): 114–65.

Useem, Michael and S. M. Miller. "Privilege and Domination: The Role of the Upper Class in American Higher Education." *Social Science Information* 14, 6 (1975): 115–45.

Veysey, Laurence R. *The Emergence of the American University.* Chicago: University of Chicago Press, 1965 .

Wechsler, Harold S. *The Qualified Student: A History of Selective College Admission in America.* New York: John Wiley and Sons, 1977 .

James R. Abbott

6. Chicago Politics and the Rise of the Boss: From Yankee and Cavalier Amateurs to Professional Politicians

Chicago's Democratic machine is undoubtedly the most inclusive, power-ful, and notorious urban political organization in America. Throughout most of this century it has set the standard by which all other urban ma-chines are judged. The machine's strong and able leaders, its paternal treat-ment of constituents, its corruption, and perhaps most importantly, its ability to quell all opposition have made Chicago political life the epitome of machine bossism. Even in light of recent Washington administrations, which challenge not so much the machine but its leadership, the Demo-cratic party organization remains monolithic. For all intents and purposes no viable second party exists in the city.[1] The last Republican Mayor, William H. Thompson, himself an aspiring machine boss, was elected in 1927. Thus, while current events in Chicago suggest a changing of the guard, the machine itself is alive and well, waiting patiently for a leader who will transcend factional disputes.

This essay examines historically and sociologically the origins of the na-tion's strongest and most durable urban political machine. Its purpose is to illuminate the uncommon conditions within which boss politics came to the fore in Chicago. The uniqueness of the Chicago experience is basically fourfold, each factor discussed in ascending order of importance.

First, most observers associate Chicago bossism—indeed, political bossism in general—with the city's two great Irish Catholic Mayors, Edward J. Kelly, who ruled the city from 1933 to 1947, and Richard J. Daley, who won the mayorality in 1955 and remained there virtually unop-posed until his death in 1976. Daley in particular is often singled out as the archetypical city boss, and Chicagoans and non-Chicagoans alike consider his name inseparable from the city's ethos. Over a twenty-one-year period Daley wielded complete power and commanded a broad appeal, regularly averaging 70 percent of the vote. In effect, Daley defined the city as no other politician was able to do. However, neither he nor Kelly was responsible for building the machine which dictates Chicago's political fortunes to this day. They were, rather, heirs to an organization which surfaced in 1931 under the leadership of a Czech Protestant, Anton Cermak, about whom more below.

Second, the late arrival of political oligarchy signifies that Chicago was one of the last major cities in America to experience machine bossism.[2] Indeed, if one were to take seriously early twentieth-century writings on the state of Chicago politics, one would be at a loss to explain how the machine ever made its presence felt. For example, of all the cities in which Lincoln Steffens "raked the muck," Chicago, strangely enough, emerged as clean and vital as many others. To be sure, in his 1903 article Steffens portrayed the city as "first in violence, deepest in dirt, loud, lawless, unlovely, ill-smelling, irreverent," and suggested that corruption was certainly a prominent characteristic of its government. However, next to St. Louis and Philadelphia, Steffens felt that Chicago's grafting was petty and, moreover, that the city's reform efforts were real and significant. He further argued that Chicago's efforts at political reform should be a "model for every city and town in the country."[3] The city had "beaten boodling," and, according to Steffens, there was little doubt "that Chicago will be cleaned up."[4]

Similarly, writing in 1929, Charles Merriam, one-time candidate for Mayor, alderman, and political scientist at the University of Chicago, boasted that Chicago had no machine.[5] There were, he conceded, petty bosses of only parochial ambition operating in and content with their respective wards, but the city was not plagued by the centralized, oligarchic structure one observed in New York or Philadelphia. Merriam, born to a prominent Iowa political family, interpreted this freedom from oligarchy as cause for a guarded optimism concerning the city's political future. The events of the past fifty years, however, suggest that both Steffens and Merriam were grossly misguided.

Third, since Robert Merton's famous article on urban political systems and their functions, many researchers conceive the machine as a feudal-like structure led by a "knight" to whom followers owe allegiance.[6] Boss politics was and is decidedly "ethnic" and indeed atavistic, a throwback to aristocratic culture in which personal loyalty and allegiance to one individual were motivations for political behavior, rather than dedication to an abstract set of values associated with middle class Protestantism. Within and through these feudal-like relations the machine provided invaluable services and functions, among which were opportunities for mobility, the mediating of conflicts, and an easing of discrimination by personalizing and humanizing the political structure (and taking good care of WASP businessmen as well).

Some authors such as Zane Miller and Roger Lotchin,[7] however, have suggested that the immigrants' role in boss politics has been exaggerated. This contention has great merit given that boss politics was alive and well in America before the period 1870–1930. Rhode Island and Pennsylvania, for example, two states with liberal Protestant heritages, have long histories of political bossism independent of the immigrant presence. I suggest that the Chicago experience follows not Merton's characterization, but the examples of Rhode Island and Pennsylvania. The initial impulse toward one all enveloping populist machine in the city was catalyzed by a group of Protestants during the late nineteenth and early twentieth centuries, among whom were politicians William Lorimer, a son of a Presbyterian minister, William H. Thompson, a renegade son of privilege born in the Beacon Hill section of Boston, and Anton Cermak; businessmen Charles T. Yerkes, a Philadelphia native of Quaker ancestry, and English-born Samuel Insull (these latter two created the mold within which Al Capone flourished during the 1920s). These individuals, among others, not the ethnics, redefined political behavior in Chicago. It is of course true that the most vociferous demonstrators against machine politics were Protestants (the Protestant reformer–ethnic boss dichotomy derived from the Hofstadter thesis), but this does not detract from the fact that individuals of like descent and circumstance were the first to transform the city's political life and structure.

Last and most importantly, the public and intellectual fascination with Daley often leaves unexamined the nature of Chicago's leadership from its founding as a town (1833) to the emergence of the machine in 1931. In my personal experience I find that many individuals (including natives) perceive Chicago politics to begin and end with Daley, or, similarly, that the city's political history is nothing more than a series of Daley-like bosses or Capone-like gangsters. Investigations into the city's leadership at its founding and throughout its development, however, suggest otherwise.

What many people do not recognize, and in direct contrast to Turner's populist and individualist thesis of frontier settlement, is that several of the city's significant nineteenth-century political leaders (economic and cultural as well) were members of upper class families of the established east. As was the case in St. Louis, Cincinnati, and Cleveland, patricians from the New England states and Cavaliers from the south played pivotal roles not only in Chicago's development, but that of the State of Illinois as well[8] (interestingly Pennsylvania provided very little to the state's and city's leadership). Although known today and throughout its history as a rough hewn and often times vulgar pioneer town, Chicago's elite structure from 1833 until 1915 was staffed by members of some of the nation's most illustrious families.

To be specific, among the town's original trustees was Gurdon Saltonstall Hubbard, a descendent of a Connecticut founder and Governor, Gurdon Saltonstall. Hubbard, who migrated to Illinois in 1818, also served in the state legislature throughout the 1830s, and established a number of Chicago "firsts," among which were the city's first bank, hotel, water system, and fire department. He also wrote Chicago's first insurance policy, was first president of the board of underwriters, and an organizer and original director of the Chicago Board of Trade.

Hubbard was soon joined by the city's founding generation among whom were Jonathon Y. Scammon, William B. Ogden, and the so-called "Chicago Triumvirate," John Wentworth, Lyman Trumbull, and Stephen A. Douglas. All of these individuals settled in either Chicago or its surrounding territory in the 1830s, and all of them were of high status if not wealthy families. Ogden, for example, was a descendant of a New Jersey first family; Wentworth and Trumbull were members of, respectively, New Hampshire's and Connecticut's foremost families; Douglas, a Vermont native, was maternally related to the Arnold family and Scammon was a college educated son of a Maine legislator. These individuals, among others, were to be found on all levels of government from 1833 to the great Chicago fire of 1871.

Following this group in politics and in law were the southern gentlemen Carter Harrison, his son, Carter Harrison II, John M. Harlan, John G. Rogers, Charles M. Walker, Henry Waller and the New England patricians George Everett Adams, Mark Skinner, Hempstead Washburne, Melville Fuller, Henry S. Boutell, and a host of others. At Hull House established in 1889 representing cultural authority, were the college educated and genteel heiresses Jane Addams, Sophinisba Breckinridge, Florence Kelly, Julia Lathrop, and Lucy Flower.

While I will have more to say about these and other individuals below, it is important to note that the Carter Harrisons, Hempstead Washburne, George Everett Adams, and Sophinisba Breckinridge were either extended or immediate members of four of the sixteen American family dynasties identified by Stephen Hess.[9] Moreover, all of them were influential during Chicago's turbulent industrial era. The Kentucky/Virginia Harrisons, for example, members of the south's most accomplished political family, were elected to a total of ten terms as Mayor between 1879 and 1911, with large support from the working classes.[10] George Everett Adams, an extended member of the Adams clan and an 1860 graduate of Harvard, served in the House of Representatives from 1883 to 1891; another Harvard graduate, Henry S. Boutell, served from 1897 to 1911. Hempstead Washburne, a Yale graduate, whose father, Elihu B. Washburne, was a prominent Illinois statesman, was elected mayor in 1891. Finally, Sophinisba Breckinridge, a member of a prominent southern planter family,[11] was a volunteer at Hull House after graduating from Wellesley in 1888. She went on to receive Ph.D. and J.D. degrees from the University of Chicago, where she was Professor of Social Work, 1904–1942.

Hence, prior to the advent of the machine, Chicago politics was significantly influenced by a group of similarly situated individuals. During this period of upper class political leadership there existed two viable parties, or at least factions, from which the constituency selected representatives. Neither party nor an individual was able completely to centralize political power. Only when these sociological types ceased to be public spirited did oligarchy triumph—and it triumphed through the activities of Protestants, not ethnics.

These four facets of Chicago's experience with boss politics serve as the impetus for this study. Following is an examination of the nature of class authority and its relationship to political democracy, and the positive function of class leadership in American political history. The absence of a dominant machine and the optimism this inspired at the turn of the century are intriguing points in themselves. However, it is the fact that upper class Yankees and Cavaliers played a crucial role in the city's evolution that lies at the heart of this analysis. My argument, however, is not simply a reiteration of the well-known urban political machine thesis of upper class decline and immigrant boss ascension. On the contrary, Chicago's machine was a Protestant creation. It is argued that at the turn of the century upper class individuals of New England descent experienced a decline. Rather than engage in the rough and tumble of institutional politics, New Englanders turned toward the reclusive and private comforts of wealth, and in the process left the Cavalier alone to do battle with the Protestant bosses. To be sure, the New Englander maintained the Protestant zeal for reform, but, as we shall see, such efforts were intermittent and usually undertaken from the periphery.

Data

To provide a general portrait of the sociological composition of Chicago's elite and upper class structure from 1833 to 1931 the *Dictionary of American Biography* (*DAB*) was employed as a "functional elite" index and the Chicago *Social Register* as a social elite or "upper class" index. The original twenty volumes of the *DAB* and its first five supplements, which include prominent figures who died prior to 1956 (Daley took office as mayor in 1955), yielded a sample of 324 elite individuals, and in the 1976 *Social Register* (the year of Daley's death) listed a group of twenty-one upper class families which could claim at least one ancestor in the *DAB*.[12] A comparative sample of 117 elite Illinoisans was taken from the *DAB* as well. The purpose of this comparison is that while Chicago is essentially a Yankee city, Illinois is a southern state, founded and led by Cavalier gentlemen. I thought a contrast between the two elite groups might reveal something of the Cavalier and Calvinist ethics as they were experienced in the nineteenth century.

As with all the individuals profiled in the *DAB,* the selection of these 441 elites, as well as the space allotted to them, was based on their importance to American history as evaluated by an editorial board—the persons listed "did something notable in some field of American life." While there is no guarantee of objectivity, the editorial board, which consisted of more than 100 accomplished intellectuals, and those who contributed biographies, were guided by that principle.

The *Social Register,* on the other hand, is a subjective index compiled in relative secrecy by individuals who ideally remain anonymous. As Harvey Zorbaugh reported years ago, criteria for inclusion and the people who determine such criteria are unknown even to those families listed. Thus, while the *DAB* editorial board is comparatively open to methodological criticism, the mystery surrounding the *Social Register* lends doubt concerning its objective utility. Nevertheless, and with full appreciation of its peculiarities, the *Social Register* is a convenient and useful tool through which the general and representative properties of an upper class can be discerned. Furthermore, it is important to note that while Zorbaugh's subjects were ignorant of the criteria for inclusion, they considered entry to the *Social Register* to be the most important symbol of upper class status.

Each elite group is well represented by the New England element. Approximately 17 percent of both the Chicago and Illinois samples were native to the New England states and 40.7 percent of the Chicago elite and 35 percent of the Illinois elite were of New England descent. In terms of the southern presence (excluding Scotch-Irish southerners) 6.4 percent of the Chicagoans and 25.8 percent of the Illinoisans were native to the South.

With little surprise, Chicago's elite is essentially an auslander group. Only 13 percent were born in the city, a contingent almost as large as that born outside of the United States. Furthermore, of the 51 percent who had some college training only 19 percent attended schools located within the state. In contrast, the Illinois group is a rooted elite; 31 percent were home grown and more than a third of the 63 percent who were college trained attended local schools (38 percent).

The mean number of lines written about the Illinois and Chicago subjects (the more lines provided the individual, the more accomplished he was thought to be) was virtually identical: for the Illinoisan, $X = 135.46$; for the Chicagoan, $X = 134.91$. A t test revealed no significant difference between the means.

Some interesting patterns were revealed when the samples were broken down into the functional categories "Politicians, Diplomats, Jurists"; "Businessmen"; "Writers, Journalists, Authors"; and "Educators." As would be expected the largest Chicago category is "Businessmen." In this instance 22.2 percent of the city's elite were involved in commerce, of which 42 percent were of New England lineage. In contrast, only 11 percent of the Illinois elite were so involved. This is of course quite understandable given that Illinois is essentially a rural agricultural state. However, it is revealing that of the state's business elite, 42 percent were of New England ancestry and only 8 percent of southern ancestry.

The categories "Writers . . ." and "Educators" were also well represented by the New England element; 47 percent of the Chicago writers and 26.6 percent of the Illinois writers claimed New England ancestry. New Englanders were even more influential in education. Over half of the Chicago and Illinois elite educators were of New England descent (53 percent and 65 percent, respectively).

The smallest Chicago functional category is "Politicians, Diplomats, and Jurists." Only 15 percent of the entire elite were engaged in the public sphere. Furthermore, it is the only Chicago category in which New England representation falls below the general sample figure. Although the difference is negligible (38 percent as opposed to 40.7 percent), when birth cohorts are considered the relative disinterest of New Englanders in public life is brought into relief. Of the New England contingent in public life, 77 percent were born before 1860 and 72 percent before 1840. This seems to indicate that the New England contingent was active in politics, diplomacy, and the bench before 1900. Of course, one could surmise that the city simply did not produce significant public servants from the birth cohorts past 1860, and therefore the decline noted is simply indicative of a general decline of notable public officials. However, when the non-New England political elite are examined we find that 75 percent were born after 1839 and 53 percent after 1859, which suggests not a general decline, but the intriguing point that after being quite active in the public sphere throughout the nineteenth century New Englanders suddenly eschewed such leadership toward the end of the Gilded Age.[13]

It is important to point out that the largest Illinois functional category (for the state as a whole in contrast to Chicago) is "Politicians, Diplomats, and Jurists." Almost half of the Illinois elite (42 percent) were involved in the public sphere, of which 33 percent was of southern and 19 percent of New England background. It will be recalled that southerners constituted 25.8 percent and New Englanders 35 percent of the entire Illinois sample. Thus, New Englanders are underrepresented here as well.

If one were to abstract from all the *DAB* entries, a typical Illinois elite was born in either Kentucky or Illinois of southern heritage. After passing the bar the individual enjoyed private law practice before entering politics or accepting an appointment to the bench. If and when necessary the individual served in the armed forces as an officer. Towards the twilight of his career he invariably wrote a book of history dealing either with his military experiences or with the founding and leadership of the state to which he dedicated his life. It is no coincidence, of course, that these "callings" tend to be associated with aristocratic, Cavalier culture. As we shall see below, all of the territory's and state's governors between 1800 and 1830, and many of the elected and appointed officials during this period and beyond, were Cavalier gentlemen who were not hesitant to take the lead, as if it were their birthright, in whatever circumstances they found themselves.

The bourgeois nature of the Chicago elite sample (as opposed to the aristocratically tinged Illinois elite) is reflected in the sociological composition of the city's twenty-one upper class families.[14] It must be emphasized that of the city's high status families these are the most accomplished, at least by the criteria used by the *DAB* editorial board. It is therefore interesting that only 33 members of these families are listed in the *DAB,* or 10 percent of the Chicago elite sample. (This is roughly the same percentage of Chicago social registrites E. Digby Baltzell found listed in *Who's Who in America* for the year 1940—the lowest percentage of all the cities he considered.)[15] Twelve of the family founders were of New England descent, three of northern New Jersey stock,[16] two of Quaker ancestry, one southern Cavalier, one Scotch-Irish southerner, one of Dutch ancestry, and only one non-Protestant, the Irish Catholic meat packer Michael Cudahy. Of the city's founding families only the New Hampshire Wentworths survive. The Scammons, Ogdens, Trumbulls, and Hubbards, among others, either drifted away from Chicago or simply died out.

The Fields (Massachusetts), Harrisons (Kentucky), Swifts (Massachusetts), and McCormicks (Scotch-Irish Virginia) are the only families to have multiple generations recognized by the *DAB*—the two Farwells, as with the Daweses, were brothers. The McCormick clan is by far the most accomplished "home grown" Chicago family (8 members are listed in the *DAB*) and the only one to approach Boston's dynastic Lodges and Cabots or Cincinnati's Tafts. However, the Harrison family, the most prolific political clan in American history, is the most illustrious of this sample, but only two of its members rose to prominence in Chicago.

Four families were more or less integrated into the eastern upper classes prior to their members' achieving functional significance in Chicago: Harrison, Wentworth, Holabird (Connecticut), and Washburne (Maine). Perhaps not coincidentally all were functionally important in categories other than business: the Harrisons, Wentworths, and Washburnes in politics, the Holabirds in architecture.

The remaining 17 families rose to prominence roughly between the Civil War and the First World War. Nine of them are of New England heritage and three of northern New Jersey stock. If we consider only the descendants of these twelve family founders, not one directly engaged in politics as a life work. Frank Lowden, son of a Minnesota Granger and husband to the daughter of railcar magnate George Pullman, was one term Governor of Illinois (1916–1920), but he was the family founder. Likewise for Charles B. Farwell (congressman 1871–1877, 1881–1883 and United States senator 1887–1893), whose brother John was a successful merchant, and Charles G. Dawes (vice president under Coolidge and Ambassador to

Great Britain), whose brother Rufus was a utilities magnate. Although periodically civic-minded, the descendants of these families along with those of the Armours, Swifts, Fields, Ryersons, Higinbothams, Drakes, Pullmans, Ayers, and Cranes did not participate directly in the political sphere.

On the other hand, two of the five non-New England, non-New Jersey families [17] produced individuals prominent in something other than money making. Medill McCormick, whose promising political career was cut short by a fatal heart attack at age 48, served as congressman (1917–1919) and United States senator (1919–1925). His cousin, Anita McCormick Blaine, was an early champion of progressive education, supporting throughout her life the educator Francis Parker and the school named for him. Ernest Poole, of Dutch descent, is the only member of this sample to pursue a literary career. Poole, whose father Abram was a successful grain broker in the city, graduated from Princeton in 1902, after which he became a magazine correspondent in Russia, France, and Germany. In 1915 his first novel, *The Harbor,* was published, followed two years later by *His Family,* for which Poole was awarded the Pulitzer Prize. (Poole's sister, Elizabeth, married Walter Weyl, whom she had met at Jane Addams' Hull House. Poole was a prominent Socialist before converting to Episcopalianism.)

It is important to point out that George Raymond, son of Benjamin Raymond, a prominent businessman and mayor (1839–1840, 1842–1843), and Edgar Rice Burroughs, son of a successful capitalist, were the only other native Chicagoans of privilege to be recognized by the *DAB* for writing or intellectualism. Raymond left Chicago at age forty (1880) for Princeton and later Oxford; Burroughs refused his father's wish for him to attend Phillips Academy and Yale, moved to California, and wrote *Tarzan of the Apes.* Both Raymond and Burroughs were of New England descent.

All this discussion is to say that the upper class sample reflects not so much an aristocracy, and certainly not a patriciate, but a plutocracy. In effect it is a list of interrelated businessmen who have all too often eschewed public responsibilities. No New England child of the gilded age pursued the public or intellectual spheres. The only families which did produce such persons were either of southern or Dutch descent, or of upper class position prior to migrating to Chicago. Furthermore, the only families to contribute political elites after 1900 (Harrison and McCormick) were of southern origin. Thus, not only did the gilded age New Englander but the established New Englander as well retreat from politics. Indeed, Chicago appears to have had two upper classes: the first, which dominated the city from 1833 to approximately 1900, was very public spirited; the second, reflected in this sample, tended toward private ambition. The essay now moves from the general to a specific treatment of Chicago leadership until the later emergence of the boss.

The Founding of Illinois and Chicago

Illinois is a southern state, ruled successively by the French, who settled in the area in the 1670s; the English, who took possession in 1763; and the State of Virginia, which organized the area as the County of Illinois in 1779 (after which it became the Northwest Territory). In 1800 the Illinois county became part of the Indiana Territory under the leadership of Virginia gentleman and future president William Henry Harrison. Nine years later the Illinois Territory was formed, and in 1818 the Territory was granted statehood. President Madison appointed Ninian Edwards[18] as territorial governor in 1809, and Shadrock Bond was elected first state governor in 1818, with Edwards becoming the state's first United States senator. Bond was succeeded by Edward Coles in 1822 and Coles, four years later, was followed by Edwards. All three individuals were upper class southerners characteristic of the sociological types who led Illinois into statehood and beyond. As historian Theodore Calvin Pease noted:[19]

> The government over Illinois in this period was more aristocratic than it has ever been since. Officials sent out by Congress to govern were accorded the position and consideration of gentlemen. The men who led the opposition claimed likewise to be gentlemen. And the rank and file of the territory willingly conceded gentlemen the right of political leadership.[20]

One such gentleman was Nathan Pope. Born in 1784 in Louisville, Kentucky (his brother was United States senator from that state), Pope was attracted to the Illinois Territory by his cousin Ninian Edwards. A graduate of Transylvania College, Pope became territorial delegate in 1816, and it was largely through his efforts Illinois was granted statehood. Moreover, he was responsible for drawing the state boundaries so that the future site of Chicago would be included within its territory.

Initially, Illinois's northern boundary ran due west from Lake Michigan's southern tip, which left Chicago in the Wisconsin Territory. But Pope, aware at that early date of the possibility of civil war over the slavery issue, persuaded Congress to push the boundary northward to include the lake's southwestern shore. Although born to a southern planter family, Pope was pro-Union, and he felt the northern section of the state was destined to attract a host of northern settlers who would, in the event of war, override the state's southern element and thus prevent secession.[21] The terrain for which he successfully fought was named Cook County after his nephew Daniel Pope Cook, an Illinois congressman and Edwards's son-in-law. After statehood Pope was appointed judge of the Federal District Court, in which post he remained until his death in 1850. He therefore never lived to see that the voters of Cook County did indeed turn "the tide for the election of Lincoln"[22] in 1860.

Pope's optimism concerning the state's northern region was hardly grounded in the realities of the time. The only permanent settlement in the area was Fort Dearborn, located in what is today downtown Chicago. The fort was built in 1803, destroyed by native Americans in the massacre of 1812, and reconstructed four years later. It served to protect a small and transient group of settlers (fewer than thirty in 1820) and their lucrative fur trade from hostile natives. One such protector was Captain John Whistler, grandfather of the famous artist and expatriot James Abbott McNeil Whistler.[23]

Among the early fur traders were John Kinzie, a native Canadian whose father had been a surgeon in the British Army, and the aforementioned Gurdon Saltonstall Hubbard. Kinzie migrated to the area as an agent for Astor's American Fur Company, and Hubbard followed in 1818. Kinzie, his son John H. Kinzie, and Hubbard became leading members of the community, such that it was in the 1820s.

The opening of the Erie Canal (1825) and the Illinois Legislature's proposal to construct a canal linking Lake Michigan with the Mississippi River[24] (1829) changed the fate of Fort Dearborn forever. Owing to these events, the area's real estate prices soared, luring Easterners west and shifting their economic focus from St. Louis and Detroit to the southwest shore of Lake Michigan. Indeed, throughout the 1830s the area was little more than a real estate lottery. In 1832 an 80 by 100 foot parcel of land was priced at $100. Three years later the same parcel sold for $15,000.[25] Accordingly, the population soared from thirty in 1829 to 1,300 in 1833.

In 1833 Chicago was incorporated as a town and in 1837 as a city. What followed was the most extraordinary rate of growth experienced by any city in the Western world. In 1850 the population had increased sevenfold to 29,963, of which 52 percent were foreign born; by 1860 to 109,260 of which 50 percent were foreign born; by 1870 to 298,977 of which 48 percent were foreign born (78 percent foreign born or of foreign parentage); and by 1920 to 2.7 million, of which 72 percent were first or second generation immigrants.[26]

For the most part, this burgeoning and heterogeneous population was governed by two auslander groups of similarly situated individuals well integrated into the historical matrix characteristic of upper class life. The first group, consisting of Hubbard, Ogden, Wentworth, Trumbull, Arnold, Douglas, and Scammon were to be found at all levels of government and set the tone of the city's political life between 1833 and the Great Chicago Fire of 1871.

While a member of a Connecticut first family (Hubbard) was among the town's original trustees, William B. Ogden (1805–1877), a member of a New Jersey first family, was elected mayor when Chicago was incorporated as a city in 1837. John B. Ogden descended from John Ogden, one of the original associates of the 1664 Elizabethtown purchase. John Ogden's grandson, Robert, continued in public service as surrogate for the County of Essex, member of the council, and, for several years, Speaker of the House of Assembly. Robert's son, Aaron Ogden, was elected New Jersey's fifth governor in 1812.

Twenty-two years after Aaron was elected governor, William B. Ogden was serving in the New York Legislature. His tenure, however, was cut short when Ogden's brother-in-law, Charles Butler, persuaded him to resettle in Chicago and attend to the Butler family real estate interests. (Charles Butler, along with his brother Benjamin, were members of Martin Van Buren's law firm. Benjamin Butler would later become attorney general under Van Buren, having served in that position, as well as Secretary of War, under Jackson.)

Ogden accepted Butler's offer and migrated to Chicago in 1835. He opened a real estate office the following year, then was elected Mayor, and in 1840, city councilman. Shortly thereafter, he was joined by his brother, Mahlon Dickerson Ogden, named, incidentally, after their father's good friend, New Jersey governor and U.S. senator Mahlon Dickerson, and the two served many terms in the city council throughout the 1840s and 1850s. In 1860 William Ogden was elected to the Illinois senate.

Perhaps Ogden's greatest contributions to Chicago's development was industrial. In 1847 Ogden induced Cyrus McCormick to establish his Reaper Manufacturing Company in the city, thus initiating Chicago's growth as an industrial giant. Thereafter, Ogden was largely responsible for transforming the city into the leading railroad center of the nation. As president and/or director of eight railroad companies, Ogden, with Congressional support from Senator Douglas, oversaw the city's infrastructural development from not one mile of rail track in 1847 to 3,000 miles of rail track by 1856, over which traveled 58 passenger and 38 freight trains every day.[27]

John Wentworth and Stephen A. Douglas were elected Chicago's first Congressional representatives in 1843. Douglas served two terms before his election as the city's first U.S. Senator in 1847, and Wentworth went on to serve six terms in the House. Wentworth also was a twice elected mayor of Chicago (1857–1858, 1860–1861), police commissioner, and superintendent of the public schools. He furthermore owned and operated the newspaper, the Chicago Democrat, the leading Free Soil journal in the area.

Douglas, a Vermont native, related to the Arnold family, initially settled in Jacksonville, Illinois (1834) where for a decade he practiced law with and before that extraordinary group of "prairie" aristocrats, Orville Browning, Ninian W. Edwards, Abraham Lincoln, David Davis, Sidney Breese, and John J. Hardin, among others. Wentworth, like Hubbard and Ogden, was a first family member—in this case, of New Hampshire. A Dartmouth and Harvard Law School graduate, Wentworth descended from Benning Wentworth, the first royal governor of New Hampshire. Wentworth's great grandfather, a Harvard graduate, presided over New Hampshire's first revolutionary convention in 1774 and later served as chairman of the Committee of Correspondence; his grandfather, John, Jr., also a Harvard man, represented the rebel colony in the Continental Congress and later signed the Articles of Confederation. His father, Paul Wentworth, was a military officer during the Napoleonic Wars, after which he served several terms in the New Hampshire state legislature.

Still another "first family" descendent was Lyman Trumbull of Connecticut. Like Douglas, Trumbull first settled in the downstate region (1837) where he assumed a prominent position among Illinois's legal aristocracy. Three years later Lyman, a grandson of the eminent minister Benjamin Trumbull, was elected to be the state legislature, after which he became secretary of state (1841–1843), justice of the Illinois Supreme Court (1848–1853), congressman (1854), and Republican United States senator from 1855 to 1873, during which time he resided in Chicago. In 1880, as a Democrat, Trumbull ran unsuccessfully for governor.

Isaac Arnold and Jonathan Y. Scammon round out Chicago's most significant early leaders. Scammon, a Maine native and graduate of the then new Colby College, established the city's first free school system, served in the city council, was a judge of the Cook County Circuit, and was elected state senator on the Republican ticket in 1861. In 1833 he established the *Chicago Journal* newspaper, the leading Whig journal in the city. Arnold, a son of a Rhode Island physician, migrated to Chicago in 1835 and a year later became a law partner of Mahlon D. Ogden, brother of the soon to be mayor. As a Free Soil Democrat and then Republican, Arnold represented Chicago in the state legislature (1842–1845) and United States Congress (1861–1865). In 1856 he helped found the Chicago Historical Society.

These seven individuals represent the nucleus of an auslander upper class. All told, the seven spent almost ninety years in public service. Socially, this group was centered in the Presbyterian Church (established in 1833), and the New England, Excelsior, and St. Andrew's clubs which were formed in the 1840s. In 1855 the Old Settlers Society was founded, the first officers of which were Hubbard, Scammon, and John H. Kinzie. Early upper class society was hardly "composed of rough and tumble pioneers." As one daughter of a leading Chicagoan wrote to her eastern friends, "There never were so many delightful and cultivated people to the square yard as there are here. They are all from the East or South, you know, and have brought the traditions and ideals of those older communities with them."[28]

Perhaps the most significant evidence of the vitality of upper class stewardship is revealed by the city's original charter. Devised in large part by New England descendant Norman B. Judd, a city alderman, state senator, congressman, and Lincoln's 1860 campaign manager, the charter was a conservative document which called for a strong legislative council, consisting of aldermen elected from the then six wards, and a weak mayor whose role was to preside over the council (in 1898 Sidney Webb remarked that this was a distinctly English practice and the only example of it he observed in America). Conceived to guard against the abuse of power by inhibiting its centralization (very much federalist) the mayor's role was simply that of a chairman of the board. All aldermen, and after 1840, the mayor, were to perform their duties honorifically. Because socioeconomic residential segregation had not yet been firmly institutionalized, each ward was consequently represented by high status individuals, or at least persons of independent means. This lack of remuneration, of course, was intended to dissuade the common and propertyless from seeking high public office, and all evidence points to the success of such a ploy. As historian Bessie Louise Pierce points out, 25 out of the 27 candidates for mayor between 1848 and 1869 were of the upper classes prior to entering politics.[29]

Without question the charter is non-democratic by contemporary standards. It was drawn up and passed by, and certainly favored, the privileged as well as those who aspired to be of that circle. Indeed, the charter actually required that the privileged be public spirited. But the document also reflected, I think, the confident spirit of a class—a spirit which was fundamental to the political decentralization enjoyed during that era and one which restrained the actions of its proponents. As odd as it appears today, the participants in Chicago's nineteenth century political contests considered public office something honorable, not a means for egoistic enhancement.

This public spirit was very much alive throughout the city's second era of class leadership, spanning the time from the fire to 1915. The most intriguing figures of this group were Carter Harrison, Carter Harrison II, and Hempstead Washburne.[30]

As mentioned, the Harrison family is the most prolific political clan in America. When the first Harrison was elected to the Virginia House of Burgesses in 1642 "he founded the longest unbroken line of politicians in American history."[31] From 1642 to 1965 every generation was represented in public life, which included two United States presidents, one signer of the Declaration of Independence, four members of the Virginia House of Burgesses, one governor of Virginia, and several members of Congress. It is not surprising then, that one of the more remarkable American urban political dynasties would be founded by one of the Harrisons.

Carter Harrison I was born in 1825 at Clifton, the family plantation outside of Lexington, Kentucky. In 1845 he graduated from Yale, after which he traveled abroad where he became fluent in German, French, and Italian—which later aided his political aspirations in Chicago. In 1855 Harrison took a Law Degree from Transylvania, moved to St. Louis, and then to Chicago where he bought a home on Ashland Boulevard, in the center of the city's upper class "Kentucky Colony." The first Yale Club meeting was held in the Harrison home in 1866.

In 1874 Harrison was elected to Congress as a Democrat by a margin of five votes, and reelected in 1876. After his second term expired he was persuaded to run for mayor, again as a Democrat, which he did successfully in 1879. Thus began the first of what would be five terms as Chicago's leading official, five terms coinciding with the city's industrial expansion and concomitant labor unrest. He was re-elected in 1881, 1883, and 1885. On the expiration of his fourth term Harrison again toured Europe, where he was entertained by royalty and heads of state, including von Bismarck, which greatly impressed Chicago's significant German population. He returned to Chicago in 1891 in time to enter the mayoralty race, but was defeated by fellow "Yalie" and Republican Hempstead Washburne.

Washburne himself was a member of a political family dynasty. His father, Elihu B. Washburne, a Maine native and graduate of the Harvard Law School, was a prominent Illinois statesman based in Galena, and among his uncles were governors of Maine and Wisconsin, a United States senator from Minnesota, and an ambassador to Paraguay. Hempstead moved from Galena to Chicago in 1875, and eight years later became a partner in the law firm headed by his father's friend, Lyman Trumbull.

It is important to note that Boston, the citadel where it is reported that "Lowells talk only to Cabots," elected only one Brahmin to the mayoralty between 1865 and 1917, Josiah Quincy, who served one three year term. In contrast, Chicago, considered the most plebian of American cities, elected the two Harrisons and Washburne to eleven mayoral terms between 1879 and 1915, and the three individuals served a total of twenty-one years in office.

Washburne's ascendancy to the mayoralty, however, symbolizes something far more than just another patrician in office. On the one hand, he represents the last New Englander of privilege to assume prominent local office. On the other, his victory relied on a novel type of Chicago politician, a type which emerged as the New England "better element" retreated: the local ward boss. Within the Republican party during the 1880s there surfaced "professional" politicians who tended to view politics as an end in itself—power for power's sake, one might say. The first and most significant Republican professional was William Lorimer, the son of a humble and poor English born Presbyterian minister. Although condemned by "amateur" Republicans as a "renegade boss," Lorimer had nevertheless built an efficient and powerful grass roots organization, so powerful, in fact, that any Republican candidate for mayor, including Washburne, had to rely on it for votes.

The Democratic party also had its bosses, most of whom were Irish-Catholic. But in contrast to the Republican bosses those in the Democratic party had only parochial ambition, content to be the knight of a particular ward, but not concerned with assuming total power over the city. Lorimer, in effect, represents the first Chicago politician to have desired to be the boss of the entire city, and a symbol of what was to come.

Perhaps one reason the Democratic bosses were held in check were the Harrisons. Carter Harrison I regained the mayoralty in 1893 on the eve of the famous Columbian Exposition. The ceremony and enthusiasm surrounding his election, however, came to an abrupt end when a city employee, unhappy over being denied a lucrative patronage position, assassinated Harrison in his Ashland Boulevard home.

However, the Cavalier presence did not end with Harrison. After his father's death, Carter Harrison II assumed a prominent position in Chicago's Democratic party. Educated abroad and at the Yale Law School, Harrison II gained the mayoralty in 1897 by defeating fellow Kentuckian, J. M. Harlan, a Princeton graduate and son of a United States Supreme Court Justice. Like his father, Harrison II served five terms, being reelected in 1899, 1901, 1903, and finally in 1911.

In *Chicago: A More Intimate View of Urban Politics,* [32] Charles Merriam, whom Harrison defeated in the 1911 election, attributed the city's relative freedom from oligarchy to the honesty and effectiveness of the Harrison administrations. Merriam's perspective on the issue was largely psychological. But a sociological interpretation of the phenomenon in question would also be useful.

A particularly striking feature of the Harrisons was the utter confidence of self and place they exuded in the political arena. This confidence, I suggest, was largely engendered by the class and familial traditions in which they were raised; moreover, this confidence enabled them to be a friend of, yet remain aloof from, the "common man"—a trait well in evidence among America's most significant assimilating aristocrats. The Harrisons were as comfortable with the ethnic groups, and for that matter, the city's resident socialists, as they were with men of their own rank, and, most importantly, they managed to gain the political vote of all three. Only with the Protestant middle classes did the Harrisons lack favor,[33] largely because they did not share the northern Protestant zeal for reform, a zeal which often took on an overly idealistic and often prejudicial dimension. This wide appeal was at once integrative and elevating. It was integrative in the sense that the authority wielded by the Cavalier mayors was a qualitative force around which various groups and strata cohered. It was elevating in the sense that the political sphere was personalized without its leaders resorting to the manipulative and demagogic tactics frequently used, perhaps necessarily, by persons claiming to be a friend and peer of the people. The Harrisons claimed to be a friend of the common man but unlike their ancestor, William Henry Harrison, they never pretended to be his equal.

Throughout the 1880s revolutionary anarchists, among them German born Johann Most and August Spies, as well as New England descended Albert Parsons, flocked to the city. These individuals and others distributed literature and "preached the gospel of revolutionary anarchism undisturbed by Mayor Harrison, Chicago's doughty champion of individual liberty."[34] Eventually, their activities found favor among those living the industrial reality, and in 1886 the workers at the McCormick Reaper factory went on strike (Cyrus McCormick, the founder, had died two years before, at which time his 26-year-old son and namesake took control of the company). On May 4, the workers assembled in Haymarket Square, and while Chicago's business elite protected themselves in their mansions on Prairie Avenue and Lake Shore Drive (Harrison liked to refer to them as the "timid millionaires"), the Mayor walked through the crowd, talking with the strikers and confirming their right of assembly and free speech. Harrison deemed the demonstration peaceful, ordered the police to retreat, and left. The workers, supposedly seething with revolt, cheered the exit of this upper class gentleman—a man they always referred to as "Our Carter."

As it turned out, of course, Harrison left too early. What began as a peaceful demonstration became the infamous Haymarket Riot. To this day we can only speculate as to why and who exploded the bomb, setting off the conflict which left several policemen and strikers dead, and why the police did not heed Harrison's order to retreat. And while I do not wish to diminish the significance of the sociological forces leading to the strike, nor the tragic execution of the anarchists, the fact that a southern aristocrat, a member of one of the nation's most illustrious families, had the confidence of place to meet the strikers face to face is surely revealing of the nature of authority. The industrial giants protected their flanks—powerful, rich, yet authorityless—and in the process estranged themselves from the working class. In contrast, the less wealthy but comfortable Harrison wielded an authority and confidence of self that comes only from birthright.

Many of the "timid millionaires," of course, are reflected in our upper class sample. As we have seen, most of them are of New England descent, defying their public spirited biological and spiritual ancestors. This private impulse, interestingly, caught the interest of their peer and contemporary Franklin MacVeigh, a Scotch-Irish capitalist from Pennsylvania. In 1896 he published a paper in the *American Journal of Sociology* in which he argued that, while the "better element" thought government should be *for* them, they no longer seemed willing that government be *of* them. He proceeded by suggesting that the best element was reduced to criticizing government from afar and had little taste for reforming government from within—content with exercising the democratic right of vocal protest, but not interested in the democratic duty of direct participation. Why is it surprising, he wondered, that Chicago politics was becoming a matter for the bribed and the briber, when "gentlemen," individuals historically above money, cease to function in that public world?[35]

MacVeigh's concern is evidenced through the activities of the Municipal Voters League, a Chicago reform group. In 1895 the MVL sought to oust many of the known grafters in city council (the vast majority were known to be crooks). To this end the members sought out and supported honest men—Republican, Democrat, or Socialist—to challenge the targeted aldermen. As it turned out, the reform crusade was successful in defeating 23 out of 26 boodlers. But the interesting point which concerns this essay is that very few members of the MVL saw fit to be candidates themselves. Only William Kent, who eventually moved to California, and J. M. Harlan actually ran for office. This is to say, responsibility for political reform was delegated from afar, not assumed directly.

The New Englander's hesitancy to engage the political domain allowed William Lorimer freedom of action. Moreover, it provided an avenue for the "Gold Plated Anarchist," those businessmen Harold Gosnell characterized as "ruthless" and publicly irresponsible.[36] The first such person to wreak havoc in Chicago's political and business worlds was Philadelphian Charles T. Yerkes. Sent west in 1882 by P. A. B. Widener to gain control over Chicago's traction system, Yerkes introduced the city to "boodling," a Swedish term used by Lincoln Steffens to denote political bribes. Yerkes's astute use of the bribe, and Lorimer's frequent acceptance, allowed the Philadelphian immeasurable political influence, and by the late 1880s the traction system was his.

There was, however, resistance to his activities. In 1898 Harrison II, serving his first term as Mayor, and J. M. Harlan, the man Harrison defeated, were among those influential in defeating legislation which would have essentially given Yerkes the city's traction rights for life. Immediately thereafter Yerkes left the city for London where he engaged in the same activity.

Eventually, Lorimer and Yerkes were followed by men who proved to be beyond restraint. Not even Harrison II could muster the strength to battle the ambitious, capable, and frequently unscrupulous William H. Thompson, Samuel Insull, and Anton Cermak. These three created the machinery which dictates Chicago's political fortunes to this day.

The political career of William H. Thompson was catalyzed by the Lorimer organization. After an unimpressive stint as alderman, Thompson joined forces with the Lorimer people in 1899. Three years later, backed by the Republican machine and displaying an unusual capacity to sway the passions of the crowd, Thompson was elected to the office of county commissioner. And as they say, the rest is history—colorful history. "Big Bill" went on to dominate Chicago's mayoralty from 1915 to 1931 during which he organized "civic plunder on a scale never before seen in Chicago, or perhaps anywhere else in the country."

Whereas Lorimer was of humble origin, Thompson was a renegade son of privilege, born in the Beacon Hill section of Boston and raised in an elite neighborhood of Chicago. On his father's side Thompson descended from a long line of land rich New Hampshire military officers and politicians, and his mother, Medora Gale, was a member of one of Chicago's founding families (Thompson's maternal grandfather had been a justice of the Illinois Supreme Court). Such a pedigree is hardly what one would expect of a Chicago political boss, but then again Thompson devoted much of his life to opposing the traditions into which he was accidentally born.

Thompson symbolized the frontier rebel. In contrast to his rival and contemporary Carter Harrison II, Thompson's life was marked by disdain for the past and all it represented. He was an individual born to uncommon circumstance who forever tried to act common, but in the end only burlesqued himself. From his teenage years when he denied his father's wish for him to attend Exeter and Yale and instead became a cowboy in Wyoming, to his adulthood when he hired professional athletes to play on his gentlemen's club teams, Thompson was never content to subject himself to form.

Throughout his public life Thompson made good use of his cowboy experiences, rarely campaigning without the symbolic cowboy hat. He presented himself as the rugged individualist during his always entertaining speeches (for which he charged admission), and showed himself a master of political manipulation in the style of Huey Long. As Charles Merriam observed, whatever the people's passions, fears, or desires, Thompson was able to formulate policies so that their votes would be secure.

Whereas Lorimer had his Yerkes, Thompson's organization enjoyed the benevolence of Samuel Insull. The road to power traveled by the English born Insull was in the Yerkes style. Insull immigrated in 1893 as the newly appointed president of the Chicago Edison Company. Within twenty years his use of the bribe allowed him a monopoly over midwestern utilities—by 1917 his companies operated in eleven states, furnishing power to

385 cities, which prompted Edgar Lee Masters to remark, "with a flick of his hand he could plunge the middle west into darkness and cold."

As Lorimer, Yerkes, Thompson, and Insull (and later Capone) wreaked political havoc, Anton Cermak (1873–1933) was working himself up the Democratic party hierarchy. The son of Hussite Protestants who migrated to America from Bohemia in 1874, Cermak spent his entire life in party politics. From 1889 onward, ironically the year Hull House was founded, Cermak served in a number of positions ranging from errand boy to mayor in 1931; Cermak was very much the professional politician.

Perhaps Cermak's most significant political act was not winning the mayoralty but in denying Harrison II the Democratic party's nomination for mayor in 1915. Four years earlier, Cermak, whom Harrison II counted as a friend and ally, had been significant in turning out the vote for the Cavalier mayor in his race against Charles Merriam. Cermak's loyalties shifted, however, when Harrison II expressed a desire to run for an unprecedented sixth term. For reasons still not understood, the Czech boss, along with the Irish Catholics George Brennan and Roger Sullivan, gave the party's nomination to a weak and insignificant figure, Robert Schweitzer, who then proceeded to lose to Thompson, thus ushering in the era during which the city's wide open reputation was earned. In so doing, Chicago politics was bereft of a class presence, leaving the struggle for power between two Protestant bosses, Thompson and Cermak.

The battle between Cermak and Thompson culminated in the 1931 mayoral election, certainly one of the most controversial and emotionally charged in the city's history. The aging Thompson felt confident that Cermak (a man he referred to as "bohunk," and as an aspiring slave master) did not present a challenge, but as election day neared it was clear the Republican machine was not as vital or popular as Thompson believed. The unexpected and broad ranging popularity of Cermak demoralized the Thompsonites and forced them to join ranks with the Czech politician. On election day a record 82 percent of all registered voters made it to the polls and gave Cermak a resounding victory. He carried 45 of 50 wards (at that time a record) and outpolled Thompson 671,189 to 476,922, a 58 percent majority considered at that time to be exceedingly large.[37] In so doing, Cermak accomplished what no political figure in Chicago history had been able to do: centralize political power completely, and do so with wide support. In other words, he was not an "ethnic" phenomenon. Although the immigrant presence in Chicago was significant, it was Cermak's appeal to

Protestant groups, particularly the Congregationalists, civic organizations, business groups, and the silk stockings, which gave him victory. Even Charles Merriam, who three years before had boasted of Chicago's relative political vitality, supported Cermak.

As the unchallenged political boss, Cermak, according to Harold Gosnell, "ruled with an iron hand, kept all patronage under his thumb, and dealt ruthlessly with those who furnished opposition."[38] In the words of Edward J. Kelly, Cermak's protegé and successor, Mayor Cermak was the most powerful figure in the State of Illinois, and in the history of Chicago.

It is important to note that when Cermak rose to power Chicago's charter had been liberalized to such a degree that the city's political structure was an incomprehensible maze of separate and independent governments. In the city alone there were eight principal and twenty-five minor governments—the metropolitan area had some 1600 governments and 7700 elective officials.[39] While space does not allow for detailed examination, suffice to say that when Cermak took office the typical voter was burdened with 161 elections every six years, which, according to Charles Merriam, even the most astute citizen could neither manage nor understand.[40] As William Kornhauser might suggest, Chicago's government in 1931 was an example of mass politics, participatory and direct in theory, where the population had comparatively radical access to both leadership positions and leaders—and perhaps more importantly, vice versa.

Cermak's reign was tragically cut short in 1933 by an assassin's bullet intended for President Franklin D. Roosevelt. Chicago's first boss mayor had traveled to Miami, Florida where, ironically, he was to discuss his prospects for controlling federal patronage with the President. After Roosevelt gave a speech in Bayfront Park, Cermak approached him to exchange greetings just as the assassin, Guiseppe Zangara, pulled the trigger. Cermak died three weeks later.

But the political machine he built survived. Kelly and Daley merely solidified its hold over political power. As for Thompson, he died in 1944, claiming to the very end that Chicago had not heard the last of him. Interestingly, his funeral was one of the least attended in Chicago political history until such time as the local press pounced on the story, prompting hundreds of Thompson's "friends" to pay their last respects. Furthermore, as Thompson's estranged wife and his mistress fought over his modest $150,000 estate, probate court officials searching for a will found that Big

Bill had scattered $1.5 million in cash (small denominations) and $352,000 in stocks and bonds in a number of safety deposit boxes around the city. Such was the pathetic end of a Beacon Hill born renegade.

Conclusion

The political history of Chicago defies conventional wisdom on three counts. First, the extent to which the city was led throughout the nineteenth century by members of the eastern upper classes belies its rough, raw, and vulgar reputation. From 1833 until 1915 when Harrison II was ousted from the Democratic party some of the more illustrious families in American history were significant in founding and developing the city of big shoulders. The settlement of the frontier by rugged and equal individualists is a thesis which simply does not hold up for Chicago. This is all the more significant given the city's place in the popular consciousness. As Kipling observed years ago, Chicago is the most American of American cities—it is the city in which the common man is celebrated, the city in which refinement takes a back seat to the natural, the city, indeed, which takes pride in its adversarial posture vis-à-vis the eastern seaboard. Nevertheless, members of this eastern establishment essentially built the city from the marshes up.

Second, the city's political machine was Protestant in origin, not Irish Catholic as is so often assumed. Republican bosses William Lorimer and William H. Thompson came to the fore between 1885 and 1900 as the privileged Chicagoans of New England descent retreated to the country. Along with Charles T. Yerkes and Samuel Insull these individuals redefined politics and political behavior, and in the process provided all other aspiring politicians with the concept of a citywide boss.

Thompson's career is particularly relevant, at least symbolically, for it was during his reign as mayor that Chicago earned its reputation as a corrupt, wide open, and coarse city. That an individual who enjoyed all the fruits of upper class WASP life assumed an antinomian and populist facade is surely an intriguing point, although it was only the action of one individual. I would suggest that Thompson's rejection of his privileged past, and all that went with it, was paralleled by the retreat of the gilded age heirs from the public domain. The Yankees reverted to type, settling comfortably into trade. The pseudo-charismatic Thompson was able to construct a centralized political machine insofar as a virtuous materialism replaced the Calvinist spirit of stewardship, and this private orientation left Thompson and Cermak the sole political powers in the city.

Cermak, unlike Thompson, was of humble origin, but like Thompson, eager for political power. The important issue to consider is that Cermak was politically socialized within a milieu created by the Lorimer-Thompson-Yerkes-Insull forces. For a significant period of time the Harrison presence kept the Democratic bosses in check, at least compared to their Republican counterparts. But once the Cavalier was disposed of, the Protestant Cermak (not the Irish Catholic George Brennan or Edward Kelly) was able to construct a machine unfettered by secondary authorities.

Finally, I have tried to suggest that insofar as the Calvinist and Cavalier ethics of stewardship were vital, Chicago enjoyed political decentralization. This is to say, when individuals who wielded authority in *society* did so in *politics,* there existed two viable parties from which the constituency selected representatives, where neither a party nor an individual could completely monopolize power. For a time the city's charter actually demanded this of persons who were authoritative independent of functional position. But as the New England public spirit declined, and as the charter was liberalized, ambitious and certainly capable individuals pursued politics, not honorifically but as an end in itself. As Chicago's elite structure democratized, its normative shroud became tattered. Whereas the Harrisons felt the normative weight of generations past, persons such as Thompson and Cermak operated within comparatively lax moral milieux which allowed them to seek power for power's sake, and to covet power once it was realized.

This interpretation speaks to the democratic paradox which caught the interest of both Tocqueville and Weber. Chicago's political machine was truly a democratic phenomenon in that it presupposed the transference of authority from social class to "the people." The people, however, were in turn represented by an oligarchic administration, one which negated the very principles which inspired its evolution.

Notes

1. Since 1959 Republicans have won only 9 percent of all aldermanic and mayoral contests. Between 1939 and 1955 the Republicans fared better, winning 24 per-

cent of these contests. Furthermore, between 1939 and 1955 the five Republican mayoral candidates averaged 44 percent of the vote, and between 1959 and 1976, only 30 percent of the vote. All ten candidates lost to their Democratic foes. See Paul Kleppner, *Chicago Divided* (Dekalb: Northern Illinois University Press, 1985), 23.

2. The year the machine won out in Chicago (1931) was the year in which Yankee gentleman Samuel Seabury forced boss Jimmy Walker from New York's mayoralty. Similarly, as Richard J. Daley assumed office, boss leaders such as Boston's James Curley, Jersey City's Frank Hague, Kansas City's Thomas Pendergast, and Memphis's Edward Crump had passed into history, and their organizations with them.

3. Lincoln Steffens, *Shame of the Cities* (New York: Hill and Wang, 1957), 163–64.

4. *Ibid.*, 194.

5. Charles Merriam, *Chicago: A More Intimate View of Urban Politics* (New York: The Macmillan Company, 1929), 18.

6. Robert K. Merton, *Social Theory and Social Structure* (New York: Free Press, 1968), 126–36.

7. See Zane Miller, "Bosses, Machines, and the Urban Political Process," and Roger Lotchin, "Rejoinder and Comment," in *Ethnics, Machines, and the American Urban Future*, ed. Scott Greer (Cambridge, Mass.: Schenkman Publishing Co., 1981), 51–84, 139–52.

8. The Mather family was strategic in building the city of Cleveland; the Eliots were influential in developing St. Louis; and the Perkins clan was involved with the development of Cincinnati. See E. Digby Baltzell, *Puritan Boston and Quaker Philadelphia* (New York: Free Press, 1979), 508–10.

9. Stephen Hess, *America's Political Dynasties* (New York: Doubleday & Co., 1966).

10. C. O. Johnson, *Carter Henry Harrison I* (Chicago: University of Chicago Press, 1928), 173–200.

11. Stephen Hess, *op cit.*, 239–71.

12. This criterion for upper class inclusion meant excluding many of Chicago's most prestigious families, for example, the Blairs, Bowens, and Fairbanks. After investigating these and other cases, however, I concluded that their exclusion did not significantly alter the fundamental character of the upper class sample. In fact, their inclusion would strengthen the nuances of my argument rather than challenge them.

13. This decline was certainly not so evident in business. Whereas only 28 percent of the New England political elite were born after 1839, 45 percent of the New England business elite were born after 1839.

14. It will be noted that the Stevenson clan is not among the twenty-one families. Although Adlai Stevenson III was residing in Chicago in 1976, his family is of downstate origin, specifically Bloomington. I therefore did not include the Stevensons among Chicago's upper class families. However, it is interesting to point out that this public spirited clan is of southern origin.

15. E. Digby Baltzell, *Philadelphia Gentlemen: The Making of a National Upper*

Class (Philadelphia: University of Pennsylvania Press, 1977; original edition New York: Free Press, 1958), 29.

16. Since northern New Jersey was essentially a New England settlement created in response to the alleged liberalism of Connecticut and Yale College, one could legitimately argue that fifteen families were of New England descent.

17. The remaining three families, Wrigley, Palmer, and Cudahy, reflect the privatism which characterizes the Gilded Age New England and New Jersey contingents. The Wrigleys, for example, are noted as much for their reclusive life styles as for their acumen in selling chewing gum, and were a Philadelphia family of Quaker stock.

18. Edwards's son, Ninian Wirt Edwards (1809–1889), was a prominent Illinois politician as well. Ninian Wirt married Elizabeth Todd, sister of Mary Todd, and it was in his home where his good friend Abraham Lincoln met his future bride.

19. Southerners were not entirely dominant. Prominent northerners included the Hudson River Patroon Sidney Breese, a United States senator, congressman, and judge; Yale graduate Elias Kent Kane, author of Illinois's first Constitution and an Illinois state secretary; and the famous band of Yale educated ministers, Edward Beecher, Theron Baldwin, Asa and Jonathan B. Turner, and David Sturtevant. In 1830 this group established Illinois College, the first institution of higher learning in the state.

20. Theodore C. Pease, *The Story of Illinois* (Chicago: University of Chicago Press, 1949), 69–70.

21. Lloyd Lewis and Henry Justin Smith, *Chicago* (New York: Harcourt, Brace, and Company, 1929), 20–23.

22. Pease, *op cit.*, 75.

23. Lewis and Smith, *op cit.*, 9.

24. Daniel Pope Cook obtained the federal land grant for this project in 1827. Gurdon Saltonstall Hubbard authored the 1836 bill which initiated work on the canal, which was completed in 1848.

25. Harold M. Mayer and Richard C. Wade, *Chicago* (Chicago: University of Chicago Press, 1969), 16.

26. Bessie Louise Pierce, *History of Chicago* (Chicago: University of Chicago Press, 1957), Vol. II: 482; Vol. III: 516.

27. Mayer and Wade, *op cit.*, 35.

28. Frederic Cople Jaher, *The Urban Establishment* (Urbana: University of Illinois Press, 1982), 471.

29. Pierce, *op cit.*, 305.

30. Others include southerners J. M. Harlan, Charles M. Walker, John G. Rogers, J. H. Lewis (all politicians and judges), and New Englanders or of New England descent, George Everett Adams, Mark Skinner and Melville Fuller. All were of high status families.

31. Hess, *op cit.*, 217.

32. *Op. cit.*

33. Johnson, *op cit.*, 201–23.

34. *Ibid.* 41.
35. Franklin MacVeigh, "A Programme of Municipal Reform," *American Journal of Sociology* (July–May, 1895–96): 551–63.
36. Harold Gosnell, *Machine Politics: Chicago Model* (New York: AMS Press, 1969), 4.
37. Alex Gottfried, *Boss Cermak* (Seattle: University of Washington Press, 1962), 235–37.
38. Gosnell, *op cit.,* 15–16.
39. Merriam, *op cit.,* 30.
40. *Ibid.,* 30–31.

Elijah Anderson

7. Moral Leadership and Transitions in the Urban Black Community *

Far-reaching social changes are presently occurring within urban black communities as a major consequence of the civil rights movement, the urban riots of the 1960s, and various governmental remedies for racial exclusion, including civil rights legislation of the 1960s and 1970s. Fair housing, affirmative action, and various "set-asides" for blacks and other minorities have made a tremendous difference in the lives of great numbers of black Americans. The black middle class has grown in size and outlook (see Sitkoff, 1981; Morris, 1984; Farley, 1984; Landry, 1987; Wilson, 1987). Many members of this group, at times against serious prejudice and racial discrimination, have risen socially and economically, while simultaneously realizing themselves as full citizens of American society.

But as the black middle class moves socially and economically, it tends to move geographically, becoming ever more distant from the ghetto communities of its origin and leaving such communities without the quality of leadership from which they have traditionally benefitted. Current relatively high rates of teenage pregnancy, a lack of motivation to work in certain jobs when they are available, a desire to "get over" on fellow residents, and a prevalence of black on black crime may be reflections of the increasing absence of the black middle class as a stabilizing social force within ghetto communities.

At the same time, opportunities for poorer blacks to participate in the regular economy are limited, as evidenced in recurrent disproportionately high levels of black unemployment and underemployment. With severely limited education and skills, numerous inner city blacks are caught up in an employment bind. As low skill inner city manufacturing jobs decline. many jobs in the emerging service economy available to young blacks tend to be low paying or located far from the inner city. The remuneration from these positions constrains many to a life of poverty. To many young inner city blacks unable to participate effectively in the regular economy, an underground economy of drugs and vice appears attractive (see Anderson, 1981). This economy pervades the ghetto community, augmenting or replacing the regular one in many instances. As this economy expands, it undermines the level of interpersonal trust and moral cohesion that once prevailed in the urban black community. Young men without legitimate opportunities become especially vulnerable. And law abiding people who remain in the community, particularly the elderly, fear crime and personal injury. An atmosphere of distrust, alienation, and crime pervades the community, thereby segmenting the social relations between and among its residents. These changes alter the social organization of the traditional black ghetto (see Wilson, 1980; 1985; 1987).

In the past, blacks of various social classes lived side by side in segregated "Negro" sections of the city. They shared racially separate neighborhood and community institutions, including churches, schools, barber shops, and even liquor stores and taverns (see Cayton and Drake, 1945; Lewis, 1951; Clark, 1965). For instance, on a visit to a local barber shop, it would not have been unusual to observe a black doctor, dressed in coat and tie, follow a black factory worker, still dressed in his work overalls, into the chair. Living in close proximity to one another, the children of working class blacks attended school with the children of black lawyers, doctors, and small businessmen; the black churches often worked to coalesce such disparate individuals into a single congregation.

Successful people in urban black communities carried wide local reputations as big shots and were treated as pillars of the community. Their behavior, mannerisms, and habits were studied, discussed, and imitated; young people paid especially close attention to them. For instance, people knew all about "Dr. Davis": where he lived, what car he drove, how he walked; they knew the same about the lawyer, "Mr. Willis." They knew "Mr. Pitts," the black pharmacist and proprietor of a local drug store, who also served as a kind of informal banker for people, cashing checks and holding money for some until they could get to the bank; at times he interceded on behalf of one of "his people" at a bank downtown, and occasionally he would give the sermon at church. They knew "Reverend James," the minister of a local church, a virtual moral force and human institution of the community; he was always ready with a good word of advice to those who sought it—and often to those who did not. He could be counted on to help people, particularly young people in trouble with the law. Until recently, these people had to reside in all-black areas of the city because of residential segregation, but they served the black community well as visible, concrete symbols of success and moral value, living examples of the fruits of hard work, perseverance, decency, and propriety. Because of their presence, and the honor accorded them, there was more cohesion among individuals and the various classes of the black community than is generally observed today. These leaders served as effective, meaningful role models for community residents, lending to the community a certain moral integrity.

But it was not solely black professionals and small businessmen who led the community. On a more informal level, there were also construction workers, factory workers, and others who had "slaves," meaning jobs that required hard physical labor. Some men would hold two jobs simultaneously, or have a "hustle" on the side, in the form of odd jobs or handyman work, in order to get ahead. Not only did such men set an example for others, who at times would compete with them, but often they actively encouraged the young to follow their lead. Imbued with a strong commitment to the work ethic, they generally viewed working hard for a living as a positive value. Their wives often worked as domestics, hairdressers, nurse's aides, or storekeepers, setting an important example for young women. In those days, people generally regarded having children out of wedlock as serious deviance. To be young, single, and pregnant was generally frowned upon and considered to be a sign of being "messed up." Moreover, to be "on welfare" was to be stigmatized in many circles.

Because of recent openings in the opportunity structure of the wider society, the urban black community has experienced an outflow of middle and upper income people such as Dr. Davis and Mr. Pitts, as well as some church leaders. Some have died, and others moved away; their children have been educated and joined the professional class of blacks, away from their original communities. For the first time blacks are theoretically able to move into almost any housing they can afford. In this social climate, even some of the construction men and factory workers have moved to "better" neighborhoods; their children, too, are becoming educated and joining middle and professional classes of blacks.

The New Black Middle Class

When young students used to leave segregated black communities for college, they would very often go to institutions such as Howard, Spelman, Fisk, Wilberforce, Central State, Southern University, or Virginia Union, the traditionally "black" colleges and universities. After graduation many of these students returned to the black community, perhaps to work as schoolteachers, social workers, dentists, doctors, or undertakers. They did this not so much because they preferred to, but because of widespread discrimination, and the fact that social rewards and economic opportunities for educated blacks were in the black community.

But today, as many black students are educated in major formerly "white" universities and colleges, they tend not to return to urban black communities. In pursuit of bright futures in big corporations, law firms, and universities, these young, educated blacks gravitate to suburbia or to trendy areas of the city. As they move into leadership positions in the wider society, many become abstractions to the local black community, leaving the poorer, uneducated blacks without tangible role models and instructive agents of social control. As described by a minister of an inner city congregation who is a part-time taxi driver:

> The black community needs these people. I know, they've worked hard for what they got. People don't resent them for it. They worked for what they got, and they're still working to keep it. They're well qualified for their jobs. But people, black children, need them. They need to be around them. How many of these kids have met a Mayor Goode, you know. They see him, you know, just sometimes. How many of these kids get close to a black businessman? Or a black lawyer, or somebody? None. They need these people right around them who will guide them and show them how to take hold of life. To teach them how to behave themselves and to teach them that they care. That's the big thing, too. People don't care. See, time was when the big people had distinguishing features about them, and they made you feel like "here's someone who is a leader of the community" and "I want to be like him" or "I want to be like her."

To be sure, newly mobile members of the black middle class often have close kinship relations with blacks of the ghetto communities. In a unique manner, they may serve as cultural brokers of a sort, linking the new black middle class with the ghetto, and more generally, the black community with the wider society. Occasionally, there are extended family reunions which may include relatives from diverse backgrounds, from members of the underclass to successful medical doctors and business executives. Such reunions may at times be centered around or related to trouble of some sort, such as sickness or death in the family or legal difficulties. During such occasions, because they are times when old ties are renewed, those in need may make outright requests for financial assistance. In these circumstances, the successful members of the family may feel some obligation to render at least token assistance. But repeated requests can discourage intimacy between well off and poorer relatives, or at least place some strain on the relationship. The successful members of these families tend to feel a deep obligation to serve as role models for younger sisters, brothers, cousins, and other kin. It is at this family level that the new black middle class may have an effective social connection with the ghetto community.

But in general, the newly educated groups appear increasingly distant and formal in their relations with residents of traditional urban black communities. There seems to be some desire among the better off simply to place social distance between themselves and those who are left behind. Many rationalize this stance as the practical need for new middle-class people to draw lines between themselves and others in order to participate more fully in the general society.

Involved in careers ranging from medical doctor to investment banker to lawyer, this new middle class group appears to be much less a merchant and service class, financially dependent upon the black community, than the middle class traditionally has been (see Frazier, 1957; Landry, 1987). Members of this class tend not to aspire to own a local restaurant, tavern, or barbershop and seldom operate the grocery, clothing, and furniture stores within the black community. In Philadelphia and other cities, other ethnic groups, including Jews and Koreans, tend to dominate in these commercial areas of the black community; such merchants, particularly the newly emerging Asians, at times incur the wrath of many race-conscious blacks.

As middle income blacks are encouraged to leave traditional black communities, they gravitate to residential areas of second and third settlement in ways reminiscent of the upwardly mobile Irish, Italians, and Jews who preceded them (see Wirth, 1928; Shaw and McKay, 1942). Ostensibly, they are moved by concerns over crime, drugs, poor public schools, poor and crowded housing, and social status; there is also sometimes a deep emotional desire to get as far from poorer blacks as possible. They are attracted as well by the prospect of good schools, "crime-free" suburban neighborhoods, good real estate investments, and the status requirements of their professional and corporate careers. They send their children increasingly to private schools. While their black peers sometimes chide them about remembering where they came from, they generally offer no excuses or apologies for their departure from the ghetto community, believing it their right to have and to enjoy success.

Education and connection with professional and corporate America contribute to gradual social, economic, and perhaps political estrangement between the black middle and upper classes and the poor, urban black communities. As these processes mature, the socially mobile group is likely to be slowly transformed from separate individuals ambivalent about their connection with ghetto communities into a class increasingly concerned with itself.

As these people leave black communities, they settle predominantly in white or ethnically diverse areas. The middle and upper income whites they join may be angry, cool, indifferent, cordial, or receptive to their presence. In some white suburban communities, the experience of ghettoization recurs, though in abbreviated form. Blacks find themselves forming exclusively black communities of communion, if not of residence; at times, they actively seek out other blacks of only casual acquaintance for sociability and friendship. As one twenty-two-year-old black female college student said:

> When I was 15, my dad was transferred from Baltimore to New Jersey. It was a big change for my family, including my mom, dad, and 8-year-old sister. We moved to this all-white suburban community. It was upper income, Jewish and Italian, mainly. We were the only blacks around. A few people were friendly, but it wasn't Baltimore. One white woman, a writer, was very friendly. At school, the students were very cold. It took a long time for me to make friends, but I managed it and graduated from the high school; it was a good school. My dad seemed not to mind so much being the only blacks there, but my mom really resented it. My parents didn't socialize or have a dinner party for two years. My mom began to meet black people on the commuter train, and so things got better. We used to get so excited when we saw another black person. It was lonely. My sister seemed to do all right. She had many white friends, and she went to the bar mitzvahs and parties. Now my dad has been transferred back to Washington. My mom is happy. My sister misses her friends, and in Baltimore many of her friends are white.

The Underclass

The prospect is for the lower income ghetto residents to become increasingly isolated, sharing neighborhood institutions with the financially desperate and the criminal element. As the black middle class gravitates to situations that promise increased opportunities, members of the underclass appear mired in poverty and second class citizenship reminiscent of the caste-like system of racial exclusion described by Cayton and Drake, (1945), Myrdal, (1944) and Clark (1965) more than a generation ago. In this situation, crime, drugs, and general antisocial behavior come to serve as social forces that work to underscore status lines drawn within the community. With the introduction of drugs and the correspondingly large incidence of black on black crime, fear and distrust abound, particularly toward the young. It is this feature of the present situation that has such fateful implications for the way in which the community itself is related to its erstwhile leadership class. Many of the better off people simply want to get as far from the community as they can. What they do not accomplish by physically moving, they work to accomplish socially: they try to distance themselves from others who do not meet their standards of behavior (see Anderson, 1978). It is through such conduct that they in fact contribute, however unintentionally, to the social construction of the underclass (see Anderson, 1980; Auletta, 1980; Glasgow, 1980; Wilson, 1980; Nathan, 1987).

The underclass in the black community is made up of people who have failed to keep up with their brethren, both in employment and in sociability. Essentially, they can be seen as victims of the economic and social system. They make up the unemployed, the underskilled, the poorly educated, even though some hold diplomas from urban high schools. Many are intelligent, but demoralized by racism and the wall of social resistance facing them. In this context, many easily lose perspective and lack an outlook and sensibility that would allow them to negotiate the wider system of employment and society in general.

Emerging from the ghetto's crippling educational experience, often lacking even rudimentary skills, and at times scorning subsistence jobs, they also tend to be discriminated against by prospective employers who find it difficult to trust them. In part, this is because of their inability or unwillingness to meet basic rules of middle class propriety with respect to dress and comportment, but it is also because of their skin color and what this has come to symbolize to prospective employers.

While it may be argued that the institutions both of the wider society and the local community have failed members of the black underclass, local working and middle class residents often hold them to blame for their predicament. Such a stance allows the better off to maintain faith in the wider institutions, particularly the work ethic, thus helping to legitimate their own positions in the local system of stratification. Hence, to many employed and law-abiding blacks residing in inner city areas, members of the underclass are viewed, and treated, as socially convenient objects of scorn, fear, and embarrassment.

In this way, the underclass serves as an important social yardstick within the community that allows working class blacks to compare themselves favorably with others they judge to be worse off. In this respect, the underclass is a category of persons stigmatized within the black community. Included in this category are the blacks who threaten and thus incur the wrath and condescension of the financially more successful who remain in the ghetto.

To the stable working class, the underclass symbolizes "how low a black person can fall from decency." On the streets, the members of this class are viewed as "trouble" and avoided. Perceived as people "doing drugs," selling drugs, and committing most of the street crime in the area in support of their habits, they are the pimps, hustlers, prostitutes, destitute single mothers, and anonymous street corner men. The easy stereotype is that such people, "think nothing of making two or three babies with no way to care for them. They don't want to work, and have no get up about themselves." In the ghetto, the very poor may reside on the streets, or in abandoned houses and automobiles, and may be seen rummaging through refuse, thus fueling the community's negative conception of them. There is little room for empathy from the stable working class.

It should be pointed out that ghetto residents seldom use the term "underclass" when referring to the poor and others having difficulty surviving by the conventional means of the system. They tend to use terms of derision, working socially to distinguish such people from themselves. Common terms are "lowlife," "street niggers," and "tacks." Hence, the category referred to by the term "underclass" is largely symbolic, informed and in effect socially constructed by the public observations of relatively better off residents who are concerned with their local status and identity.

The underclass thus comprises a highly stigmatized group within the ghetto community. This kind of stigmatization is widely shared, as indicated in the following field note:

> On a Friday morning at approximately 11:00, I caught the number 34 trolley at 47th and Baltimore Avenue, just on the edge of the sprawling black community of West Philadelphia. I paid my fare and looked for a seat. It was a rainy morning, and people were dressed in rain gear; some carried umbrellas. The passengers were mostly blacks, a quarter white, and about three Asians.

The back of the trolley is usually informally reserved for blacks; whites are reluctant to venture beyond a certain point unless other whites inhabit the rear section in numbers. The ecology of seating is influenced by the color of passengers, the symbols they display, and the time of day. The front of the trolley is generally considered safer than the back, for social control is believed to be a function of proximity to the driver. In the back region, young black men sometimes play radios, the sign proclaiming "radios silent" notwithstanding. At times, there is a noticeable odor of marijuana and tobacco smoke; I have, on occasion, observed people sharing liquor. Young black men and women sometimes talk loudly to the person sitting next to them in what is to blacks nothing more than sociable and polite conversation though whites at times take it for a disturbance. There is a clash of cultures here. But proper blacks seem to "understand," as they roll their eyes or avert their gaze in an effort to place distance between themselves and those making too much noise.

On this day, the only available seats were at the very rear of the trolley. As I stumbled through the moving car toward a seat, I passed a black foursome near the rear door. They seemed to be having a good time, talking and laughing loudly, at times arguing. Three men and one woman made up the group. They seemed to be in their early to mid-twenties. I moved by them and took a seat at the rear. I sat between two young black men, one of whom carried a radio that was turned off. I began a conversation with the young man to my left. "Is it really that difficult to find a job?" I opened. He looked at me with surprise. Smiling, he shook his head, "Naw, not really." I said, "Do you work?" He said, "Yeah, with my uncle. A lot of people don't wanta work." After a short pause, I asked, "Do you go to school?" "Yeah, I go to West Philly High." "How old are you?" I asked. "I'm seventeen," he said. We had easy conversation for a while. Soon the four loud persons became louder as they discussed an upcoming baseball game. One person shouted at another, "I ain't gon' spot you shit!" Other passengers cringed. Some looked nervous but interested in the conversation. Still others seemed to pay them no attention. The four persons became even louder. Attempting to collude with me, the youth with whom I had been speaking whispered, "Ignorant niggers. Boy!" He seemed embarrassed. I pressed him on his feelings. "Where do you think they're going, to work?" I led. "Work!?" he exclaimed. "They don't work no where, and probably don't want no job. People like that just care 'bout gettin' high, hanging on the corner, and stuff. Wastin' their lives," he said. "Yeah," I said, gently affirming his comments. My stop was coming up. "Be cool," I said to the young man. "You too," he offered. I pulled the cord, rose, and stumbled toward the door. As I passed the loud four, I got a strong whiff of liquor. The trolley stopped, I got off and went on my way.

Blacks who achieve middle class or even solid working class status often become, of their own volition, culturally estranged from the underclass. In pursuit of status opportunities and fuller participation in the wider society, and out of concern for their own physical survival, the middle class, and those who aspire to it, tend to leave the black underclass increasingly alone.

Of "Old Heads" and Young Boys

The relationship between "old heads" and young boys represents an important institution of the traditional ghetto community. It has always been an important aspect of the social organization of the segregated black community. This institution assisted the transition of young men from boyhood to manhood, from idle youth to gainful employment and participation in the regular economy. The old head's acknowledged role was to teach, support, encourage, and in effect socialize young men to meet their responsibilities with regard to the work ethic, family life, law, and decency. But as meaningful employment opportunities have become increasingly scarce for young black males, drugs accessible, and crime a way of life for many, this institution has undergone stress and significant change.

In the past, an old head was known as a man of stable means who believed in the work ethic and was strongly committed to family life, to church, and, most important, to passing on his philosophy, developed through his own rewarding experience with work, to young boys whom he found worthy. He personified the work ethic and equated it with value and high standards of morality; in his eyes, an employed, working man was a good and decent individual (see Anderson, 1978). The old head and young boy relationship was essentially one of mentor and protégé. The old head could be two years older than the young boy or as much as thirty or forty years older; the young boy was usually at least ten or older. The young boy readily deferred to the old head's chronological age and worldly experience. The nature of the relationship was that of junior/senior, based on junior's confidence in senior's ability to impart useful wisdom and practical advice for getting through the world successfully and living well according to the values of decency, family responsibility, and regular work.

The old head was a kind of guidance counselor and moral cheerleader who preached anticrime and antitrouble messages to his charges. Encouraging young boys to work and to make something of themselves, he would try to set a good example by living, as best he could, a stable, decent, worry-free life. His constant refrain was, "Get yourself a trade, son " or

"Do something with your life" or "Make something out of yourself." Displaying initiative, diligence, and pride, as a prime role model, he lived "to have something," usually something material, but an intact, nuclear family counted in the picture he painted for the young boys. On the corners and in the alleys, he would point to others in the community who worked, using them as examples of how hard work and decency could pay off. Of such a person, he might urge the young boys to "pattern yourself after him." In these conversations and lectures, he would express great pride in his own outstanding work record, punctuality, good credit rating, and anything else reflecting his commitment to honesty, independence, hard work, and family values.

The old head could be a minister, a deacon in the church, a local policeman, a favorite teacher, an athletic coach, or a cornerman. He could be the uncle or even the father of one of the local group of young boys. Very often, the old head played the role of surrogate father for many he determined to be in need of such attention. A youth in trouble would sometimes discuss his problem with an old head before going to his own father, if he had a father. And the old head would be ready with a helping hand, sometimes in the form of a loan for a worthy purpose. The following interview with a twenty-nine-year-old man gives a glimpse of the relationship between an old head and a young boy:

> Yeah, I got three of my boys in the service right now, and another is on the way. Just the other day, a young boy come up to me in the neighborhood and say he need 25 dollars to get some underwear and toiletries so he can get ready to leave for the army. We talked for a while, and then I reached into my pocket and came up with two tens and a five and handed it to him. He said, "Thanks." And I said, "I'm gettin' ready to go downtown, you want to come along? We can pick up that stuff you need." He said, "O.K." We got the trolley, and went on downtown. We got his stuff, and came on back home. I was glad I could do that for him, help him out. Now he gone to the army. He's one of my young boys. I been knowin' him since he was very young, and now he's nineteen. I don't worry 'bout my money. He'll pay me. I don't worry 'bout it.

The old head would often be well prepared to tell the youth what was good for him. Through this kind of extension of himself, the old head could gain moral affirmation that would be his reward for saving another young boy. The reward served as an important if subtle incentive for helping young boys.

It was not uncommon for young boys to gather around an old head on a street corner or at a gathering place after Sunday school to listen to his witty conversations and moral tales on hard work and decency. The young boys truly felt they were learning something worthwhile from someone whom they could look up to and respect. One of the primary messages of the old head was of manners and the value of hard work: how to get a job, how to keep a job, how to dress for a job interview, how to deal with a prospective employer. Through stories, jokes and conversational exchanges, the old head would attempt to convey his own conception of the "tricks of the trade."

On occasion he might be seen walking through the community streets with one or two of his young boys, showing them how to "hustle," to make money by doing legal odd jobs for community residents. This kind of hustle can be seen in the young boys who meet strangers at urban supermarket doors offering to carry groceries to their car for money, or at self-service pumps offering to pump gasoline for a small fee. There is often an old head in the background, encouraging the boys to earn spending money through honest work. If the old head owns his own business, in auto repair, general hauling, cleaning services, or yard work, the boys might serve as his apprentices.

The old head would sometimes refer to his recruits and apprentices affectionately as "my boys." Some of them would become runners, young boys who took the lead in being publicly responsible for the neighborhood, but often under the control or at the direction of an old head. Whenever the old head needed a favor or an errand run, one of his protégés would be eager to carry out his wishes. Moreover, the old head would keep an informal record of how well they had learned their lessons—which ones had gone on to college, to successful employment, to the military, or to jail.

Within the traditional black community, the old head served as an important link to the more privileged classes. Often he could be seen at a local barber shop pointing out and speaking of the big shots in glowing terms to the youth. Through his example, he offered moral support to both the local and wider system of social stratification. In this way, he inspired and taught his boys to negotiate the system through legitimate means.

Today, as economic and social circumstances of the urban ghetto have changed, the traditional old head has been losing something in the way of prestige and credibility as a role model. One of the most important factors in this change is the glaring lack of access to meaningful employment opportunities for black youths in the regular economy. The result is an increased number of unemployed and demoralized black young people. When gainful employment and other rewards are not forthcoming, young boys easily reach the conclusion that the moral lessons of the old head concerning the work ethic, punctuality, and honesty do not fit their own circumstances. In turn, the old heads' attitudes toward young people have been modified to reflect current employment realities, particularly the youths' adaptation to them.

For instance, Mr. Hamilton, a 70-year-old wallpaper hanger who has taken on young black men as apprentices over the years, laments the way things have changed with the young boy–old head relationship and says that he's not able to find honest, hardworking young men the way he used to. He begins his day at about 6:30 in the morning, arriving at his job promptly at 7:30. Wearing a brown work uniform, he is spotted with paint and stains. On his head is an old, beat-up white hat, and at his side is his lunch pail. He works steadily until lunch time, rests for about thirty minutes over lunch, and then goes right back to work. Some nights it is 6:30 before he has cleaned up and is ready to go home, and this is a schedule he follows every day, regardless of the weather. At times, he makes as much as $100 per room, and he has more than enough work. He fails to understand why there is a youth employment problem, saying simply:

> These young boys today just don't want to work. They could work if they wanted to. There's plenty of work to do. Today, they just don't want to work. That's all there is to it. They could do alright if they wanted to. They just want somethin' give to them, wanta get on welfare, I think. I did it [made a living] and they can too.

The following interview with a forty-year-old black man who works two jobs to make ends meet is relevant:

> This used to be a heavily industrialized nation, but now all that's done changed. Now it's technology. There's a lot of unemployment, but the statistics just give one picture. I think that's overblown, 'cause there are a lot 'o guys out here who just don't wanta work. There are cats who can barely read and write, and they wanta come in and take over. There's a lot o' young men doing the dope thing. They sell it, get high on it. But I'd rather work hard

on a grind; the money's better. That dope money is fast, quick money. And, you know, easy come, easy go. Can't depend on it. When they doing good, they doing real good, but when they doing bad, they doing real bad. I still try to talk to the youngsters that I run into, but it's hard to talk to these young boys. I tell them to go and try to learn something, but they don't want to listen. There's a different kind of black man today. And I'll tell you something, as quiet as it's kept [between you and me]. There are some old heads out here selling that dope, and they know better. They sho' know better.

The Impact of Drugs

With the massive introduction of drugs into the black community, a drug culture as well as a drug economy has developed within the ghetto. The attendant financial opportunities compete effectively for the hearts and minds of young boys. The roles of drug pusher, pimp, and (illegal) hustler have thus become increasingly attractive. People who work in this underground economy are apparently able to obtain big money more easily and glamorously than the traditional old head. It is this sort of role model that traditional old heads find themselves competing with. Many become very cautious or simply withdraw from any involvement with young boys.

Community residents believe that much street crime is drug-related. This general perception has contributed to the flight of many from urban black ghettos. Those who remain and might serve as self-conscious and upright role models for youth are often reluctant to become involved, or do so only with much hesitation. Many say that "The young boys have changed," or, "I can't take the chance." Their general tendency is to define the young boys pejoratively, as "mannish," crime-prone, aggressive, and unpredictable.

The traditional old heads, like most others of almost any urban community, possess a heightened concern about street crime. Furthermore, they have reason to believe that many of the young boys they encounter may be mixed up in the drug and alcohol culture. They believe a person on drugs is dangerous and out of control and thus capable of robbing his own family members and friends or turning on them in a violent manner. The following are comments of a self-employed carpenter who resides in the black community of West Philadelphia:

Oh yeah, the hard-working men used to be free with time to help anybody they could help, help 'em to gain a skill or a trade. Even now, we'll sometimes get some of 'em through OIC [Opportunities Industrialization Center], or somewhere. At least then we know they into it [serious] and not just messin' around. These young boys, they all into the drugs, that's all they do. I get so I don't even want 'em around me. They'll be doing drugs right on the job.

The concern about youth involved in the drug culture mixed with a certain general distrust of young people has augmented the atmosphere of estrangement, segmentation, and social distance in the black community. The drug culture and its organization is related in the following account by a former dealer:

The way I see it there's top dogs, middle dogs, and low dogs. In the neighborhood, right? The top dogs are the guys with the money, dudes with the cars. The majority of them sell drugs. They got the big money. They drive Caddies, El Doradoes, Rivieras. They selling drugs in the bars. There's not many of them that work at regular jobs. They dress casual. Then on weekends they go on out, they can show off their suits, walk in the neighborhoods. They sell cocaine mostly and heroin. They're in their late 30s, 36 to 38 range. They make big money. They have a little war here and there, when they sell bad stuff; they get their cars shot up. They stand on the corner and someone come shooting at them.

Mostly you see top dogs at after-hour spots after the bars close. I went to one, they had a gambling spot upstairs. They go to them all morning. They're located in somebody's house, one of the top dog's houses. They sell foods, and they have liquor at a bar upstairs. They have a little whore room where the whores give you a little action. To me it was nice, but I knew everybody in there, just about. Everybody want to be tough; they got guns. But as long as you mind your own business, you're cool. All of them are black people. They had a couple of white guys in there one time, they were nice. They sat around, talking shit. Nobody went up to them and say, "White mother-fucking shit," like that. All was cool. I spoke to them, laughed, talked shit with them, take a hit from their smoke. That's the way it was. They knew the top dog. Someone starts in with them, well they knew they came with a certain person. Don't fuck with them. He told me, "You have no problems with them, they with me." That's the way it was. They was nice people. That's the top dogs.

The middle dogs are the ones who sell drugs for the top dogs. They're trying to be like them, trying to get like the top dogs, selling drugs for them, shit like that. They range from 17 to late 20s. They get their supply from the top dog. They're selling drugs. When they sell out, they give him the money, they get their half, and they give them some more drugs to sell. You get the drugs first. Then you bring in the money when you sell the drugs.

He gives you like 10 or 15 bags of cocaine to sell. That's $20 a bag. So you make from 15 times $20. When he gets out there, he give you $5 off a bag, the middle dog. And they make pretty good money, I assure you. You know, the top dog, he'll take care of you. You say you owe money here, he trusts you and he'll give you money. But don't burn him, shit like that. 'Cause he'll burn your ass. He'll get you shot. But it hasn't happened lately; they don't want to go through all this shit. He'll get a bunch of gang boys together and they'll sell drugs. There're certain bars. There's one gang be in a bar. Another gang member can't come in and sell drugs. I saw a guy go in one time and try to sell drugs in the wrong place, wrong turf. They said, "Hey, you can't sell that shit in here. Go to your own space. You want to sell, get to your own space. We sell the shit here." There was a big fight. And I knew the guy. I swung around and say, "Hey, this is their territory. It ain't yours. They my allies. You can't do it. You do, and you'll get hurt, I assure you."

The middle dogs ask or the top dog asks the guy, "Do you want to sell for me?" Everybody knows the top dog. The guy wanted me to sell for him. He knew I knew a lot of people. And I said, "No, that's not my style." I used to sell speed pills, but I can't go through that shit. People can knock on your door and they can't give you the money they owe. "You buy me out. I need you this time." Then they want more and you say, "You can have this shit. I don't want it to more. I don't need you in my shit, and I don't want to be in your shit." So, I was proof. So the middle dog gets a lot of the young boys who come out of school and want to make some money. They can make some money. They can make $150 a day selling that shit. And they sell it to the low dogs, 'cause the low dogs are the guys that want to buy it.

They buy the shit from the middle dog. Then they become middle dogs, a majority of them do. Some of them even become top dogs. That's the way it is. Just like climbing a ladder. They got these jobs at McDonald's, places like that, or they may be unemployed, getting money from their father and mother, or they stealing. Stealing money, ripping people off, going around town snatching pocketbooks and stuff like that. That's the low dogs for you. They hustle downtown. They steal gold chains and sell them. They steal shit and sell it. They want some cocaine. They get the money together, they get half a gram of cocaine, get it from the middle dogs. When I see a transaction, I just sit back and laugh. 'Cause I buy from the middle dogs sometimes, too, when I want something. I want a joint and I didn't know nobody to go to so I go to the middle dogs and they make a bag. That's all that I need. I get some grass, some cocaine. They make a bag of cocaine. No selling nickels, just twenties. Sometimes they're nice. If the guy know you good and he like you, you can get it for ten. Like a half a gram will cost you $50. You know, you five dollars short: "All right, man, here." Only if he like you, if he know you good. A gram costs a hundred. If you're a good friend of the person or you grew up with the person, he say, "O.K., give me $90."

Crack is out there too. I took that shit one time, almost killed my damn self. If my friend at home had not poured milk down my throat, man, I woulda been gone. That costs $10 a bag. That's some nasty stuff. That shit'll turn your keys green. We snort that shit. That will hook us up. And I took too much of it. I realized that I was on my way but my boy Steve saved me. He's in jail now for shooting two guys already. Well, he knew I was fucked up. He said, "Come on, Bird, where you going?" I took too much, and I'm lucky to be alive. But he knew I was having a hard time. He knew something was wrong, 'cause he'd used it before. So he ran to the corner store and snatched the guy at the counter, grabbed a half pint of milk and poured the shit down my throat. You see, if you drink milk, the shit brings you down. Milk brings you down like that. I was fucked up. My heart going real fast, you know. That shit could bust my heart. I never fucked with any more of that stuff since. No more. You call it crack, call it crank, monster, or beast. Them four names. They take them pills for downers. I can't take that shit.

The low dogs never get completely off that shit. When they like it, they like it. Some of them will get off crack maybe and do regular cocaine. You know I have these boys, 8, 9, 10, 11, 12 ask me for rolling paper. I was shocked. I said, "How old are you?" He said, "I'm 10." I said, "Man, you're crazy. What are you going to do with the paper?" "Smoke a joint, man." Eight, 9, 10 years old. I was shocked. I didn't know they did it that young. Ten years old? Man, that freaked me right out. Cute little guy. Dressed nice in his FILA sweatsuit. Nice. I'd say he was wearing $200 worth of clothes, easy. Shit, a FILA sweatsuit is $200. FILA sneaks on, they $70 a pair. FILA hat, another $5. Ten years old, smoking a joint, had over $300 worth of clothes on. He come with a 16-year-old guy and a 15-year-old girl. He got the shit from a middle dog. They don't care who they sell that shit to. You got the money, you can have it. Tiny dog, I call him. That's a lot of money for a little boy like that, a 10-year-old boy. I didn't believe it, I looked at him. He had to be selling something, or he had a good mother and father, one or the other. I didn't picture him selling drugs really. I just pictured him. Young guy. You should have seen him sitting like this, rolled that shit like a pro, two hands and tongue in it. I said, "Jesus. Oh, my God." That freaked me out, that did. Street kid.

Tales such as these, related through a network of associates, friends, and relatives, help to interpret and define the drug culture in the ghetto community. At other times, the culture is objectified by the proliferation of "drug houses" in poor inner-city neighborhoods, through drug-related violence, including killings and crime on the streets in which innocent people, including bystanders and children, are victims. When an unexplainable murder or break-in occurs, residents often conclude that it was drug-related. Such reports and their interpretations have worked to inhibit spontaneous social relations among anonymous residents.

The fear and concern of drug-related behavior serves to inhibit the traditional old heads, making them reluctant to assume the role they played in simpler times and altering their relationships with young boys. With limited employment opportunities available, the old heads assume young boys are likely candidates in the marketing and selling of drugs. In this context, the old head does not easily trust the young boy.

New Old Heads

Traditional old heads seem genuinely puzzled by their changing relationships, or lack of relationships, with young boys. When they observe unemployment, they are likely to blame the victim for "not wanting to work." So strong is their commitment to the work ethic and a belief in the infinite availability of traditional work that they have great difficulty understanding how anyone could be unemployed for long. Their common view of the unemployed is that "they don't want to work." As these men approach young boys with such views, the young boys tend to ignore them or patronize them. In response, the old heads sometimes accuse the youth of arrogance toward their elders. One detects hurt feelings among many old heads who openly complain that the young boys of today fail to listen to them the way they listened to their elders and the old heads who raised them. The following interview with an old head of fifty-eight years is relevant:

> I was sitting in the back of the bus the other day down in South Philly and three young boys (anonymous) were sitting across from me. We had stopped, and a crippled man was getting on the bus. I looked over at these young boys and said, "Now, ya'll watch this man." They look at me and then they looked at him. I said, "Now, just watch. I'm gon' show you something." We all watched the man get on the bus. It must've took him seven or eight minutes. Then I said, "Ya'll see that? That man is independent. He ain't got as much as you got. You got all yo' health and strength, and what ya'll doing, huh?! That man is independent, he's taking care of himself. That ought to give you some inspiration to go out and do something worthwhile. If he can do it, why can't you?"
>
> You know, them young boys just looked at me and laughed. That's what they did. They weren't listenin' to anything I said. I could tell by the vibes, though, that they weren't studyin' me. They were being disrespectful. Now, in the old days, they, at least one of 'em would have stopped and come over to me and heard me out, and listened to what else I had to say. But today, I

just don't know 'bout these young boys. They don't care. They don't listen to their elders.

In the old days, the old head had such legitimacy on the ghetto streets that he could chastise anonymous young boys, thinking that he knew the young man's relatives, or knew someone who knew them, and that they knew him in the same way. In his efforts to put the young boy in his place, he could expect the parents "to take his side against the child." But today, given the segmentation and anonymity of the black community, and also the unpredictability of the young men, the elders are not likely to become very involved with anonymous youths. As one middle aged old head told me:

> I have to watch what I do today, because you just don't know what you gettin' into when you speak to these youngsters. You could get cussed out, or cut up. You just don't know, and many of the old heads are not saying anything.

Along with the influx and expansion of the drug culture, a new role model is being created. Displacing the traditional old head, a standard bearer of yesterday who worked hard in the factories and mills and valued his way of life, the emerging old head is often younger and the product of a street gang, makes money fast, and scorns the law and traditional values. If he works, he does so grudgingly. He makes financial ends meet by involving himself in the underground economy. He may dabble in the drug trade or be a full-time participant. As far as family life goes, he shuns the traditional father's role. His is a "get over" mentality, and, as the traditional old heads comment, he is out to beat the next fellow.

This emerging figure is in many respects the antithesis of the traditional old head. He derides family values and generally feels little conventional responsibility to the family's financial welfare. He hardly thinks he has any obligation to his string of women and the children he has fathered. In fact, he considers it a measure of success if he can get away without being held legally accountable for his out-of-wedlock children. In his hustling mentality generosity is a weakness. Given his unstable financial situation, he would feel used when confronted with the prospect of "taking care of someone else." For him women are conquests, to be obtained by mentally "running a game," by feigning to love and care for them to get what he wants, only to discard them at the merest adversity. His self aggrandizement consumes his whole being and is expressed in his penchant for a glamorous lifestyle, fine clothes, fancy cars. On the corner he attempts to influence people through displays of the trappings of his success. Eagerly awaiting his message are the young unemployed black men, demoralized by a hopeless financial situation but inclined to look up to this figure and, if they can, to emulate him. For his recruits a trail of broken lives, trouble, jail and even death may be in store.

As this kind of person proliferates on the street corners of the ghetto community, he works to blur the line between the traditional old head and himself. Many of the young boys fail to draw a distinction, having never known any old head other than the one they now see. Consequently, many young men who are looking for direction from available male role models to achieve a more conventional life have little direct and personal support.

Conclusions

Regardless of personal values, many disadvantaged, poor young blacks living in the ghetto find themselves surrounded by an extremely complex world that seems arbitrary and unforgiving. Major changes in the regular economy, including automation and cybernation of industry as well as the development and elaboration of a service industry whose lowest levels encourage subsistence wages—combined with the massive influx and proliferation of drugs into the urban black community—have all exacerbated social conditions in urban black communities. Although inner city manufacturing jobs have declined, the poorest segments of the urban black community have yet to make an effective adjustment to this reality. As far as many impoverished young blacks are concerned, the underground economy competes effectively with the regular economy. All of this has worked to undermine traditional social networks that formerly brought youths into the world of legitimate work and family life.

A good job is important to anyone, but particularly for someone trying to establish a family and become a productive citizen. But what constitutes a "good job"? Thirty years ago, a black migrant from the South could find a job at a factory and take home about $100 per week, amounting to some $5,000 per year. This is equal to approximately $22,000 in today's dollars. In those days, a man of the working class on such a salary could look forward to starting or raising a family with little financial strain. Today, jobs for unskilled workers with salaries even approaching this figure are scarce.

Good jobs exist in offices, hospitals, factories, and other large institutions that provide not only good pay but also increasingly important health care and other benefits. Since these jobs require training and are scarce, many young black men work instead at fast-food concerns to make $5,000 to $6,000 per year, an amount that would not encourage a responsible person to attempt to establish a family. Many people will not accept such low paying jobs; they gravitate to the military or to the underground instead (see Anderson, 1980; 1985).

Yet there is more to a "good job" than money. Let us return for a moment to Mr. Hamilton, the self-employed paper hanger in West Philadelphia. Many young black men in today's urban settings would not aspire to work as he does. They prefer not to engage in such "hard" and "dirty" work. A great number of the young men want not only a secure job that pays well, but also one that provides "good benefits." Yet such jobs are scarce.

It is not so much that the work ethic has declined in the black community as it is that good jobs are unavailable. When good jobs are unavailable, the work ethic loses its force, for there is a basic incompatibility between theory and reality. At the same time, there are those remaining within the black community as leaders who continue to believe in the infinite availability of work in the traditional sense, high-paying jobs that required little in the way of training and skill. They tend to be diehards of a sort, people wedded to a mentality perhaps best suited to the manufacturing era, who uncritically and strongly believe in the work ethic. The words of the minister of an inner city congregation who is a part-time taxi driver, are worth recalling:

> There are jobs out here for people who want to work. It may not be just what they want, but there is work to be done, if you want it bad enough. Honest and honorable work. Something has happened to our community. Now you see a lot more violence than ever before. The drugs are everywhere, taking over our neighborhoods. A lot of our young people don't respect themselves today. Many of them don't know the value of work. Why, when I was growing up, the grown-ups taught us the value of work. I have a deep respect for it. Any man should want to work hard, for dignity comes with a job that enables a man to provide for his family.

But because of the lack of jobs, and the seductive pull of the underground economy, the youngsters to whom he preaches do not believe him. His message falls on deaf ears, and his example is not fully trusted.

To be sure, there are varying conceptions of work in the black community, and whether a person holds one or another of these conceptions may very well relate to whether he holds or does not hold a good job. Many of the employed consider the jobless to be personally at fault, their condition the result of a character flaw. Those without a job, on the other hand, are inclined to say how tough it is for a young black man. These varying conceptions are frequently voiced in charges and countercharges that pit one segment of the community against the other. The urban ghetto community suffers from a host of strains, the most pressing of which are exacerbated by a profound lack of fit between the newly emerging service economy and potential workers who would fill its jobs.

The social networks that would connect many of the unemployed to good jobs are difficult for outsiders to penetrate. The community wisdom is that "you have to know someone." The common story is that you put in your application, but "you don't hear anything," but even when "someone" is known the employment problems of a black youth are further complicated by issues of prejudice and distrust, especially as to whether he will be a good worker and can be effectively managed by the person sponsoring him. If the person sponsored appears to be unmanageable, erratic, unreliable, then the sponsor, who is likely to be a traditional old head, "looks bad" or is "messed up." Sponsors thus husband their reputations and are constrained to limit their recommendations of those who seem the least bit marginal. Hence, increasing numbers of hard core unemployed black youths have little use for the traditional old head, and he has even less respect for them.

As indicated above, the traditional old head is gradually being replaced by a younger person often with a checkered past in the underground economy. Yet, traditional old heads remain the immediate hope of the black community. They continue to serve many young black males as highly effective role models, emphasizing their strong affiliations to the regular economy. Their mission of connecting youths to work in the regular economy must be encouraged. What is required is a serious federal job training program geared to inner city communities. The training effort would have to lead to placement in jobs that pay a substantial amount of money and offer a certain amount of job security, thus allowing its recipients to support and maintain a family—a situation that often does not exist today. With effective employment, many of the problems faced by young, poor, ill educated black people would at least be correctable.

References

* The material for this essay was drawn from my earlier studies, "The Social Context of Youth Employment Programs," commissioned by the Committee on Youth Employment Programs (1985) and "Of Old Heads and Young Boys," commissioned by the Committee on the Status of Black Americans (1987), The National Research Council, The National Academy of Sciences, Washington, D.C.

Anderson, Bernard and Isabel Sawhill, eds. *Youth Employment and Public Policy.* Englewood Cliffs, N.J.: Prentice-Hall, 1980.

Anderson, Elijah. *A Place on the Corner.* Chicago: University of Chicago Press, 1978.

———. "Some Observations on Black Youth Employment." In Bernard Anderson and Isabel Sawhill, eds. *Youth Employment and Public Policy.* Englewood Cliffs, N.J.: Prentice-Hall, 1980.

Becker, Howard S. *Outsiders.* New York: Free Press, 1973.

———. *Sociological Work.* Chicago: Aldine Publishing, 1970.

Blackwell, James. *The Black Community: Diversity and Unity.* Second Edition. New York: Harper and Row, 1984.

Bluestone, Barry and Bennett Harrison. *The Deindustrialization of America.* New York: Basic Books, 1984.

Cayton, Horace and St. Clair Drake. *Black Metropolis.* New York: Harper & Brothers, 1945.

Clark, Kenneth. *Dark Ghetto.* New York: Harper and Row, 1965.

Dollard, John. *Criteria for the Life History.* New Haven, Conn.: Yale University Press, 1932.

DuBois, William E. B. *The Philadelphia Negro.* Philadelphia: University of Pennsylvania Press, 1899.

Farley, Reynolds. *Blacks and Whites: Narrowing the Gap?* Cambridge, Mass.: Harvard University Press, 1984.

Fogelson, Robert. *Big City Police.* Cambridge, Mass.: Harvard University Press, 1977.

Frazier, E. Franklin. *Black Bourgeoisie.* New York: Free Press, 1957.

Freeman, Richard B. "Create Jobs That Pay as Well as Crime." *New York Times,* Sunday, July 20, 1986.

Goffman, Erving. *Stigma.* Englewood Cliffs, N.J.: Prentice-Hall, 1963.

Landry, Bart. *The New Black Middle Class.* Berkeley: University of California Press, 1987.

Liebow, Elliot. *Tally's Corner.* Boston: Little, Brown, 1967.

Morris, Aldon. *The Origins of the Civil Rights Movement.* New York: Free Press, 1984.

Myrdal, Gunnar et al., *An American Dilemma.* New York: Harper & Row, 1944.

Nathan, Richard P. "Will the Underclass Always Be With Us?" *Society* 24, 3 (March/April, 1987).

Peterson, Paul, ed. *The New Urban Reality*. Washington, D.C.: The Brookings Institution, 1985.

Radzinowicz, Leon and Marvin Wolfgang, eds. *The Criminal in the Arms of the Law*. New York: Basic Books, 1971.

Shaw, Clifford, Henry McKay, et al. *Delinquency Areas*. Chicago: University of Chicago Press, 1929.

Shaw, Clifford and Henry McKay. *Juvenile Delinquency and Urban Areas*. Chicago: University of Chicago Press, 1942.

Short, James and F. L. Strodtbeck. *Group Processes and Gang Delinquency*. Chicago: University of Chicago Press, 1965.

Sitkoff, Harvard. *The Struggle for Black Equality*. New York: Hill and Wang, 1981.

Suttles, Gerald. "The Defended Neighborhood." In Gerald Suttles, *Social Construction of Communities*. Chicago: University of Chicago Press, 1972.

Wilson, William. *The Declining Significance of Race*. Chicago: University of Chicago Press, 1980.

———. "Cycles of Deprivation and the Underclass Debate." *Social Service Review* 59, 4 (December, 1985).

———. *The Truly Disadvantaged*. Chicago: University of Chicago Press, 1987.

Wirth, Louis. *The Ghetto*. Chicago: University of Chicago Press, 1928.

Samuel Z. Klausner

8. *Jews in the Executive Suite: The Ambience of Jewish and Gentile Firms*

Baltzell and the Mission to the Jews

In *The Protestant Establishment,* E. Digby Baltzell quotes from a chastising sermon by the Rector of St. James the Less in Scarsdale, New York. With a "heart overflowing with sorrow," the rector condemns some parishioners for preventing a young man "of Jewish parentage whom I baptized at the font" from escorting a young lady of his parish to the annual Holly Ball of the Scarsdale Golf Club, an organization, in this heavily Jewish New York suburb, that apparently excludes, or in 1961 excluded, Jews. According to Baltzell, the young man's father was born of Jewish parents and married a Roman Catholic. Presumably, the son had not been baptized into the Catholic faith since the rector had considered a visit to the font necessary. As the son of a Christian mother he would not have been Jewish.

Baltzell's "Jews" are often Christian with a Jewish ancestor or outright apostates from Judaism. A very few are wealthy Jewish arrivistes who preserve "Jewish convictions" or "ethnic characteristics." The implied a fortiori argument is that if such people are rejected, how would a Jew with "ethnic characteristics" fare? Baltzell might, but does not, assert that the rejection of Jews with such characteristics is ill-conceived. Cultural assimilation is expected.

The Protestant Establishment, racily written, naming names, anecdotal and sociologically insightful, is, among other things, a secularized homily on the Christian mission to the Jews. Jewish penitents, whose business success evidences their election, are, nevertheless, denied membership in the gentlemen's club if not in the Kingdom. Why would a Jew with "Jewish convictions" want to be co-opted by the establishment? Could a Christian establishment share power with Jews who do not enter the kingdom of cultural assimilation? The Jewish community has no death wish, especially in this period of recovery from the Holocaust, a period of national renaissance in Israel and of the deepening quality of its religious culture in America. How should Jews feel about Baltzell's biographies of modern Marranos?

Jewish communal interest is piqued because, aside from Jewish commitment to "equal opportunity," the exclusion of the apostate implies that the practicing Jew may also be excluded from the personal and material resources needed to compete equally in the economy. The exclusion of Jews from education and political leadership hampers their economic contribution and well-being. Jews do remember that oppression of the Marrano heralded the expulsion of practicing Jews from Spain.

America has a Jewish business elite, unconverted. Baltzell attributes their "gilded ghettos" and "opulent synagogues" to disappointment at exclusion from Proper Philadelphia or from Proper Boston society. In truth, though, the large institutional synagogues are a response to the liberal Jews' current willingness to drive on the Sabbath to a center that meshes Jewish communal activities with worship. The investment in communal institutions is a commitment to an integral community life.

Properly, Baltzell accepts the failure to absorb Jews, or former Jews, as a Christian problem. The failure to absorb the most talented among the Jews threatens the authority and the leadership of the upper class. In his earlier *Philadelphia Gentlemen* Baltzell wrote that when an upper class is not a ruling class it will be replaced with another upper class. The gentlemen's club in a capitalist free economy is a device for transmitting power but, ultimately, not a source of economic power. Economic power is grounded in economic performance, whether by Christians, Jews, or Japanese. Baltzell sends a deeper message. A decline in general social authority and, as a result, a debasing of the moral society ensues from a loss of authority by the current upper class.

Baltzell berates Christians who fail to receive the convert, less for moral guilt than for failure to act on self-interest. The failure of absorption is a two-sided affair. Not inconceivably, the failure of Jews to accept conversion or cultural assimilation, to use the secular term, can rebound as Jewish guilt, even as an incitement to attack Jews. History is heavy with this sequence of spurned invitation followed by anger—from Rome to Medinah to Berlin.

The study reported here compares the ambience of Jewish and non-Jewish firms. It is not a study of elites and the national upper class, but of Jews and Gentiles in middle management and as directors of modest firms in a small sector of the economy. In a general way, the theme confirms Baltzell's prediction of the rise of alternate elites. This study displays Jewish firms that do very well. The business styles of these firms are somewhat more universalistic, their hiring practices more meritocratic and more "rationalized" around shareholder interest. The particularistic social ties, such as those represented in the gentlemen's clubs, become less relevant for economic dealing in such an ambience.

The style of sociological analysis of this paper differs somewhat from Baltzell's. He is a masterful observer of the behavior of institutional leadership and an astute historian. His writing style involves the presentation of individual biographical sketches to illustrate general themes. The method here is more positivistic, nearer the quantitative, conceptually abstracting approach popular in the natural sciences. But, sociology is, at times, historically concrete and, at times, conceptually abstract.

The study data are drawn from a survey of 444 MBA graduates of three business schools, one local and two elite, in the northeast. About half of the respondents had received degrees in 1974, the other half in 1979.[1]

On the Method for Studying Jewish Firms
Defining a "Jewish" Firm

The traditional test for discrimination in the executive suite has concerned the experiences of individuals. How do Jews fare in Gentile firms or women in male dominated occupations? Firms, too, are economic actors. One can think of black owned and directed factories, of a bank directed by women, and of Jewish operated textile mills. How do these firms fare in an environment of white, male, Christian dominated businesses in each area? What is the nature of the ambience within each type of firm? How is the career of a white executive influenced by the characteristics of black enterprise, or what is it like to be a Christian in a Jewish firm?

Management as well as work force may be Jewish or Gentile. We will compare Jewish and Gentile firms in terms of their locations in the economy, their authority hierarchies, and the career paths of a sample of MBA executives through those hierarchies. The ambience of a firm is also influenced by the family and individual characteristics of its recruits; the way firms may be bound to one another socially and culturally; and the status in them of Jews, Catholics, and Protestants, blacks and whites, women and men.

How may we, given our data, define a "Jewish" firm? Commonly, firms are classified by their product, as a steel producer or a law firm, or, in broader classes, as a manufacturing, commercial, trade, or public service corporation. The government's Standard Industrial Classification takes such production goals as its criteria. Firms are also classified according to the religious or ethnic group that controls or inhabits them, for instance, as a "minority" enterprise or under the leadership of blacks or women. Presently we have a federal legal definition of these classes. A firm may also be thought of as Jewish, Catholic, or Protestant. The Jewish family business or businesses conducted by members of the Hasidic community in the New York area are nearly unambiguous cases of Jewish businesses. Antisemitic pamphleteers and journalists unabashedly designate firms as Jewish on the basis of individual Jewish executives or owners to whom they attribute strategic "control," obviously for malevolent purposes. An objective quantitatively based classification could consider ownership, or principal stockholders, officers, and directors of the corporation, or the staff and line employees.

Two types of classificatory indicators will be used here. The first rests on the presence of Jewish employees, the second on the representation of Jews among officers and directors. For this analysis we consider only the firms in which the respondents were currently employed, in 1985–86, at the time of the survey. For an analysis of firms in which the MBA respondents served at earlier stages of their careers, see the report to the American Jewish Committee cited earlier.

A Jewish Firm is a Place Where Jews Work

The first measure classifies a firm as a *Jewish worksite* if it has at least one Jewish officer or director and the respondent (who may be Jewish or non-Jewish) reported three or more Jewish coworkers. This is a "value added" classification, the presence of, at least, one Jewish member of the board being an initial requirement for a firm with at least three Jewish coworkers to be called Jewish.

Essentially, this classification reflects the presence of Jewish employees, first, in a token way, at the directorial level, and then, in a more substantial way, as fellow workers of the junior executive. These indicators use attributes of individual members of firms to classify the firms as collectives. The firm, classified as a Jewish or non-Jewish worksite, is the unit of analysis. Data sufficient for this classification are available for 111 current worksites, 50 percent of which are classified as Jewish.

The firms are not a sample of a defined population of firms, but are simply those in which our respondents are employed. As a consequence, any generalization of the results of this analysis for some larger population of firms must remain tentative.

The meaning of this classification will emerge in the course of our analysis. A few correlates may help initiate clarification of that meaning. Firms classified as non-Jewish worksites have an average of 1.9 (s.d.=3.5, N=55) Jewish officers and directors compared with 4.6 (s.d.=7.3, N=56) for the Jewish worksites, a statistically significant difference (F=6.12, P<.02).

While Jewish managers are more prominent in firms with more Jewish employees, they do not constitute a large proportion of officers, a controlling force in their firms, a matter that distinguishes this classification from the subsequent one. The Jewish worksites have a mean of 19.7 percent (s.d.=22.6, N=54) of their officers and directors who are Jewish, while the proportion for the non-Jewish worksites is 9.2 percent, (s.d.=17.6, N=54), a statistically significant difference (F=7.3, P<.01).

The second element in this "value added" classification is the number of Jewish coworkers. By definition, in all of the Jewish worksites (56), respondents reported three or more Jewish coworkers. Only 23.6 percent (55) of firms classed as non-Jewish worksites had as many Jewish coworkers, while 58.2 percent had one or two and 18.2 percent had no Jewish coworkers. The difference is statistically significant, not giving us new information, but revalidating the distinctiveness of the classes (chi sq.=68.79, P<.001).

A Jewish Firm is One Directed by Jews

The second classification is based on the proportion of Jews among directors and officers of the firm. A count of directors and officers of each firm was accomplished by name identification from lists of officers in the reference books on American corporations such as Standard and Poor's.

An average of 13.3 percent (s.d.=22.1, N=220) of officers in the respondents' places of current employment were identified as Jewish, as noted above, by a judgment of the ethnicity of their names. The population of firms was divided between those with 20 percent or more Jewish officers (the 20 percent figure was a half standard deviation above the mean) and those with less than 20 percent Jewish officers or board members. These will be termed *Jewish and Gentile managed* firms, respectively. The proportions of Jewish officers are 46.6 percent (s.d.=27.3, N=40) in the former and 5.1 percent (s.d.=5.1, N=177) in the latter firms. The classes are quite distinct in this respect (F=357.8, P<.001).

This difference in proportions is also a difference in numbers. Jewish managed firms average 6.3 (s.d.=9.2, N=37) Jewish board members while Gentile managed have a mean of 1.4 (s.d.=1.5, N=163), again a significant difference (F=41.5, P<.001) and one which validates the original classification.

The two measures overlap. Jewish worksites average just under 20 percent Jewish officers, while nearly half the board members of Jewish managed firms are Jews. Three or more Jewish coworkers are reported in 75 percent (24) of Jewish managed and in 58.3 percent (84) of Gentile managed firms, a difference short of statistical significance ($P<.15$). No Jewish coworkers at all were reported in 11.9 percent of the Gentile managed firms. No Jewish managed firm reported a complete absence of Jews in the workforce.

Thus, we have two perspectives on the Jewishness of the firm, first, as a place where Jews are employed and, second, as a place in which Jews are a significant proportion of management, and may exert policy control. The following pages examine characteristics, other than the presence of Jewish officers and employees, which distinguish each type of relatively Jewish firm from a relatively Gentile one. We will refer to the distribution of Jewish and non-Jewish or Gentile firms. This will be shorthand for a distribution of respondents associated with these types of firms.

The Sample is Northeastern

Three-fourths of the firms in which the MBAs are employed are located in the northeast. This is not surprising since the three schools providing the graduates are located in that section of the country. Even elite business schools are regional schools, neither recruiting students nor providing executives equally to all parts of the country.

Jewish worksites are more likely than non-Jewish firms to be in the northeast. Of respondents in Jewish worksites 85.7 percent (56), but 72.7 percent (55) of those in non-Jewish worksites are in the northeast, a statistically significant difference (chi sq.=3.9, $P<.05$). Comparing Jewish with Gentile managed firms, we also find a bias toward northeastern location, with 70.6 percent (163) of the Gentile but 89.2 percent (37) of the Jewish firms in that region (chi sq.=5.46, $P<.02$).

This concentration is also no surprise. In fact, one might have anticipated an even greater tendency for Jewish firms to be in the northeast, given the concentration of Jewish population in that area. Social analysts call this an "edge effect;" with almost all already there, it is difficult to increase the proportions. Factors drawing firms to other parts of the country, such as location of markets and raw materials, must have some effect on the geographic distribution of firms.

The American economy is regionalized, each area serving different functions for the nation as a whole. Primary industry is in the south central and mountain states, mining and oil production having declined in Pennsylvania and West Virginia. The north central states remain the hub of heavy manufacturing. The northeast is a center of the federal government, port activities, finance and the Wall Street complex, and the managerial headquarters of many of the nation's leading businesses. If Jewish managed firms are in the northeast, this would reinforce a tendency toward commerce and service functions.

The Economic Locations of Jewish and Gentile Firms
The Preference for Commerce and Service

The ethnic division of labor was a commonplace expected in the Orient and in Europe of earlier centuries. Jewish economic specialization in trade and commerce has been continuous since the Biblical period. Yet commerce has never exhausted Jewish economic activities. Over the past couple of centuries Jews have been in textile manufacture in Poland, distillation of liquors, forest harvesting, and lumber production in the Ukraine, and extending financial credit in the Low Countries. Jews were typically underrepresented in agriculture and the public sector occupations, the civil service, and the military. In the Islamic world, Jews were prominent in jewelry crafts, domestic retail trade, import and export trade, and management of credit. Here and there in the Moslem world we find Jewish peasantry.

Jews were everywhere a minority; never outnumbering Christians and Moslems, they never had economic predominance in any of these areas. In some areas of Jewish population concentration, Jews had a sizeable share of some specific economic activity on a local level, such as the nineteenth-century textile industry in Lodz or silversmithing in San'a. In North America, the New York garment industry of the first half of the twentieth century had significant Jewish participation, first as workers and later as owners, and Jews pioneered the west coast movie industry, though, one could not say that a significant proportion of Jews would be found in either of these commercial endeavors.

Jewish firms, in contemporary America, are unevenly distributed in the economy. Our data cannot show the full extent of Jewish economic participation, only their share in business to which an MBA is attracted. Thus, we will see nothing of the Jewish role in the professions, in law, medicine, the academy, or creative arts, other than as an occasional medical administrator and artistic impressario.

TABLE 8.1.   Jewish and non-Jewish worksites (first positions after MBA) in three industrial sectors (percents)

INDUSTRIAL SECTOR	NON-JEWISH	JEWISH
Manufacturing	47.0	35.8
Commerce	47.0	43.3
Service	6.1	20.9
	(66)	(67)

chi sq. = 6.5, P <.04

Table 8.1 shows the proportion of firms in manufacturing, commerce, and service among Jewish and non-Jewish worksites. The data here refer to 133 firms engaging our respondents immediately after graduation.

The non-Jewish worksites are a bit more likely to be in manufacturing, and the Jewish in the service industries. Service here includes public employment as well as private agencies such as hospitals and advertising. Manufacturing fields in which Jews concentrate, such as textiles, are a minority of all such firms, and do not absorb large numbers of MBAs. The media have a Jewish presence, especially in television and advertising. Over a fourth of the MBA respondents are in investment banking, significantly more than are found in commercial banking and insurance.

This distribution is not fixed. An individual entering either a non-Jewish or Jewish worksite after the MBA is about as likely, six or eleven years later, to be working in any of the three industrial sectors. Firms employing a number of Jews are no more concentrated in commerce than firms with few Jews in their workforce either at the initial stage or in current employment. The highly aggregated level of our categorization obscures differences in specific commercial ventures, the tendency of Jewish firms toward investment banking and of the non-Jewish toward commercial banking.

However, a sharper economic sectoral difference exists between Jewish and non-Jewish firms as categorized by the number of Jews on the board. Table 8.2 shows the industries of current employment in which at least five respondents (of 163), in the relatively Gentile managed firms, and two respondents (of 37), in the Jewish managed firms, are found.

Nine-tenths of the respondents work in only nine industries. The appearance of natural gas in the Gentile managed column reflects the general low rate of Jewish participation in primary industries, such as mining. The

TABLE 8.2.   Gentile and Jewish board members by
kinds of firms

INDUSTRIES	PROPORTIONS OF RESPONDENTS
Gentile managed	
Natural gas	3.8%
Telephone company	3.8
Commercial banking	14.5
Investment firms	9.2
Holding companies	4.6
	35.9%
Jewish managed	
Computing equipment	16.7
Investment firms	20.0
Data processing	6.7
Advertising agencies	10.0
	53.4%

telephone company, before divestiture, had a reputation for resisting Jewish participation. The transformation of this communications industry by
computer technology is changing this situation. Advertising and investment banking remain important Jewish managed areas. Investment banking is prominent as a place both where Jews work and where they are
managers. (One could not reverse the statement to assert that Jews dominate investment banking, since the percentages shown in the table represent fifteen Gentile but only seven Jewish firms.)

Table 8.3 compares the industrial sectors of Jewish and Gentile managed
firms. These are places of current employment. The Jewish managed firms
are underrepresented in manufacturing and overrepresented in commerce
and service. The difference is statistically significant, as shown at the bottom of the table.

These distributions do not demonstrate a Jewish propensity for or
avoidance of certain types of work, of an "elective affinity" between commerce and Jewish personality. MBAs are engaged in the abstract activity of
the top floor office. They are, in a sense, Jew and Gentile, symbol manipu-
lators devisors of plans and strategies, writers of memoranda, signers of
checks, and political debaters in the boardroom.

The founding of Jewish firms, or the conversion of Gentile to Jewish

TABLE 8.3.   Gentile and Jewish managed firms (current employment) in three industrial sectors (percents)

INDUSTRIAL SECTOR	GENTILE	JEWISH
Manufacturing	50.0	24.3
Commerce	40.6	56.8
Service	9.4	18.9
	(160)	(37)

chi sq. = 8.63, P <.02

firms, unlike the seeking of individual employment, is less subject to prejudicial attitudes. Some Jews may go into business for themselves in order to avoid a prejudicial encounter. The American business licensing system, unlike the European, is not given to ethnic discrimination, and Jews have had access to investment capital even when banks were not Jewish managed. They were good credit risks.

The MBAs in our sample were born in the 1940s. The firms in which they seek employment are dominated by a generation born in the 1920s, or a bit earlier or later. The Jewish firms are managed by a second and third generation of American Jews. They built on the capital of their parents. Those who went into business in the postwar era found the "smokestack" industries cutting back production while high technology industries were emerging and Wall Street was opening to new capital.

Jewish firms follow economic opportunities. Economic opportunity for Jews wears two faces. On the one hand, opportunity is at the "frontier," the development of a new field. In the past this was the movie and the broadcast industry; currently it is the computer industry; they have all ridden on new technology.

The other face has to do with a "breakage" point; cities grow at times when there is a break in transportation patterns say, from land to sea. Trade, too, is a brokering of a commercial relationship between diverse social sectors, originally between tribes and more recently between producers and consumers. Currently, investment banking is an example of activity at such a "breakage" point between accumulators of capital and producers.

Jews Are at Headquarters

The sectoral and regional locations of firms are characteristics they present to the external world, their market positions. Jewish and non-Jewish firms may also differ internally in worksite organization, size of firm, and growth rate. Any particular worksite may fulfill a special function for the firm as a whole. Availability of labor or efficiency in transporting goods to a local market may determine which worksites house production and which administration. Managerial functions may be divided, with payroll handled by one office, personnel by another. One site may be designated corporate headquarters and others branches.

Jews are more likely to be employed at headquarters sites. We find that 51.9 percent (54) of the non-Jewish but 78.6 percent (56) of the Jewish worksites are headquarters for their firms, rather than branches or an only location. The difference is statistically significant (chi sq.=9.90, P<.01).

In general one might expect MBAs to be drawn by a headquarters site, given their skills in financial management and planning. That the firms where Jews work, at least where they are moving into middle management, are more likely to be headquarters is partly due to the tendency for headquarters to be in cities, the centers of Jewish population. In part, also, this may reflect the association of Jews with commerce, an activity planned and supervised at headquarters.

Having a headquarters and branches is usually a sign of a larger and more complex organization. An indicator of the complexity, and perhaps of the size, of a corporation is the size of its board of directors. This is not a perfect measure: Membership on the board of directors is a function both of structure and of volume of business. More divisions require more officers. The non-Jewish firms have a mean of 22.5 (s.d.=18.1, N=54) officers and directors, and the Jewish ones a mean of 29.4 (s.d.=19.7, N=54), a nearly statistically significant difference (F=3.7, P<.06). The Jewish firms seem by this measure to have larger boards.

Organizational structure differs across industries and is influenced by patterns of ownership. Using our measure of Jewish management, we obtain a reverse result. Jewish managed firms have an average of 15.2 (s.d.=18.7, N=37) officers and directors in all, Gentile managed ones an average of 26.4 (s.d.=19.0, N=163). This difference is statistically significant (F=10.6, P<.002). Gentile firms have larger boards.

The apparent discrepancy, that boards are larger where Jews work but smaller where Jews manage, can be understood in the light of the different sizes of the corporations. Jews, like other minorities, tend to find employment in large corporations, perhaps even in manufacturing. These tend to be Gentile managed, and, particularly if they are in manufacturing, customarily have larger numbers of officers. Jewish owned firms are more likely to be involved in commerce, smaller firms with smaller boards. Jews may begin as employees of large corporations, but when they are directors, prefer smaller boards. A Jewish preference for a more limited authority hierarchy will be illustrated below.

Gentile managed firms may have more directors, but Jewish managed firms grow more rapidly, at least in accreting employees. Our measure is the percentage increase in number of employees between 1972 and 1982. The non-Jewish and Jewish worksites do not differ in this respect. Employment of Jews is not associated with business expansion. However, Jewish managed firms experienced an average of 5.9 percent (s.d.=3.5, N=18) increase in employees between 1972 and 1982 compared to only 3.6 percent (s.d.=3.2, N=98) for Gentile firms. The difference is significant (F=8.2, P<.005). This finding is consistent with the notion that Jewish managed firms are at the frontier of newly opening areas such as high technology. This may also help explain why salaries in Jewish firms are higher; the latter may also reflect Jewish opportunism, the flow of Jewish entrepreneurship in the direction of greater reward. But more on this later.

Recruits to Jewish and Gentile Firms

Religion and Race: Jews Are Not Preferred by Jewish Firms—Nor Rejected by Gentile Firms

Jewish and non-Jewish firms compete for the same MBA graduates but, here and there, with different emphases. At first, recruitment is not a matter of religion or ethnicity, but of technical competence. Firms must ultimately succeed as productive organizations in a competitive marketplace. Success, though, is holistic and depends on team performance. Competence, the promise of productivity, is even more difficult to measure in the executive suite than on the assembly line. Selection criteria for corporate leaders vary from a subjective sense of personality and cultural styles to an objective judgment of productive experience. One firm seeks a broadly educated liberal arts student; another wants the practical undergraduate business major. Compatibility of members, and this may include social compatibility of the team, may be as relevant to productivity as individual competence in technical tasks.

Recruitment is a two sided affair, the outcome of negotiation. The MBA recruits the firm in terms of compensation, work satisfaction, and the social climate of the workplace, among other things. Social climate may directly influence the candidate's ability to perform, and indirectly influence his or her belief in mobility opportunities within the firm. The candidate, too, is concerned with matters beyond the technical facilities provided for work. The employer interviews several candidates, and each candidate interviews several firms. The conclusion follows give and take, offer and counteroffer, between firm and candidate.

The result of this social process is something other than random selection by firms and by applicants. Different family background experiences, cultural commitments, ethnicity, and gender are associated with work opportunity, just as industrial type, growth potential of the firm, and promise of career mobility are associated with the attractiveness of the firm to recruits. Religious or ethnic prejudice may be a consideration for both parties to the negotiation. How does the Jewish or non-Jewish character of the firm affect the outcome?

The religion of the candidate, surprising as this may be, does not distinguish between the recruits of the two types of firms. Jews, as indicated, flow more to one sector of the economy than to another, more to commerce than to manufacturing, more to investment banking than to commercial banking. Whatever the reasons for these choices, Jewish firms in each of these areas do not behave differently from non-Jewish firms in the same areas. Using either measure of Jewishness of firm, the presence of Jewish employees or the proportion of Jews among officers and directors, shows no statistically significant difference in the likelihood of either type of firm attracting Jewish or non-Jewish graduates.

Jewish MBA respondents are not more likely to be found in Jewish firms. No difference was found in the proportions of Jewish respondents employed in the non-Jewish and Jewish worksites. We found that 17.9 percent (156) of the respondents working in Gentile managed firms are Jewish, compared with 34.3 percent (35) of those in Jewish managed firms. This difference, which in the superficial comparison of percentages appears substantial, is nevertheless short of statistical significance.

These correlations were examined for manufacturing, commerce, and service industries, comparing Jewish and non-Jewish firms in each case, without discovering statistically significant differences. It must, however, be kept in mind that with so small a sample, fine distinctions might have been missed. To that extent the issue awaits further exploration. These findings do not gainsay the possibility that in a somewhat larger population of firms the percentage differences displayed above could be statistically significant, but we do not at present have such results.

This provides one answer to a question of discrimination toward Jewish executives, a null finding in that respect. This interpretation is bolstered by findings in other parts of this study showing that the earnings of Jewish MBAs is above that of Gentiles and that very few Jewish respondents reported a subjective sense of discrimination in hiring and promotion in their firms.

Conceivably, anti-semitic attitudes might be found in certain specific industrial sectors, as has been asserted in the past about commercial banking. Conceivably, also, Jewish firms in such a prejudiced sector might follow the practice of their industry, thus erasing any apparent differences between Jewish and non-Jewish firms. This suggestion seems perverse. Specific firms, perhaps even a specific class of firms, might discriminate, but there is no discriminatory climate in the field, insofar as this sample at this time is concerned. Jewish executives may be exposed to social anti-semitism on the part of their peers or superiors, but to the extent that this occurs it is not translated into decreased work opportunities.

Doubtless, there are still firms that reject Jews, and others, including Jewish firms, that show a preference for Jews. Such preferences average out in the aggregate of firms in our major industrial sectors. The uneven distribution of Jewish executives among industries is to be explained in other than specifically Jewish ethnic or religious identity terms.

Nondiscrimination in favor of Jews in Jewish managed firms reflects an element of universalism in employment practices. Since Jews are a minority, Jewish firms having more than a few hundred employees would have difficulty remaining competitive if they excluded Gentiles. This problem is less pronounced for a firm that hires only Gentiles, because the pool of Gentile MBAs is comparatively larger. In fact, earlier studies of employment discrimination showed such religious preferences in hiring. That such discriminatory hiring is not widespread in this population suggests a move toward meritocratic universalism.

Gender: Women Serve on the Boards of Jewish Firms

Is gender an element in recruitment? Doubtless it is for some positions. The question here is whether Jewish and non-Jewish firms differ in this respect. Does the Jewishness of the firm influence the hiring of women beyond the usual sex segregating biases of the American corporate world? We will analyze first the proportion of women board members and then that of women in the executive workforce.

The number and proportion of women among officers and directors of firms is a bellwether. It is a measure of their economic power. The relative proportion of female to all officers does not differ between Jewish and non-Jewish worksites. In both cases it averages 3.4 percent (s.d.=6.6, N=109).

Jewish and Gentile managed firms, on the other hand, differ in proportions of women on their boards. Women constitute 9.9 percent (s.d.=14.5, N=37) of officers in Jewish and 2.3 percent (s.d.=4.9, N=162) in Gentile managed firms, a statistically significant difference (F=30.0, P<.001).

Jewish and Gentile firms differ in the proportion but not in the numbers of women on their respective boards. Jewish managed firms, as we saw above, have smaller boards and so, relatively, the two or three women on them constitute a higher proportion. This, though, is a significant difference. The relative economic power of women is greater in Jewish firms. In Gentile firms the same number of women are outnumbered and overpowered by a large board.

The proportion of women on the board differs by industrial sector, kinds of professions drawn upon by management, and geographic location, among other factors. Thus, women are less likely to be managing an oil company in Oklahoma than a banking firm in New York City, and more likely to bring expertise in economic theory than in engineering.

The Jewish character of the executive workforce, our first measure of Jewishness, is weakly related to the presence of women on the board. This may be a matter of timing, since women are too recent in executive roles to have worked up through the ranks to board status. Some women on boards have been appointed because they are major stockholders or relatives of stockholders.

Jewishness of worksite does not influence the likelihood of its having women in the executive workforce. In places reporting women coworkers the figures are respectively 82.0 percent (41) in Jewish and 73.5 percent (49) in non-Jewish firms, a difference that is not statistically significant.

Jewish management is, however, associated with women in the executive workforce. We find that 81.5 percent (27) of Jewish-managed firms have three or more female coworkers compared with 60.7 percent (107) of Gentile-managed, a statistically significant difference (chi sq.=5.0, P<.05). It may be that female board members promote a female executive labor force, at least in Jewish managed firms.

Further, Jews, who are more patriarchal in religious and family life are less so in the economy. In this they contrast with Catholics, as shown in the fuller study report, who extend familial patriarchy into the economy. Even in East European settings, Jewish women would often "mind the store." Jewish boards are more liberal than Gentile ones with respect to women. Jewish managed firms are also in this instance more universalistic than are Gentile firms, seeking competence and engaging competent women.

Education and Age

A white Protestant elite has played a significant role in the control of American corporations, bequeathing positions from father to son. Dynasty is no longer a link among industries. The "community" of business school graduates links contemporary firms. Students at business schools are by no means a cross section of American society. They are all college graduates, though they include sons and daughters of blue as well as white collar parents. Jewish and non-Jewish firms do not differ with respect to occupations of fathers and mothers of the MBAs they engage. Class, in a traditional sense, is not an issue.

The educational histories of recruits to Jewish firms differ from those of the recruits to Gentile firms. The undergraduate subject matter makes a difference. Some MBA respondents majored in business and engineering while in college, others majored in arts and sciences. Of those engaged in non-Jewish and Jewish worksites, 58.5 percent (53) and 84.9 percent (53) respectively majored in arts and sciences, a statistically significant difference (chi sq.=7.9, P<.01). The Jewish firms attract arts and science students, social science majors in particular, and these latter tend to be economics majors.

The same finding holds for the management classification. Of those in Jewish managed firms, 85.3 percent (34) took undergraduate degrees in arts and sciences as compared to 62.2 percent (156) in Gentile managed firms, again a statistically significant difference (chi sq.=5.6, P<.02). Gentile firms lean toward engineering and business graduates.

Arts and science students defer their entrance into a vocation while they deepen their cultural preparation. To the extent that the major is economics, and the employer requires commercial know-how, the preparation may appear practical. Yet Jewish firms select economics rather than finance majors. Nearly all MBAs study finance at the graduate level. Jewish managed firms are not simply attracting economics undergraduates; they are avoiding the vocationally trained undergraduate. They seek greater understanding of society as a system, not just the technology of work. The educationally well-rounded person should have a sense of the way the society works, sensitivity to its cultural and value nuances and, perhaps, even some foreign language training. These are the men and women of the world who will ultimately rise to more responsible positions than those who acquire mere technical competence. For the more worldly young men and women, getting along in business is getting along with people, and being able to take on the role of the high-level negotiator.

Jewish worksites hire younger MBAs, a matter related to the educational characteristics they seek. The proportion of MBAs hired before their twenty-fifth birthday is 17.0 percent (53) for the non-Jewish and 37.5 percent (56) for the Jewish firms, a statistically significant difference (chi sq.=6.8, P<.01). Jewish and Gentile managed firms do not differ in the age of MBA recruits.

The younger MBA is more likely to have gone straight through school without pause, a situation less common among engineering and business students who are more vocationally committed and probably more likely to work between college and business school. In the balance between education and experience, Jewish worksites give relatively more weight to the former.

Educational differences in personnel signal different social milieux, and thus different cultural milieux. Firms that employ Jews also employ more women and Catholics, a finding reported in our fuller report, and seek executives with a broader cultural background, whatever the religion of those executives. Jewish managed firms, while not biased toward hiring Jews, engage women for positions of power and prefer younger, more broadly cultured entry level executives.

Traditionally, a good humanistic foundation prior to a technical education has been the aristocratic choice. If so, Jewish firms have a more aristocratic ambience. In this case, though, the criteria of class differ from those of the older Gentile aristocratic firms. Aristocratic qualities include competence defined by higher cultural attainments, not by ethnicity, family, or technical experience.

Careers in Jewish and Gentile Firms
Passage Through the Network of Firms

Networks of firms may be based on dynastic familial links, interlocking directorates, or class or ethnic group capture of sets of firms. This study, beginning with a sample of MBAs, was not designed to locate such palpable networks.

Firms in a particular industrial sector are linked in their market relations. Some are key suppliers of parts, others are assemblers; several firms competing in the same market take account of one another or meet in a trade association.

In this study, we glimpse organizations linked through sharing an executive labor pool or bound in culturally based networks. Common cultural characteristics designate a category of firms. People move in their careers through firms with cultural commonalities. To consider these firms as a network we should locate actual social connections between them. The Jewishness or non-Jewishness of firms and the ambience implied is a cultural distinction for which we must yet seek the social correlate.

Those who enter Jewish worksites initially tend to continue with such firms. Table 8.4 shows how respondents in Jewish worksites in their first positions reported more Jewish coworkers in their current positions.

Of those whose first position was a non-Jewish worksite, one that had no Jewish officers and fewer than three Jewish coworkers, 45.2 percent are currently employed in firms with three or more Jewish coworkers. But of those who began in Jewish worksites, having a Jewish officer and at least three Jewish coworkers, 80.3 percent are currently in firms with three or more Jewish coworkers. Very few MBAs are in the same firm five to ten years later, so in the majority of cases we are dealing with different employers.

The linkage is transitive, working in the reverse direction from that presented in Table 8.4. A classification by current position "predicts" the character of the first position. Of those currently in Jewish worksites 82.4 percent (51) reported three or more Jewish coworkers in their first place of employment, compared with 42.6 percent (54) of those currently in non-Jewish worksites, a statistically significant difference (chi sq.=18.2, P<.001).

The common cultural characteristic of having Jewish employees, as mentioned above, does not prove the existence of a network, but only of a class of firms. The common pool of employees offers the possibility of such a connection. A respondent who worked in two of the firms in our population of firms is a social link between them.

The data of the above table refer to all employees, Jews as well as non-Jews. If a Jew begins in the non-Jewish network, he or she is likely to remain there. Similarly, a non-Jew entering a Jewish worksite will likely be found later in his or her career in a firm with more Jewish coworkers.

The cultural commonality among sets of firms is not limited to characteristics of the work force. Consistency in character of officers and directors, specifically, the propensity to have Jewish board members, also appears to link firms for which MBAs work at these two points in their

TABLE 8.4.   Employment in Jewish and non-Jewish worksites for first position and Jewish coworkers in current position (in percents)

JEWISH COWORKERS IN CURRENT POSITION	NON-JEWISH	JEWISH
None	14.5	6.6
One or two	40.3	13.1
Three or more	45.2	80.3
	(62)	(61)
	chi square = 16.40, P <.001	

careers. Those in Jewish worksites immediately following receipt of their MBA are currently in firms with a mean of 4.7 (s.d.=7.8, N=45) Jewish officers. Those whose first position was in a non-Jewish worksite are currently in a firm with 1.8 (s.d.=1.9, N=44) Jewish officers, a statistically significant difference (F=5.89, P<.02).

The reverse is also true, as this relation too is transitive. Those currently working in non-Jewish worksites were in firms with 1.8 (s.d.=2.6, N=42) Jewish officers when first employed. Those currently in Jewish worksites worked under 5.1 (s.d.=7.6, N=47) Jewish officers at that time, a statistically significant difference (F=7.2, P<.01).

The results are similar when we take the proportion of Jewish officers as the criterion. Those who worked in their first position in a non-Jewish worksite currently are in firms in which 7.3 percent (s.d.=10.9, N=44) of officers are Jewish, whereas those who worked first in a Jewish worksite are currently in firms in which 19.4 percent (s.d.=25.1, N=43) of officers are Jewish, a significant result (F=8.6, P<.005). Contrariwise, those now in non-Jewish worksites worked for firms with 8.0 percent (s.d.=14.6, N=42) Jewish officers in their first job as compared with those now in Jewish worksites having had 19.1 percent (s.d.=22.9, N=45) Jewish officers, again significant (F=1.20, P<.01).

Comparison of Jewish and Gentile managed firms reveals the same consistency. To take but one example, those currently in Jewish managed firms earlier worked for firms with an average of 5.4 (s.d.=8.0, N=31) Jewish officers. Those currently in Gentile managed firms earlier worked in firms that averaged 1.7 (s.d.=2.0, N=132) Jewish officers, a statistically significant difference (F=23.0, P<.001).

The results are similar if we take proportion, rather than number, of

Jewish officers as the criterion. Those currently in Jewish managed firms began their careers in firms in which, on average 45.7 percent (s.d.=32.8, N=31) of the officers were Jewish. Those now in Gentile managed firms began in firms that averaged 6.0 percent (s.d.=8.2, N=131) Jewish officers, a significant difference (F=155.56, P<.001).

Firms whose officers are Jewish, as we now know, present a distinctive ambience, have more women on the board, are in the commercial more than the manufacturing sector, are relatively more universalistic in their personnel selection, and more often recruit those who majored in arts and sciences as undergraduates. This cluster of characteristics defines a type of setting to which a candidate may or may not be drawn. One may imagine a mentor in one firm referring a junior executive to another with a similar ambience, or working alongside persons who can report on another firm in the same cultural sphere and who, in this way, may help channel people from one firm to another of similar ambience and so materialize a network. The network may be industry defined, but in which ethnicity, Jewish or non-Jewish, as represented by a cultural ambience, constitutes a subsidiary network.

Mentoring: The Social Connection

A senior executive who guides a junior executive has been termed a "mentor." The mentor may even intervene to facilitate the junior executive's advancement. Jews mentor Christians and Christians mentor Jews, but an earlier analysis in this study showed there is a tendency toward consistency between religion of the mentor and the junior executive. A Gentile firm is more likely to have Gentiles mentoring than a Jewish firm, simply in response to the distribution of religions among the senior personnel or the directors.

Table 8.5 shows the religions of our respondents' mentors in firms classified by the religions of their officers and directors.

This is a bit surprising. Firms were classified according to the proportion of Jews on the board. We do not know the distribution of members of each religious group among relatively senior personnel in each type of firm. Distributions of respondents of these three faiths did not differ significantly between Jewish and Gentile firms. The predominance of Catholic and Protestant mentors in Gentile and of Jewish mentors in Jewish managed firms is a result not simply of the concentration of senior executives of each faith in those firms, but of their influence. The prominence of Jewish mentors in Jewish firms may be due to their greater political influence in these settings,

TABLE 8.5.   Religions of mentors of respondents employed in Jewish and Gentile firms in first and current positions (percents)

RELIGION OF MENTOR	FIRST POSITION		CURRENT POSITION	
	Gentile	*Jewish*	*Gentile*	*Jewish*
Catholic	34.9	17.4	39.2	28.6
Protestant	51.9	39.1	45.0	14.3
Jewish	13.2	43.5	15.8	57.1
	(106)	(23)	(120)	(28)
	chi sq. = 11.8, P <.003		chi sq. = 22.5, P <.001	

a result of their prominence on boards. In firms with influential Jewish board members, they are sought as mentors by both Jews and Christians.

We can surmise the direction of such intervention from the following results. Mentoring by a Jew in the respondent's entry position increases the likelihood that the respondent will be in a Jewish managed firm later. Of those who, in their first position, were mentored by Catholics, 12.2 percent (49) are currently in Jewish managed firms. This compares with 14.1 percent (71) of those mentored by Protestants; but 38.7 percent (31) of those mentored by Jews are currently in Jewish managed firms, a statistically significant difference (chi sq.=10.6, df=2, P<.01)

The association is transitive. Those who were in a Jewish-managed firm for their first position, are more likely to be mentored by a Jew in current employment. Respondents who began in a Gentile managed firm, are currently more likely to be mentored by Protestants (though not so much by Catholics). This association is also statistically significant (chi sq.=14.8, P<.001).

Mentoring may have a role in sustaining a tendency for individuals beginning in Jewish firms to remain in Jewish firms. Jewish mentors, in the first position, whether in a Jewish or non-Jewish firm, direct an executive to a Jewish firm for later employment. The executives mentored include Jews and non-Jews. The latter, we suspect, are as likely to be directed to a Jewish-managed firm as the former.

Women mentors are relatively more frequent in Jewish than in Gentile firms. Thus, 19.2 percent (26) of those currently employed by Jewish managed firms have a female mentor as compared to 6.0 percent (100) of those in Gentile managed firms, also a significant result (chi sq.=4.5, P<.04).

Jewish managed firms are more likely to have women on the board, and so, in general senior women executives, whether Jewish or Gentile, are sought as mentors.

In part, too, the association between female mentors and Jewish firms may be related to the fact that Jewish firms are more likely to be in commerce, trade and service sectors in which more female executives are employed. The number of cases is too small to test the interplay between Jewish and Gentile women and men mentors and mentored.

Authority: Jews Are Ambitious

MBAs absorbed into Jewish firms are given greater authority than those absorbed into non-Jewish firms. Authority is here defined as rank in the hierarchy. Such a measure has some limitation when comparing industries whose authority structures are of different sizes.

The number of levels of authority in the firm was reported by the respondent. Non-Jewish and Jewish worksites do not differ in this respect. Jewish and Gentile managed firms, on the other hand, have different numbers of levels of authority. Gentile-managed firms average 10.1 (s.d.=8.09, N=77) levels, Jewish-managed firms have 6.5 (s.d.=2.2, N=20) levels. This is a significant difference (F=4.06, P<.05). Gentile managed firms have a steeper hierarchy. This is consistent with the earlier finding that Gentile managed firms have larger boards of directors and are more organizationally complex.

Respondents indicated the number of authority levels of their position below the CEO. In Gentile managed firms respondents' positions averaged 5.0 (s.d.=3.6, N=91) levels below the chief executive, and in Jewish managed they averaged 3.5 (s.d.=2.1, N=24) levels below. This just misses statistical significance (F=3.6, P<.06). It is difficult to say that the latter, though closer to the top rank, outrank the former since they are in organizations with fewer levels of authority. Does a third level below the CEO in a six-rank organization have more or less authority than a fifth level below in a ten-rank organization? The former would seem to offer a wider scope of authority and the climb to the top may be shorter. Yet that top position controls a simpler system. MBAs in Jewish firms, therefore, are closer to top management, and have more authority as we have defined it, albeit in smaller firms.

Despite the longer road, those in Gentile firms have more confidence in their eventual rise to the top than those in Jewish firms. Respondents were asked about the position they expected to hold at the peak of their careers, and are classified as expecting to be leaders (to be a corporate president or a CEO) or expecting to be subordinates (to hold technical positions such as corporate accountant or divisional head). No difference appears in this respect between non-Jewish and Jewish worksites. In Gentile managed firms, however, 73.1 percent (26) of the respondents expected to achieve a leadership position. This expectation is shared by only 25 percent (8) of those in the Jewish managed firms, a statistically significant difference (chi sq.=6.0, P<.02). If respondents in Jewish firms are nearer the top, in a smaller organization one would expect them to have a greater expectation of reaching the top of the ladder. The number of cases is quite small, however, so the finding should be considered tentative.

Several explanations are possible. Smaller hierarchies may be more rigid, making it more difficult to ascend from one rank to another. In this type of organization, respondents have less opportunity for each promotion. On the other hand, as we will see, those in Jewish managed firms anticipate a significantly higher salary than those in Gentile managed firms. Thus, the executive in a Jewish managed firm exchanges inter-organizational authority for a position in a high paying elite firm.

Compensation: Jewish Firms Pay Better
Working in a Jewish firm seems to offer a distinct salary advantage. The study provides data for comparisons at each step in the career ladder. Our survey instrument asked for starting and ending salaries for each place of employment since earning the MBA. All salary figures are deflated to allow comparison in constant 1972 dollars. Sometimes reference is to starting salary, the entering salary in the current position, and sometimes to ending salary, that is, to salary at the time of the study. Where no point in time is given, reference is to salary at the time of survey.

Respondents working in non-Jewish worksites earn a mean of $73,396 (s.d.=65,854, N=46) while those in Jewish worksites earn $131,011 (s.d.= 158,001, N=45). The salary advantage of those in Jewish worksites is statistically significant (F=4.50, P<.04).

Respondents working in Gentile managed firms began with a mean salary of $56,666 (s.d.=52,629, N=129) whereas those in Jewish managed firms began with a mean salary of $84,166 (s.d.=104,420, N=30). This too is a statistically significant difference (F=4.3, P<.04).

Three or four years later, on average, those in Gentile managed firms earn a mean of $81,123 (s.d.=77,410, N=160) and those in Jewish managed firms earn an average of $142,841 (s.d.=164,580, N=36), also a statistically significant difference ($F=11.42$, $P<.001$). The average increase for those in Jewish managed firms of some $59,000 dwarfs the increase in Gentile managed firms of about $24,500. The gap widens over time.

These are not the salaries of Jews as compared to Gentiles. That matter is dealt with elsewhere in this study. These are the salaries of MBAs, regardless of their religion, who work in either Jewish or Gentile firms. In fact, we have already noted that Jewish firms do not overselect Jews.

Why are salaries higher in Jewish firms? In part, this could be due to the concentration of Jewish firms in commerce. This would not explain all of the difference. In general, salaries in commerce are not two-thirds higher than those in manufacturing and service. Another possibility is that as non-Jewish firms are larger corporations and there is a longer road to the top, the MBA in the first few career years is not yet as far along as he or she might be in a smaller firm.

The salary differential is consistent with the cultural characteristics of Jewish firms described above. These firms emphasize labor, especially executive labor, above land and capital. Being competitive means commanding the most competitive labor and that means offering better salaries. This last explanation seems most in line with what we have discovered about the ambience of Jewish and Gentile firms thus far.

The salary advantage of executives in Jewish firms is carried over to an anticipation of further advantage. Asked to estimate their earnings at the peak of their careers, the difference between those in Jewish and Gentile firms remains. (These figures are not deflated.) Executives currently working in non-Jewish worksites anticipate a mean peak earning of $226,764 (s.d.$=205,746$, $N=51$) while those in Jewish worksites anticipate $340,729 (s.d.$=238,864$, $N=48$), a statistically significant difference ($F=6.5$, $P<.02$).

Respondents in Gentile managed firms expect an average of $257,448 (s.d.$=207,913$, $N=96$) while those in Jewish managed firms expect an average of $335,870 (s.d.$=261,101$, $N=23$). This difference, although apparently large, falls below statistical significance ($F=2.4$, $P<.13$). Were a difference of this magnitude to hold constant in a survey of a larger number of cases, given the size of variation around the mean, the difference would attain statistical significance.

As a proxy test for this last assertion we took all positions respondents occupied, neglecting the sequence, whether first or current, but not allowing more than one position for each, thus picking up the additional respondents. MBAs who were at any time in Gentile managed firms anticipated a peak of $270,588 (s.d.$=244,338$, $N=136$) while those at any time in

Jewish managed firms anticipated \$367,580, (s.d.=271,277, N=31), a statistically significant difference (F=4.4, P<.04). In the Jewish managed firms executives earned more and expected to continue to earn more.

Salaries are a function of a norm within a particular industrial sector, an aspect of the labor market. Although Jewish and Gentile firms may be in different labor markets, skills of the executives are not specific to a particular industry. Business schools train for general administrative skills, which it is believed may be applied in a range of positions. In this case we could have a single labor market for executives, at least for those in the two elite schools in the sample. The evidence above of networks of firms suggests there may be some labor market segmentation separating Jewish from Gentile firms. These networks seem to be based more on differences in cultural ambience than directly on religious identification of board members.

The Jewishness of the Executives: Affirming Jewishness Among Gentiles
Acceptance of Jews in Gentile corporations has sometimes hinged on identifiable Jewishness of the candidate. In nineteenth century Europe it was not unusual to hear of Jews converting to Christianity to facilitate their careers. Gustav Mahler's appointment as director of the Vienna Court Opera required such conversion. In the more secularized United States, the 1920s and the 1930s were times of name changing for immigrant Jews seeking acceptance in the American corporate world or simply admission to college. Our opening comments on Baltzell's work refer to these assimilatory adjustments, sometimes honest, sometimes a masquerade.

Anti-semitism in the western Christian world is a religious prejudice; Jews are cast in a mephistophelian role. In a secular society the symbols have been transformed into cultural and personality matters, to matters of Jewish business ethics or Jewish corporate loyalty or, in Baltzell's term, "ethnic characteristics." Even after Jews abandoned a Jewish language for English and the western business suit supplanted orthodox black gabardines, private ritual distinctions have remained. Some religious observances have been considered to inhibit Jewish mobility, if only for logistical reasons, in this secular corporate world. Thus, Sabbath observances or observance of *kashrut* have been thought of as objective barriers to corporate assimilation because of their influence on social relations and work schedules. Some who thought that a Jew's career chances would be better in a Jewish setting have sought to work in Jewish firms or become entrepreneurs. Such adaptations also have been thought to protect the expression of Jewish identity and resist compromising Jewish cultural forms.

For the MBA population, these issues seem close to irrelevant. Gentile and Jewish firms differ in the social and cultural types they recruit, but religious or ethnic background is not among the discriminating standards. Have the MBA Jews become indistinguishable from Christians, or have Gentile firms come to accept MBAs who identify themselves as Jews?

The MBA population included eighty Jewish respondents, male and female. The survey instrument included several measures of Jewish cultural involvement, including measures of Hebrew knowledge, level of Jewish religious observances, and attitudes toward Israel.

In many senses, Jewish society is less differentiated along the secular/religious dimension than Protestant, or even Catholic, society. The line between secular and religious Jewish culture is not always clear and the contemporary role of Hebrew illustrates this. The Hebrew language has been revived as a living language in the context of a secular Jewish renaissance, as a vehicle for discovering world news and for writing works on economics. Yet, most of those in our population who have learned Hebrew have learned it in connection with Judaism as a religion, as preparation for participation in synagogue liturgy, or for reading sacred text at a Bar or Bat Mitzvah.

Respondents' knowledge of Hebrew was assessed first by asking whether they had ever learned to read the language, and then by asking them to transliterate a voweled line of text (a test of simple ability to decode), and to translate a simple voweled line. (An earlier version of the scale included the translation of an unvoweled line of text, but few in this population proved able to perform at that level.)

Hebrew knowledge scores vary from 0 to 3, from no successful responses to an ability to translate the text presented. Jews employed by non-Jewish firms are superior in Hebrew knowledge to those employed by Jewish firms. Jews in non-Jewish worksites, for their first position, scored a mean of 1.2 (s.d.$=$.87, N$=$21) whereas Jews in Jewish worksites scored 0.7 (s.d.$=$0.8, N$=$20), a statistically significant difference (F$=$4.2, P$<$.05). This difference does not seem to hold for current positions, suggesting that the difference may be related more to recruitment decisions immediately after school than to transfers after job experience.

This same finding holds for Jewish managed firms. Respondents whose first position was in a Gentile managed firm had a mean Hebrew score of 1.2 (s.d.$=$0.9, N$=$32) while those in a Jewish managed firm achieved a mean of only 0.2 (s.d.$=$0.4, N$=$11), also a statistically significant difference (F$=$12.3, P $<$.002). Again, in current positions, Jewish and Gentile management drew executives of equivalent Hebrew knowledge.

Why the greater Hebrew knowledge on the part of those in non-Jewish settings at the time of professional entry, but not five or ten years later? No change takes place in Hebrew knowledge over this time. Most of what the respondent knows was learned in childhood, though the more culturally involved may use Hebrew in the interim and recall more. Gentile firms, for whatever reason, hire Jews from the MBA pool who are more Hebraically educated than do Jewish firms. As their careers advance, other factors emerge to control job tenancy, such as performance and reward, which outweigh this early sorting.

The religious observance scale is based on adherence to five traditional religious activities such as participating in a Passover seder, eating kosher food, and lighting candles on the Sabbath and on Hanukkah. Scores ranged from 0 to 5, from a respondent's practicing none of the rituals to practicing all those on the list. A difference in scores of those hired for first position after the MBA survives to current employment, but not at a statistically significant level. The means are respectively 1.7 (s.d.=0.9, N=15) for executives in non-Jewish worksites and 1.4 (s.d.=1.1, N=17) for those in Jewish worksites. The difference is not statistically significant, but this tabulation is based on only 32 cases.

When we compare the scores of executives of Jewish and Gentile managed firms, a sharp difference emerges, for places both of initial and current employment. In current positions the means are respectively of 2.0 (s.d.=1.0, N=24) for the Gentile managed firms and 0.7 (s.d.=0.8, N=10) for the Jewish managed, a statistically significant difference (F=13.2, P<.001). Jews who work for Gentiles are more observant.

All of these means are quite low in an absolute sense. A score of 2.00 implies attendance at a seder without defining it as a ritual seder, and probably the lighting of Sabbath candles, but excludes token observance of dietary laws or marking of their door with a mezuzah—thus a ritual life limited to several occasions a month. At the same time, given that the standard deviation is 1.0, only a scattered few would have a score of 0, no observance at all. Almost every Jew employed by a Gentile managed firm publicly identifies himself or herself as Jewish in religion, in this sense. On the other hand, a mean of 0.7 and a standard deviation of 0.8, for those in Jewish managed firms, implies that a significant minority observe no rituals. In light of this finding it should be noted that all eighty MBAs considered here identified themselves as Jews in their returned questionnaires. Any respondent who though a child of a Jewish mother, checked Christian or none on the item asking for religion, was not counted.

We may specify the meaning of these rituals by examining a few individually. Eight of ten Jewish respondents report attending a Passover seder. There is little difference in this respect between Jews in non-Jewish and Jewish worksites. Comparing those in Jewish managed environments we note a real difference. Of those in Jewish managed firms 58.3 percent (12) attend a seder as compared with 94.6 percent (37) in Gentile managed firms, a statistically significant difference (chi sq.=9.73, P<.002).

The religious form of the seder differs for individuals with different overall scale scores. A person attending a seder but observing none of the other rituals likely has a modified seder, perhaps blessing the matzah but probably not reading through a traditional Haggadah. One with a high score, perhaps eating kosher food, probably has a full traditional seder. In any event, the seder is a ritual of solidarity for a Jewish family or friendship circle. It asserts the Jewish dimension in intimate relations, but does not publicly declare one's Jewishness.

The display of mezuzah is a public statement of Jewish identification. Taking that item alone from the scale, we found no difference between Jews working in non-Jewish and Jewish worksites. However, 62.5 percent (24) of Jews working for Gentile managed firms but only 20 percent (10) of those working for Jewish managed firms display a mezuzah, a statistically significant difference (chi sq.=5.0, P<.03).

These observances communicate between a Jew and the Gentile firm that the Jew is permitted, if not invited, to publish his or her identity, and that the Gentile finds it acceptable, or even desirable, to have an executive with that identity. Jewish firms do not suppress Jewish cultural expression, but the absence of a religious boundary in the firm allows such assertions of identity to sink into the background. In addition, the greater particularism of Gentile firms supports religious expression. Adherence to nearly any accepted religion is viewed as culturally positive, affirming virtue. Denominational religion is more likely a matter of indifference in the more universalistic Jewish firms in which attention is riveted, paradoxically, on broadly shared western humanistic culture and on economic performance.

The scale measuring attitudes to Israel consisted of three items: helping needy Jews settle there, sending Jewish children to summer camp there, and feeling an obligation to spend a part of one's life there. Scores varied from 0 to 3, from disagreement with all to agreement with all items. On the whole, few Jewish respondents considered it an obligation to live part of their lives in Israel, but most believed in financial support of the Zionist experiment. Scores on this scale did not differ between those who worked in non-Jewish or Jewish worksites or between executives of Jewish or Gentile managed firms.

The Israel attitude is secularized, more statist than messianic. Apparently, only religious attitudes are more intense among Jews in non-Jewish settings. This is consistent with suggestions that Jewishness is not inhibited in Jewish firms, but religious Jewishness is permitted and elicited in Gentile settings. Eliciting of a pro-Israeli attitude, a Jewish nationalist position, would be more controversial in such settings.

In a simpleminded way, one might have anticipated more Jewish religious expression in a Jewish firm on the basis of religious conformity. But the expectation of religious expression is low in these settings so that any conformity is to the simplest of token expressions. The corporate environment, whether Jewish or Gentile, would not condone strict Sabbath observance if it would interfere with the needs of business. Nor would strict observance of dietary laws be supported in either case if it were to limit social interaction among business colleagues. (Jewish or non-Jewish), particularly clients. Religious expression is permissible if it is slight; in that sense, the ticket of admission for Jews has been the thinning of culture. Yet this thinning cannot be attributed to demands of the corporate world, since Jews themselves, when in Jewish firms, are ready to shed their cultural identities. Orthodox Jewish firms, supporting strict observance, are few in number and so carry no numerical weight in this population.

In sum . . .

Jewish managed firms are a mature, though not the definitive expression of Jewish participation in the American economy. Firms distinguished by the employment of Jews are the setting for an earlier, perhaps an apprenticeship, stage of participation in the economy. Characteristics of contemporary Jewish-American economic behavior may be identified in these Jewish worksites but are more complete in the Jewish managed firms.

Keeping in mind that we have been observing the behavior of MBAs— not of all Jews nor even of all Jews who enter the world of business and administration, the findings reviewed in this chapter suggest seven points about Jewish, and non-Jewish, economic behavior. (1) An ethnic division of labor remains, though not a firmly segregated system. (2) This ethnic division of labor is more apparent as a division among firms than as an ethno-religious division of employees within firms. (3) The economic activities preferred by Jewish firms are at the frontier, especially businesses built around technological innovation and those associated with areas of "breakage," the areas of economic exchange more than of economic production. (4) Jewish firms compete for the best personnel as judged by economic performance and broad culture, and pay higher salaries to recruit them. (5) Jewish firms, more than Gentile, limit the influence on business of particularistic relations and obligations in favor of meritocratic and performance considerations. (6) Networks of firms of similar ambience, in the sense indicated above, define career paths. Mentors in these firms support these social connections. (7) The more Jewishly cultured Jews are more likely to be working in Gentile firms.

A few concluding comments on each assertion. First, the ethnic division of labor is reflected in the concentration of Jewish managed firms in the commercial sector and, secondarily, in the service sector, with the Gentile managed firms more numerous in manufacturing. Nearly half the Jewish firms in which our MBA respondents work are in a single subfield, investment banking. Media related activities, such as advertising, are a second major area.

The second point is that the division of economic labor is defined by the firm. Within firms of each category, Jewish and non-Jewish, we found no significant difference in the employment of Jewish and Gentile MBAs.

The third point is that Jewish sector businesses tend to be in areas of "breakage" and in areas that developed through technological innovation. Trade is always a point of "breakage," being traditionally a link between ethnic groupings, producers and consumers, and hinterland and cities. East European Jews were in trade in this sense. New opportunities that develop around technological innovation draw Jewish firms. An earlier generation entered the Hollywood movie industry, combining Jewish organizational and entertainment backgrounds with the new technology.

Investment banking, a form of trade, is not a new career among Jews. For generations Jews have been involved in finance and in stock exchanges. In the early modern period they pioneered letters of credit. The current population of Jews in these fields in the United States are descendents of East European immigrants, while in an earlier generation Western European Jews were the financiers. We may be seeing a social synergistic effect of the amalgamation of these two Jewries. Investment banking has been spurred by the introduction of computers and telecommunications, dramatically reducing the time for information to be exchanged and the geographic reach over which it is exchanged. It is also a branch of the new information revolution. Jews have been prominent in the communication industry, in radio and television, advertising, and the computer industry.

The fourth point concerns the cultural ambience, the preference given to educational, especially liberal arts, background, over experience and a more vocational college training. Jewish firms stress the human relations aspect of business interactions, negotiations, and deal making, over the craft aspect of production. The relatively high salaries paid in these settings are a response to their rapid growth and the demand by Jewish firms for the most competitive employees. Jewish firms pay the highest salaries. Executives working for Jewish firms expect that in the future they will be earning higher salaries than their colleagues in Gentile firms.

The fifth point refers to the universalistic-performance character of the firm's behavior. By this technical term, the sociologist means that general attributes of people become relevant to their role performance rather than some particular personal relation between the role occupants. Competent performance is such a general attribute. Religion and family ties illustrate the particularist relation. Neither Jewish nor Gentile firms show a preference or dislike for executives of one or the other religion. Jewish firms do not prefer Jewish employees nor do Gentile firms avoid them. This signals a weakening of particularism in the executive market place. The suspected tendency for Jewish mentors of entry level executives to direct their protégés to Jewish firms is based, we believe, on a judgment of competence and broad general culture rather than on religious identification.

Sixth, findings regarding networks of firms and mentoring illustrate a mechanism supporting not the ethnic division of labor, but a division among firms based on cultural ambience. We did not show that the MBAs who entered a given industry remained with that industry, but that they tended to remain within a cluster of firms of a similar cultural type. If they began with a firm that had a goodly proportion of Jewish officers, they would, currently, be found in the employ of another firm having Jewish officers. Other network identifiers were the presence of female officers, high salary levels, and minority group coworkers. The prominence of Jewish mentors in Jewish firms reflects their position in the power structure of those firms.

The seventh point is that the relatively particularistic Gentile firms are more supportive of religion. Religious Jews are not excluded from this advantage. Jewish employees of Gentile firms are more culturally Jewish, in knowledge of Hebrew and in ritual observances, than Jewish employees of Jewish firms. This may be, in part, a form of Jewish identity expression in a non-Jewish environment and be itself particularistic in nature, a special group membership becoming relevant to the job situation. Notably, the depth of involvement in Israel is no different among Jewish MBAs in Jewish and Gentile firms. Perhaps an orientation to Israel, as it is secular and nationalist, is not especially elicited by a climate generally receptive to religious orientations. Also, within the Jewish community, loyalty toward Israel has come to function to some extent as a religious expression, and this expression of identity is acceptable, even desirable, in Jewish firms.

The Jewish labor force, of course, goes well beyond MBAs and the business world. Paralleling entrepreneurial activity, and not well reflected in the MBA population, is a tendency of Jews to enter community service, to apply technical expertise and professional training in what in America is the nonprofit sector. Jewish corporate organization also encompasses these endeavors.

Jewish entrepreneurial and service sector firms are linked in a dialectic between individualism and collectivism. These two cultural trends are commonly antithetical. They remain that way in the larger society because each becomes institutionalized in a separate societal region, pitting individualists in business against collectivists in the service sector. In Jewish society the powerful individualistic Jewish entrepreneur, with his name on the sign outside the shop, is the same person who assumes the noblesse oblige of a community benefactor, contributing significant portions of his (rarely her) wealth to hospitals, community welfare organizations, and educational institutions. The Jewish entrepreneur creates a nonprofit sector with its positions for those of his brethren who seek more professional expression. The entrepreneur, now in the form of lay leader and major contributor, seeks to maintain control over these community institutions. Collectivism is then neither that of religious clerical control nor that of political control pitted against economic control. It is parallel behavior by the same individualistic people within the same economy. At least, this is the case in the American diaspora. Jewish economic behavior in Israel, in the diaspora of the Soviet Union, or in the historical Islamic world, is a subject for another inquiry into the socio-economic life of Jewry.

Returning to *The Protestant Establishment*, we note that our finding supports Baltzell's advice to the old upper class that failure to absorb the most competent members of the new group will lead to upper class loss of power. Actually, several processes are proceeding simultaneously. Jews are being absorbed into the establishment. Some are apostates, co-opted by the establishment, but some are Jews who remain identified with their "Jewish convictions" and even with their "ethnic characteristics," sharing power with the old establishment. Sometimes this Jewish elite challenges the establishment. American diversity is at work.

Note

1. The study was sponsored by the American Jewish Committee, Philadelphia Chapter, with funds from the Muriel and Philip Berman Foundation and the Sun Oil Company. The methodology and further data analyses are described in the author's report to the American Jewish Committee entitled *Jews in the Executive Suite* (1987). I am grateful to Michael Eleey and Hein Cho, both of the University of Pennsylvania, for their contributions to survey data collection and data processing.

Jerry A. Jacobs

9. The English Landed Aristocracy and the Rise of Capitalism: Status Maximization and Economic Change

Explanations of social change examine the relationship between developments in the economy and social structure and transformations of values, ideas, and ideologies. Both Marxian and Parsonsian perspectives posit the existence of a basic congruence between value structures and social structures, and hold that value systems change in step with changes in the social system. However, an historical examination of normative systems reveals a more complex picture. Some beliefs evolve in form and content as the social situation changes, while others prove remarkably intractable in the face of seemingly incompatible circumstances. This paper is intended to contribute to the development of a framework to describe changes in the value structure of the European aristocracies which may be extended to other status groups. The development of this framework should be useful not only to students of ideas, but also to students of the social and economic history of the industrial revolution. I draw on a range of historical sources and offer a reinterpretation of this material from a sociological vantage point.

The English landed aristocracy played a vastly different role in the emergence of a market economy than did its French counterpart. However, I believe that these two aristocracies responded in fundamentally similar ways to the emergence of a market economy despite the marked differences in their eventual fates. In each case, the landed aristocracy made concessions to economic reality in seeking to preserve and enhance its social status. My concern is to elucidate in a systematic manner the interplay of social status and its economic underpinning.

Max Weber distinguished class, status, and party as three separate but related aspects of inequality (Gerth and Mills, 1946). While these distinctions are familiar to students of sociology, they are rarely employed in actual sociological research. In this essay I show that the continuity of one of these dimensions, status, is crucial to understanding the motivation of the English aristocracy during the transition to the modern economic era. The English aristocracy, I argue, unwittingly aided in the fundamental alteration of class relations in its efforts to preserve its social status.

I propose a model of status maximization that distinguishes the obligations of conspicuous consumption from prohibitions on inappropriate acquisitive behavior. One aspect of this value structure can take on a modern form while the other remains locked in a more traditional orientation. In England, the aristocracy rationalized its acquisitive practices in order to underwrite traditional consumption patterns. The English aristocracy was willing to relax its disdain for detailed attention to estate administration. Thus, it played a crucial role in the emergence of agrarian capitalism, not as a capitulation to bourgeois values but as a means of maintaining its traditional conception of social status.

The Landed Aristocracy and the Rise of Capitalism

The focus on status maximization stems from my dissatisfaction with the two prevailing approaches to understanding the historical role of the English aristocracy. The Marxian view sees the English aristocracy as a capitalist agricultural class that ruled on behalf of capitalist interests. The "open elite" view maintains that the distinctive feature of the English aristocracy was its willingness to accept the successful merchants into its ranks.

The Marxian approach to the emergence of capitalism holds that during decisive moments of conflict the bourgeoisie seized the political reigns of society, and transformed the world in its own image. The English Civil War and the French Revolution are two crucial instances for the application of this thesis, especially the former, since England was the site of the emergence of the modern capitalist order (Moore, 1966).

There are many difficulties with this view. The historiography of the English Civil War remains contested: many historians, for example, dispute the social composition of various factions in the conflict (Hexter, 1961; Stone, 1985; Goldstone, 1986). The bourgeoisie itself, however, appears to have played a relatively minor role in this episode. Equally problematic is the fact that political power in England remained in the hands of the landed aristocracy from the late seventeenth through the eighteenth and even into the nineteenth century (Cannon, 1984).

If the English Civil War is to be called a bourgeois revolution, it must be because the conflict set the stage for the economic emergence of the bourgeoisie. Both political power and social preeminence remained in the hands of the landed aristocracy. While the Marxist approach is of undoubted value in focusing attention on the discontinuities of change, especially on the decisive transformation of class relations, elaboration of the role of particular institutions and values inevitably draws on Weberian concepts.

The "open elite" view has a long history and a coterie of noted proponents, including Tocqueville (1955). This view assumes that the presumed acceptability of business for the English aristocracy resulted from the entrance of sons of commerce into its ranks. Yet there are even more serious difficulties with this view than with the Marxian. Stone and Stone (1984) have presented impressive empirical evidence indicating that this elite was not nearly so open as has been assumed. Further, the English aristocracy remained quite ambivalent about industrialization well into the nineteenth century (Mingay, 1976).

Did the English landed aristocracy aid in the emergence of industrial capitalism? Did the great English landlords acquiesce in this change, or did the wheels of history turn despite their efforts to hold them back? How can we understand the value structure of the English aristocracy that held merchants and industrialists in disdain while it advanced policies that promoted business and commerce? I will examine the value structure of the English landed aristocracy in order to understand its economic and social contributions to the transformation of the English feudal order to capitalism. The contrast with the French nobility will put the case of England in comparative perspective.

Status Ethics Require Consumption and Restrict Acquisition

The term "status ethic" refers to various norms governing the conduct of a status group. I am particularly concerned with norms of consumption and norms of acquisition. Certain expenditures are expected of members of a status group, but there is only a limited range of acquisitive practices that is acceptable to them. Aristocrats must live lavishly, but must not concern themselves with acquiring "filthy" lucre. As Weber defines a status group:

> In contrast to classes, status groups are normally communities. They are, however, often of an amorphous kind. In contrast to the purely economically determined "class situation" we wish to designate as "status situation" every typical component of the life fate of men that is determined by a specific,

positive or negative, social estimation of honor. . . . In content, status honor is normally expressed by the fact that above all else a specific style of life can be expected from those who wish to belong to the circle. (Weber, in Gerth and Mills, 1946:186–87)

A status ethic, then, includes a set of prescriptions and proscriptions relating to carrying out the style of life of the status group. For present purposes, acquisition encompasses all action that increases or is intended to increase the income or wealth of an individual or his or her family. Consumption encompasses all expenditures except those intended to increase income or wealth.

The distinction between acquisition and consumption is needed to avoid confusion about the nature and extent of the transformation of the values of the English landlords. It is clear that their attitudes concerning consumption remained firmly aristocratic: oriented to the conspicuous demonstration of status. The transformation of their values involved the limited acceptance of new approaches to acquiring money, and this change occurred precisely to provide the economic basis for their conspicuous consumption.

The aristocratic emphasis on display sets the group apart by indicating its power and social preeminence (Elias, 1983). The restrictions on acquisitive behavior, however, may be more difficult to understand. Why should a dominant group restrict itself from potential sources of income such as industry and trade? This question takes on particular interest in historical hindsight, for the acquisitive practices scorned by the aristocracies of Europe became the basis for riches beyond their imagination.

There is a religious element in the ambivalence toward money makers, as the Catholic Church has historically looked with disfavor on materialism (Weber, 1958; Nelson, 1969). However, the incompatibility of aristocracy and "mean" occupations dates back to ancient Greece, and thus is not simply an artifact of Christian theology (Finley, 1973; Weber, 1976). The aristocratic disdain for commerce and industry goes beyond a religious rejection of worldly affairs: it is a central aspect of its claim to purity, and high status.

The systematic pursuit of money interferes with the leisurely pursuits that distinguish the truly established from the merely wealthy. Being rich is the source of admiration, but *acquiring* great wealth makes one suspect because it is incompatible with a life devoted to refinement. Further, the aristocratic rejection of commerce originated at a time when the profitability of such endeavors was far smaller than that of a great estate.

There is a fair degree of autonomy between acquisition and consumption. For example, a group may display a systematic, calculating, and innovating attitude toward acquisition while maintaining a traditional pattern of consumption. Still, the notion of autonomy cannot be taken too far. Total expenditures cannot stray far beyond the limits of total income for very long, only as long as credit holds out. Thus, while attitudes concerning acquisition and consumption are somewhat independent, they also act as constraints on one another. Conspicuous consumption will quickly foil the most systematic and persistent attempts to accumulate wealth, as an empty purse will sooner or later frustrate the extravagant spender. However, the balance of income and expenditure that is of primary interest here is the balance for the status group as a whole. Individuals or families may fall out of the group without significantly lowering the expected levels of consumption for the remaining members. Only when the sources of income of the group as a whole fall, or the levels of consumption rise, are the values of the group modified.

If consumption and acquisition come to be imbalanced, how will the conflict be resolved? Will consumption fall into line with a lower level of acquisition, or will income, through unflagging efforts, be brought up to the level of expected expenditure? Is there autonomous movement of consumption that acquisition must follow? Or does consumption faithfully follow income, increasing as income increases but never acting as an independent agent?

This paper offers a framework for analyzing the choices status groups make in response to these dilemmas. I will argue that consumption may have an independent effect on acquisitive behavior. The demands of conspicuous consumption may help to create a more systematic, calculating concern for ways to increase income, as was evident in the English case. The group temporarily sacrifices one component of its status system in order to preserve the larger whole.

It is ironic that the demands of lavish aristocratic lifestyles—virtually the polar opposite of the Protestant work ethic that Weber described—made a historically important contribution to the emergence of the modern economic order. However, changes in accepted practices of acquisition, historically important or not, need not change the nature of a status group if these changes are designed to maintain other elements of the status ethic.

In the framework I am proposing, Weber's third element, political power, plays a role in helping to set the context for both status and economics. The conflict between nobility and monarchy is a central feature of

European politics, from the rise of the absolutist state through the First World War (Anderson, 1974; Mayer, 1981). The crown can be of decisive importance in the status maximization equation. By requiring attendance at court, for example, the king can preclude serious attention to details of estate administration while requiring major outlays for conspicuous display, as was the case in France under Louis XIV (Elias, 1983). Granting of titles was a constant source of concern to the European aristocracies, for it threatened the stability of the status hierarchy (Goodwin, 1967; Spring, 1977). Finally, the legal basis of noble status, including the extent of tax exemption, terms of inheritance, and enforcement of these regulations, were vital to the social standing of the landed nobility and central in their calculations of status. A more complete model of status groups would have to pay greater attention to the political role of the nobility that can be done here.

The Transformation of the English Landed Aristocracy

I will outline the principal elements of the status ethic of the English aristocracy as these existed in the sixteenth century. Subsequently, the effect of changing economic conditions on acquisition and consumption will be sketched. Finally, I will compare these developments with those of the French aristocracy.

The Peerage in England was a much smaller group than the titled French nobility. Moreover, membership in the Peerage did not carry the privilege of tax exemption as in most other European countries. Thus, it is appropriate to include the wealthiest gentry along with the Peerage in the English aristocracy. Many historians have made such a grouping on the basis of important similarities in the social situation of the gentry and the Peerage (Bush, 1984; Stone and Stone, 1984).

By the sixteenth century, the English aristocracy had long since lost its military role, and had become transformed into a landed nobility controlling local politics and influencing national affairs. Remnants of an ideology of chivalry remain to this day as part of the value orientation of English elites, but this is not of concern to this study.

It is not difficult to demonstrate that the great English landlords constituted a relatively unified status group. Several types of conspicuous consumption characterized this group. First, the great landlord was expected to own and maintain a great house.

> The other, unacknowledged, reason for extravagant building was in order to satisfy a lust for power, a thirst for admiration, an ambition to outstrip all rivals, and a wish to create a home suitable for the residence of a noble-man—a particularly urgent incentive to one whose patent was still fresh from the mint. (Stone, 1965:551–52)

A stay in London during "the season" was a second type of expected consumption. The annual stay in London, together with the ownership of a great house, has been described as the essential status symbol of this group. The practice developed in the late sixteenth century as London grew in economic and political importance, and was well established by the beginning of the seventeenth century (Fisher, 1948).

A third important aspect of the expected consumption of the great landlords was the education of its youth (Stone, 1977). Education is included as consumption because it constituted a considerable expenditure that helped to separate members of the group from outsiders. The English elite's commitment to education also distinguished it from many of the continental nobilities, many of whom remained poorly educated through the eighteenth century (Goodwin, 1967). Even before 1600, the practice of educating the sons, and sometimes even the daughters, of the aristocracy was prevalent. Whether educated by private tutors or at a university, followed by a stay at one of the Inns of Court or a tour of Europe, the aristocracy reinforced its distinctive social position by conferring the refinements of education on its youth.

The English aristocracy was also characterized by certain expected methods of acquisition. The predominant source of income was the reliance on rent from landholdings. The English landlord was expected to be paternalistic toward his peasants, coming to their assistance in difficult times. The land provided great security, but typically only relatively modest rates of return on investment.

A second characteristically noble method of acquisition was the courting of royal favor. Most of the truly large landed fortunes were acquired, at least in part, in this fashion. Such a tactic, however, required a heavy outlay that was difficult to limit once begun. Frequently, the would-be favorite left the court far worse off than when he arrived (Habakkuk, 1967; Stone, 1965:445).

A third aspect of aristocratic attitudes concerning acquisition is related to marriage. Endogamy is often seen as the defining characteristic of a status group. Yet the emphasis on a proper marriage had pronounced economic implications. The landed aristocracy preferred to marry its children to other members of the squirearchy, while a marriage to a merchant family might bring with it a sizeable fortune. The practice of marrying for money was always present, but was viewed with varying degrees of disfavor. This disfavor was relaxed during periods of economic stress, as were other components of the acquisition ethic. Marriage also involves a specific type of expected consumption. Expenses for jointures and dowries were among the most difficult burdens for the aristocracy to bear (Mingay, 1976; Stone, 1977).

Industrial activities, including coal mining and iron smelting, were considered an acceptable part of the exploitation of one's estate. The great landlords invested in canals and other commercial ventures, as is often noted. Yet the income from such sources rarely amounted to more than a modest percent of an aristocrat's income. Investment in certain business ventures was more compatible with elite status than was active management of a business enterprise. Although there may not have been a clear prohibition of industrial and commercial activity, these sources of income could hardly compete for prestige with the rolling acres of an estate (Mingay, 1976; Stone, 1965: 335–85; Habakkuk, 1967: 6).

In the sixteenth century there began a period of sustained inflation. Prices rose 500 percent between 1500 and 1650 (Goldstone, 1984). This inflation seems to have been caused partly by the influx of precious metals from America and partly by a swelling population, although Goldstone emphasizes the increased velocity of money produced by growing commerce.

What was the effect of this inflation on the great landlords? The aristocracy by and large received its income from rents set at customary levels. In a period of inflation, reliance on relatively fixed sources of income creates a decline in real income. Given this situation, either traditional consumption patterns must be sacrificed or a new method of acquisition found.

Income from royal favor remained inadequate to fill the gap until after 1602, and even then large sums and privileges were conferred on just a few families. Marriage took on an increasingly economic character. The aristocracy began to invest in industry and commerce in a limited way. Most significantly, the landed aristocracy began to rationalize estate management. The paternalistic character of landlord-tenant relations gave way to more careful calculation of profit and loss, to increasing rents, entry fines, and enclosures (Stone, 1965: 307, 375–81, 504).

The growth of markets created financial difficulties for the aristocracy but also offered them a solution. The decline in noble incomes coincided with new opportunities for growth. However, to take advantage of these opportunities, the proscription of certain types of acquisition had to be overcome. Paternalism toward tenants, preference for status over wealth in marriage, reluctance to participate in commerce and industry—all these components of the noble code of honor gave some ground during this period.

Standards of consumption were preserved at the expense of certain rules of acquisition. In fact, there is some evidence to suggest that the level of extravagance increased during this period. The epidemic of house building, an increase in the size of dowries, and the growth of importance of the London "season" appeared at the same time that the traditional sources of income were being undermined (Stone, 1965:550; Fisher, 1948; Mingay, 1963:59–76).

There is a debate among historians of the English Civil War as to whether or not noble incomes actually declined (Stone, 1973). The present argument assumes a marked decline, but does not depend on a "crisis" in incomes or a subsequent crisis in power and influence of this group. There were some landlords who were more responsive than others to the new market situation. The general level of income of this group would not suffer as dramatic a decline as would those individuals who lagged behind.

One statistic, however, does merit particular attention. The greatest landlords, those with the largest holdings and the most wealth, did not continue to emphasize acquisitions after they had secured a level of income sufficient to sustain their social position. Stone reports:

> There was little sign of active accumulation of more landed capital by the greater families, a policy which was well within their means. There was a financial plateau between 6,000 and 10,000 pounds a year which was ample for all reasonable needs and at which most great families were content to rest. Once arrived at this level by diligent exploitation of what they possessed, they used their income to maintain status rather than to save and reinvest so as to hoist themselves to new heights of affluence. (1965:162)

Acquisitiveness in this group was instrumental for the realizations of status goals, but did not constitute the primary driving force for change. If a landlord would cease to pursue a perfectly accepted mode of acquisition when his status was insured, it is not difficult to believe that nobles would pursue less favored activities only for as long as they needed the added income to preserve their position.

In Weber's terms, the landed elite, while creating agrarian capitalism, did not develop the "spirit of capitalism" that Puritanism bequeathed to the middle classes. The relentless, systematic pursuit of economic gain remained foreign to the orientation of English landed society, even as late as the nineteenth century. Rationalized estate management, so closely related to the fostering of agrarian capitalism, was adopted as part of an effort to preserve an aristocratic ethic. This group remained pre-capitalist in its value orientation, even while it instituted capitalist economic relations and provided a crucial stimulus to the emergence of a capitalist society.

The situation stabilized somewhat after the Restoration. The modified consumption and acquisition patterns of the early seventeenth century became entrenched. The nobility was able to moderate the level of extravagance somewhat with the development of the strict settlement. Prices began to rise again after 1750, with a steady increase in the population pushing up food costs. The English aristocracy was now in a position to take advantage of price increases by adjusting rents upward and enclosing more land. Enclosure increased the value of land two- to threefold by allowing the tenant to use more productive techniques. Enclosure, was, indeed, an expected response from landlords who had become accustomed to calculating in terms of market prices.

The substantial profit now obtained from agriculture was not reinvested in a profit-maximizing manner. Instead, profits were spent to increase consumption. The evidence suggests a sharp increase in conspicuous consumption after 1780 (Habakkuk, 1967:10; Habakkuk, 1979–81; Mingay, 1963:48). Thus, acquisitive behavior for this group can only be understood in light of the consumption patterns expected of it. Consumption and acquisition constrain one another: both must be considered if the economic behavior of the aristocracy (or any group) is to be understood.

The lifestyle of the nineteenth-century English landed elite is further evidence for the usefulness of this framework. Far from adopting bourgeois manners, nineteenth-century English landlords maintained and elaborated a country lifestyle far removed from middle class values. They were not averse to profiting from the burgeoning industrial economy, as their investments in railroads and other commercial ventures attests. However, they were unlikely to pursue venture capitalism very far, and failed to dominate industries such as coal mining in which they had been early participants. The profitability of English agriculture provided a sufficient economic base for leisure pursuits until the 1870s when a prolonged depression quickly followed by political reform changed the terms of English agriculture forever (Thompson, 1963; Mingay, 1976; Stone and Stone, 1984).

A long lineage is a status resource employed by aristocratic groups, even when the lineage in question may be quite recent. In his study of the English Peerage, Cannon found that relatively few families maintained a representation in the Peerage for as many as four generations (Cannon, 1984: 224). The great prestige of tradition was a status resource that all landed elite could draw on, even if a particular family's prominence was of recent vintage.

Yet the circulation of elites should not be understood to imply the unique openness of the English landed classes. Cannon notes that most entrants were scions of well established families, not founders of commercial fortunes. Stone and Stone have emphasized the limited mobility of founders of commercial fortunes into the higher reaches of English landed society. Recent historical accounts have emphasized the similarity in the rate of social mobility for English and continental landed elites (Cannon, 1984; Bush, 1984).

The English landed elites played a decisive role in the emergence of capitalism in transforming the countryside from a feudal to a capitalist system. Whereas feudalism rested on a set of mutual rights and obligations between lord and serf, capitalist agriculture paired independent owners and workers with no mutual obligations other than contractual ones. The decisive change was not cash versus in-kind payments, but the freedom of landholders to maximize their returns from the land, and the freedom of the agricultural workers to take whatever position paid the most. The transformation of agriculture was the precondition for the development of the industrial proletariat. As rationalized agricultural production produced a surplus of agricultural goods to feed the cities, so it produced a surplus of laborers to run the factories. The enclosure of common lands was part of a general movement to change peasants into agricultural wage laborers, a first step on the road to the industrial factory.

Why did English magnates rationalize their estate management and engage in enclosing the commons lands on such an extensive scale? English elites were able to enclose the commons partly because they were the local magistrates; as such they were in a position to advance the interests of the landed aristocracy. The weakness of the crown in protecting the peasantry was no doubt a crucial condition which facilitated this transfer. Of secondary importance was the absence of legal boundaries between the English landed elite and other social strata. Since there were no special tax exemptions linked to a titular nobility, as in most continental nobilities, the rationalization of estates was not encumbered by complication of land changing juridical status as it changed hands.

Thus the English landed classes primarily played a role in the transformation of the countryside. However, the English aristocracy acted more because there were structural opportunities for change than from a distinctive value orientation. As we will see in the comparison with the French pattern, there is a similarity in motives if not outcomes.

The response of the English elite to the crisis of declining incomes in the sixteenth and seventeenth centuries was unique in its consequences, but the framework developed here will apply to other European nobilities as well. Let us turn to the French case for comparison.

The French Nobility

The French nobility was a large group with a complex system of social ranking. There were three major legal divisions: the *noblesse d'épée*, the members the military caste turned into a landed aristocracy; the *noblesse de robe*, the officers of the sovereign courts; and the *noblesse de cloche*, the municipal officials. The three groups shared the common privilege of exemptions from taxes (the *taille*). The nobles increasingly monopolized the higher positions in the army and the church. There was no English group quite comparable to the *noblesse de robe*, and an analysis of the unique economic and political situation of this group would divert the course of our presentation (Ford, 1965; Chaussinand-Nogaret, 1985; Elias, 1983).

Within the French nobility there existed widely disparate levels of income. As the split between court and country was much greater in France than in England, it might be appropriate to consider the gilded nobility and the provincial nobility as two separate but related groups.

The level of extravagance of the provincial nobility in France could not compare with that in England or Versailles. This fact, however, does not mean that the provincial nobility did not constitute a status group. In the context of the provinces their style of life was extravagant. More important, the expenditure of this group was intended for display, and as such can reasonably be termed conspicuous consumption.

The information on the provincial noble is rather sketchy. One study of the city of Toulouse has helped to fill this gap (Forster, 1960). The nobles in Toulouse enjoyed unchallenged social preeminence during the seventeenth century. They typically owned a summer and a winter home, had four to six servants, a pantry and an extensive wardrobe, and could afford an occasional trip to the seashore. The average noble in Toulouse had his own library, which suggests a fair degree of education. This portrait undoubtedly varied from region to region in France.

The provincial noble obtained the bulk of his income from the land. Sharecropping arrangements prevailed over most of France, although regional variations in practice abounded. It is difficult to discern any specific practices which were frowned upon in the administration of estates. The paternalism of England was much less evident. There seemed to be no inhibition concerning selling the produce of the land on the market.

Provincial nobles who had fallen into destitution sought assistance from the crown, perhaps to place a son in the army or the church, or to grant some direct aid. The crown was seen as "necessary, because without it poverty was usually inescapable" (Behrens, 1967:58). Resorting to marriage of a non-noble for financial gain was considered somewhat of a last resort to serious difficulty (Barber, 1955:99–106): this practice was viewed as a way for "old stock to 'manure its lands'" (Chaussinand-Nogaret, 1985:123).

The aspect of the aristocratic acquisition ethic that most significantly restricted their income was in the area of industry and commerce. Derogeance, the formal loss of title, was the possible consequence of engaging in occupations thought unfitting for a noble. The institution could not exist in England in a formal sense because there was no juridical status to lose, but was common in other European monarchies (Goodwin, 1967).

How did this system originate? In 1561 and 1583 the French monarchs issued proclamations prohibiting nobles from engaging in retail trade or manual labor, on pain of losing noble status. One explanation for these rules was that the crown wanted to protect merchants from the difficult task of competing against noble businessmen who would be tax exempt. The crown thus preserved commerce as a source of income. Another view is that the enactment of formal rules in this era was a product of renewed interest in Roman law, which had similar provisions. A third view is that derogeance was a creation of the nobility itself for the purposes of justifying its tax exempt status and for defending its honor against the claims of the nouveaux riches (Forster, 1960; Grassby, 1960). If this last view is correct, it would suggest that the nobility did not foresee the extent to which commercial fortunes would rise nor did they see that they would require more flexibility than this restriction would allow.

Whatever the historical roots of derogeance, it is clear that the support of the nobility was instrumental in its continued effect. The poverty-stricken rural nobles resisted the opportunities available in commerce and industry to preserve their status. Mining, again considered a legitimate part of estate exploitation, was exempt from derogation and was carried out mainly under royal monopolies. Glassmaking was also exempt, probably due to the interest of the crown in promoting artistic products (Mc-Manners, 1967; Nef, 1940; Foster, 1950; Moore, 1965).

The nobility of Paris and Versailles were more unified by the expected manner of consumption than by the expected manner of acquisition, the reverse of the provincial situation. Louis XIV undercut the political position of the nobility, and brought many of the wealthiest and most powerful to Versailles to compete for social position and royal favor. Yet it was not solely the court that was responsible for extravagance. Presentation at Versailles required proof of lineage dating before 1400. This requirement excluded many who had more recently attained high social position. These great nobles gathered in Paris. The ostentatious lifestyle of the Parisian salons may have been comparable to that of Versailles. Education was increasingly important in the life of the gilded nobility since wit held priority in the salons.

A high level of income was required to preserve such levels of consumption. The gilded nobility was thus greatly concerned with making money, but not with its sordid details. The bulk of income came from a variety of feudal dues collected from the peasants who worked the land by agents.

> The prejudice against trying to make money out of farming was probably very influential among the highest nobility and those subject even less directly to the mores of court life. A life of strenuous indolence and intrigue at Versailles would certainly be vastly more exciting than superintending cows and peasants, and would soon teach a man to be embarrassed at the smell of manure on his boots. (Moore, 1965:44)

The inefficiency in agricultural administration was thus less a case of paternalism than of disdain directed to showing active attention to moneymaking. Land was inherited through a system of entailments similar to that in England, although somewhat less rigid, and with a less pronounced emphasis on primogeniture.

A second source of income was the crown itself. The enforced conspicuous consumption of the court impoverished many of the great nobles. The crown thus increased its power over the nobility, conferring favors and grants on whom it pleased. Marriage with rich merchant heiresses was viewed with the same ambivalence for this group as for their country counterparts.

Increases in prices in the sixteenth and seventeenth centuries occurred throughout Europe and affected France as well. The position of the French nobility was already weakened by the deaths and expense of the Thirty Years War. Reliance on the inelastic base of feudal dues during this inflationary period undermined the solvency of the French nobles. The crown courts did not allow charges and fines to be changed into flexible rents. The French aristocracy responded by increasing the intensity with which the dues were collected. Precedents were discovered on which to base additional charges (Bloch, 1970).

The differences in outcomes between English and French agriculture are thus best understood with reference to the structural positions of these two groups. The same pressures that led to agrarian capitalism in England produced an intensification of feudalism in France. This explanation is consistent with the provocative and influential analysis of Brenner (1976; 1982). Yet economic change is not an automatic response to circumstance. The model proposed here provides a context in which to understand the motives of the groups involved.

The prohibitions on commerce and industry were modified as the economy developed. The gilded nobility was more active in these areas. The typical case, however, involved investment, not management, and even the investments were often concealed. The policy of the crown on derogeance was ambivalent. It wanted a prosperous nobility, but not one with an economic base independent of the crown. Through a series of halting steps, the crown decided in favor of increasing national wealth. In 1701, restrictions on trade, on land as well as sea, were lifted. Yet, the nobles did not respond well to these new opportunities. The belief that certain practices are inherently degrading is not easily dispelled. "Fifty years after Colbert the only possibility was for a merchant to become a noble, not the reverse" (Barber, 1955:52). The crown initially reinforced the bias against commerce, but the perpetuation of the value was reinforced by the nobility itself.

In the eighteenth century the French nobility increasingly accepted marriages with wealthy commoners. However, this pattern of intermarriage increased despite the persistence of status differences, not because these differences had disappeared.

> The tendency towards noble endogamy was offset by the need to rebuild compromised fortunes, by the narrow range of choice, and by the social importance of a middle-class elite who lorded it in the towns. Marriage be-

tween nobles, however, remained the norm which was not flouted except with extreme care. (Chaussinand-Nogaret, 1985:127)

I have characterized the nobility as status maximizers, not profit maximizers. They were willing to forego certain base acquisitive activities if the proceeds were insufficient to purchase more status than was lost through participation in such activities. They would venture into unacceptable fields if those ventures held the promise of revitalizing their ability to spend lavishly. The provincial nobles stood to gain less income and lose more status by their participation in petty retailing and small-scale manufacture than the gilded nobles by their underwriting overseas trading ventures. Thus, the more liberal attitude of the gilded nobles toward commerce and industry becomes comprehensible.

Throughout the eighteenth century the income of both groups probably rose moderately, due primarily to squeezing increasing amounts of profit out of agriculture (McManners, 1967; Forster, 1960). The French aristocracy reinvigorated feudalism even as its English counterpart helped to set the stage for the industrial revolution. A desire to solve the same dilemma—maintaining the aristocratic status structure—led the English to become capitalist farmers, while the French intensified the feudal system in the waning years of the ancien régime.

Discussion

The division of values into a consumption ethic and an acquisition ethic is a useful way to analyze the evolution of economic attitudes of these aristocracies. Regulations on acquisition were somewhat flexible, more in agriculture than in commerce and industry. Evidence of this flexibility does not demonstrate that the professed standards were a sham, nor does it show that the view of the aristocracy on economic issues in general had changed. Consumption and acquisition constrain one another: each provides the context in which the other operates. Status-based consumption patterns can foster changes in acquisitive behavior.

This formulation resolves a number of unfortunate complications in the normal discussion of the emergence of the modern economic order. It shows that the transformation of aristocratic values is not necessary for the aristocracy to contribute to economic change: it is precisely the attempt to preserve its status ethic that prompted the aristocracy to transform the countryside. The structural position of the English landed aristocracy, its ability to transform the nature of social relations in agriculture, enabled it to play a progressive historical role.

Moore considered the English Civil War a bourgeois revolution by emphasizing the transformation of the English landed elites into a capitalist elite. But he then restored the schism between landed and commercial interests in order to account for the nature of eighteenth- and nineteenth-century English politics. The problem is solved by noting that this status group changed its economic base without changing its status-group character. This framework helps to clarify the relationship between landed and industrial interests: there was a congruence of class position between industrialists and agriculturalists, even as a huge social chasm between them remained.

Weber observed that the spirit of capitalism may be threatened by its own success (Weber, 1958). The relentless pursuit of profit is a peculiarly ascetic approach to acquisition. It is a pursuit which, if truly single-minded, resists the temptation to enjoy the fruits of one's acquisitions. Weber noted that such asceticism may not withstand the unparalleled prosperity that modern industrial society produces, and that over time capitalism may give way to hedonism. Bell (1978) worries that the incompatibility of the hedonistic orientation of leisure pursuits and the strict economic calculus of the productive sphere has created a fundamental tension in modern capitalist society.

I am suggesting something slightly different. The continuity of aristocratic values results not in hedonism but in a desire to distance oneself from acquisitiveness. By all accounts, after 1880 English businessmen succeeded in entering the landed gentry and buying up country houses, if not maintaining the massive estates which were rapidly becoming an economic burden (Stone and Stone, 1984; F. M. L. Thompson, 1963). It has been suggested that this pattern of mobility tended to limit economic growth in England, as the energies of the business elite were directed to acquiring social prestige rather than expanding their holdings (Wiener, 1981). The durability of the English landed aristocracy through the nineteenth century may have contributed to the industrial decline of England in the twentieth. The lingering prestige of aristocratic living may have dampened the motivation for economic enterprise. A similar ambivalence toward acquisitive behavior may have contributed to the relative slow growth of France in the nineteenth century.

Paradoxically, it was the very gulf between aristocratic values and the emergence of the Protestant work ethic among the English middle class that constituted a powerful impetus to capitalist development. Rather than encouraging economic growth, a relatively open landed nobility would tend to draw money and energy out of enterprise and into their own rentier class. The contrast with the eighteenth and early nineteenth century is striking: not only did relatively few English businessmen enter the higher echelons of the English gentry but those that did often sojourned only briefly with the country aristocrats (Stone and Stone, 1984). The business elite were not thoroughly imbued with aristocratic values.

The contrast between tradition and modernity is thus overdrawn. Traditional elites were capable of transforming their acquisitive orientations, but seemed less able to transform their desire for social preeminence. The latter changed its form, from chivalrous knight to country lord and eventually to London gentleman. The emergence of a spirit of systematic acquisitiveness was not a permanent feature of modernity, as this can be transformed into hedonism or aristocratic elitism with equal facility.

I am optimistic about the applicability of this framework to other aristocratic groups. Each would require a detailed analysis because the economic and political position of each differed. Yet there are similarities in the dilemmas faced by Belgian (Clark, 1985) and other European aristocracies (Spring, 1976). My emphasis on the continuity in the value orientation of the aristocracy is broadly consistent with Mayer's emphasis on the continued political influence of the European aristocracies through the First World War (1981). Azarya's fascinating account of the Fulbe aristocracy in West Africa also strikes a responsive chord (1978). In all of these cases the continuity of aristocratic status and lifestyles is primary; these groups search for an economic base compatible with this goal. A thorough comparative analysis of aristocratic groups must be left for further studies.

References

Anderson, Perry. *Lineages of the Absolutist State*. New York: New Left Books, 1974.

Azarya, Victor. *Aristocrats Facing Change: The Fulbe in Guinea, Nigeria, and Cameroon*. Chicago: University of Chicago Press, 1978.

Barber, Elinor G., *The Bourgeoisie in Eighteenth Century France*. Princeton, N.J.: Princeton University Press, 1955.

Behrens, C. B. A. *The Ancien Régime*. London: Harcourt, Brace and World, 1967.

Bell, Daniel. *The Cultural Contradictions of Capitalism*. New York: Basic Books, 1978.

Bloch, Marc. *French Rural History: An Essay on Its Basic Characteristics*. Los Angeles: UCLA Press, 1970.

Brenner, Robert. "Agrarian Class Structure and Economic Development in Pre-Industrial Europe." *Past and Present* 70(1976): 30–74.

———. "Agrarian Roots of European Capitalism." *Past and Present* 97(1982): 16–113.

Bush, M. L. *The English Aristocracy: A Comparative Synthesis*. Manchester: Manchester University Press, 1984.

Cannon, John. *Aristocratic Century: The Peerage of Eighteenth Century England*. Cambridge: Cambridge University Press, 1984.

Chaussinand-Nogaret, Guy. *The French Nobility in the Eighteenth Century*, trans. William Doyle. Cambridge: Cambridge University Press, 1985.

Clark, Samuel. "Nobility, Bourgeoisie and the Industrial Revolution in Belgium." *Past and Present* 105 (1985): 140–75.

Elias, Norbert. *The Court Society*, trans. Edmund Jephcott. New York: Pantheon, 1983.

Finley, M. I. *The Ancient Economy*. Berkeley: University of California Press, 1973.

Fisher, F. J. "The Development of London as a Center of Conspicuous Consumption in the Sixteenth and Seventeenth Centuries." *Transactions of the Royal Historical Society*, 4th Series XXX (1948): 37–50.

Ford, Franklin L. *Robe and Sword: The Regrouping of the French Aristocracy After Louis XIV*. New York: Harper and Row, 1965.

Foster, Charles. *Honoring Commerce and Industry in Eighteenth Century France*. Ph.D. dissertation, Harvard University, 1950.

Forster, Robert. *The Nobility of Toulouse in the Eighteenth Century*. Baltimore: Johns Hopkins University Press, 1960.

Gerth, Hans and C. Wright Mills, eds. *From Max Weber*. Oxford: Oxford University Press, 1949.

Goldstone, Jack A. "Urbanization and Inflation: Lessons from the English Price Revolution of the Sixteenth and Seventeenth Centuries." *American Journal of Sociology* 89(1984): 1122–60.

———. "State Breakdown in the English Revolution: A New Synthesis." *American Journal of Sociology* 92(2)(1986): 257–32.

Goodwin, A., ed. *The European Nobility in the Eighteenth Century*. New York: Harper and Row, 1967.

Grassby, R. B. "Social Status and Commercial Enterprise under Louis XIV." *Economic History Review*, Second Series XIII (1960): 19–38.

Habakkuk, H. J. "The Rise and Fall of English Landed Families, 1600–1800." *Transactions of the Royal Historical Society*, 5th Series, 29–31(1979–81)[29: 195–217, 30: 199–221, 31: 187–207].

———. "England." In A. Goodwin, ed., *The European Nobility in the Eighteenth Century*. New York: Harper and Row, 1967.

———. "Marriage Settlements in the Eighteenth Century." *Transactions of the Royal Historical Society*, 4th Series XXXII (1950): 15–19.

Hexter, J. H. "Storm over the Gentry." In J. H. Hexter, *Reappraisals in History*. Evanston, Ill.: Northwestern University Press, 1961.

Mayer, Arno J. *The Persistence of the Old Regime: Europe to The Great War*. New York: Pantheon, 1981.

McManners, J. "France." In A. Goodwin, ed., *The European Nobility in the Eighteenth Century*. New York: Harper and Row, 1967.

Mingay, G. E. *English Landed Society in the Eighteenth Century*. Toronto: University of Toronto Press, 1963.

———. *The Gentry: The Rise and Fall of a Ruling Class*. London: Longmann, 1976.

Moore, Barrington. *The Social Origins of Dictatorship and Democracy*. Boston: Beacon Press, 1966.

Nef, J. U. *Industry and Government in France and England, 1540–1640*. Lancaster, Pa.: Lancaster Press, 1940.

Nelson, Benjamin. *The Idea of Usury*. Second Edition. Chicago: University of Chicago Press, 1969.

Spring, D. *European Landed Elites in the Nineteenth Century*. Baltimore: Johns Hopkins University Press, 1977.

Stone, Lawrence. *The Crisis of the Aristocracy, 1558–1641*. Oxford: Oxford University Press, 1973.

———. *Family and Fortune: Studies in Aristocratic Finance in the Sixteenth and Seventeenth Centuries*. Oxford: Oxford University Press, 1973.

———. *Family, Sex and Marriage in England, 1500–1800*. London: Harper and Row, 1977.

———. "The Bourgeois Revolution of Seventeenth Century England." *Past and Present* 109(1985): 44–54.

Stone, Lawrence and Jeanne C. Fawtier Stone. *An Open Elite? England 1540–1880*. Oxford: Clarendon Press.

Thompson, F. M. L. *English Landed Society in the Nineteenth Century*. London: Routledge & Kegan Paul, 1963.

Tocqueville, Alexis de. *The Old Regime and the French Revolution*, trans. Stuart Gilbert. New York: Doubleday, 1955.

Veblen, Thorstein. *The Theory of the Leisure Class: An Economic Study of Institutions*. New York: B. W. Huebsch, 1918.

Weber, Max. *The Protestant Ethic and the Spirit of Capitalism*, trans. Talcott Parsons. New York: Charles Scribner and Sons, 1948.

———. *Agrarian Sociology of Ancient Civilization*. trans. R. I. Frank. New Highlands, N.J.: Humanities Press, 1976.

Wiener, M. J. *English Culture and the Decline of the Industrial Spirit, 1850–1980*. Cambridge: Cambridge University Press, 1981.

Harold J. Bershady

10. The Cities of Nations: A Comparative View*

Introduction

European tourists who have traveled widely in the United States often remark on differences between American cities and their own. The recent founding of American cities in comparison to the long history of many of the European ones is commonly mentioned. Also noted is the stark contrast of new and old in American cities for which there is no real counterpart in Europe—the proliferation of new shopping centers, office buildings, parking lots, sporting and entertainment facilities, restaurants, and houses in some parts of a city and the decay of abandoned factories, empty warehouses, dilapidated houses, and filthy potholed streets in others. The contrast between new and old in American cities corresponds to the contrast between rich and poor, with the rich living in new housing, the poor in old. European cities also have slums, but housing arrangements are often the reverse of the American—either the poor are in the newer housing or rich and poor alike live in old, if differently appointed, quarters. Moreover, the immense scale of building and *re*building in American cities, none of which has been devastated by war, is cited by European visitors as testimony to the fact that America is indeed a rich nation, as they have heard.

There is, however, more to the difference between American and European cities than any of these observations brings out. European visitors also note that the hustle and bustle of American cities, the pace of activity even in smaller ones and in so-called sleepy towns, exceeds by far that of most European cities—with the exception of the great metropolises: Paris, London, Rome, Amsterdam, Copenhagen, Berlin. But these are world cities, as is New York, for whose characterization national stereotypes are inadequate. Further, the ethnic diversity of American cities of even moderate size (population about 200,000)—the Polish, Irish, black, Greek,

Italian, German, Hispanic, Slavic, Jewish, Scandinavian, Asian neighbor-hoods—is found only, and then rarely to the same extent, in the European metropolises. The inhabitants of American cities, large or small, are "city-centric," as it were, and often act as though their city were the world, independent of other cities as well as of the nation. However, this indepen-dence, as Americans know, is only one side; the intense rivalry between American cities, for example, in sporting contests, implies they are also keenly aware of one another. But even this more visible intercity awareness usually takes several weeks to decipher, longer than the average tourist's stay. As is said by many Europeans in an effort to summarize their Ameri-can experiences, it is a difference between the American way of life and the European. There is a truth to this cliché which American tourists voice equally often when they are in Europe. But of what does this truth consist?

Although not addressed to this question, the comparisons made by E. Digby Baltzell in *Puritan Boston and Quaker Philadelphia* can put light on it.[1] Baltzell traced the stamp of two Protestant ethics on the character of the two cities. In part, his book was a jeremiad, excoriating the failure of Philadelphians, who cultivate the pleasures of private well being, to enter national life and of Bostonians, so self-assured if not arrogant in their leadership, to be responsive to achievements of others. But the book was much more. However different Philadelphia is from Boston—and many who have lived in both cities acknowledge Baltzell's book captured sharp cultural differences—it is nevertheless remarkable that so many of the *same* measures could be taken of each. Consider merely the kinds of facilities, not their quality or ethos, Philadelphia and Boston have in common: a great number of churches, synagogues and temples of each denomination of the major faiths, universities and colleges, professional schools, sym-phony orchestra, ballet and opera companies, theatres, art museums, sports teams, hospitals, libraries, banks, radio and television stations, news-papers, public parks, civic associations, charitable agencies, chambers of commerce—to mention merely the more prominent. If not for the fact these cities are so similar Baltzell would have been unable to draw so many comparisons between them. Can similar comparisons be made of other American cities?

Philadelphia and Boston are old, large in numbers and hundreds of miles apart. A certain amount of duplication is to be expected. Yet even smaller, younger cities, nearer to one another, are constantly being com-pared in newspaper and magazine articles, television and radio programs to larger, older cities—not necessarily for the want of facilities that the larger cities have, although often in this too, but in the degree to which their hospitals, schools, musical organizations, sporting grounds, museums, parks, among other things, measure up to those of the larger cities. In whatever city they live, large or small, Americans want for their city the things other cities have. This desire is, I believe, the spur for a great many of the physical and cultural changes that take place in American cities. It is as though Americans' belief in equality—that the "little guy," and by extension the little city, are as good and deserving as the "big guy" and big city—has given them a sense of entitlement acted upon whenever it can be afforded. But this anti-elite attitude also means that Americans view their cities as individual entities, worthy in their own right.

American cities are among the major institutions of American life. They have the right to own buildings and land, employ persons, regulate trade, tax their citizens, and not least, pass and enforce laws. They are largely responsible for the well-being of their citizens—their health, education, conditions of livelihood, recreation, safety. They are chartered by federal, state, and county law, but only under carefully regulated conditions is their jurisdiction over their own territories and facilities partly ceded to other governing bodies. They are a separate, legitimate form of government. The institutional character of American cities proper—not simply of the facilities in their territories, but the fact that American cities are the rightful possessors and regulators of these facilities—is, I think, one of the features that most sharply differentiates them from the European. If these propositions are true, the measures taken of Boston and Philadelphia by Baltzell are likely applicable to a great many other American cities.

Individuality, Equality, and Achievement in America

Several salient characteristics of the American outlook were surveyed by two of the more famous, sharp-eyed travelers to the United States, Alexis de Tocqueville, fifty years after the founding of the republic, and Max Weber, at the turn of the twentieth century.[2] Their well-known studies inform much of Baltzell's work. A few of the main points and implications of these studies will be summarized here as they figure in the analysis to follow.

In Tocqueville's view, Americans were driven by an equalitarian passion to eliminate differences in wealth, privilege, power and status. Such hierarchies were—and are—not suffered long or in silence. Continual efforts were made to curb the powerful and trim the rich. But the equalitarian aim was not merely to bring down the high; more important was to improve the lot of the weak and poor. The extent to which Americans endeavor to achieve a democratic condition among their citizens in social, moral, educational, political and economic spheres has been explored by native scholars ever since.[3]

However, equalitarian standards in American life have not just inspired the effort to level differences. Equality has also been interpreted to apply to opportunities and rights. This second principle of equality serves as a standard of fairness, and its violation, sooner or later, is protested. In its terms the civil rights and women's movements were launched and gained legitimacy. In its terms also entrance to political life was shifted from the holding of private wealth to party membership and service, admission to elite colleges from standards of privilege to standards of merit, funding of school tuition from family resources to government grants and loans, provision of infant care and health services from predominantly private to public facilities, job training from the exclusive apprenticeship pattern to programs for the generally unskilled—to mention a few notable examples.[4] But equality of opportunities and rights does not imply equality of results; in the application of this principle different outcomes may be expected. Thus, equality of opportunity supports another, related principle, the principle of individuality.[5] However, given the high value placed upon equality of conditions, individual differences in achievement are often viewed ambivalently. Superior achievements of individuals are accepted as legitimate only if there have been equal opportunities for their attainment. Although distinct and sometimes in conflict, the principles of equality and individuality are firmly bound together.

Americans are problem solvers. They seek to improve the situations in which they live, and their situations are ever changing. Weber saw in the Americans' zeal to find better solutions to their problems a secular version of earlier religious, specifically Puritan, injunctions. But the individual was not moved to master the world and complete God's work solely out of religious duty or the hope of attaining salvation, powerful though these reasons were. Weber also observed that successful achievements—good works—were among the major ways Americans had of participating in a community and gaining social esteem.[6] However, as the need for new achievements was reborn with each change in situation, one's social esteem had constantly to be won anew. The Americans' penchant for self improvement that Europeans remark upon—whether in body, mind, habits, neighborhood, city, or nation—is not solely an expression of their sense of entitlement to such things, but in part also driven by the dual needs to better themselves and the world and to gain esteem.

Tocqueville and Weber were struck by the ubiquity of these attitudes, the fact that wherever they traveled in the nation, among different religious sects, communities, and groups, each person to whom they spoke, regardless of attainments or station, held individuality, equality, and achievement among their dearest values. However rooted in Puritanism they may once have been, these values were no longer the expression of one, or indeed of any, religious view, but part of a general secular morality. The characterization of the culture of the United States and the attitudes of the individual citizens in this broad way has become a commonplace of sociohistorical analysis.

In respect to their cities, small, large, prominent or obscure, Tocqueville observed, these attitudes have produced among Americans a "booster" spirit. Independent and equal, not oppressed by others, the American is more readily attached to his or her city and its interests, and cooperates with fellow citizens in endlessly improving the city's welfare. The sharpest contrast to this restless American spirit is found among the inhabitants of many European cities who have neither the right nor the inclination to enter into and affect the course of civic life.[7]

The Symbolism of American Cities

Baltzell's methodological innovation was, in part, to treat Philadelphia and Boston as individuals and the nation as the community of which they are constituents. In this way, he could compare the extent of certain contributions each city made to the national community and also the esteem in which it was held.

To treat cities as individuals is to suppose they have distinctive identities. But if each city is genuinely unique, different in kind from all others, it is not possible to compare cities along the same dimensions. This is an elementary logical point equivalent to the hoary dilemma of attempting to compare apples and oranges; the final arbiter of such a comparison cannot be a common measure, but, perhaps, taste.

All cities in the United States have many features in common, although these features occur in varying degrees. It is in the degree these features occur, I believe, that much, if not all, of the uniqueness of each city can be found. Thus, although the Puritan culture of Boston places a high premium on a variety of individual achievements, this does not mean these achievements are without value, and not represented, in Quaker Philadelphia or in other American cities. It is because there is a common value on achievements in learning, science, and law that Boston, in its long-standing excellence in such things, can serve as a national symbol of them. Thus too, the Quaker culture of Philadelphia prizes equality of persons and groups, and the city is to the nation a chief incarnation of this value. This is not solely because Philadelphia was the site of the writing of the Declaration of Independence and the Constitution. Philadelphia has been known from its beginnings as a domicile for strangers, and this reputation continues to be exemplified in the variety of its churches, the preponderance of its family dwellings, and the *relatively* peaceful coexistence of its numerous ethnic inhabitants. These too are "achievements" commonly valued. As Tocqueville, Weber, and other investigators have found, individuality and equality, represented in extreme measure by Boston and Philadelphia, cannot be ranked, one placed over the other, but stand as independently sustained values in our national culture.

The two cities have specialized, as it were, divided the labor of representing these values to the national community. Sociologists have long known that each community, small or large, requires for its continual affirmation and identity many kinds of "collective representations" of the things that it is.[8] The Constitution is to Americans the most sacred of such representations, but not the only one. For in a community as large and complex as the United States no one symbol is sufficiently rich *and* clear in meanings to represent all the elements of the national identity.

Americans, for example, have thought of themselves from the start as pioneers who seek new territories to tame. However, the definition of a territory, and of the frontier between tame and untame, has shifted. When the nation was expanding geographically, one city after the other, Cleveland, Chicago, Denver, was defined as *the* frontier city, at the edge of civilization and wilderness. But "civilization" and "wilderness" are not terms of mere geography. They are moral terms, part of a rhetoric of conduct. Since the continent was settled, vast new territories have emerged in business, style of life, self expression, and education, among others, and prompted the movement of people from one part of the country to the other. To tame these territories has meant extending the rule of law over them, improving the opportunities, redressing the inequalities and guaranteeing the liberties and well-being of their inhabitants.

Several American cities in their patterns of activity, housing and working arrangements, demographic characteristics, kinds of industry, products, and buildings are specialized in representing one or another new territory. New York City, for example, has been known since the turn of the century as the cultural and commercial capital of the nation, at the frontier of art and acquisition, and drawn an endless stream of pilgrims and pioneers to its territories. Los Angeles, since the conclusion of World War II, has been heralded as the frontier city of new chances in livelihood and lifestyle, and lured hundreds of thousands, indeed millions, of settlers to its territories. Containing many rich inhabitants, Los Angeles is nevertheless without a developed upper class, in Baltzell's sense, and this equalitarian feature of the city may be a source of its significance and appeal. So too, the nation's singularity in being a "melting pot," its ability to produce enterprising factory managers, or its industrial strength have been projected in the figures of Chicago, Pittsburgh, and Detroit respectively. Indeed, in an earlier period Chicago was hailed by its poets as hog butcher to, and transportation hub of, the nation; Pittsburgh was called "steel city" and continues to pride itself on the banking and educational institutions of its native sons, Carnegie and Mellon; and Detroit, frequently called "Motown," remains known as the city that put America on wheels. These few cities are hardly an exhaustive list of positive representations; many more could be given. In any case, New York, Los Angeles, Chicago, Detroit, Boston, Philadelphia, Birmingham, Montgomery, Miami have also been symbols of features in each of our cities all of us condemn: bigotry, violence, crime, prostitution, drug traffic, gambling, illiteracy, slums. These are wildernesses in our national moral landscape.

Positive and negative images of American cities are invoked incessantly in newspaper and magazine articles, short stories, novels, television programs, movies, and not least, scholarly studies. These images serve to objectify America and thus help clarify the nation to its citizens. In their symbolic and rhetorical roles American cities provide a common vocabulary, a moral lexicon, as it were, by which to refer to the successes and failures in our national life. The esteem of our cities is thus measured by the extent to which they have tamed their territories and brought them into conformity with American values and norms. However different they are, the fact that each of our cities can be gauged by the same moral standards means that at least in these terms they are all equal.

Foundings and Features

The cities of the occident, Max Weber held in his study of ancient and medieval cities, have been deeply influenced by the conception of *res publica*, developed in Greco-Roman antiquity. This conception holds the city to be an entity distinct from its inhabitants, a republic, possessing property for public use, and concerned with the general welfare—health, safety, education—of its citizens. Neither the features nor the idea of *res publica* are found in the cities of the orient. [9]

All nations of the west partake of the heritage of Greece and Rome—they are members of a common civilization. Yet no two nations of the west have had an identical history. The idea of *res publica*, although found everywhere in the west, has worked itself out differently in the different nations. In the following, I will sketch briefly the distinct national patterns of city life found in four democracies.

1. American cities. The first immigrants to the American continent modelled the governance of their settlements on the English villages and towns of their origins. These settlements were self governing and, as far as possible, autonomous from English colonial rule. However, relationships among inhabitants of American settlements soon developed along lines more extreme than in England or Europe. In American settlements and towns, for example, disagreements not resolved to each party's satisfaction were sometimes terminated by the expedient of one of the parties, individual or group, moving elsewhere. The resources of a dissatisfied party, other settlements with need of the party's skills, or unclaimed territory not far distant, made moving feasible, but these were hardly sufficient reasons to move. The largely unstated premise of movement and settlement, serving as goad and legitimation of each, was belief in the right of individuals to direct their lives in light of their own conscience.[10] Persons of like mind, of like views, of like interests, although strangers to one another, considered it their right, indeed won the right legally, to congregate—the Puritans, for example, in Boston, the Quakers in Philadelphia. Rhode Island was settled, in these terms, by groups that withdrew their association from Massachusetts Bay. This pattern of voluntary association transcended class differences and has prevailed throughout the nation's history.[11]

The class consciousness of Europeans, based on stable and diffuse class membership and long, well established patterns of prerogative and deference in class relations, is much more well defined than among Americans. As social researchers have found innumerable times, Americans in all walks of life think of themselves as belonging primarily to the "middle class." There is no doubt, however, that an upper class presence developed in American cities, as Baltzell's and other studies have shown. Members of this class have made notable contributions to the political and cultural life of the cities and the nation. However, the more permeable class structure of American society, and the greater mobility of its members, have doubtless facilitated association of Americans along voluntary lines. This pattern of association, coupled to the belief in the worth of individual persons, has contributed to and reinforced the egalitarian and individualistic terms in which Americans view their cities.

2. *French cities.* The French situation was, and I believe continues to be, in several respects the polar opposite of the American. In *The Old Regime and the French Revolution,* Tocqueville described the steady diminution, beginning in the thirteenth century, in the self rule, rights, and wealth of French localities—provinces, manors, cantons, towns—and the corresponding rise in power, perquisites, and holdings of the monarchy seated in Paris.[12] Already by the sixteenth century, as Weber also noted, French cities were, with the exception of police matters, divested of legal control over their own affairs; indeed, permission of the state authorities was required for any financially important act.[13] By the seventeenth century French localities were ruled by the bureaucracy in Paris, the governance of towns was sold by the king to the highest bidder, and the central government alone maintained order in the provinces. By the eighteenth century the royal parish, similar in organization to the New England township, was dead. There was no township in France, said Tocqueville, no "borough, village, or hamlet, however small, no hospital, factory, convent, or college which had a right to manage its own affairs as it thought fit or to administer its possessions without interference."[14]

Paris stood at the apex of the nation, in which all power was held and administered and many of the splendors of France were housed. In overturning the monarchy, however, the revolution of 1789, directed from Paris and affecting all of France, aimed at and succeeded in increasing the power of central authority. The hold of the church, virtually the sole religious body of France for centuries and deeply entwined in French life, was also broken. However much equalitarian standards, fortified and borne by the Reformation, and culminating in the revolution, may have helped to level social hierarchies, the position of Paris as the nation's center of administration and wealth was not merely untouched by the revolution, but strengthened. Originally fostered by, but now freed from, monarch and church, the life of the mind and the arts and the locales in which this took place—universities, opera houses, theaters, galleries, museums, newspapers, cafés—flourished in secular Paris, and the city was the most glittering and cosmopolitan in all of France—indeed in all of Europe.[15] Thus, whether in the older terms or the new, the regions, villages, boroughs, towns, and cities of France continued to be, for the most part willingly, politically subservient and culturally secondary to Paris, and were prevented from emerging as competitors in any field of high culture. This pattern was invested with the weight of hundreds of years of tradition, which no doubt lent it some authority. But the pattern was also given new vitality in the nineteenth century by the charisma of Paris' revolutionary role. The luster of this role has faded, but Parisian dominance remains.

3. *English cities*. The pattern of English city life combines elements of the American and French. England and France were politically unified at approximately the same time. Yet, unlike the situation in France, the power of the English monarchy never fully usurped the power of locally based aristocrats. English aristocrats were able to maintain self-governance in their shires—the city and county corporations—in part because these were electoral bodies for parliament. Able to defend their interests in parliament, the cities and counties had no need to develop political ambitions separate from, and in opposition to, the state. Indeed, city and county corporations retained an effective local base of power, independent of parliament and king. Their governing councils, whose members were selected on the basis of neighborhood and class, had the right to levy certain taxes and spend tax monies for local purposes, such as sewage disposal, schools, and hospitals. Thus, the English state and the localities were able to coexist and develop without the sacrifice of one to the other. Growth of county and city corporations in membership and in numbers took place alongside growth of the state, many of whose branches were designed to provide services to the localities.[16] Aristocrat, cleric, merchant and commoner remained tightly bound to one another in a complex system of duties and rights, and were integral to the corporations for centuries.

Standards of equality and individuality, championed by the Puritans, did their part in weakening, if not completely destroying, the old order. In the aftermath of the rebellions of the seventeenth century, the prestige and power of the king declined and those of parliament rose. By the eighteenth century an *exclusively* hereditary aristocracy was abolished, and nobility and commoners joined in business, entered the professions, and intermarried.[17] The immense growth of social, political, and civil rights in England since the seventeenth century served to amplify features already present. Proliferation in numbers of courts, extension of the reach of law, broadening of the right to elect to, and hold, office, establishment of universal education, and provision of a large range of social services was the work of the central government.[18] Parliament was composed of representatives from city and county corporations into which, over time, a larger share of the population was moving.

Although in power and privileges considerably greater than in the United States, the central government in England acts on behalf of, and in cooperation with, the localities. The larger the population of a locality, the more numerous and various are the facilities it may legitimately claim. The central government remains the owner, purveyor, distributor, and regulator of a great many facilities. Yet, English localities are more autonomous than the French. Many retain an identity established centuries earlier—for example, as the domain, of a noble family or the site of a Roman settlement or a cathedral—and have ancient buildings such as church, castle, aqueduct, and houses within their territories. Indeed, the importance of the older English cities, particularly those with a cathedral, is not limited to their historic associations; they are places in which to congregate, not merely reside, and this strengthens the attachment of their citizens. But English cities are not nearly so autonomous as the American. Indeed, as the new English cities have no ties to tradition, class, church, or territory with which to forge an identity, they are, in comparison to the older cities as well as to the American, culturally bereft. Such cultural life as the new cities have, musical, theatrical or literary, is distributed to them through an agency of parliament; this is true also of such facilities as hospitals and universities. English localities and cities have plural, not equal, definitions, and thus plural rights and access to facilities. The English pattern falls between the extremes of the near monopoly of a great many facilities enjoyed by Paris, and the equal entitlement to all facilities held to be a right by each American city.

4. *German cities.* The pattern of German city life was formed in a long, often bloody, history that extended from medieval times well into the modern period. Oscillating between separation and temporary unity, the German member states did not become a nation until late in the nineteenth century. For centuries many of the Germanic territories shared a common language, religion, and culture. Rulers of German principalities could determine the religion of their subjects. But as medieval Germany was part of the Holy Roman Empire, the religion common to the territories was that of the Roman church. The princely city was thus a center of state administration and worship. Noblemen, advisers, clerics, functionaries, jurists, merchants, and soldiers, and the appurtenances these required—castles, churches, workshops, markets, and barracks—were concentrated in the princely cities. This pattern was repeated in each of the territories as well as the free city-states.[19]

The Lutheran branch of the Reformation, however, split the principalities religiously and broke the tenuous unity of the empire. Emphasizing solitary faith, inner spiritual sanctity, and the charity and brotherliness of closely-knit communities, the Lutheran doctrines furthered particularistic interests of German dukes, princes, and territorial and city lords. Moreover, in accepting government authority over church affairs in return for the prince's protection of the "freedom of a Christian," the Lutheran attitude made individual political rulers the highest authorities of the church. This served to dissipate resistance to local princes among Luther's followers and strengthened the princes' hold over their territories.[20]

The Counter-Reformation further exacerbated religious and political divisions. In the seventeenth century, at the conclusion of the thirty years war, the Treaty of Wesphalia established a loose confederation of German states in which each had direct jurisdiction only over its own inhabitants. At the time local powers were falling in France, and central power was rising in England, the principalities in Germany grew stronger and the rifts among them became more extreme.

In the eighteenth century, under Frederick the Great, Prussia emerged as a formidable military power and became, for a time, the supreme German state. In setting out to unify the principalities, Prussia's disciplined army, efficient bureaucratic administration, and responsible, if authoritarian, leadership was the model of government for the nation and the territories. Even after the Napoleonic conquest, and the revolution of 1848, Bismarck's consolidation of the empire was achieved on the Prussian model; the imperial constitution of 1871 consisted of laws binding on each citizen, but sovereignty rested in the princes of each state. The princes were represented in the Federal Council which checked the power of the emperor, the Kaiser. The federal government had authority to legislate civil, commercial, and criminal law, and jurisdiction in certain economic and foreign affairs. But the right to administer and execute federal laws was left to the member states. Thus, each member state—Prussia, Bavaria, Hesse, Mecklenburg, Thuringia, Saxony, etc.—developed its own executive machinery and bureaucracy. Indeed, "state" meant to Germans even before Bismarck, and perhaps continues to mean, not so much the federal government, but the individual member states. Through centuries of common dialect, religion, family history, relatively stable residence, social standing, occupation, and not least, distinctive cuisine, the inhabitants of each member state formed deep bonds of identification with and loyalty to each other and their state. These were not easily displaced.[21]

The Weimar government, erected after the First World War, endeavored to overcome the particularism of the territories and to develop a representative national government, a republic. But in 1919, one year after the new government was formed, Bavaria seceded and declared itself a communist state. Although ideological passion in this rebellion was no doubt authentic, the line of cleavage followed old territorial boundaries; Bavaria was largely Catholic, much of the remainder of the republic Protestant. The unification of Germany during the Nazi period, in which, at first, Bavaria also played a leading role, was won at the cost of at least temporarily subduing many distinctions—territorial loyalty, class membership, religious identity, and political affiliation. Yet east Germany today consists of formerly Protestant territories. But west Germany is hardly of a piece, religiously or politically. In taking many powers unto itself, the central government of west Germany has developed an extensive bureaucratic machinery and an elaborate civil service. But the many branches of the central government are poorly coordinated, and the territories may legislate on their own accord should the central government not do so. The lineaments of the old territories, and, therefore, of old loyalties and identities, are still operative in Germany.

Each territory and its capital city—often the residence of a former or living prince—is in tradition and culture distinct from the others. No one capital city in Germany—Munich, Cologne, Frankfurt, Nürnberg, Hamburg, Hannover, Düsseldorf, Mainz, Stuttgart, and so on—has a monopoly on goods, services, and facilities, as does Paris, but each is similar in the kinds of facilities it possesses. There is hardly one without its own opera company and art museum, for instance. The German pattern of city life is characterized by a repetition of like aggregates, a form sociologists call segmental. Because capital cities are different, they do not lose themselves in each other and become effaced, as do many English new towns or French provincial cities. Although the capital cities in Germany stand above the others in prestige, authority, and entitlements, they are in many respects equal to one another; each capital city holds itself entitled to all things other capital cities have. The fact that each capital city is formally similar makes it possible for them to be united.[22] This pattern of German city life is a distinctive combination, quite unlike that of the English, of elements found in the American and French. However pale in comparison to earlier times, the particularism that has played so large a part in German history is still discernible.

The Cities of Nations

The patterns of city life that have been discussed—egalitarian/individualistic, hierarchical/central, pluralistic, and segmental—are features specific to the United States, France, England, and Germany. They have emerged in the course of the religious, social, political, and economic history peculiar to each nation. The patterns of one nation cannot be generalized to another. But at the same time the pattern of any one nation, and its actual extent, cannot be well discerned by examining that nation in isolation from others; comparison with other nations is essential to bring the patterns of each into sharper relief.

This is also one of the lessons of Baltzell's study; the distinctive patterns of Philadelphia and Boston emerge more clearly when each is compared with the other. But although his first interest was in sources and kinds of democratic leadership, Baltzell emphasized the significance of the particular institutions of each city—indeed the city itself as an institution—in generating kinds of leaders. This methodological innovation has yielded fresh insights and provides another lesson.

The categories of national city patterns developed in this study are a theorist's contribution to urban sociology. They are derived by considering cities as institutions, as patterns of human relationships held to be valuable and normative by their inhabitants. They are collective, not aggregative, categories, and their empirical deployment requires quite different sorts of data from those commonly found in the census tracts.

American urban sociologists have a propensity to differentiate city life merely in demographic and ecological terms—for example, by variation in density of population per square mile. Variations of this sort are valuable in assembling regional and national economic and political indicators. They are also useful in yielding a demographic morphology of cities and nations. Such variations are derived by assuming each person is equal, in the sense that he or she has the same numerical weight as any other, and each person is an individual who can be counted. These individualistic and equalitarian assumptions are consistent with an American democratic view, and have become institutionalized as a principle of much American research. But to limit analysis of cities solely to data selected on the basis of these assumptions is unnecessarily to restrict our understanding of city life.

A typical census category, for example, "urban agglomeration," tells us something about size, but little of significance, little of the place and meaning of a particular "urban agglomerate" in any nation. Indeed, the *exclusive* use of this and kindred categories results in a reification of cities, a taking of a part for the whole, and thus obscures the fact that in a particular nation some cities are more venerated, therefore not equal to others, and, in respect to size, often disproportionately influential and powerful in their relations to other cities.

As the nations of the world come into ever closer, more frequent contact it behooves American sociologists who wish to develop a "generalizing" discipline to challenge and rethink their fundamental social categories. They cannot hope in any other way to capture the variety of the social world.

Notes

* I wish to thank Matthew Bershady, Stuart Bogom, Richard Farnum, Jo Gullo, Victor Lidz, Samuel Preston, Jeremy Tanner, Karen Walker and Adam Weissberger for their helpful comments.

1. E. Digby Baltzell, *Puritan Boston and Quaker Philadelphia* (New York: Free Press, 1979).
2. Alexis de Tocqueville, *Democracy in America*, 2 vols. ed. Phillips Bradley (New York: Vintage Books, 1954); Max Weber, *The Protestant Ethic and the Spirit of Capitalism*, trans. Talcott Parsons (New York: Charles Scribner and Sons, 1930).
3. *Cf.* Seymour Martin Lipset, *The First New Nation* (New York: W. Norton & Co., Inc., 1979), xxxiff., 279ff.
4. *Cf.* the essays by Samuel Preston, Richard Farnum, Elijah Anderson, and Victor Lidz in this volume.
5. *Cf.* Louis Dumont, *Essays on Individualism* (Chicago: University of Chicago Press, 1986), 76ff.
6. *Cf.* Max Weber, "The Protestant Sects and the Spirit of Capitalism," in H. H. Gerth and C. W. Mills, eds., *From Max Weber, Essays in Sociology* (New York: Oxford University Press, 1946.)
7. Tocqueville, *op. cit.*, vol. 1, p. 69ff., vol. 2, ch. XIII.
8. Emile Durkheim, *The Elementary Forms of the Religious Life,* (Glencoe, Ill.: Free Press, 1947), ch. VII.
9. Max Weber, *Economy and Society,* ed. Guenther Roth and Claus Wittich, (Berkeley: University of California Press, 1978), vol. 2, ch. XVI.
10. *Cf.* Michael Zuckerman, *Peaceable Kingdoms* (Westport, Conn.: Greenwood Press, 1983); see also Arthur M. Schlesinger, *The Rise of the City* (New York: Macmillan, 1933), and Richard C. Wade, *The Urban Frontier* (Chicago: University of Chicago Press, 1959).
11. *Cf.* the discussion of the associations developed between the Irish immigrants and the New England Protestants in the United States in the mid 1800s, in Stephen Thernstrom, *Poverty and Progress* (New York: Atheneum, 1975), ch. 6.
12. Alexis de Tocqueville, *The Old Regime and the French Revolution,* trans. Stuart Gilbert. (Garden City, NY: Doubleday Anchor Books, 1955.)
13. Weber, *op. cit.*, 1325ff.
14. Tocqueville, *op. cit.*, 51.

15. *Cf.* Walter Benjamin, "Paris, Capital of the Nineteenth Century," in Walter Benjamin, *Reflections,* trans. Edmund Jephcott, ed. Peter Demetz. (New York: Harcourt Brace Jovanovich, 1978.)

16. Weber, *op. cit.*

17. Tocqueville, *op. cit.,* 79ff.

18. *Cf.* T. H. Marshall, *Class, Citizenship and Social Development* (Chicago: University of Chicago Press, 1964), ch. IV.

19. See, for example, A. J. P. Taylor, *The Course of German History* (New York: Coward McCann, 1946), ch. 1.

20. Taylor, *op. cit.,* 230ff; *cf.* G. Barraclough, *The Origins of Modern Germany,* 2nd ed. (Oxford: Blackwell, 1949).

21. See Golo Mann, *The History of Germany Since 1789* (New York: Frederick A. Praeger, 1966), 131ff; *cf.* Hajo Holborn, *A History of Modern Germany* (Princeton, N.J.: Princeton University Press, 1964); see also the discussion of "pluricentric" language use by Michael Clyne, *Language and Society in the German Speaking Countries* (Cambridge: Cambridge University Press, 1984).

22. Emile Durkheim, *The Division of Labor in Society* (Glencoe, Ill.: Free Press, 1947), pp. 175–177.

Fred Block

11. *Modernity, Democracy, and the Problem of Authority**

Modernity, Democracy, and the Problem of Authority

The writings of E. Digby Baltzell can be understood as an extended commentary on the problem of authority in modern societies.[1] As with other scholars of his generation, Baltzell's intellectual concerns were shaped by the horrors of European fascism. In responding to the experiences of the 1930s and 1940s, Baltzell's central concern became the issue of how it is possible to have legitimate and effective political authority in a secular era marked by continuous social change. Baltzell proposes a solution to the problem of authority that is grounded in his interpretation of several centuries of English and American history—the reconstitution of aristocratic authority based on a meritocratic elite. In the essay that follows, I will argue that Baltzell has correctly identified a problem in the modes of authority delineated by Max Weber. However, I will argue that Baltzell's solution is not adequate, and I will suggest an alternative conception of authority that is more consistent with modernity.

The Necessity of Authority

While conservatives have long upheld the value of authority, theorists in various radical traditions have had a very different position. Critics of existing authority have often taken the position that it is possible to reconstitute society without relations of authority. Marx and Engels' vision of "the withering away of the state," and of the end of politics in a socialist society, can be understood as an effort to imagine a society without authority. More recently, American radicals and counterculturalists attempted during the 1960s to prefigure a society without authority through the creation of alternative institutions that dispensed with hierarchy and formal rules. Radicals attempted to build "organizations without authority"[2] in free schools, communes, alternative newspapers, law firms, and other settings.[3]

Significantly, both of these strands of radicalism have begun to reconsider the issue of authority. In the Marxist tradition, a great deal of recent research has emphasized that Marx and Engels were misguided in believing that the end of capitalism would bring an end to the problem of politics. Alvin Gouldner, in particular, has been most trenchant in analyzing the connections between the deformation of Soviet-style socialism and the failure of the Marxist tradition to recognize the inevitability of authoritative relations in the organization of any society.[4] Many contemporary Marxist analysts have come to recognize that the coercive power of the state cannot be reduced to class power and that it is a fundamental theoretical task to find ways to control that power in a post-capitalist society.[5]

In this respect, many contemporary Marxists have returned to a position advanced by Karl Polanyi in the 1940s.[6] Polanyi developed his own socialist position in opposition to both the Communist and Socialist traditions. Central to this position was the argument that political power was indispensable for the organization of any complex society, and that the beginning of freedom in a complex society came with the mature acceptance of the existence of that power. Implicitly, Polanyi was suggesting that the Marxist beliefs about the withering away of the state was the mirror image of the laissez-faire ideal of a self-regulating market which would obviate the need for political power. He saw both as forms of magical thinking that interfered with effective responses to the problem of state power.

Similarly, recent theorists within the communitarian and cooperative tradition have also come to recognize that the effort to build institutions without authority is problematic. In an often cited article on "The Tyranny of Structurelessness," Jo Freeman[7] argues that when organizations lack structure, informal modes of authority substitute for formal authority. But those who exercise this informal authority are not easily held accountable for their actions; they are able to hide behind their lack of a formal position while continuing to exert great power. The obvious solution to this problem is to re-establish formal roles and formal lines of authority, while simultaneously attempting to make those with authority accountable to the group.

But while many radicals have come to accept the necessity and even the desirability of authority, there have been few systematic efforts to theorize about how this authority should be exercised. To be sure, radicals believe that authority should not be abused, and that it should be subordinated to democratic control, but there are few specifics beyond this. In this sense, those on the political left now share the problem of conservatives: the inadequacy of Weber's typology of modes of authority.

The Weberian Typology

While Weber posited three distinct ways to legitimate authority,[8] it is obvious that all three of his types are problematic when faced with the realities of modernity. Modernity means, above all, an acceleration in the pace of social change, so that the process of revising existing social arrangements must occur at progressively shorter intervals. Much of Weber's analysis of the dynamics of authority in traditional societies rested on the long intervals between periods of social crisis. During these long intervals, traditional authority worked well; society would be ruled according to long established procedures. However, after generations of stability, problems could develop that required significant adaptation. This was the occasion for charismatic authority; a leader would emerge with the personal authority to persuade the society to change its established practices. But the brief period of disruption would be followed by a routinization of the new practices, and there would be the creation of a new set of traditions and a new period of stability.

With modernity and a continuous process of adaptation, traditional authority is obviously inappropriate. Similarly, reliance on charismatic authority to carry out frequent adaptations is far too dangerous. According to Weber, charismatic authority is exemplified by the biblical prophets who declare, "It is written, but I say unto you . . ." But since this rejection of established law is central to the exercise of charismatic authority, there is the continuous danger that charismatic leaders will transgress all kinds of moral and political restrictions. There is no way to defend a society against the abuse of charismatic authority since its essence is the surrender of the society's judgment in the face of the leader's moral claims to be followed.

But if traditional and charismatic authority are inadequate or unreliable in the modern world, legal rational authority is only marginally better. Legal rational authority provides society with protection against the excesses that can occur when authority is embodied in an individual rather than in the office. However, legal rational authority also lacks the adaptability that is necessary when change is continuous. The effort to respond to new historical circumstances simply through the interpretations of an existing body of law always poses the danger that adaptation will occur far too slowly. The bold measures that the charismatic leader can propose will be lacking from political leaders schooled in the incrementalism of a legal rational order. Paralysis and drift are likely to predominate over effective adaptation.

For American social scientists in the immediate post-World War II period, the collapse of Weimar Germany and the rise of Hitler represented the classic instance of the paralysis of legal rational authority and of the profound danger of charismatic authority. These experiences posed the stark question of how stable and flexible authority could be reconstituted in a modern, mass society.

It was in this intellectual context that Baltzell elaborated his response to the limited options that Weber provided by constructing a fourth type of legitimate authority. For convenience we can call this model aristocratic authority, but Baltzell did not have in mind a return to traditional aristocracies. Baltzell's aristocracy exercises its power within a formally democratic institutional framework with the legal safeguards of the Anglo-American tradition. Unlike traditional authority, Baltzell's aristocratic authority is capable of providing adaptability and, as with legal rational authority, it places constraints on the abuse of authority. This type of authority is an attempt to theorize the most positive moments of the last several hundred years of English and American history when political life was dominated by an enlightened elite that was capable of taking bold action to maintain the social order in the face of historical transformations. The English elite that carried out the great electoral reforms of 1832 and 1867, the Puritan Bostonians who dominated Massachusetts life in the nineteenth century, and the elite group around F.D.R. that carried out the New Deal are archetypes of the proper exercise of aristocratic authority.

Baltzell is well aware that the possession of wealth and social prestige in themselves are not sufficient to generate aristocratic authority or effective leadership. His model requires two critical features for its effectiveness. The first is a relatively meritocratic selection system that screens out less talented members of the upper class and allows for the entrance of a number of highly talented individuals from humbler social backgrounds. One part of this selection mechanism is a system of elite education that maintains high standards and provides some openings for children from non-elite families. Another part is the existence of social clubs and informal associations that are flexible enough to include successful individuals from non-elite backgrounds. Without this capacity to coopt new members an elite, in Baltzell's view, loses both its legitimacy and its creativity, since the capacity to recognize and reward merit is the only way to assure that the right people get put in the most important positions.

However, Baltzell is also clear that too rapid entrance of new members can undermine the second critical requisite for aristocratic authority—a strong ideology of service. Without some measure of social exclusivity, it is difficult to maintain and reinforce any shared perspective, particularly one that stresses the obligation that members of the group have to place broader interests ahead of personal gain. The idea, in short, is that the boundary between the elite and the rest of the society must be well established in order to maintain a common elite ideology, but the boundary must be permeable enough so that the common ideology emphasizes the importance of merit.

This model proposes to resolve the problem that Weber's typology poses. The self-confidence and intelligence of this aristocracy creates the potential for strong adaptive actions; there is not the dependence on incrementalism of legal rational leadership. On the other hand, the service ideology helps to protect society against the abuse of leadership positions. Also, authority is vested in the collective leadership, so it is relatively simple for the group to ease out individuals who have lost their effectiveness or have become corrupted by power.

Table 11.1 shows how Baltzell's aristocratic authority fits within the Weberian typology. The first variable is the adaptability of a form of authority to changing circumstances. The second variable is the extent to which the exercise of authority is bounded and constrained. The box that Weber left open and that Baltzell has sought to fill with an aristocratic elite is a mode of authority that is highly adaptable to changing circumstances, but which places severe constraints on the exercise of authority.

But is Baltzell's solution persuasive? One can hardly deny the historical achievements of the Anglo-American elites that Baltzell so much admires; the history of enlightened reform has produced remarkable institutional and social stability. But neither can one overlook the darker side of this history; particularly the impact of these elites on non-European peoples over the past three hundred years. The very self confidence that characterizes an aristocratic elite made possible centuries of imperial conquest of extraordinary violence and brutality. In fact, the relationship between Anglo-American civilization and the indigenous populations of Asia, Af-

TABLE 11.1.   Weber's types of authority

		ADAPTABILITY	
		Low	*High*
BOUNDEDNESS	*Low*	Traditional	Charismatic
	High	Legal-rational	Aristocratic

rica, and the Americas points to the fundamental defect in Baltzell's position—the reliance on a service ideology to constrain against abuses of power.

Here, it is worth looking briefly at a recent moment in American history—the post-World War II period that culminated in the Vietnam debacle. It is in this period that one can see the distinct outlines of the kind of political aristocracy that Baltzell admires. While most of the post-World War II American presidents were men with relatively tenuous elite connections, the same cannot be said of the men they appointed to play critical roles in the shaping of American foreign policy. Men like Dean Acheson, John McCloy, Douglas Dillon, the Dulleses, the Bundys, and many others shared membership in a social upper class and common socialization in elite private schools and colleges. The cohesiveness of this group was such that when Richard Rovere wrote his famous article on "The Establishment," his attempt at humor was seen by many as a serious analysis.

This was a group that met all of Baltzell's criteria. There was enough exclusivity to maintain a common ideology that emphasized service and enough openness to facilitate the entrance of men of socially marginal background such as W. W. Rostow and Henry Kissinger. And, to be sure, this American aristocracy did have its moments of triumph, such as the development of the Marshall Plan as a multilayered and ingenious initiative to secure a variety of American foreign policy objectives.[9] Yet it was this same group—"the best and the brightest"—that engineered the growing United States involvement in Vietnam and presided over a war effort of startling cynicism and stupidity. Some might treat this as an unfortunate aberration, but it was an aberration of enormous consequences. For one thing, the social divisions that erupted with the war destroyed the cohesiveness and political effectiveness of that American elite, one consequence of which has been the political triumph of the far Right. When an aristocracy engages in self destructive behavior, some explanation is in order.

The problem is that intelligence and an ideology of service do not protect a society against the abuse of power. The very cohesiveness of such an elite makes possible a collective myopia in which the entire group shares a fundamentally mistaken perception of reality. Since the self confidence of the elite implies a contempt for democratic opinion, there is no reason to question one's fundamental assumptions when one is challenged from outside the elite. On the contrary, the elite's impulse is to do everything it can to manipulate public opinion since the populace's inadequate grasp of the situation might prove to be an obstacle to the elite's capacity to carry out its plans. All of these patterns are clear in the Vietnam record; the foreign policy elite enforced a kind of tunnel vision on itself until the American involvement had escalated disastrously.

In some historical situations, aristocrat elites have produced individuals who are able to break with the rest of the group in protest against mistaken policies as when Churchill challenged the appeasement policies of Chamberlain. This kind of public elite defection was strikingly absent in the Vietnam experience. But even when such elite defections do occur, they hardly indicate the strength of aristocratic rule. On the contrary, without democratic opinion on their side, these elite defectors would be powerless. The lesson is that democratic restraints on elite power are indispensable to avoid the systematic abuse of power. Yet there is a fundamental conflict between the maintenance of a cohesive and homogeneous elite and the existence of effective democratic restraints. In sum, the Vietnam debacle reveals one of the key flaws in the aristocratic mode of authority. The very elite cohesiveness that is the strength of this form of authority is also its undoing.

But there is also another important problem with aristocratic authority—there are formidable obstacles to the continuing legitimacy of such an aristocratic grouping. Distrust of established authority is a critical aspect of modernity, so it is hardly surprising that the political right and the political left now compete with each other in their denunciations of "establishment" groups like the Council on Foreign Relations and the Trilateral Commission. In contemporary American politics, almost everyone is a populist who denounces established centers of power. This kind of distrust is intensified in periods of social dislocation, but it is a fundamental part of the temperament of modernity. In retrospect, the brief dominance of American foreign policy by an aristocratic elite now appears more an aberration than a sustainable pattern. Those who would restore aristocratic power have no real answer to the problem of dispelling this kind of distrust.

An Alternative Solution

There is, however, an alternative way to fill the missing box in Weber's typology. The fourth type of authority that is both bounded and adaptable can best be termed postindustrial authority, since it emerges in the most modern work settings that rely heavily on the appropriation of advanced technology.[10] I want to suggest that this new form of authority, which currently exists only in some work settings, might be the characteristic form of political authority in an emergent postindustrial society. Such a development, however, would require significant institutional and cultural changes.

One virtue of the label "postindustrial" is that it suggests that this new form of authority is a relatively recent invention. It must be remembered, however, that Weber's typology does incorporate the idea of change in modes of authority; in Weber's account, legal rational authority evolved over many centuries. It is not inconsistent with Weber to argue that modernity leads to the invention of an additional type of authority.

The content of postindustrial authority is most immediately grasped in the growing management literature on post-bureaucratic forms of organization. This literature is grounded in the familiar insight that bureaucratic forms of business organization are insufficiently adaptive to fit "turbulent" environments.[11] In business settings where both technologies and markets are changing rapidly, the inertia and incrementalism of bureaucratic organizations becomes highly problematic.

One useful formulation for understanding the problem is provided by Rosabeth Kanter.[12] Drawing on Parsons's nonzero sum view of power, she argues that power in an organization increases with the capacity of people to get things done. She then delineates two different styles of management—which could be called authoritarian and authoritative management. Authoritarian management is close to the standard image of bureaucratic or Taylorist practices; the manager closely supervises subordinates whose knowledge and responsibilities are quite limited. Total power in the organization is reduced by this style of management because the capacities of the subordinates are minimal. In contrast, authoritative management is concerned to increase the knowledge and capacities of subordinates, so their ability to get things done is enhanced. Authoritative managers do not engage in close supervision and monitoring of their subordinates; they are more like resource people who provide their employees with advice, information, support, and access to others in the organization that they need to complete their tasks.

While authoritarian management styles with their reduction in overall power work when a bureaucracy faces a stable task environment, they become problematic when the organization must adapt. In the latter context, it is highly desirable to increase power in the organization to assure effective responses to a changing environment.

What Kanter describes can be seen as a modification of legal rational authority, since the authority of the manager still derives from his or her position within a bureaucratic hierarchy. But one comes closer to the pure type of postindustrial authority if one adds the idea that the managers do not know the correct solutions to the problems their subordinates face. This point emerges most sharply in discussions of the management of engineers in high technology settings. The organization will be faced with choices between different technical solutions to a given problem. Someone will have to decide which path to choose, because resource scarcity precludes pursuing both options at the same time.[13] In this case, the manager's credibility in relation to his or her employees depends on making a decision that is based not on arbitrary grounds but on a careful review of the different arguments. This pushes the situation closer to one in which the authority of the manager derives from the subordinates rather than from hierarchical position.

A further step in the direction of the dissociation of hierarchy and authority is visible in some of the more advanced quality of work life experiments that have been carried out in a number of North American settings.[14] These experiments generally occur in technologically advanced, continuous process, production facilities. Blue collar workers are organized into autonomous work groups that are responsible for managing the production process in a particular part of the enterprise. The role of first line supervisors is eliminated completely; the managers who work with the autonomous work groups are supposed to be support personnel who help the group manage its tasks and help with the process of coordinating with other parts of the organization.

In some of these settings, the work groups elect representatives to a plant-wide committee that meets with the plant manager to set overall policy. While the plant manager is still appointed by people higher up in the organization, his or her effectiveness is directly linked to the capacity to work out problems with the autonomous work groups and with the plant-wide committee.

There is further evidence of how far things can evolve away from legal rational authority in these kinds of settings. There exists a detailed report of labor-management relations within one of the most advanced of these quality of work life experiments—the Shell Oil plant in Sarnia, Ontario.[15] Over a period of time, the union and management have agreed to a dramatic reorganization of the pattern of collective bargaining. The old union contract involved pages of detailed rules governing pay, promotion, work rules, and other issues. This document has been abandoned and in its place, union and management have agreed to a set of "constitutional" documents that set out principles for running the plant and managing conflict. In contrast to legal rational arrangements, the emphasis in the documents is not procedural but substantive—the emphasis is on a vision of how the plant should function.

This development in labor relations moves the situation even closer to the ideal type of postindustrial authority. Managers are now constrained both by their need to cooperate with employees and by the existence of a shared vision of how the plant should run. Nominally, their authority is derived from a bureaucratic hierarchy, but in practice, they derive their authority from the consent of their subordinates and from their ability to adhere to the principles embodied in the "constitutional" documents.

By now it should be clear how postindustrial authority fits the empty box. Those who exercise it are able to innovate without being constrained by the normal bureaucratic limitations—detailed procedural rules or opposition from people further up in the hierarchy. On the contrary, they have won their position precisely because of their capacity to innovate. But the capacity to innovate depends upon winning the consent of others in the organization—subordinates and peers. There must be a process of dialogue through which many of those others come to be persuaded that the proposed innovations are rational and desirable.

The contrast with charismatic authority is critical here because the exercise of charisma also involves winning the consent of others. The critical difference is that the charismatic leader insists on generalized deference—there are no boundaries separating legitimate and illegitimate claims on followers. The postindustrial leader, however, is constrained by the reality of specialized deference that is a critical element of modern professional authority. Just as people are likely to be suspicious of legal advice that is offered by a medical doctor, so they are unlikely to take seriously a manager's proposals about how they should live their private lives. But the postindustrial manager is even more constrained than the professional because he or she lacks a definitive area of specialized expertise. His or her claims that a particular innovation is correct cannot simply be based on one body of expert knowledge, but must involve weighing a number of different types of expertise. But for such a process of adjudication to be persuasive, a serious effort must be made to explain the criteria—the decision rules—that were used to reach a final decision.

Until quite recently, the doctor who told a patient that a particular procedure was needed was unlikely to provide a great deal of technical information to justify the decision. Instead, the doctor assumed that the patient would defer to his or her medical expertise in the relevant specialty. The postindustrial manager, in contrast, attempts to provide others in the organization with enough technical information to make a reasonable assessment of the soundness of his or her decision. While not all of those whose consent is being asked for will understand all of the complexities of the final decision, they will have the opportunity to assess the views of a number of people who are better informed than they are. The result is a decision-making model that is close to the model of collegial decision making in the university. When, for example, faculty from different disciplines sit on a schoolwide committee to evaluate candidates for promotion, there are vast differences in their ability to evaluate the work of particular individuals. There is also a lack of formal authority; one need not defer to the judgment of a particular colleague just because he or she is a physicist. The result is a situation where authority is earned as a result of the quality of the arguments that individuals make and where less knowledgeable colleagues can make a significant contribution by posing key questions about the strengths or weaknesses of a candidate's work.

This kind of collegial decision making must be supplemented by formal lines of authority, so that decisions are actually implemented. The idea is that postindustrial authority is similar to the combination of collegial decision making with formal lines of authority. The leader is effective to the extent that the decision is consistent with the collegial process and he or she is not able to exercise undue influence over the group's deliberations.

Postindustrial Authority and the Political Arena

Even if one is willing to grant the claim that there is some evolution in the workplace towards the development of the kind of postindustrial authority that I have described, it is a further leap to argue that the same type of authority might become the dominant model in the society as a whole. In fact, it is difficult to see how such a transition could occur since the existence of postindustrial authority in the workplace appears to rest on a stable community in which people have come to know each other on a face to face basis. How could the same model apply to representative politics in which leaders are chosen by extremely large and heterogenous populations?

The question is particularly difficult to answer at a time when the dominant tendency in American politics is for the level of political participation to decline and for serious discussion of issues to be replaced with clever advertising and the manipulation of images. The most critical aspect of this debasement of political life is the decline of a public sphere in which issues of collective importance are discussed and debated. Instead, we have a headlong retreat into privatism, and an environment where politics is reduced to the question of which politician has "made you better off than you were four years ago?" The same danger of a slide from mass democracy to authoritarianism that theorists of mass society feared in the 1950s appears even more acute today.

But the theorists of mass society failed to understand accurately the reasons for the fragility of mass democracy. Liberal capitalist societies have been built around a fundamental division between the political realm and the economic realm. The economic realm is supposed to operate according to the logic of the market, and political interventions into this economic realm are to be kept to a minimum. This means that the democratic electorate has little influence over the decisions of corporations to invest in certain places, to produce certain goods or services, or to disinvest. The result is a situation in which many of the most important decisions that affect people's lives lie outside of the sphere of democratic politics. At the same time, business interests that fear any expansion of the government's role in regulating the economy have poured huge sums of money into the political process to gain influence and further debase politics. The result is that most people experience a structured powerlessness that weakens the commitment to the political process and opens the way to demagogic manipulation.

This situation was brilliantly grasped in Sheldon Wolin's prophetic insight that Ronald Reagan, as president, would continually evoke the myths of small town American life at the same time that he removed any obstacles to a ruthless process of capitalist modernization that would destroy forever the economic foundations of American traditionalism.[16] The plight of the family farmer during the Reagan years is only one evidence of the gap between a rhetorical commitment to traditionalism and an actual commitment to unimpeded markets.

The only way out of this morass is through a revival of democratic politics that expands popular control over economic decisions. I have argued elsewhere that, without such a democratic revival, there is little prospect that the macroeconomic problems of a postindustrial economy can be solved.[17] But it also seems likely that people will find the retreat into privatism increasingly unsatisfactory, because modernity increases our interdependence and makes the quality of life dependent on what should be collective decisions.

If this democratic revival occurs, one of the central questions will be what kind of political leadership people want. Our recent models of political leadership all depend on fairly high levels of generalized deference; while there are general institutional constraints on what a president can do, the public's orientation has been to give the people it elects a great deal of leeway to choose a particular set of foreign and domestic policies. Unless these policies produce disaster in the form of significant American casualties or highly visible domestic economic difficulties, approval ratings tend to remain quite high. This is precisely the context in which image management and public relations become more central to the exercise of presidential power than policy initiatives.

There has been, then, an isomorphism between the kind of authority that people experience in the workplace and in the political arena. In both cases—but perhaps for different reasons—individuals defer to authority and collude in maintaining their own powerlessness. But as increasing numbers of individuals come to experience new types of authority in the workplace, and perhaps in other social arenas as well—schools, voluntary associations, and churches—their expectations about political authority might change. They might well come to demand new forms of political leadership that involve less generalized deference and greater responsiveness to public concerns.

While postindustrial authority must operate somewhat differently in the public arena than it would in a workplace setting, the basic elements are the same. There would have to be a revived public sphere in which there could be genuine debate over the comparative desirability of different policies. Political leaders who entered these debates would not be able to claim deference simply by virtue of their incumbency, but would have to persuade publics of the value of their proposals. The present reification of "expertise" would be replaced by clashes among competing experts who would be forced to explain the intellectual logic of their differing positions. Moreover, political leaders would be expected to become adept at making state entities—at various levels—effective as organizations; they would be pressured to be postindustrial managers.

Conclusion

While the emergence of postindustrial authority might appear wildly utopian in the present historical context, it is the form of authority that gives actual content to democracy. As Schumpeter has argued,[18] that which we call democracy is really elite democracy, in which electorates are able to choose among competing political elites that want to control the state. The elaborate structure of legal rational authority is designed to place limits on what this elite is able to accomplish and to assure that the public will have further opportunities to choose among competing elites. Yet as many have noted, this is an impoverished vision of democracy; it falls far short of popular sovereignty. Only when people have learned new models of leadership and followership that are based neither on generalized deference nor on high levels of distrust, can one imagine progress toward a more meaningful form of democracy.

This is the promise of postindustrial authority. While modernity has tended to increase distrust of established authority, this emergent form of authority can disarm that distrust by allowing individuals to experience their own authority and efficacy. In sum, the logic of modernity points beyond elite democracy to popular democracy, and postindustrial authority is a requisite for democratic advance.

Notes

* I am grateful to Ann Swidler and Larry Hirschhorn who suggested some of the ideas that are developed here.

1. *Philadelphia Gentlemen: The Making of a National Upper Class* (Philadelphia: University of Pennsylvania Press, 1977; original edition New York: Free Press, 1958); *The Protestant Establishment: Aristocracy and Caste in America* (New York: Random House, 1964); *Puritan Boston and Quaker Philadelphia* (New York: Free Press, 1979).

2. The phrase is the title of Ann Swidler, *Organizations Without Authority* (Cambridge, Mass.: Harvard University Press, 1979).

3. See Frank Lindenfeld and Joyce Rothschild-Whitt, *Workplace Democracy and Social Change* (Boston: Porter Sargent, 1982); John Case and Rosemary C. R. Taylor, *Co-ops, Communes and Collectives* (New York: Pantheon, 1979).

4. Alvin Gouldner, *The Two Marxisms* (New York: Oxford University Press, 1980).

5. Mihaly Vajda, *The State and Socialism* (London: Allison and Busby, 1981); Carmen Sirianni, *Workers' Control and Socialist Democracy* (London: New Left Books, 1982; Ernesto Laclau and Chantal Mouffe, *Hegemony and Socialist Strategy* (London: Verso, 1985).

6. Karl Polanyi, *The Great Transformation* (Boston: Beacon Press, 1957; originally published in 1944).

7. Jo Freeman, "The Tyranny of Structurelessness," *Ms.* (July 1973).

8. Max Weber, *The Theory of Social and Economic Organization*, III (New York: Free Press, 1964).

9. Fred Block, *The Origins of International Economic Disorder* (Berkeley: University of California Press, 1977).

10. For more on a theory of postindustrial transition, see Fred Block and Larry Hirschhorn, "New Productive Forces and the Contradictions of Contemporary Capitalism," *Theory and Society* (May–June 1979): 363–95; Fred Block, "Postindustrial Development and the Obsolescence of Economic Categories," *Politics & Society* 14 : 1 (1985): 71–104; Larry Hirschhorn, *Beyond Mechanization* (Cambridge, Mass.: MIT Press, 1984).

11. F. E. Emery and E. L. Trist, *Towards a Social Ecology* (New York: Plenum, 1975); Warren Bennis and Philip Slater, *The Temporary Society* (New York: Harper and Row, 1968).

12. Rosabeth Kanter, *Men and Women of the Corporation* (New York: Basic, 1977).

13. See Tracy Kidder, *The Soul of a New Machine* (New York: Avon Books, 1981).

14. Hirschhorn, *Beyond Mechanization*.

15. Thomas Rankin, "Unions and the Emerging Paradigm of Organization: The Case of ECWU Local 800," Ph.D. dissertation, Social Systems Science, University of Pennsylvania, 1986.

16. Sheldon S. Wolin, "The New Public Philosophy," *democracy* (October 1981): 23–36.

17. Fred Block, *Revising State Theory*, Chapter 1 (Philadelphia: Temple University Press, forthcoming).

18. Joseph Schumpeter, *Capitalism, Socialism, Democracy* (New York: Harper and Row, 1962; originally published 1942).

Victor M. Lidz

12. Founding Fathers and Party Leaders: America's Transition to the Democratic Social Condition

In the collective consciousness of American society, the Founding Fathers are objects of special veneration. Their actions are regarded as standing above all ordinary events in the national history. Along with Abraham Lincoln, they are accorded quasi-sacred status. The record of their conduct is celebrated for revealing timeless principles of civic life. The nation they founded is affirmed to hold special promise as a model for the affairs of all nations. That nation bears a duty of commitment to principles of public liberty, individual freedom, equality, justice, and material well-being. Through their achievements, culminating in the Constitution, the subsequent history of the American republic has been cast as a tale of the trials confronting a people burdened by a transcendental, though secular, covenant. Americans ritually remind one another of their covenanted burden on practically every occasion of public ceremony and whenever they deliberate matters of high policy.[1]

The collective belief in the Founding Fathers has the form of myth. The Founding Fathers are known to have been highly cultivated, wondrously steadfast in character and in devotion to the national welfare, supremely moral in dedication to liberty, and perhaps even divinely guided in judgment. Their conduct is thus elevated above profane history to appeal directly to Americans of all eras for emulation. Identification with the political principles of the Founding Fathers, known through the oft-taught stories of the Revolution and its aftermath, is a path to public rectitude and leadership. The myths of the Founding Fathers serve also to legitimate an order of public institutions. They elevate the institutions by associating them with the fundamental principles of the nation's creators. Life within authentically American institutions derives moral authority from being seen as continuous with the heroic achievements of the Founding Fathers.

All myth uses mystery to fascinate a community of believers. The stories of the Founding Fathers revolve around the central mystery of the nation's extraordinary fortune in the quality of the leadership under which it was unified.[2] How did so small a nation, living on the margins of European civilization, gain such leadership? Why was the nation so fortunate as to find such leaders precisely at its time of greatest vulnerability? How could the principles of the Founding Fathers have so profoundly unified a far-flung, diverse, and contentious nation with little previous experience of political coordination? How did that small group develop political principles that have been so enduringly valuable? How did the founders set a group of small colonies in modest circumstances on a path of national development that would prove to be prosperous and powerful? Why has no other nation or group of leaders been comparably "chosen" to serve the principles of liberty, democracy, and justice?

The myth of the Founding Fathers responds to these mysteries, but does not explain them away. It provides vivid details of heroic characters, exceptional fortitude, and great achievements that authenticate attitudes of reverence for the Founding Fathers and deepen fascination with the mysteries. The mysteries are profoundly bound up with and supportive of Americans' attachment to their national ideals.

American historical writing of the twentieth century, committed to the rationalism of modern scholarship, has faced difficulties in freeing itself from the myths of the Founding Fathers. A variety of tactics have been tried. The Founding Fathers have been debunked and portrayed as all-too-human. It has been shown that in actuality they followed the same baser motives as other figures in history.[3] The enduring myths of the Founding Fathers have themselves been subjected to close analysis and their formal similarities to myths of other peoples scrutinized. Perhaps most important has been the effort to portray the founding of the nation strictly according to Ranke's historiographic dictum, "as it actually happened." American historians have devoted great energy to interpreting the institutions, beliefs, anxieties, motives, and customs of the early Republic in the terms of that era, cut free, so far as possible, from the biasing beliefs of later eras.[4]

And yet the presuppositions deriving from the common myths surrounding the Founding Fathers continue to define many of the problems on which historians focus their studies. What we value in American history and wish to comprehend about it—for example, liberal institutions, democratic social arrangements, structures of opportunity, the dynamics of change and development—have sources in the common culture and have been precoded, as it were, in the myths surrounding the Founding Fathers.

The strongest symbolic link between veneration of the Founding Fathers and legitimation of the civic order is the Constitution. The Constitution is, to the public, the masterwork of the founders and the vital embodiment of their durable principles. The modalities of this embodiment, the actual workings of the Constitution as the central legitimator of authority, are so complex that they strain several basic categories of social theory. The Constitution is a product of eighteenth-century faith in social design by Reason and abstract principles, but carries the moral authority of a charismatic entity. It is the skeletal structure of the nation's normative order, but also protects a seemingly boundless interplay of the most powerfully vested interests. Advocacy in Constitutional cases involves the specialized or "artificial" reason of the law and a myriad of formal technicalities, but may also activate the strongest passions and sentiments of civic life. The heart of the Constitution remains an overall plan of self-government esteemed for simple elegance and coherence, yet is connected to values, ethical maxims, and technical rules that reach into practically each institution of American life. The Constitution stands as an emblem of continuity across epochs of vast social change, representing the design of the Founding Fathers through two centuries of national growth. But it is also a symbol of flexibility and assimilation, having absorbed principles of morality and law from each era in the life of the Republic. It has been a constant force of tradition and yet remained open to reinterpretation and reformulation in each cultural epoch of American history. By its growth into an organic combination of these many functional modalities, the Constitution has sustained the moral authority of the Founding Fathers and maintained this as an irreplaceable groundwork of practically all wealth, power, and prestige in the nation.

Given the pragmatic cast of American culture, the Constitution has been celebrated to an important degree for its success. It has provided a continuous and stable framework for law and government in a free and thriving republic for two hundred years. Deep within the mystery by which Americans identify the living Constitution, as they currently experience it, with the work and principles of the Founding Fathers, however, something crucial for the understanding of American public institutions has been concealed. As recent scholarship has uncovered through study of the ideals and concerns of the early republic, the Constitution actually failed to work as the Founding Fathers intended. They designed the Constitution to secure a kind of social order—a kind of relation among the distinct status groups of civil society—that they believed necessary to protect freedom and liberty in a republic. The special insecurities that characterized a republic or commonwealth stretching over much of a continent, encompassing peoples diverse in customs, and resting on innumerable local political communities were thought to heighten the need for that firm social order. Yet the social order that the founders hoped to consolidate started to disintegrate soon after the Constitution was set in operation. In less than a decade, the civic life of the new republic began to fill with alarms, recriminations, and confusions over its condition and fate. The turmoil and upset continued to grow for several years and soured a fateful period in the nation's history, the transition from the Federal to the Jeffersonian era. In crucial respects, the outcries were echoes of the ideology that had generated the Revolution, though now American rather than British conditions came under anxiety-ridden attack.

The crisis was not fully and stably resolved for several decades. By then, the ideals of social order that held moral authority in America had been greatly transformed. The Constitution, along with much else in American moral, legal, and political culture, had assimilated more democratic ideals of the status order of society. As the ideals of a democratic social order were joined to the Constitution, its symbolic powers of mystery and charisma covered over its early failure. Far from losing its moral authority as a failed political framework, the Constitution came to be revered for the democratic principles it was believed to have liberated. It has ever since been a premise of the American civic faith that the Constitution is essentially democratic. During celebrations of the bicentennial of the Constitution, nearly every suggestion that the founders' original plan of government had flaws as a democratic framework, even Justice Marshall's moderate criticism of the racial and gender discriminations it embodied,[5] provoked public expressions of anxiety. Thus, the mystery of the Constitution has created what we may consider a collective amnesia of American consciousness, a shared inability to recall in a coherent way the non-democratic past of the nation.

Among social scientists, too, the collective amnesia has distorted the understanding of the American experience. The distortions are perhaps most evident in the comfortable reading that has conventionally been given to Tocqueville's analysis of the "social condition of democracy" in America.[6] Tocqueville's suggestion that the democratic condition grew out of circumstances present in the earliest colonial settlements has been unduly highlighted. It has often been exaggerated into an argument that the American experience was essentially democratic from earliest times, however inconsistent certain particular institutions, such as indentured servitude, religious establishments, or the limited franchise, may appear with the overall pattern of democracy. American history has thus been interpreted, in a "Whiggish" manner, as revealing a general progression toward ever more thorough institutionalization of democracy.[7] Alternatively, but with hardly less distortion, undemocratic or antidemocratic events have been presented by more critical authors as simply "betrayals" of the essential American heritage.[8] This perspective, too, is "Whiggish" in concealing a major period of discontinuity and problematic transformation in American history, an epoch in which democracy was not simply purified out of older materials but established as a new principle of structure.

I will argue that American democracy and its import in American experience over the longer run can be grasped only if special attention is given to the dynamics of its emergence during the first several decades of the nineteenth century. My argument will be consistent with Digby Baltzell's long-standing effort to identify the distinct principles and patterns of social hierarchy that have predominated in different epochs of American history.[9] What Tocqueville called the "social condition of democracy" in American society will be portrayed as only in part a natural consequence of the absence of a "social condition of aristocracy" from the colonial settlements. Neither colonial society nor the society of the Revolution and its immediate aftermath closely fitted the type of "democracy" in Tocqueville's sense. The society envisioned in the Constitution itself was not yet democratic, but an ordered hierarchy of distinct status groups based on ideals quite different from the "equality" that Tocqueville identified in America.[10]

The social condition of democracy was a product of a tense, often bitter process of competitive struggle and institutional transformation. This process of change culminated roughly at the time of Tocqueville's visit to America. Tocqueville himself seems to have overestimated the extent to which the democratic condition had become well established before the period of his visit, even though he called attention to the differences between the popular party-based politics he observed and the politics dominated by a leading status group (in his terms the politics of noble leaders and great parties) that had prevailed in the first years of the Constitutional republic.[11]

The Tocquevillian period itself—roughly, the 1830s or the "Jacksonian era" and its aftermath—was a time of critical change. It was then that the social order and institutional pattern of American society took on distinctive qualities that have marked it as democratic ever since, and that, in particular, set it sharply off from the kind of society envisioned by the Founding Fathers. All the major institutional spheres of American society were drawn into the processes of change—religion, law, social hierarchies, political life, economic entrepreneurship and relations of production, education, consumption patterns, and so forth.[12] Everything that Tocqueville associated with the "social condition of democracy" was affected. Many of the distinctive features of democratic culture that Baltzell, following Tocqueville, has criticized in his discussions of American society also originated in this era. Thus, the democratization of American society provides a dynamic case of what Marcel Mauss called a "total social phenomenon," an institutional arrangement that can be understood only through its connections to the organization of the entire society.[13]

However, as an "index" of the general or total transformation and as analytical means of cutting into the entire complex of changes, I will focus on one highly apparent, because strongly contested, part of the emergence of a frankly democratic social order, namely, the rise of competitive political parties.

Leadership by Aristocrats of Talent and Virtue

The political party system developed in a setting where the general political culture was at the outset firmly opposed to parties and competitive politics. Not only did the Constitution fail to envision a role for parties in American political life, but the Founding Fathers had designed it to prevent the emergence not only of party alignments but also party spirit and partisan feeling as significant factors in public life.[14] None of the authors of the Constitution would, in public, have accepted as legitimate partisan opposition to governmental leadership that was itself regarded as legitimate. To be sure, some of the framers, such as Madison, were beginning to view the political processes of republics in dynamic terms. They perceived politics as a matter of factions working actively to bend the use of public authority to self-interested purposes. However, they hardly conceived of continuously organized associations that would appeal to almost all groups within the community for electoral support as a means of gaining control of practically every public office. In particular, they would never have condoned political associations devoted to challenging the right of legitimately seated authorities to remain in office. Organized partisan activity contradicted ideals of civic polity that were strongly held when the Federal government was first established, and we should not wonder that its legitimation, though utterly elementary to us, was not consolidated until a generation and more had passed. Even after competitive politics had become institutionalized in national politics, many Americans, especially among the educated and reflective status groups, long entertained nagging worries about party organizations and partisan political activities.

To the framers, "party" evoked the narrowly self-interested factions, usually based in familial, affinal, ritual, communal, and other particularistic solidarities, that had proved destructive of civic harmony in the ancient Greek *poleis,* and in the city-republics of the Renaissance. The term also evoked the cliques and cabals through which it was believed the British crown and its ministries had used patronage to corrupt Parliament in the course of the eighteenth century. People who viewed all concentrations of power as corrupting to traditions and constitutions and as inherently destructive of liberty, saw parties merely as devious tools by which great leaders could subordinate others to their will and thus build up large centers of personal power. The British parties were regarded as an underlying cause of the oppressive policies that had required Americans to resort to revolution as the only means of protecting their liberties. Similarly, the "factions" or "parties" that emerged in the political life of a few larger American towns, notably Philadelphia, were viewed suspiciously either as tools of rich and powerful families, or as disruptive agencies of an ambitious mob. A susceptibility to factions and parties was commonly believed to be a characteristic weakness of republics as a form of governance.[15]

Given these beliefs, it followed that the political design of the Constitution should embody the purpose of protecting the American republic and its fragile liberties from the bane of parties. To be sure, it was understood that despotism could be exercised through means other than parties. Conspiratorial oligarchies, tyrannical kings, and ambitious demagogues could destroy freedom even without the tool of a party. Yet, the complex machinery of government ordained in the Constitution—the divisions of powers among the branches, the distinctions among the forms of power exercised in the different branches, the checking and balancing of powers, and the resort to legal principles and usages in restricting powers, among others—was intended largely to keep faction and party from emerging or, at least, from becoming weighty forces in political life.[16]

The conviction about the political evil of parties went unchallenged. Neither the convention in Philadelphia nor the public debate over ratification of the Constitution brought out favorable views of parties. Party organization was regarded by practically all as leading naturally to the rise of factions and the outbreak of civic disorder. It evoked a chilling Hobbesian specter of the war of each against every, with the well-known history of the Puritan Revolution and its bitter conflicts in the background. Even the practical experience with political organization in the years leading up to and through the Revolution did little to dispel the fear. The organizational activities of the Revolutionary movement had been legitimated as drastic measures to protect imperiled liberties. Committees of Correspondence, Sons of Liberty, and Minutemen, among others, had been organizations of vigilant patriots opposing an illegitimate regime. However proudly remembered, they were hardly models to guide a citizenry's participation in the routine life of a peaceful republic that properly protected liberties.[17]

The Founding Fathers did have positive ideals about how political associations should be formed and political leaders chosen in free republics. Like their fears of parties, these beliefs were based on their concern over the fragility of liberty, even in republics, and perhaps especially in a republic that would not be confined to one town or city, but would extend across a vast territory, many hundreds of local communities, and a number of semi-sovereign "states." They knew that liberty was threatened whenever power was concentrated in the hands of one or a few. They knew that liberty was also threatened whenever power fell into the hands of the democracy, that is, the large numbers of common people, for the multitudes were believed to lack the self-restraint essential for civil conduct in a republic. At least, the democracy was believed to be unreliable in exercising self-discipline unless effectively constrained by the guidance of the leading status groups in society. Thus, power in a republic should be neither too highly concentrated nor too widely distributed. A republic would have the best opportunity to protect its freedoms and exercise its authority on behalf of the commonweal—the good of the people as a whole—if power were held mainly by the advantaged "natural leaders" of society. A status group of the wealthy, educated, and politically experienced, one that could consolidate authority while being sufficiently diverse, responsible, and self-disciplined to restrain itself from becoming an oligarchic faction, should serve best. People with the benefit of wealth were also thought, by virtue of their relative freedom from need, to be more capable of setting aside private interests and devoting themselves without compromise to the public interest.[18]

The emphasis on the role of "natural leaders" of society arose out of the tradition of political thought concerning mixed regimes and constitutions. That tradition dated back to ancient figures such as Aristotle, Polybius, and Cicero, but included many modern authors ranging from Harrington and the British Commonwealth pamphleteers and Country moralists to Montesquieu.[19] It was a tradition that, with the best of Enlightenment culture, drew both on hallowed antiquity and on the most acute modern rationalism. In this tradition, properly constituted polities mixed monarchical, aristocratic, and democratic elements together in complicated ways. These elements were understood to be distinct and in contention with one another, yet ideally balanced in a fashion that could preserve the coherence of the society as an organic whole.[20]

The Constitution drew on this tradition for certain aspects of its design of governmental powers. The presidency was conceived in part as responding to a universal need for a "monarchical" concentration of power, the Senate and judiciary were regarded as "aristocratic" in form, and the House of Representatives was thought to fulfill a "democratic" function.[21] As the new government was established under the Constitution, Americans continued to think in these terms. Washington, in establishing precedents for the public conduct of presidents, followed an etiquette that, although modest in a way befitting the leader of a free republic, drew on old customs concerning the special respect due a monarch as a central figure of authority.[22] The Senate in its early days tried to follow ideals dating back to the Roman republic, ideals concerning both the personal stature of senators as guardians of civic order and the ways aristocratic bodies should deliberate on matters of high policy. Men appointed to the Federal judiciary were also expected to conduct themselves as members of an exclusive group of dignitaries. The first Congressmen, sensitive to their standing as the only Federal officials to be elected more or less popularly, regarded themselves as representatives of the people at large, including especially the common people. Their role permitted them to be democratically responsive to the practical needs, interests, and wishes of citizens in a way deemed inappropriate for senators or the president as well as judges.

Under the influence of Montesquieu's celebrated treatment of the British Constitution, however, the generation of the founders also thought of the society at large in terms of mixed regimes and constitutions. In this context, the concept of mixture applied not simply to powers of governmental bodies but more deeply to the balancing that ought to obtain among constituent "orders" or "estates" of the republic.[23] The social values involved in this conception of a mixed constitution were in crucial respects static, for they presupposed that only an enduring and generally continuous relationship among the "orders" of society could be ideal. The decline of this relatively static outlook during the next generation became an important factor in the legitimation of political parties. Indeed, this change in outlook and perception was perhaps a cultural precondition of a more dynamic and democratic evaluation of political conduct.[24] But even at the time of the establishment of the Federal government the general conditions characteristic of American society created difficulties as to how the ideal of a mixed constitution could be made to work.

American social conditions and cultural orientations sharply limited the role of the monarchical order in society. There had been no consolidated monarchical or executive order in colonial America. There had only been weak governors who, whether selected by the crown, proprietors, or the colonists themselves, had not been able to represent the crown with vigor in trying to make extensive groups dependent on their authority and forge them into a unified social interest. Neither governors nor the distant kings had built up a large and well coordinated body of officials to achieve their policies expeditiously. Nevertheless, Americans believed that the crown's corrupting force in England, acting in part through the leadership of Parliament, had seriously endangered their liberties. The monarchical order in any society was feared as a danger to liberty unless it was closely restricted. Americans were agreed that they must avoid a concentrated executive which might command many officials and vast patronage, reducing large numbers of citizens to dependency on and servility to a monarchical interest or establishment. They were also wary of creating traditions of loyalty and devotion to leadership that might create a strong interest or establishment out of the executive branch of government.[25]

By contrast, American conditions gave a large and expansive role to the democracy as an order of society. As Tocqueville later argued, the original settlement of the American colonies had not reproduced the monarchical and aristocratic orders of Europe. On the contrary, it had left many opportunities for the democratic order to grow under conditions of much reduced constraint from higher orders.[26] Nevertheless, the term "democracy" still referred in the time of the Founding Fathers to a distinct order or status group of disesteemed persons, not to the general character of a society or its political regime. Care must be taken not to project a Tocquevillian concept of a democratic social condition back into the colonial or even Federal periods.

The common people or democratic order at the middle of the eighteenth century was far from being a self-reliant social entity, to say nothing of a confident social group imparting its moral qualities to society as a whole. Commoners understood, despite ambiguities about the status of some of their wealthier or better educated members, that they comprised the humble order of society. Many of them lived under conditions of oppressive poverty inconsistent with a belief in the dignity and self-reliance of the democracy. The largest number were, to be sure, independent farmers. Yet they supported themselves on small plots of land, worked with their bodies to the point of physical exhaustion, lived in cramped housing with minimal furnishings, wore crude homemade clothing as an outer sign of their status, worried about supplies of food for the coming year, and saw little prospect of a better future. Most other commoners were physical laborers, household servants, or artisans who worked for their betters. They served on a basis of free agreement (formally free contract, in Max Weber's term), despite diffuse personal relations of disadvantage and disesteem that often limited their choices. Like the free farmers, they, too, had a positive status that set them apart from the peasants, serfs, and hereditary servants in European societies of the "aristocratic social condition." However, they lived under harsh material conditions and often experienced considerable insecurity about their futures. Many commoners had undergone the humbling and physically wearing experience of indentured servitude and emerged in utter poverty, or had been raised in homes humbled by their parents' earlier servitude. Pride in their status as free persons was often measured in comparison with the condition of slaves. Most attended town and church meetings where seating arrangements, procedures of discussion, and patterns of influence ratified their low standing. They knew that as commoners they owed deference and personal loyalty to the religious and secular leaders of their towns and villages. Institutions of personhood, kinship, and marriage reinforced a sense of diffuse belonging in and identification with low social standing. Heritability of status, including humble status, remained a general social expectation, giving a corporate quality to the make-up of the commons as a democratic order.[27]

Nevertheless, several cultural forces were already converging to transform members of the democracy into more independent and effective agencies of social action. The ascetic Protestant heritage of most of the colonies had established a belief in the dignity and even ultimate equality of every responsible conscience.[28] The widespread sympathy for the Puritan revolutionaries, and then for the Commonwealth pamphleteers and Country publicists, had started to elaborate the political implications of the Puritan doctrines of conscience.[29] These ideologies elevated notions of individual liberty to the point of treating them as transcendental principles of social and political life.[30] They also tended to strengthen trust in members of the democracy by lending new importance to questions of their political freedoms. Ever since the Great Awakening of the 1740s, the evangelical strains of American Calvinism had stimulated commoners to take more assertive roles in public life.[31] Though the increased religious and political activity of commoners was most apparent in frontier communities, it had been felt in the larger towns as well. This trend was further invigorated by the Revolution and its enthusiasms. From the middle decades of the eighteenth century, the Scottish doctrines of "common sense" had also exerted a growing influence in favor of commoners and their political participation.[32] These doctrines provided a persuasive foundation in secular moral philosophy for viewing the ordinary citizen's judgment as sufficient to make the sorts of decisions requisite to an active consent of the governed.

Thus, several elements in American culture had combined with one another and, perhaps by an "elective affinity" with practical social conditions, created new reasons to accord the common people a more active role in political life. The democratic order had gained a strength, vitality, and status of trust that was perhaps unique even among republics. From the standpoint of a belief in a mixed constitution of society, however, the democracy had grown worrisomely prominent. Practically all Americans were concerned, at least, that new political institutions must encourage virtue, modesty, and self-restraint among the people in order to protect the liberties of the republic. The vigor and relative autonomy of the democracy were widely viewed as a potential danger. Many of the disorders of political life under the Articles of Confederation appeared to be just the sort of difficulty that ambitious democracies typically create.[33]

Given the weakness of every component of monarchical establishment and the growing strength of the democracy, it appeared obvious to the generation of the Founding Fathers that an orderly republic would require, in some sense, a firm aristocracy. In the theories of mixed constitutions, the aristocratic order was viewed as the moderating and integrating element. Only an aristocracy devoted to virtue and self-discipline could overcome the tendencies of both monarchy and, under American conditions, more ominously, the democracy, to be ambitious and grasping of power. Such an aristocracy could assure that power would not become overly concentrated, but remain distributed among a number of independent and civic-minded leaders. By drawing on its solidarity as an exclusive and advantaged status group, a virtuous aristocracy could also assure that the leaders of the nation would extend trust and mutual respect to one another. Thus, the balance and coherence of a properly constituted society seemed to depend on a stable, self-confident aristocracy.[34]

The difficulty, as the Founding Fathers were quite aware, was that America lacked an aristocracy in a strict sense. There was sensitive ambivalence about the weaknesses of groups and institutions considered to be aristocratic in type. When traveling in Europe, the founders were often overwhelmed by the sophistication and self-assurance of the aristocrats as well as by the grand roles that some of them played in national affairs and national culture. Nevertheless, the true aristocracies, with positions of leadership secured by heritable privileges, appeared to ascetic American eyes as a major source of the corruption and lack of vigor in the politics of the Old World.[35] Inherited status, great wealth and the ease it brought, arrogant exclusion of new talents and ideas from the circles of leadership, and exploitation of laboring classes held in positions of dependency had reduced too many European aristocrats to ineffectiveness and often sheer laziness. Instead of bulwarks of liberty, the aristocracies had become passive tools of absolutist monarchies.

In sum, the same ascetic Protestant culture that had strengthened democratic groups in America by articulating individualistic principles of legitimacy had also weakened the confidence in all leadership based on claims of aristocratic privilege. Few Americans wished to establish an actual aristocracy in the New World. Even those who harbored strong anxieties over their ability to fulfill the aristocratic function in a free republic recognized the evils of the European experience with aristocracy. The Constitution accordingly banned titles and privileges, and it codified strong sentiments among Americans in doing so. Nevertheless, these measures did not satisfy all Americans. Many of the Anti-Federalists who opposed ratification of the Constitution did so out of a fear that it would introduce an aristocratic establishment.[36] While the Anti-Federalists were defeated, their concerns framed a widely shared, if largely suppressed, undercurrent of discomfort with the Constitution. Awareness of this undercurrent placed the nation's new leadership in a posture of caution about its exercise of authority.

That America lacked an aristocracy propped up by encrusted tradition, privileges, great concentrations of wealth, dependent serfs, a national court "society," hereditary civil and military leadership, and national class-based intermarriage, thus seemed a special opportunity. Americans could form a new sort of aristocracy on the basis of talent, virtue, and energy. This "natural aristocracy" would exercise leadership not by inheritance, but by qualification. In every generation leadership might go to the individuals who had the most talent, virtue, education, and devotion to the common welfare and who were wealthy enough to be "disinterested" in shaping public policy. If advantages of birth would allow many sons to succeed their fathers in roles of public prominence, opportunities for new talent must also be secured, and leadership acquired sheerly by inheritance should not be tolerated.[37]

The theory of leadership and authority embedded in the concept of a natural aristocracy had a large fiduciary component. To be sure, public uses of power were understood to be acts of the people. A conception of the ultimate sovereignty of the people acting corporately played a leading part in the Constitution. This idea is implied in the opening phrase of the preamble, "We the people . . .," but it did not imply then what Americans usually presume it to mean today. The "people" did not mean an aggregate of autonomous individuals each of whom, with right, acts as a self-reliant conscience when participating in public decision making. The Constitutional phrase implied, rather, a conception of rule by the people as a whole—with the people viewed as a public unified through its organization into "orders" or status groups.[38] The common people or democratic order in this understanding played a limited and mainly subordinate role. The democracy's legitimate part in public life depended largely on its being under the influence of a proper leading status group, the group that could wield power on behalf of the whole community in a judicious fashion. The natural aristocracy must be sufficiently self-disciplined and self-confident to protect the republic against the dangers presented by the common people. Moreover, the social discipline should be realized in personal relationships. Political leadership and authority exercised over the lower orders and groups should be rooted in the face-to-face settings of local communities.[39]

This leadership ethic was obviously a demanding one, and only select groups in the society of the early republic could put themselves forward as having the status characteristics to fulfill it. In socio-economic terms, these groups were somewhat diverse, but reflected the still limited pluralism of the society around them. They were large landowners, wealthy merchants, and lawyers, with a few prominent ministers, educators, and publicists also taking part. In Marxian or Weberian terms, they did not comprise a social class. Their positions within the relations of production were not unitary, but pluralistic. They did not have unified economic or socio-economic interests, and there were many occasions when they had to confront the fact that they were sharply divided in terms of economic interests. The merchants of the Mid-Atlantic and New England states, and often the lawyers who were closely tied to them, frequently entered economic relationships with European markets that conflicted with the interests of the Southern planters. Nevertheless, these various economic groups tended to regard themselves as a fairly unitary status group of gentlemen having a right of near monopoly over prominent public leadership. This status group is properly called a "natural aristocracy" or "aristocracy of virtue and talent," phrases that Jefferson favored for their idealism, to avoid misleading implications of "aristocracy," "gentry," or simply "upper class." As compared with the national "upper class" that, as Baltzell has shown, consolidated itself on the basis of a rising industrial economy late in the nineteenth century, the "aristocracy of virtue and talent" held more diffuse and more firmly established positions of leadership, but operated within a less differentiated, smaller scale society.[40]

The ideals of leadership followed by the "aristocracy of talent and virtue" derived from the fiduciary conception of its political role. In the ideal-typical terms of Weber's contrast between personal and impersonal relationships, the "natural aristocrats" claimed the right to fill roles of political leadership as an element of essentially personal status. The crucial qualification of the leader was a personal capacity to exercise disinterested judgment on behalf of the body politic as a whole. Family prominence, education, qualities of character, personal connection to other "natural aristocrats," experience in public affairs, sufficient wealth to support the appropriate style of life and a presumption of disinterest in the economic effects of public policies, and, more fortuitously, the community's lack of a gentleman with seniority who wished to serve were the major qualifications for high office. The ideal leader was a gentleman of highly cultivated conscience who could act in an independent manner and fulfill public duties defined in terms of generalized standards of reason and virtue. A leader represented a community by placing his superior judgment at its service. He was expected to avoid any compromise of the autonomy with which he might exercise his judgment. He ought to conduct himself in a way that dramatized his status as a patron of his constituents, known to them and trusted by them in personal terms. He should also manifest his superiority in character and status and his freedom from *quid pro quo* arrangements with and constraining promises to others in the community.[41]

A man who commanded these qualifications could gain election by "standing" for office. He might circulate word of his interest in serving, usually after checking that no one having seniority within the local "natural aristocracy" intended to stand for office. He might then permit his friends to praise his personal qualities among other leaders of the community and wherever citizens gathered to discuss public matters. He would not actively "run" for office, for example, by giving speeches, canvassing the voters, or otherwise publicizing his views on matters of policy. In particular, he could not issue policy statements as promises to his constituents about his conduct in office, should he be elected. Any such campaigning would be viewed as pandering to the masses and as tending to disqualify the candidate by compromising his independence of judgment and hence the necessary claims about his qualities of character.[42]

It was permissible for a candidate to demonstrate his good will as a patron of his constituents by providing drink and possibly food for the voters on election day. Their willingness to receive food and drink from him would be a sign of their acceptance of his leadership. He might then anticipate election by acclamation or by public submission of ballots bearing his name. A proper election was not so much a contest as it was a ratification of a strong claim to office, performed publicly by the assembled electorate. The public act of voting ideally affirmed the harmony of the community in choosing its leaders, a harmony colored with the constituents' deference to their natural leaders. Once in office, leaders typically expected to remain in office unchallenged until they decided to step up to higher office or step down after having done their best to fulfill the duty of "natural aristocrats" to provide public leadership.[43]

Elections were, to be sure, sometimes contested. However, open competition was deemed improper. The feeling against competition was especially strong for contests that became sufficiently heated to divide the loyalties of the community. Often the divisions resulted from clashes between the ambitions of prominent groups of kin seeking to bring the glory of leadership to their family names, as in the long-lasting factional conflicts between Livingstons and Clintons in New York.

Political rule by an "aristocracy of virtue and talent" faced several difficulties. In some parts of the country, especially on the frontiers, people of appropriate background were too scarce to fill the positions of leadership. Moreover, significant portions of the frontier communities, especially where evangelical religions were strong, no longer observed the standards of deference to a "natural aristocracy." They were comfortable in having leaders who lacked the qualities of "natural aristocrats."[44] In some of the more thickly settled areas, tensions among classes and status groups had generated distrust toward the "natural aristocracy" among craftsmen, shopkeepers, and small independent farmers. Particularly in the towns of the Middle States and on the frontiers, some commoner groups were disposed to claim leadership roles. When they joined together in "factions" or "parties" to do so, as happened in a few of the largest towns, they precipitated anxieties among other citizens that the common good would be endangered by people whose political motives lacked the discipline of proper education and experience.

An even more disturbing threat to the rule of a "natural aristocracy" was the prospect of factionalism among the leaders themselves. Whether arising from rivalries among leading families, among different alliances of economic or regional interest, or among adherents of different political ideologies, the specter of factionalism cast a pall over the principles legitimating the authority of the "natural aristocracy." Factionalism would suggest that restricting leadership to "natural aristocrats" would not suffice to preserve the harmony and welfare of the people. Given the widespread disposition to regard all organized political competition as evidence of the factionalism that had brought so many other republics to ruin, any sign of active competition created anxiety about the future of the republic.[45]

However unevenly institutionalized the leadership of a "natural aristocracy" was after the adoption of the Constitution, confidence in the new system of authority, not least because it was in tension with the Anti-Federalist distrust in semblances of aristocracy, depended remarkably on the prestige and semi-official standing of the advantaged status group. The purest symbol of the prestige of the leadership was George Washington's election as the first president. He gained office by acclamation of the Electoral College, which was itself filled with "natural aristocrats." Washington then selected people who were evidently "aristocrats of talent and virtue" to staff his cabinet and practically all major administrative offices. The etiquette that he designed to govern presidential conduct, the conduct of cabinet members, and the communications of his administration with the other branches of government and the public at large presupposed the code of honor of a modest but secure and advantaged status group—gentility, rights to exercise leadership, and personal honor.[46] The leaders and most members of the House of Representatives, practically all the Senators, the justices of the Supreme Court, and most district judges were also well qualified "aristocrats of virtue and talent." Those bodies then devised procedures of operation and styles of communication that also followed the customs of the leading status group, distinguished by honorability and deference from the styles of commoners but modest as compared with the styles of European aristocrats. The lifestyle of the English gentry perhaps provided the primary model. At any rate, the new national leadership, Washington as President above all, brought confidence to the new republic by making a specific pattern of moral virtue, deemed appropriate for civic leadership in American culture, manifest to all. Thus, following the adoption of the Constitution, American political life rested heavily on the status honor of the "natural aristocracy." The deference that status group was accorded for maintaining its code of honor was a key to civic order and civil conduct.

In its original meaning, and as it was originally put into operation, the Constitution presupposed the vital presence of an estate of "natural aristocrats" at the head of American society. By entrusting authority to an "aristocracy of virtue and talent," Constitutional governance was to avoid the factionalism that had brought decline to many other republics. The impediments to the emergence of parties that were built so deeply into the Constitution had as their counterpart a confidence that leadership by a "natural aristocracy" could manage the affairs of the republic and protect its freedoms. Signs that its governance was not operating effectively, harmoniously, or freely, provoked grave anxieties over the workability of the Constitution. The early history of the American republic shows a number of outbreaks of anxieties over factionalism and disorder. The reactions were often passionate, even over events that modern eyes interpret as simply showing a growth of healthy political competition. We can understand the gloomy interpretations of contemporaries only by understanding the events as they appeared at the time, as portents of breakdown in the secure political control of the "natural aristocracy" and hence impending Constitutional crisis. To the common understanding of Americans at the close of the eighteenth century, and of many Americans through the first decades of the nineteenth, the Constitution was not viable unless a leading status group of special talent and virtue continued to dominate political life.

At the highest levels of government, the rule of "natural aristocrats" sustained itself into the 1820s. Every president down through John Quincy Adams displayed unambiguously the qualities of "natural aristocrats." Almost all cabinet officers, the leadership of both Houses of Congress, a large majority of Senators, and practically all members of the federal judiciary were "natural aristocrats" throughout this period as well. Deference to the leading status group remained a vital factor in American political life for nearly four decades after the Constitution was ratified.

A comparison may highlight the importance of the leading status group's effort to constitute itself as an "aristocracy of talent and virtue." The wealthy and powerful *criollo* groups who led the Latin American independence movements were also motivated by feelings of inferiority, jealousy, and rivalry toward European aristocracies. Their sentiments toward aristocratic institutions were even more complicatedly ambivalent than those of their North American counterparts, but upon gaining independence they developed a profoundly different culture of leadership.[47]

Before the revolutions, the *criollos* had for generations been sensitive about their status inferiorities relative to the Spanish aristocracy. From early in the colonial period, only aristocrats born in Spain had been qualified to hold office in the royal administration. Given the unitary nature of the imperial administration, all high officials of the colonies had to be appointed from the born-in-Spain aristocracy. Members of colonial families were disqualified not only from filling offices in Spain but also from high governance of their regional societies in the New World. Even *criollos* who were descended from leaders of the Conquests, who exercised mastery over vast plantations, whose wealth was far greater than that of leading Spanish aristocrats, and who had achieved distinction in colonial society were barred from holding royal appointments. Moreover, they remained the formal inferiors of the Spanish aristocracy in social terms, bound to display deference in all meetings, even to figures holding new and low titles. These conditions bred profound resentments among the leading *criollo* families, who felt themselves entitled to royal appointments and aristocratic honors in every respect except the accident of colonial birth. No matter how successfully they lived up to aristocratic traditions in managing their affairs, they always found Spanish aristocrats, often petty aristocrats, imposed over them in the political and social hierarchies. They were institutionally prohibited from consolidating the control over their own societies to which, in hallowed European traditions, aristocracies were entitled.

Accordingly, in leading the revolutions, the *criollos* sought independence from Spain largely to establish their own aristocratic control over the new nations of Latin America. Although they often emulated the North American revolutionaries in adopting republican forms of rule, their deeper aspiration was to establish themselves as aristocracies in a rather strict sense. They expected to secure their advantages through heritable privileges, control of the land and means of production, monopoly of political leadership, rights to personal deference from other social classes, and exclusive access to education and high culture. Little emphasis was placed on the universalistic and achievement standards that were prominent in North America. Talent and virtue were not emphasized, nor was openness to progressive change. Instead, personalism and traditionalism were imposed.

The Rise of Political Parties

Competitive party politics oriented to a mass electorate, though it now approaches being an "evolutionary universal"[48] of modern democracies, was largely an American innovation. What Tocqueville observed of American politics during his visit in the 1830s had no close parallel in any other nation during his lifetime. Despite a relatively small and scattered population, decentralized political structure, and peripheral position in the European system of "modern" nations, the United States developed a stably competitive, mass-oriented party system, at the federal level, and within many states and localities as well, a generation or more ahead of any other nation.[49]

But how did this situation arise? Scarcely a generation before Tocqueville's visit, as we have seen, American politics were dominated by a status group of "natural aristocrats" who abhorred parties and factions. Why did this group fail to consolidate its control of national leadership? How were its standards of political conduct, including distrust of parties, competition, challenges to elected leaders, open electioneering, and promises to constituents about matters of future policy, overturned so rapidly? How could the revered Constitution have failed so dreadfully as to have permitted competitive parties to become established institutions of political life?

The social setting in which political parties first emerged continues to have structural consequences for American political life. Definitional problems often obscure the point, but the United States is unique among the large nations of our time in having created and stabilized a competitive, democratic party system before it became highly industrialized and developed the class system (and struggles) of an industrial society. The middle class style that predominates in American politics, including notably middle class control of the policy programs of both major parties, can be traced back to the fact that the basic patterns of political competition were created before the rise of a large industrial working class. American political life still adheres to a unique tradition of resisting explicit class appeals and class divisions. The parties renounce close and exclusive alignments with social classes. Parties compete to attract followings among the broadest range of groupings, but with the understanding that a majority following can be put together only if it is centered firmly in the middle class.[50] Policy appeals may be directed to a variety of regional, ethnic, and industrial interests and to many different social values, but care must be taken not to alienate those who identify with the core of middle class culture. One goal of the present analysis is to place this middle class control of American politics in historical and institutional perspective.

The political parties began to emerge, much to the dismay of the national leadership, soon after the Constitution was ratified and the Federal government established. Despite the discomfiture of practically everyone involved at the start, the growth of the parties proceeded rapidly, though far from evenly, through several distinct phases. After the bitter election of 1800 (during which distrust of parties helped to precipitate a national crisis) and the "Era of Good Feelings" marked by one-party domination, competition between parties began to receive general acceptance. Overt party organization and party loyalties captured a key role in the coordination of practical politics, not only in shaping policies and lists of candidates before elections, but in the legislative and administrative work of running the government as well. Parties also mediated a crucial transformation of political life by vastly expanding popular participation in electoral politics and in efforts to influence public policies. These developments culminated in the presidential election of 1840. That election—the famous Log Cabin Campaign—resulted in a new level of legitimation, first, of competitive political parties as organizations and, second, of mobilizing popular participation as a means of winning elections.

After 1840, party connections, tactics, and sentiments were widely and openly accepted as grounds of political conduct. By mid-century, older politicians could reminisce about their early party enthusiasms without fear of discrediting themselves.[51] It had by then become difficult simply to think of political life and active political leadership, even retrospectively, without reference to the motive of advancing party interests. Nevertheless, ambivalent attitudes toward parties still remained notable forces in civic life. This could long be seen in the reluctance of some political leaders to acknowledge the partisan elements in their own motives and in the ethical condescension of many upper class groups toward party politicians.

Tocqueville already encountered most elements of the American party system in the 1830s. Indeed, he was able to observe many basic features that still characterize it today, a circumstance that gives a haunting quality to his analysis. He noted the structure of two-party competition, the efficacy of the franchise in assuring that public policies are popular, but also constantly in flux, the vast number and impressive energy of voluntary associations attempting to influence public policy, the decline in the quality of leadership to mediocrity or worse, the growth of a well-informed and active citizenry, and the curiously emotional and seemingly irrational techniques and ceremonies of popular electioneering.[52] He recognized the historical originality of the democratic parties and saw clearly that they were affecting almost every aspect of political life. He probably did not appreciate the full variety of the dynamic changes that had brought the parties so dramatically into control of American politics, nor did he grasp how deeply and irrevocably institutionalized they were becoming. He seems to have envisioned a political future in which the parties might play a greatly reduced role. Our sense, today, that Tocqueville was so confidently prescient of the future of American politics certainly points to some striking institutional continuities. However, it may also derive as much from the political situation in which we read him retrospectively, where competitive parties are fully accepted, as from his own understanding of how fundamentally American democracy rests on the party system.

Based as it was on fundamental political principles, rule by "aristocrats of talent and virtue" was not displaced easily. Nevertheless, nearly from the start, it failed to operate with the noble decorum that the framers had anticipated. Already during the first Congress, the genteel conduct of the nation's leaders, though nearly all were "natural aristocrats," was marred by disturbing appearances of political competition. Almost as soon as serious differences of policy emerged at the seat of government, congressmen and cabinet members were lining up coalitions to advance interests and outlooks that were decidedly partisan.[53] A number of leaders attempted to develop a personal following in the Congress, but the patterns of alliance soon polarized between one group headed by Jefferson in the Cabinet and Madison in the House, and another group, probably smaller but more tightly knit, with Hamilton as Secretary of the Treasury serving as its leader. By the time of the second Congressional elections, influential congressman, senators, and cabinet members, though affirming the ideals of nonpartisan conduct, were also encouraging prominent citizens with views similar to their own to stand for election, especially where a figure in the opposing alliance might be displaced.[54] Thus, efforts to increase influence within the policy-making machinery of government were already extending into the electoral process. Despite their distrust of competitive politics, "aristocrats of talent and virtue" found themselves developing electoral alliances in order to strengthen the representation of views with which they identified.

Washington, as president, persistently showed his sensitivity to the political competition that seemed to threaten the republican virtue of the nation. He repeatedly urged restraint on all leaders, especially the members of his cabinet. At first, he tried to stand impartially above the growing turmoil. Eventually, reacting to Jefferson's ties with Madison as a particularly dangerous violation of his expectations for cabinet solidarity, he accepted Jefferson's resignation. This step appeared to place his influence behind Hamilton's alliance. While giving warrant to Hamilton's claim of acting on the president's wishes, a claim Jefferson had previously contested but now fearfully conceded, it did not end the divisions.

The political alliances became ever more influential as Washington's second term unfolded. Practically every event in legislative and administrative politics now took place in a context of competition between the alliances. Despite the apparent success of Washington's administration, therefore, many people familiar with the inner workings of the new government were disturbed by the activity of the new political alliances and especially by the energy and strength of feeling shown by their adherents. The rising fear was that these alliances were rapidly becoming indistinguishable from the factions so long regarded as malignant to republics.[55]

In 1796, with Washington retiring from the presidency, the new political alignments created a contest over the election of a successor. As vice-president and as a loyal member of the administration, Adams was commonly regarded as having seniority in the national leadership. Qualified by personal status, character, experience, and office, he was the natural successor to Washington. Adams seems at first to have expected, along with many others, that he would be named president by acclamation of the Electoral College much as Washington had been. Jefferson, however, using the alliance he and Madison had been building, began discreetly to inform potential supporters around the country that he, too, wished to stand as a candidate. Soon associations were being formed in communities all over the nation under the leadership of local "aristocrats of talent and virtue" to proclaim Jefferson's fitness for the presidency.[56] Jefferson understood from the start that he was challenging a figure whom many thought entitled to office, but believed the challenge necessary due to policy considerations and his own doubts about Adams's personal suitability for leading the nation.

The ensuing contest focused on seats in the House and in the state legislatures, which controlled, in most states, the selection of members of the Electoral College as well as United States senators. Both alliances pursued the goal of controlling the executive and legislative branches of the Federal government with extreme discretion, wary that their conduct might appear to be partisan. Jefferson, for example, exchanged letters about his candidacy with supporters in distant states, but he cautiously limited his correspondence to a small number of people with a proven sense of political tact. He preferred to entrust messages to traveling friends who could convey his thoughts orally after sizing up the situation in which they would be received. When committing his plans to written letters, he sent them privately through friends, for he feared that his candidacy would be discredited if postmasters favoring Adams opened them and revealed his efforts to gain election.[57]

For the most part, the two candidates "campaigned" by modestly deferring to friends who could speak about the issues for them, both adhering broadly to the established custom of "standing" for office as gentlemen. Nevertheless, policy differences between the two alliances were effectively placed before the electorate as grounds for voting. The initial, tentative steps were taken toward constructing party organizations as means of effective electoral competition. Both alliances tried to enlist influential figures and candidates from many communities across the country in support of their respective aspirants to the presidency. They attempted to coordinate, even if loosely, the policies with which their candidates aligned themselves across voting districts, states, and even regions of the country. In some locales, "tickets" of candidates were printed and publicly distributed as means of advising sympathetic voters. Both alliances took their boldest steps to appeal to editors, thereby drawing newspapers into advocacy for their policies and candidates. Nevertheless, a wary feeling that these developments were at most partly legitimate was reflected in the caution with which the alliances kept their activities largely hidden from the electorate. The entire election left the nation with an aftertaste of unseemly, but perhaps only temporary, display of factionalism and partisan conduct.[58]

A deeper crisis arose in 1800, when Jefferson, displeased by Adams's leadership of the nation, again arranged for his name to be put forward for the presidency. Four years earlier he had cautiously contested the succession to Washington, but in 1800 he was challenging Adams as an incumbent. He could gain office only by appealing directly over the head of government to the sovereign electorate, an act that was difficult to legitimate under established political beliefs. It was apparent that Jefferson's challenge could succeed only if he undermined Adams's entitlement to continue in office by bringing dramatic issues of public policy before the people. Moreover, Jefferson would need a strong political organization to reach the electorate with his appeal.

By this time, Americans were beginning to acknowledge alliances and organizations as factors that shape political life. As the election year approached , the term party was coming into more general use, along with such others as alliance, interest, and faction. There was widespread, though imprecise, understanding that major political issues pitted a party around the president, usually called the Federalists, against another one led by Jefferson, called the Republican or increasingly the Democratic if not simply the Jeffersonian party. Thus, for many citizens, it was quite apparent that Jefferson would proceed to seek election by attempting to firm up the organization of a party. Nevertheless, the term party still aroused discomfort about the health of the polity. Grave anxieties hung over the land as it ventured into its first deeply competitive election.[59]

Dissatisfactions with Adams's administration gave the Jeffersonian party a number of important issues, but the conduct of the election campaign itself became the critical issue of 1800. The leading Federalists, most of whom were less moderate than Adams, reacted to Jefferson's challenge as simply an attack on governmental authority—as sedition threatening the harmony of civic life in the Republic. They persuaded Adams to bring prosecutions under the Common Law of sedition to suppress the bolder figures in the Jeffersonian press. They also planned broad measures, of which the Alien Act was merely a part, to limit the effectiveness of the emerging Jeffersonian party organization. The Jeffersonians in turn interpreted the Federalist reaction as the desperate effort of a tyranny to sustain unwanted power over the nation. Each party came to view the other as a conspiratorial faction willing to sacrifice the civil accord of a free republic in order to grasp power for itself. The major issues of the Revolutionary ideology were resurrected, but with the extreme sensitivities over corruption, conspiracy, tyrannical attack on liberty, and grasping for power now serving to set each party self-righteously against the other. The contest for the presidency and other high offices became bitter, each side fearing that victory for the other would bring down the free republic.[60]

Both sides attempted to develop more effective party organizations and, in particular, to use the press and voluntary associations led by figures widely trusted in their local communities for partisan appeals to the electorate. Yet, the work of organizing parties and planning partisan strategies, especially the overall coordination of the many activities visible to the public, was kept largely under cover. Neither party was comfortable in asserting the legitimacy of its own organizational activities, to say nothing of conceding the propriety of organizing to the other party. Leaders of both sides exonerated their partisan activities mainly by pointing out the threats to liberty posed by their opponents.[61]

The Jeffersonians enjoyed the advantage in their organizational efforts of making a stronger appeal to the larger body of common citizens—an advantage they pressed by expanding the franchise wherever possible. They also succeeded in portraying leading Federalists as distrustful of common citizens and even republican forms of government. In extreme moments, the Republicans artfully hinted at Federalist ambitions to protect their social advantages by reestablishing the privileges of European aristocracies and possibly a new monarchy as well. Nevertheless, the Jeffersonians were also inhibited by the fear that, being an opposition, they would find the legitimacy of their organizational activities more readily questioned. The Federalists exploited this weakness by alleging that the Jeffersonians were organizing a conspiracy against the Constitutional order as well as its elected representatives. Extreme Federalists charged that their opponents were atheists and Jacobins intent on destroying social order and establishing "mobocracy."[62]

The profound departure in practice from the Constitutional ideal of genteel rule by an "aristocracy of talent and virtue" was now apparent to all. To be sure, nearly all prominent figures in both parties represented the status group and values of a "natural aristocracy." But the civility and clear direction of policy anticipated in the Constitutional theory had been lost. Irrepressible conflict dominated the scene. Policy differences between Federalists and Jeffersonians seemed ever more bitter, the rifts within the national leadership had become a growing part of routine politics, and the political stakes in organizing parties mounted relentlessly. Politics had become a matter of parties and partisan loyalties, factional interests and corruptly expanding political organizations—just what the Constitution had been designed to avoid. The conventions of mutual respect among "natural aristocrats" and common devotion to the public welfare seemed utterly ineffective as barriers to the rise of parties, as were the elaborate checks and balances of the Constitution. Recognition that a Constitutional crisis had been reached could no longer be repressed.[63]

The heavy air of crisis cleared only partially with Jefferson's narrow victory. The close election and confusions in the Electoral College left the outcome uncertain nearly to Inauguration Day. But when Adams surrendered the presidency to Jefferson, it was the first peaceful transfer of high authority in history to result from a competitive campaign oriented to the freely given votes of a mass electorate in a large nation-state.[64] There was little doubt that Jefferson was actually the favorite of the majority. He came into office at the head of a party that jubilantly interpreted its new power as a vindication of republican institutions. But its efforts to consolidate its authority were resented and distrusted by most of the Adams coalition. Federalists who remained in office tried to secure their powers—Adams's effort to "pack" the Federal courts just before leaving office was prototypical—but offered little cooperation to the incoming Jeffersonians. There was no preparation for playing a role of loyal opposition in building the powers of the nation.

The aftermath of the election makes clear that only limited legitimacy had been gained for principles of competitive politics. The Federalists for the most part regarded their defeat in national politics as permanent. They did not prepare to contest the next presidential election, but rued their loss and withdrew to regional, state, and local politics, often in great bitterness. The Federalist Party remained active in some states and, indeed, attempted with energy to bend the organizational tactics of the Jeffersonians to their own ends.[65] Some Federalists remained an organized voice in the Congress for a decade and a half, but their effective power dwindled rapidly. The Jeffersonians also regarded their victory as permanent. They proclaimed themselves the winners of a "Revolution of 1800," with overtones of having won just the sort of final triumph over tyranny that the Revolution itself represented to all Americans. They realized that they would face new Federalist challenges in some states and communities. But they were growing confident of their capacity to suppress effective Federalist participation in national politics.[66]

Jefferson's confidence rested primarily on his party's newly won control of electoral processes. Still, despite his eloquence in favor of unfettered speech and press in 1800, he briefly followed Adams's model in permitting prosecutions for sedition when angered by attacks on his leadership. He retained an underlying suspicion that committed Federalists dissented from the ideology of liberty that Americans had developed through the Revolutionary movement, hence were untrustworthy as citizens. Although he continued to foster the growth of his own party, Jefferson gave no sign of valuing the Federalist Party as an organization having a continuing importance in American politics. Most Federalists felt themselves at a loss about what to do beyond holding onto whatever offices they retained. Neither Federalists nor Jeffersonians thought of elections based on competition between parties as a permanent form of political life. It had been an evil that could be tolerated only under the special circumstances of 1800.[67]

As the Jeffersonians consolidated power, they did not abandon efforts to maintain their party. The crisis of 1800 was past, but they did not return to the ideal of politics without parties. Instead, they used the slogan of the "Revolution of 1800" to connect their party with the heritage of republican freedom. The Democratic Party was proclaimed a protector of freedoms that should continue to play a vital role in politics. A critical step was thus taken in legitimating party organization, and the Democrats were freed to set about strengthening their party in an open fashion that had been unthinkable before 1800. During the years of the Jefferson and Madison administrations, the Democrats established a national coalition among high office-holders, promoted the formation of sympathetic voluntary associations, firmed up alliances with newspaper publishers, used the party to popularize policies designed to please a broad-based electorate, developed continuing loyalties among the voters, and did their best to exclude everyone but party members from offices at all levels of government. By these means they were able to consolidate a near monopoly over promising political careers. To gain offices of any importance or exercise effective influence on matters of public policy, it now became necessary to be a reliable Democrat. Old Federalists and their political heirs gradually understood that they had to join the Democrats in order to hold open possibilities for political careers. Yet, figures who had once been strong Federalists remained under a cloud of distrust, much as former Tories fell under suspicion in the years after the Revolution. A continuing rejection of competitive struggle between parties seems to have been an important condition for general acceptance of a strong party organization.[68]

With the Federalists and their distrust for the common people discredited, the Jeffersonians were able to open political life up to greater activity on the part of the democracy. Closely tied to the new legitimacy of party organization was a new encouragement for more widespread participation by common citizens. In the absence of strenuous competition between parties, the Democrats could experiment with techniques of party organization in local communities relatively unhindered by charges of sedition, suppressing the free activities of others, or excessive devotion to narrow self-advantage. While the strength of party organization varied across the country, and among regions of particular states as well, many communities began to produce political leaders with experience in what we would call grass roots organization.

Many of the new leaders of the party, especially those filling the lower offices, were no longer drawn from the "natural aristocracy," but from more modest social circles. Their political strength was based on closer ties to majorities in the electorate. More immediately related to the common people in social background, sentiment, and practical interests, they were often more successful in asking the democracy for its votes. As the evolution of political customs permitted more forthright appeals to the self-interests of voters, these new leaders focused attention on issues that would attract popular support and produce secure majorities on election day.

By the 1830s, the nation had developed a large cadre of experienced party-based political leaders. Within a Democratic Party that still remained under the control of "natural aristocrats" at its highest levels, these men had explored new ways of appealing to a popular constituency within a mass electorate. They were learning the techniques—and ethics—of putting together tickets of candidates who would appeal to a variety of interests and solidary groups, including religious, sectional, and ethnic groups. They were beginning to experiment with ways of framing policies and party platforms that could mobilize the political energies of the common people. Their symbolic styles of leadership were less genteel, but generally more effective in attracting the popular vote. The competitive pressures under which a party organization began to emerge, however, were almost entirely local, state, and regional, not pressures that placed the leadership of the entire nation at stake. Such extreme tensions as those of 1800 were not involved in the processes by which the new leaders experimented with party organization.[69]

The period centering in Monroe's administration that was long called the Era of Good Feelings exhibited in fact neither political peace nor effective national leadership. However, this period did accustom the nation to practical, vote-getting party organization and to party feeling and loyalties. A fateful transition was made in most parts of the country from leadership focused on the person of a "natural aristocrat" to leadership resting on party allegiance and discipline. The solidarity of the Democratic Party became a major mechanism through which leadership attracted votes and the citizenry could voice its views on public issues. This more impersonal mechanism of political communication soon unleashed the forces of associational activism that Tocqueville found so extraordinary in the American democratic condition. The 1820s and 1830s became times of extremely creative civic activity.[70]

Political crisis emerged again in the 1820s, brought about by a fragmentation in the Democratic Party which could not maintain its unity in the face of the associational energies it had set free. Without an active and well organized competitor attempting to attract the loyalties of constituents, the Party had increasingly succumbed to the political temptations of trying to represent all causes to all people. It did not stand for a clear platform of policies to the exclusion of alternatives, but used its newly democratized apparatus to articulate practically all publicly voiced policies into the political arena. As a consequence, a sort of stalemate on matters of high national policy had come to prevail in Washington. The "good feelings" arose primarily from a comfortable accommodation to a weak policy agenda, an agenda that resulted from an inability to set priorities among widely divergent political hopes. The underlying sociological reality was that the Democratic Party had fragmented into several regional alliances who maintained an unstable peace with one another, but could no longer produce a concerted program of action. This weakly integrated party was susceptible to collapse once it came under stress.[71]

During Jefferson's, Madison's, and Monroe's administrations, the nation seemed to settle into a custom of electing the incumbent president's secretary of state as his successor. The unity of the Democratic Party as a loose alliance of substantially independent local, state, and regional organizations served to mobilize support for this procedure of selection, one still predicated largely on the qualifications, as "natural aristocrats," of the individuals who served as secretaries of state. By the election of 1824, however, the Democratic Party had become sufficiently fragmented that several regional candidates were pushed forward to compete with the secretary of state, John Quincy Adams, for the presidency. That Adams remained suspect as a former Federalist, regarded by some as a covert Federalist more than two decades after his father's defeat, increased his vulnerability as a candidate. Party discipline, as exercised in the customary manner through a Congressional Caucus acting as the leadership of the Democratic Party, was not sufficient to consolidate support behind any one candidate. A rather disjointedly competitive election was the result, with four candidates drawing popular support and gaining votes in the Electoral College. Each of the four affirmed loyalty to the Democratic Party, but represented largely regional interests and groups.

Adams gained the most votes in the Electoral College and became president. However, his election was clouded by the regional nature of his power base and by the fact that Andrew Jackson had received more popular votes. A feeling lingered across the land that perhaps Jackson's claim to office had been improperly overridden. The movement toward democratic politics in which popular support as expressed by a majority of votes provides the final claim to office is well indexed by the sentiment for Jackson. Adams lacked the political skills to rid his administration of the stain on its legitimacy and overcome the practical disadvantages stemming from its minority political base. Despite his exceptional qualifications as a "natural aristocrat" and the brilliance of his prior achievements, he was doomed to an ineffective presidency.[72]

Jackson easily defeated Adams in the election of 1828. Both candidates claimed to represent the political heritage of the Jeffersonian party, although Adams's claim was widely questioned. Jackson presented himself as a national hero, the victor of the Battle of New Orleans and of bloody Indian wars in the South, as a man of the rising West, and as a commoner in social background who had gained wealth and prominence through personal energy, shrewdness, and strength of will. By contrast, Adams's uncommon background, learning, and talents became disadvantageous symbols of his Federalist upbringing and leanings. They seemed to underline his apparent distrust for the common people. For the first time in a presidential election, the qualities of a "natural aristocrat" were transformed into a political liability. Jackson and his advisors, conveniently overlooking the family connections that had advanced his career at crucial points, dramatized his ties to the common people and his achievements as a self-made man. Their success in framing an electoral appeal undermined the old standards for evaluating leadership and created elements of a new, frankly democratic political culture.[73]

Jackson also benefited from the efforts of younger politicians with a new kind of experience in party organization. They were able to construct a national alliance that supported him with direct "grass roots" connections to the electorate. The most important of these politicians was Martin Van Buren, then senator from New York, but whose relationship with Jackson was destined to make him secretary of state, vice-president, and then president. Van Buren was at a distance from and had slight knowledge of Jackson's personal staff and coterie of advisors and politicians, but became the key person in pulling together the Democratic Party on a national basis. Jackson grew indebted to him and, after assuming office, relied increasingly on his advice, influence with other leaders, and ability to strike political deals in order to maintain the efficacy of presidential leadership.[74]

The relationship between Jackson and Van Buren had its origin in the debacle of the 1824 election. Recognizing the political weakness that resulted from John Quincy Adams's election, Van Buren, working from his base in the Senate, made a cautious study of the situation and gradually decided that Jackson had the best opportunity to win the election of 1828 and provide forceful leadership for the nation. By the end of 1826, Van Buren was corresponding and traveling across much of the country, including the south, to consolidate an alliance behind Jackson. His decision to offer his support seems to have rested mainly on the belief that Jackson alone had the potential for winning so decisively as to forge a new, more democratic unity for national politics.[75]

Van Buren's contribution to Jackson's cause was primarily one of mediating in party organization. Physically small but flamboyant in dress and personal manners, he was already famous as the "Little Magician," noted (and sometimes feared) for his mastery of organizational techniques and his imagination in dealing with different factions and groups in a constituency. In an age of entrepreneurial innovation, Van Buren was a political entrepreneur. His forte was creating new forms of political organization, and his leadership of the "Albany Regency" made him one of the nation's first "machine bosses." Yet, true to that type, he incited fear as well as respect, and much of his conduct was widely regarded as skirting the edges of legitimacy. From time to time, despite cautious calculations, he overreached himself and revealed the sort of underlying ambitions that repulsed more genteel politicians. Nevertheless, during his years in the senate, Van Buren had been able to project his machine-based influence into the national arena and establish himself as a leader of the Democratic Party with a reservoir of trust respected by leaders almost everywhere in America. This trust was mixed with fear of his enmity as well as hope for the powers that might be gained through alliance with him. It served to give him influence over leaders in the south and west as well as the middle states and New England.

Leaders of the Democratic Party looked to Van Buren for guidance in making political deals, but less for his insights into sound policy than for his reputation as a mediator with integrity. In an era when new sorts of deals were being struck, Van Buren's strength was his reputation as a man of his word who held all sides to a deal once it had been reached. On behalf of Jackson's alliance, he exercised a political influence rooted in party organization and designed to mobilize party loyalties to secure thoroughly practical advantages to those who joined up. It was an influence that would have been repugnant to the Founding Fathers and was quite unthinkable even in the era of Jefferson and Madison. Van Buren's sort of integrity was not one that received appreciation when "aristocrats of talent and virtue" still dominated political life. But during the late 1820s and 1830s, when party organization was growing rapidly and coming into control of national politics, it suddenly represented a strategic resource for leadership. It also received a new, if yet partial and hesitant, legitimacy. Van Buren's key role in Jackson's victory thus provides a measure of how rapidly politics and leadership were moving toward a new base in party organization. His very prominence on the scene highlights the new importance of "professional politicians" who built middle-class careers on party loyalties and connections, using them to gain advancement through increasingly powerful offices.[76]

Jackson's candidacy was also aided by innovations in the practices of conducting a political campaign. Jackson departed daringly from the genteel customs of "standing" for high office and experimented with a variety of techniques for stimulating popular involvement in electoral politics. On the pretext of celebrating an anniversary of the Battle of New Orleans, he had earlier visited many parts of the south and west, giving speeches to enthusiastic crowds. The deliberate scheduling of his public appearances made clear that they were intended to demonstrate his personal popularity and produce a political advantage. In 1828, though he remained at home during most of the political season, his supporters in hundreds of communities organized popular rallies to promote his candidacy and mobilize the enthusiasm of the citizenry. The rhetorical styles, emotional outpourings, and public exhibitions of popular revivalism were soon made over into new techniques for demonstrating political support for Jackson and other candidates. Criticism of Adams's administration and proposals for new policies were synthesized into pointed symbols with powerful emotional appeal: the slogan "Jackson and Reform" carried complicated meanings focused on needs to restrain banks and printed-money finance, limit the power of distant authorities, and gain more democratic control over the nation's affairs. Campaign pamphlets and bills heroized Jackson's achievements in a most brazen fashion, while also characterizing him in ways that underscored his attachments to common citizens. Jackson and democracy were set off boldly against Adams and aristocracy, a winning measure in a campaign for a majority of the votes in the land of common people. The clever manipulation of popular symbols to merge commitments rooted in strong moral sentiment with pragmatic calculations of advantage gave Jackson's cause the quality of a true campaign in the modern manner. This new political style was a key factor behind Tocqueville's worry that Jackson was a demagogue, but also his recognition that American citizens maintained a unique involvement in the nation's political affairs. Through Jackson's leadership, national affairs had become *res publica* in a far more democratic sense than before.[77]

The electoral campaigns in which Jackson won reelection in 1832 and Van Buren gained the presidency in 1836 saw a consolidation of the Jacksonian innovations in political style and organization. However, the campaign of 1840, the famous "Log Cabin" campaign, became the crucial landmark in the permanent institutionalization of the new, more democratic procedures. As 1840 approached, Van Buren's prospects for reelection were weakened by lingering effects of the severe depression of 1837 and by the continuing regional factionalism within the Democratic Party. His vulnerability provided encouragement to the newly formed Whig Party, which mounted a vigorous campaign in the new style to elect William Henry Harrison. Though an Ohio-raised scion of a long established dynasty of Virginia "natural aristocrats," Harrison's campaign presented him as a log cabin born commoner who had risen to the rank of general as a frontier Indian fighter and was happiest when drinking hard cider with his men. The Whig Party drew much of its leadership and policies from an alliance among Easterners from established families, rising entrepreneurs from modest backgrounds who identified with policies that would encourage business, and leaders of various popular religious and moral "causes" who sought public encouragement for reforms of character. Yet Harrison's victory was won by a conscious and energetic imitation of Jackson's candidacy. The political competition of 1840 focused on dramatizing the candidates' democratic belongingness to the common people.[78]

The outcome of 1840 was to establish two fundamental principles of American political institutions. The first was that political life is essentially a competition between two parties. In losing the "Log Cabin" campaign, the Democrats lost their monopoly of the heritage of 1800. The Whigs, soon succeeded by the Republicans, gained formally equal legitimacy as a party attempting to mobilize popular support. The second was that leadership arises from a democratic social condition. The leaders of the nation were no longer "aristocrats of talent and virtue" drawn from an exclusive status group of superior value. Instead, leaders were now to present themselves as "from" the democracy or common citizenry. They typically drew the greatest political advantage from dramatizing their roles as ordinary folk who understood and sympathized with the problems, outlooks, and interests of the majority of their constituents. To be sure, exceptional ability, achievement, and energy were still valued in political leaders, who now took pride in showing themselves to be "self-made" men. But self-made men who had risen from the common people by their own achievements alone comprise a fundamentally different social type from "natural aristocrats."[79]

To summarize, we can index the changes in political leadership that accompanied the rise of a competitive political party system if we consider briefly a sketch of Van Buren's early career. It will be apparent that he is representative of a type of leader who could not have gained national prominence in the years before the growth of the Democratic Party.[80]

Van Buren had been born the son of a tavern keeper in a small Hudson Valley town. It is likely that his father also owned land around the village of Kinderhook and was more prosperous than the designation "tavern keeper" might imply. He was certainly a respected citizen and his tavern served as the center for political discussion in the community and perhaps surrounding villages as well. Nevertheless, the younger Van Buren received a modest upbringing and education. His personal background and status were humble in contrast with those of New York's leading political families of "natural aristocrats," e.g., the Livingstons or Clintons. Throughout his career, Van Buren felt the insecurities of a self-made man who must attend closely to the impressions he creates in others. His dress, personal manners, and calculated speech were all designed to impress. He seems never to have spoken or written freely and entirely frankly; even his most personal exchanges with others and his journals convey only calculated thoughts.

Van Buren began his career early by seeking out, possibly using his father's connections, prominent attorneys in whose offices he could study the law and whose sponsorship might then improve his professional prospects. Admitted to the bar at age 20, he soon complemented the practice of law with public service as a state legislator. Born in the same year as Daniel Webster, he was among the first self-made men to gain security in his career as well as wealth by pursuing politics and the practice of law in parallel. His growing political prominence brought him clients and large cases, while his successful legal practice brought him the wealth and security that a career in elective offices might otherwise preclude. Van Buren was thus an early creator, along with Webster and others, of the pattern that most American politicians have since used (and refined) as a way of limiting the impact of electoral defeats on their careers.

In Albany, Van Buren became a youthful prodigy. After serving briefly as protege and precocious lieutenant of Governor Dewitt Clinton, he struck out on his own in seeking positions of leadership. By the time he was 30, he had put together the political alliance that captured control of the New York Jeffersonian Party from Clinton, its long-established leader whose entitlements as a "natural aristocrat" had not previously been questioned despite bitter factional disputes over state leadership within his own status group. Van Buren became an early "boss," playing a large part in politics throughout the state from his position of leadership in the legislature. In an era distrusting of leadership that was not restrained by genteel codes of honor, Van Buren experimented actively with behind-the-scenes co-ordination of policy platforms, deals among coalitions of legislators, and tickets of candidates. He continued to develop these practices during his brief period as Governor. By the time he arrived in the United States Senate, he was preceded by his reputation as the "Little Magician," and other Senators held no little curiosity about how he would conduct himself. His shrewdness in devising compromises on matters that affected each region of the country differently, notably, tariffs, trade laws, and credit policies, rapidly made him a leader of the Senate. But his politics involved more than legislative brokerage. He gained wide respect for his ability to discern potential voting coalitions and convert them into political realities. He was also admired for his sensitivity in mobilizing and responding to constituent pressures.

Van Buren made his position in the Senate a base for exercising leadership in the Democratic Party on a national stage, just as earlier he had exercised statewide leadership in New York from his position in the legislature. While in Washington, he remained cautiously attentive to the organizational groundwork of his power at home. He exchanged frequent letters with followers and collaborators in Albany, travelled across the state to visit politicians and make public appearances at nearly every opportunity, and tried to control the policy agenda of the state party in the power interests of his own faction. In all these respects, Van Buren seems closer to modern democratic politicians than to Washington, Adams, or Jefferson. His rise to the presidency, following the political innovations of the Jacksonian period, represented a deep-seated shift in the social composition of the nation's leadership. Without changing the words, it brought a newly democratic meaning to America's republican Constitution, a meaning the Founding Fathers hardly anticipated and would certainly have reproved.

Two Modes of Social Integration

A central institution of modern liberal democracies is a system of continuously organized, competitive political parties. Competition among parties is typically directed toward control of public offices and positions of leadership by obtaining the voluntarily given votes of citizens in the role of an electorate or constituency. An effective party system mediates between two major institutional complexes, the institutions of political office, public authority, and leadership, on the one hand, and the institutions of citizenship, on the other hand. To be credibly regarded as voluntary acts, the electoral choices of the citizens at large must be protected by the freedoms of conscientious belief, speech, publication, assembly, petition, and association as well as by regulation of the franchise.[81]

In the United States, a competitive party system emerged as a legitimate institutional complex during the first several decades of the nineteenth century. It was a complicated arrangement and rested on many independent elements, ranging from a structure of offices based on limited powers and a calling to act on behalf of the public to a broad tolerance of open competition among diverse social groups. In the first decades, controversy attached to features of competitive politics that Americans now accept as routine matters of political life. Public relationships of mutual support among like-minded candidates for different offices, tactics designed to derive partisan advantages from discussion of public policies, open criticism of public officials and their intentions, the formation of associations to challenge the re-election of seated officials, and appeals to party loyalties, though ventured by political figures from the earliest days of the Republic out of a variety of motives, were all activities or arrangements whose legitimacy was widely challenged. By 1840, the nation having experienced a whirlwind of political change, these competitive practices had become firmly legitimated and a two party system had emerged as an established institution of American political life.[82]

By the election of 1840, the political party system had replaced the status group of "natural aristocrats" as the principal institution regulating the exercise of political influence in America. To gain access to a position of public authority and leadership, one could no longer "stand" for office as an individual of exemplary merit, but had to "run" for office as a member of a political party. All but a handful of the "aristocrats of talent and virtue" had retreated from public life, frustrated that their standards of personal honor inhibited them from playing the sorts of political roles that were necessary to gain election.[83] They had been replaced by new group of "professional politicians" whose claims to office were closely tied to their experiences in operating political parties. Private citizens, interest groups, or voluntary associations found that to influence elected leaders in favor of one policy or another, they had to invoke social ties organized through a political party. Moreover, the leaders of the nation found that they could bring their opinions on matters of policy effectively before the public at large only by speaking through the political parties. Thus, the party system had become an established institution that firmly dominated, in a sense monopolized, public manifestations of political influence, however active the relations of political competition within the party system. With the centrality of parties that linked together leaders who were building middle class careers and followers who sought melioration of their personal life situations, middle class culture became the established framework of political activity. Its peculiar mixture of sentimentality and pragmatism, concern for liberties and interest in economic improvement, set the main agendas for politics.

The parties also constituted a mechanism for stratifying political influence. To rise in the ranks of a party had become a necessary condition for rising to high position in the political system. Having served in lower office after developing appeals to constituents and receiving a majority of their votes became the chief qualification for higher office. The means of gaining office focused on appeals to an electorate and a candidate's established popularity with his constituents. The parties coordinated the uses of political influence and the policy appeals to constituents, extending them, albeit loosely and accommodating many differences, across states, regions, and even the entire country. Both of the major political parties had organized themselves as diverse alliances of many interests. Both attempted to appeal to citizens of many regions, many economic interests, and many cultural backgrounds in order to compete effectively for majority support in elections. Few large groups in the society found themselves for long without a political home in at least one of the two parties. Together, the two competing parties integrated practically every substantial group into the political process, giving voice to their interests and providing channels of communication for them to exercise influence in the public arena. Figures attempting to rise to positions of power had to manage their public images for breadth of social appeal as well as personal connection with party organizations. The control of the votes by vast numbers of independent citizens—despite some circumstances where landlords, employers, or party bosses compromised independence—assured that the base of the political pyramid remained broad and the means of climbing it competitive.

Thus, the shift to political integration mediated through the parties from integration dominated by "natural aristocrats" had vast consequences. Leadership no longer rested on matters of personal status; the emphasis was shifted to popular appeal. Candidates came under new expectations of appealing to the interests and judgment of their constituents, while the electorate emerged as the higher arbiter of policy. Parties developed policies and programs in directly competitive ways to enhance their appeals to the electorate. The formation of associations and interest groups in the citizenry at large, groups that could effectively influence the parties, their candidates, and their policies, was encouraged. Recruitment to political life came through different career lines, and people of different backgrounds gained access to the highest offices.

The political party system, as a structure of social stratification, became the center of a new and more highly specialized institutional arena. The parties organized only political influence and leadership. They did not constitute a diffuse status group exercising leadership over all sectors of society in the manner of the "natural aristocrats" during the first years of the Republic. The new leaders of the nation were not necessarily well educated, nor wealthy, nor owners of large farms or plantations, nor heads of prominent economic enterprises. Hence, the politicians needed connection with the leaders of other sorts of social institutions—connection to replace the unifying force of the "natural aristocrats'" solidarity as a status group. The social coordination of a society so large and so diverse, and with institutions differentiating so rapidly, required new mechanisms of solidarity. The democratic social condition, viewed as a general pattern of societal organization, a total social phenomenon, constituted a system of such connection or solidarity.

The political innovations of Tocquevillian America had economic counterparts that were also bound up with the emergence of the democratic social condition. The displacement of "natural aristocrats" from positions of economic leadership opened up the business world to middle class entrepreneurs. As the privileges of limited liability incorporation, bank franchising, loans from banks, and the sale of stock were democratized, i.e., extended to entrepreneurs strictly on the basis of business calculation and without a requirement of genteel status, a flood of economic forces was loosed.[84] Economic stability was sacrificed along with the restraints that had accompanied the old monopoly of leadership by natural aristocrats. A boom and bust economy emerged. (Van Buren's fall from the presidency in the wake of the crisis of 1837 is perhaps symbolic of the connections between the new economic and political orders.) However, a take-off into an industrial economy and sustained growth also occurred. The broad democratization in social condition was as essential to these processes as to the rise of political parties and "professional politicians."

In sum, the America of the Revolution and the adoption of the Constitution was not yet more than partially democratized. The social condition of democracy characterized by Tocqueville emerged only through rapid changes in the first decades of the nineteenth century. It consisted, as Tocqueville argued, in a principle of the essential equality of citizens. Intolerant of privileges and differences, it set citizens in permanent competition with one another for advantages. Moreover, it extended this competition into every sphere of societal organization. Thus, religion, law, the academy, high culture, and so on involved the same sorts of status rivalries as economic and political institutions. Benevolent in many respects, the life of equality also imposed burdens of loneliness, rootlessness, and anxiety over issues of personal achievement on practically all Americans. In the political sphere, these burdens entailed a sense of weakness which individuals can compensate only by finding like-minded or like-situated peers with whom to associate in an effort to gain influence. As Tocqueville made clear, this drive to form associations is the engine of American political life. It flourished with the displacement of the "natural aristocracy," just as, in the economic domain, the drive for achievement swept the restraints of gentility and patronage out of business practices.

Once established, the social condition of democracy became the enduring foundation of American society. It still provides today the common frame of personal relationships that has unified the American experience from the Age of Jackson to the present, despite the vast changes we speak of as industrialization, bureaucratization, urbanization, and pluralization, all of which existed only in rudimentary degree at the time of Tocqueville's visit. When we read Tocqueville's pages, we recognize ourselves on them. We still participate in the social condition of democracy that he first characterized, and we still hold—though in broadened terms regarding race and gender—the same principles of equality and endure the same burdens of isolation, rootlessness, and insecurity over efficacy and achievement. The history of American politics from Van Buren to Nixon, Carter, or Reagan is in key respects merely a retelling of struggles with the same "total social phenomenon."

The present essay has attempted to lay bare the structural origins of these struggles. It is offered to the reader with a salute to E. Digby Baltzell, the scholar who has done the most to show contemporary sociologists the vitality of Tocqueville's conception of democracy.

Notes

1. Wesley Frank Craven, *The Legend of the Founding Fathers* (Ithaca, N.Y.: Cornell University Press, 1956); Robert N. Bellah, *The Broken Covenant* (New York: Seabury Press, 1975), esp. chaps. 1 and 2; Robert N. Bellah and Phillip E. Hammond, *Varieties of Civil Religion* (New York: Harper and Row, 1980), esp. chap. 1; Bernard Mayo, *Myths and Men* (New York: Harper Torchbooks, 1963); Ernest Lee Tuveson, *Redeemer Nation* (Chicago: University of Chicago Press, 1968.)

2. Craven, *op. cit.*

3. For example, Charles A. Beard, *The Economic Interpretation of the Constitution* (New York: Macmillan, 1913) and *Economic Origins of Jeffersonian Democracy* (New York: Macmillan, 1915).

4. See, for example, Bernard Bailyn, *The Ideological Origins of the American Revolution* (Cambridge, Mass.: Harvard University Press, 1967) and *The Origins of American Politics* (New York: Knopf, 1968); Gordon S. Wood, *The Creation of the American Republic* (Chapel Hill: University of North Carolina Press, 1969); Lance Banning, *The Jeffersonian Persuasion* (Ithaca, N.Y.: Cornell University Press, 1978); Ralph Ketcham, *Presidents Above Party* (Chapel Hill: University of North Carolina Press, 1984).

5. Thurgood Marshall, speech on shortcomings of the Constitution overlooked in the Bicentennial celebration, May 6, 1977. *New York Times,* May 7, 1987.

6. Alexis de Tocqueville, *Democracy in America,* two vols. (New York: Knopf, 1945, Vintage, 1954; originally published, 1835 and 1840). The basic concept of the social condition of democracy is introduced in volume I, Chapter 3.

7. On the Constitution specifically, a classic example is Edward S. Corwin, *American Constitutional History* (New York: Harper Torchbooks, 1961). In sociological analysis, this perspective can be found in Seymour Martin Lipset, *Political Man* (Garden City, N.Y.: Doubleday, 1960) and *The First New Nation* (New York: Basic Books, 1963). It is also present in the writings on American society by my teacher, Talcott Parsons. See his forthcoming posthumous work, *The American Societal Community.* In political science, an influential

"Whiggish" study has been Louis Hartz, *The Liberal Tradition in America* (New York: Harcourt, Brace and World, 1955).

8. For example, C. Wright Mills, *The Power Elite* (New York: Oxford University Press, 1956). But in promoting this outlook Mills has been influential on many other sociologists.

9. E. Digby Baltzell, *Philadelphia Gentlemen: The Making of a National Upper Class* (Philadelphia: University of Pennsylvania Press, 1977; original edition New York: Free Press, 1958).

10. Bernard Bailyn, *The Ordeal of Thomas Hutchinson* (Cambridge, Mass.: Harvard University Press, 1974); Richard Hofstadter, *America at 1750* (New York: Knopf, 1971); Jackson Turner Main, *The Social Structure of Revolutionary America* (Princeton, N.J.: Princeton University Press, 1965).

11. Tocqueville, *op. cit.* volume I, Chapter X.

12. Marvin Meyers, *The Jacksonian Persuasion* (New York: Vintage, 1960); Perry Miller, *Life of the Mind in America* (New York: Harcourt, Brace and World, 1965); Arthur M. Schlesinger, Jr., *The Age of Jackson* (Boston: Little, Brown, 1945); Daniel J. Boorstin, *The Americans: The National Experience* (New York: Random House, 1965).

13. Marcel Mauss, *The Gift* (London: Cohen and West, 1954), 1.

14. Bailyn, *Ideological Origins, op. cit.,* for the feeling about parties in the Revolutionary ideology. See Wood, *op. cit.* on the Constitution itself. Also, Forrest McDonald, *Novus Ordo Seclorum* (Lawrence: University of Kansas Press, 1985).

15. Bailyn, *Ideological Origins, op. cit.*; Richard Hofstadter, *The Idea of a Party System* (Berkeley: University of California Press, 1969).

16. Wood, *op. cit.*

17. *Ibid.* See also Pauline Maier, *From Resistance to Revolution* (New York: Knopf, 1972).

18. Bailyn, *Ideological Origins, op. cit.*; Wood, *op. cit.*; Rhys Isaac, *The Transformation of Virginia 1740–1790* (Chapel Hill: University of North Carolina Press, 1982). See also Dixon Ryan Fox, *The Decline of Aristocracy in the Politics of New York* (New York: Harper Torchbooks, 1965; first published in 1919).

19. J. G. A. Pocock, *The Machiavellian Moment* (Princeton, N.J.: Princeton University Press, 1975).

20. Paul Eidelberg, *The Philosophy of the American Constitution* (New York: Free Press, 1968).

21. Eidelberg, *op. cit.*

22. Marcus Cunliffe, *George Washington, Man and Monument* (New York: Mentor Books, 1960); Leonard D. White, *The Federalists* (New York: Free Press, 1965; first published in 1948); Barry Schwartz, "George Washington and the Whig Conception of Heroic Leadership", *American Sociological Review* 48 (Feb. 1983): 18–33.

23. Bailyn, *Ideological Origins, op. cit.*; Wood, *op. cit.*; Henry F. May, *The Enlightenment in America* (New York: Oxford University Press, 1976).

24. Yehoshua Arieli, *Individualism and Nationalism in American Ideology* (Baltimore: Penguin Books, 1966).

25. Bailyn, *Ordeal of Thomas Hutchinson, op. cit.*

26. Tocqueville, *op. cit.*, volume I, Chapter 3 and *passim*.
27. Hofstadter, *op. cit.*; Isaac, *op. cit.*; Fox, *op. cit.*
28. Max Weber, *The Protestant Ethic and the Spirit of Capitalism* (New York: Scribner's, 1930); Perry Miller, *Errand into the Wilderness* (Cambridge, Mass.: Harvard University Press, 1956) and *The New England Mind, From Colony to Province* (Cambridge, Mass.: Harvard University Press, 1953); Sacvan Bercovitch, *The Puritan Origins of the American Self* (New Haven, Conn.: Yale University Press, 1975).
29. Bailyn, *Ideological Origins, op. cit.*; Wood, *op. cit.*
30. *Ibid;* Ralph Barton Perry, *Puritanism and Democracy* (New York: Vanguard, 1944); Edward S. Corwin, *The "Higher Law" Background of American Constitutional Law* (Ithaca, N.Y.: Cornell University Press, 1955).
31. Alan Heimert, *Religion and the American Mind* (Cambridge, Mass.: Harvard University Press, 1966); William G. McLoughlin, "Enthusiasm for Liberty: The Great Awakening as the Key to the Revolution" in Jack P. Greene and William G. McLoughlin, *Preachers and Politicians* (Worcester, Mass.: American Antiquarian Society, 1977).
32. Garry Wills, *Inventing America* (New York: Vanguard, 1974); May, *op. cit.*
33. Benjamin Fletcher Wright, *Consensus and Continuity, 1776–1787* (Boston: Boston University Press, 1958); Corwin, *American Constitutional History, op. cit.*; McDonald, *op. cit.*
34. Wood, *op. cit.*
35. Adrienne Koch, *Jefferson and Madison* (New York: Oxford University Press, 1964).
36. Jackson Turner Main, *The Anti-Federalists* (Chicago: Quadrangle Books, 1964); Herbert J. Storing, *What the Anti-Federalists Were For* (Chicago: University of Chicago Press, 1981).
37. Wood, *op. cit;* Isaac, *op. cit.*
38. *Ibid;* Fox, *op. cit.*
39. Charles S. Sydnor, *American Revolutionaries in the Making* (New York: Free Press, 1965); Isaac, *op. cit.*; Daniel P. Jordan, *Political Leadership in Jefferson's Virginia* (Charlottesville: University Press of Virginia, 1983).
40. Compare Baltzell, *Philadelphia Gentlemen. op. cit.*
41. Sydnor, *op. cit.*; Isaac, *op. cit.*; Fox, *op. cit*
42. Sydnor, *op. cit.*; Jordan, *op. cit.*
43. Sydnor, *op. cit.*
44. Isaac, *op. cit.*
45. Sydnor, *op. cit.*; Isaac, *op. cit.*; Bailyn, *Ordeal of Thomas Hutchinson, op. cit.*
46. White, *op. cit.*; Ketcham, *op. cit.*
47. My analysis rests above all on William Spence Robertson, *The Rise of the Spanish-American Republics* (New York: Free Press, 1965; first published in 1918). See also Salvador de Madariaga, *The Rise of the Spanish-American Empire* and *The Fall of the Spanish-American Empire* (New York: Free Press, 1965; first published in 1947).
48. Compare Talcott Parsons, "Evolutionary Universals in Society", *American Sociological Review* 29, 3 (June, 1964): 339–57.

49. William Nisbet Chambers and Walter Dean Burnham, *The American Party Systems* (New York: Oxford University Press, 1967).

50. Seymour Martin Lipset, *The First New Nation, op. cit.*

51. Martin Van Buren, *Inquiry into the Origin and Course of Political Parties in the United States* (New York: Augustus M. Kelley, 1967; first published in 1867).

52. Tocqueville, *op. cit.*, volume I, Chapters 9–17; volume II, Second Book and Fourth Book.

53. Joseph Charles, *The Origins of the American Party System* (New York: Harper Torchbooks, 1961).

54. Ibid; John C. Miller, *The Federalist Era* (New York: Harper and Row, 1960).

55. Ibid; Richard Buel, Jr., *Securing the Revolution* (Ithaca, N.Y.: Cornell University Press, 1972); William Nisbet Chambers, *Political Parties in a New Nation* (New York: Oxford University Press, 1963).

56. Philip S. Foner, *The Democratic-Republican Societies, 1790–1800* (Westport, Conn.: Greenwood Press, 1976); Noble E. Cunningham, Jr., *The Jeffersonian Republicans: The Formation of Party Organization* (Chapel Hill: University of North Carolina Press, 1957).

57. Cunningham, *op. cit.*

58. Ibid; Chambers, *op. cit.*

59. Chambers, *op. cit.*; Cunningham, *op. cit.*; Stephen G. Kurtz, *The Presidency of John Adams* (New York: Barnes and Company, 1961).

60. John C. Miller, *Crisis in Freedom* (Boston: Little, Brown and Company, 1951); James Morton Smith, *Freedom's Fetters* (Ithaca, N.Y.: Cornell University Press, 1956; Leonard W. Levy, *Legacy of Suppression* (Cambridge, Mass.: Harvard University Press, 1964); and, especially, Lance Banning, *op. cit.*

61. Foner, *op. cit.*; Cunningham, *op. cit.*; Banning, *op. cit.*

62. Banning, *op. cit.*; Buel, *op. cit.*

63. Ibid; Chambers, *op. cit.*; Cunningham, *op. cit.*

64. Chambers, *op. cit.*; Kurtz, *op. cit.*

65. David Hackett Fischer, *The Revolution of American Conservatism* (New York: Harper and Row, 1965).

66. Noble E. Cunningham, Jr., *The Jeffersonian Republicans in Power* (Chapel Hill: University of North Carolina Press, 1963).

67. Banning, *op. cit.*; Richard Hofstadter, *The Idea of a Party System, op. cit.*; Leonard W. Levy, *Jefferson and Civil Liberties* (Cambridge, Mass.: Harvard University Press, 1963).

68. Cunningham, *The Jeffersonian Republicans in Power, op. cit.*; Hofstadter, *The Idea of a Party System, op. cit.*

69. Ibid; Fox, *op. cit.*

70. George Dangerfield, *The Era of Good Feelings* (New York: Harcourt, Brace and World, 1952).

71. Ibid; Hofstadter, *The Idea of a Party System, op. cit.*

72. Robert V. Remini, *The Election of Andrew Jackson* (Philadelphia: Lippincott, 1963).

73. Ibid; Robert V. Remini, *Andrew Jackson and the Course of American Freedom, 1822–1832* (New York: Harper and Row, 1981); John William Ward, *Andrew Jackson—Symbol for an Age* (New York: Oxford University Press, 1962).

74. Remini, *Andrew Jackson, op. cit.*; Donald B. Cole, *Martin Van Buren and the American Political System* (Princeton, N.J.: Princeton University Press, 1984).
75. Remini, *Andrew Jackson, op. cit.*; Cole, *op. cit.*
76. Cole, *op. cit*; Hofstadter, *The Idea of a Party System, op. cit.*
77. Remini, *The Election of Andrew Jackson, op. cit.*, and *Andrew Jackson, op. cit.*; Ward, *op. cit.*; Richard P. McCormick, *The Second American Party System* (Chapel Hill: University of North Carolina Press, 1966); Ronald P. Formisano, *The Birth of Mass Political Parties* (Princeton, N.J.: Princeton University Press, 1971).
78. Robert Gray Gunderson, *The Log Cabin Campaign* (Lexington: University of Kentucky Press, 1957).
79. Robert A. Dahl, *Who Governs* (New Haven, Conn.: Yale University Press, 1961) documents a change in the social class of leaders in early 19th century New Haven. A classic analysis of the revolution in the social backgrounds of political leadership is provided by Fox, *op. cit.*
80. My account relies principally on Cole, *op. cit.*, and Edward Pessen, *The Log Cabin Myth* (New Haven, Conn.: Yale University Press, 1984).
81. Cf. Talcott Parsons, *Politics and Social Structure* (New York: Free Press, 1969), Chapters 8, 9, 13, 14, and 17. Although Parsons places electoral politics in the functional position of mediating between two institutional complexes in modern societies, he conspicuously underemphasizes the importance of political parties. See also Stein Rokkan, *Citizens, Elections, Parties* (New York: David McKay, 1970), and Seymour Martin Lipset, *The First New Nation, op. cit.*, esp. Chapter 9.
82. Hofstadter, *The Idea of a Party System, op. cit.*; Roy F. Nichols, *The Invention of the American Political Parties* (New York: Macmillan, 1967).
83. Henry Adams, *Democracy; An American Novel* (New York: Airmont, 1968; first published anonymously in 1880) is a bitter expression of the sentiments felt by later nineteenth-century gentlemen who believed themselves "aristocrats of talent and virtue" entitled to lead the nation but could not bring themselves to enter democratized politics.
84. A suggestive study is James Willard Hurst, *Law and the Conditions of Freedom* (Madison: University of Wisconsin Press, 1956).

RT. HON. A. LEON HIGGINBOTHAM, JR. AND LAURA B. FARMELO

13. *Racial Justice and the Priorities of American Leadership*

The 1976 Bicentennial celebrations marking the signing of the Declaration of Independence had scarcely subsided when the United States Constitution took center stage as the nation celebrated the two hundredth anniversary of its adoption. Celebrations of our nation's origins and heritage are appropriate. There is much of which we as Americans can be justly proud—our economic power here and throughout the world, our level of social justice, our leadership in the world community—and we must strive to honor and preserve these virtues. Most important, we can be proud of carrying out the guarantees of the Constitution and the subsequently enacted Bill of Rights for over two centuries, particularly the protection of these rights by the Federal courts.

One way to mark the Constitution's Bicentennial is to review the contributions of our nation's most revered leaders during the time of both the Declaration of Independence and the Constitutional Convention and ask: "What was their contribution in shaping America? What lessons can be learned from them and those who followed them that can be applied today?"

Yet it is to be hoped that bicentennial scholarship and oratory will not lapse into mere self-congratulatory back-patting suggesting that everything in America has been, or is, perfect. During our euphoria as well as our solemn moments of rededication to the wisdom and ideals of our forefathers, we must not concentrate solely on the strengths of America, but, somewhat like physicians examining a patient, we must also diagnose and evaluate the social pathologies which have disabled our otherwise healthy institutions. Though it is painful to acknowledge deficiencies in ourselves as a nation, we must have the courage to confront such deficiencies once they are shown to exist, and work to eliminate them. I suggest we reflect on one particularly grave delinquency on the part of our nation in its practical accomplishment of the American dream—its failure on the issue of racial oppression.

Although the legislation of black suppression is tightly woven into the history of our country, many Americans still have difficulty accepting the truth of racism as it has existed under "the rule of law." For many, the primary conclusion of the National Commission on Civil Disorders in 1968 is still too painful to accept:

> What white Americans have never fully understood—but what the Negro can never forget—is that white society is deeply implicated in the ghetto. White institutions created it, white institutions maintain it, and white society condones it.[1]

We must face the fact that just as our heritage includes the great documents of freedom, the defeat of the British at Yorktown, victories in two world wars, and many other successes, it also includes a darker aspect. Despite our many virtues, we must recognize that as a nation we have gravely wronged innocent individuals, condemning them to lifelong servitude solely because of their race. Based on that single unalterable criterion, we established the institution of slavery, one of the harshest systems of oppression known to humanity. For at least two and a half centuries of our history we profited from, tolerated, sanctioned, and encouraged it. And although slavery was legally abolished by the Emancipation Proclamation in 1863, and although we have added the thirteenth, fourteenth, and fifteenth amendments to the Constitution, we often have been ambivalent about whether black Americans should be full beneficiaries of the American dream.

As we set our goals for the future, we must examine our national behavior and the frequently disparate treatment blacks have received throughout our history. We cannot act as though the present era began with a clean slate and that through some miracle we are devoid of a past that shapes and limits our future. We must put some of the issues and problems we now confront into historical perspective so that we may better understand how to chart our course.

This article will examine the history of some aspects of our racial prejudices and practices that still undermine the health of our nation and stunt our potential. By first looking at earlier eras, one can better analyze the continuing struggle this nation has undergone in determining its commitment to equal justice under the law for all Americans, and in setting the pace for fulfilling that commitment. With regard to blacks, the issue of equal justice can be reduced to the questions of race, values and priorities embodied in the query, "Why has full equality for blacks always been shunted aside until 'more important' problems were solved?"

Thomas Jefferson, George Washington and Patrick Henry: Architects of National Values and Priorities; Personal Profiteers of Racial Oppression

All three of the most revered leaders of the rising nation—Thomas Jefferson, George Washington, and Patrick Henry—eloquently avowed the ideals of liberty and justice for all, and took bold action to achieve those ideals—for *white*, male Americans. The importance of their declarations notwithstanding, there was a great disparity between the principles these men professed and their efforts to live up to those ideals. This disparity exemplifies the conflict between national priorities and concern for the human rights of American blacks. The human rights of blacks occupied the bottom rung on the ladder of values and priorities when our leaders sought to build a better nation for themselves. These attitudes have been the base elements from which our nation's racial problems have crystallized.

Of course, Washington, Jefferson, and Henry were great leaders and great men. But historians have often given these distinguished early statesmen an exaggerated reputation for impartiality and fairness which masks their involvement in slavery and in the systematic degradation and denigration of blacks. Most of our forefathers had certain moral blind spots which allowed them to focus only upon their own rights and interests and ignore the needs and entitlements of others, particularly black Americans. These blind spots are of crucial importance for they greatly influenced the quality of life—and life itself—for millions of blacks.

In questioning whether there was a valid basis for leaving the matter of black independence out of the new nation's agenda of priorities, the response may depend upon whether one identifies with the economic needs of the slave master or with the personal misery of the slave. Whether one looks at the uniqueness of enslaving only nonwhites in the Americas in the eighteenth century or whether one views slavery in an historical perspective spanning millennia[2], the lens through which one looks, and the time period one considers, define and color the image.

In 1776, when Jefferson wrote his most egalitarian lines, the system of slavery had been sanctioned, promoted, and guaranteed by the laws of the colonies for more than a century. At the height of the American Revolution, the colonists' values and priorities concerning the rights of men were at fever pitch. Jefferson declared to the world that "all men are created equal"; yet, at the same time, by his ownership of slaves, he implicitly repudiated that ideal of equality. How does one reconcile Jefferson's moving lines in the Declaration of Independence recognizing man's inborn yearning to be free, with his advertisement in the *Virginia Gazette* laying down a dragnet for the capture of a runaway slave, a fellow creature with those same understandable yearnings?

Run away from the subscriber in *Albemarle,* a mulatto slave called Sandy, 35 years of age, his stature is rather low, inclining to corpulence, and his complexion light; he is a shoemaker by trade, in which he uses his left hand principally; can do coarse carpenter's work, and is something of a horse jockey; he is greatly addicted to drink, and when drunk is insolent and disorderly, in his conversation he swears much, and his behavior is artful and knavish. He took with him a white horse, much scarred with traces, of which it is expected he will endeavour to dispose; he also carried his shoemaker's tools, and will probably endeavour to get employment that way. Whoever conveys the said slave to me in *Albermarle* shall have 40 s. reward if taken up within the county; 4 l. if elsewhere within the colony; and 10. l if in any other colony, from

Thomas Jefferson[3]

Jefferson's Virginian contemporary, Patrick Henry, faced the same conflict. On March 23, 1775, standing before the Virginia Convention meeting in St. John's Episcopal Church in Richmond, Henry exhorted his colleagues to support his resolutions for organizing and arming the Virginia Militia, with these famous words:

Is life so dear or peace so sweet as to be purchased at the price of chains and slavery? Forbid it, almighty God. I know not what course others may take, but as for me, *give me liberty or give me death!*

Patrick Henry's eloquence should not be permitted to obscure the fact that he himself was an owner of slaves, a participant in a system which owed its very existence to the principle that certain persons would forever be deprived of their liberty. On that selfsame historic day in March 1775, while the rafters of St. John's rang with this great patriot's stirring call for freedom, he had slaves back on the plantation for whom it would have been a severely punishable act to heed his call. He protested that the colonists were held in "chains and slavery" by the King of England, but seemed to be blind to the fact that thousands of blacks were suffering in the chains of a much more invidious and palpable slavery.

George Washington, in at least one public statement, revealed that he could be quite firm in insisting on his rights as a slaveowner; this was in a published notice offering a bounty for the return of three of his slaves who sought freedom by running away.

> They went off without the least suspicion, provocation, or difference with any body, or the least angry word of abuse from their overseers . . .

> Whoever apprehends the said Negroes, so that the subscriber may readily get them, shall have, if taken up in this country, forty shillings reward . . .
>
> *George Washington*[4]

It is intriguing to note Washington's stress that his four slaves had gone off "without the least suspicion, provocation, or difference with any body, or the least angry word or abuse from their overseers." His bewilderment and lack of understanding reflect a dual standard of expectation—that the white colonists were rightly provoked when the King taxed them while denying them representation, but that it was a baffling mystery when blacks did not silently tolerate or even enjoy the permanent degradation imposed upon them by the colonial masters who enslaved them.

The colonists often were ridiculed in England because of their distorted and contradictory values. In response to one of their protests against the King for his alleged denial of liberty and adequate representation, Dr. Samuel Johnson asked, "If slavery be thus fatally contagious, how is it that we hear the loudest yelps for liberty among the drivers of Negroes."[5] Dr. Johnson summed up the colonists' arguments as "too foolish for buffoonery and too wild for madness."[6]

Yet these patriots were not so altogether hypocritical as really to believe that anyone had an absolute right to demand liberty for himself and a concurrent right to enslave others. Jefferson, because of his knowledge of the principles of natural law and his purported commitment to its "self-evident truths," perhaps easily recognized the great contradiction between his rhetoric and his behavior. Shortly after writing the Declaration of Independence, in reflecting on slavery, he wrote:

> [I]f a slave can have a country in this world, it must be any other in preference to that in which he is born to live and labor for another; in which he must lock up the faculties of his nature, contribute as far as depends on his individual endeavors to the evanishment of the human race, or entail his own miserable condition on the endless generations proceeding from him.

*   *   *

> *Indeed I tremble for my country when I reflect that God is just; that his justice cannot sleep forever.*[7]

*   *   *

Patrick Henry also confessed to the contradicting distortions and inconsistencies in his values when he asserted, "[W]ould anyone believe that I am master of slaves of my own purchase! I am drawn along by ye general inconvenience of living without them; *I will not, I cannot justify it.*"[8] Thus his convenience (not to mention his economic well-being) took priority over the promptings of his nobler sentiments. Washington, the astute military leader, made fewer public comments than the idealists Jefferson and Henry about the double standard of words and actions in relation to freedom and slavery. Yet, while he participated in the slave system during his lifetime, unlike his two presumably more conscience-stricken colleagues, he willed all his slaves their freedom on his death.

But even though they recognized the disparity between their rhetoric and their actions, perhaps none of our esteemed forefathers understood fully the significance of a letter which Benjamin Banneker wrote to Thomas Jefferson in 1791. Banneker was one of the outstanding black intellectuals of the Revolutionary period. He was an astronomer and mathematician and assisted in the official survey of the city of Washington in 1790. In his letter to Jefferson, Banneker entreated the author of the Declaration of Independence to end the hypocrisy by ending slavery.

> Suffer me to recall to your mind that time, in which the arms of the British crown were exerted, with every powerful effort, in order to reduce you to a state of servitude; look back, I entreat you . . . you were then impressed with proper ideas of the great violation of liberty, and free possession of those blessings, to which you were entitled by nature; but, sir, how pitiable is it to

reflect that although you were so fully convinced of the benevolence of the Father of Mankind, and of his equal and impartial distribution of these rights and privileges which he hath conferred upon them, that you should at the same time counteract his mercies, in detaining by fraud and violence, so numerous a part of my brethren under groaning captivity and cruel oppression, that you should at the same time be found guilty of that most criminal act, which you professedly detested in others.[9]

Good Men, Evil Institutions, and Priorities

What is the lesson that each of us, whatever our racial or ethnic heritage, can learn from these tragic tales of distorted priorities? The first and most important message is that the institutions we condemn as evil were not the products solely of "evil" men. They flourished in the presence of "good" men who acquiesced to and supported them. Generally it is not the venal characters in history alone who determine the quality of life in a society; much harm is done by respected leaders of good intention who by their silence and inaction implicitly give encouragement to the perpetrators of injustice and inequality.

Many of our nation's leaders who sanctioned, tolerated, and participated in slavery were well meaning men like Washington, Jefferson, and Henry, who could scarcely be branded as evil. These honorable statesmen made many valuable contributions; often they recognized and deplored the immorality of slavery. But one must ask why they tolerated such pervasive degradation of other human beings, especially if they acknowledged its immoral nature. Perhaps their tolerance of what was morally repugnant can best be explained through one word—priority—a word which is one of the most deceptive masking terms in the English language. As the direction of the new nation was being charted, it was simply "more convenient" and thus of higher priority to maintain and support slavery than to grant freedom to black Americans. Because racial equality and justice ranked so low on the new nation's priority scale, it was argued that blacks and their allies should be patient and understanding, and in essence don masks of happiness while accepting as a fact that "now is not the time."

The word "priority" often camouflages evils sanctioned under the guise of "national purpose" and masks values underlying the hierarchy of interests. At no time since the founding of the Republic—with the notable exception of the Kennedy-Johnson era—have options for blacks been a continuing priority. In 1776, the Revolution was given priority over blacks' shaking off the chains of slavery. In 1787, the country's major priority was the drafting and adoption of the Constitution. From 1789 to 1860 we addressed other major priorities threatening the new nation's stability: the War of 1812; the problems of depression and inflation; the Monroe Doctrine conflicts with Spain, England, and France; and the admission of new states (free and slave) to the Union. Throughout this time of pursuing "vital" national goals, the eradication of slavery was of secondary importance, if it had any priority at all. In the meantime, blacks remained powerless to help themselves.

The Priorities of Abraham Lincoln

In the opinion of many, Abraham Lincoln was our nation's greatest president. He was a public official who apparently placed concern for human welfare high on his list of personal and presidential priorities. Since most of us have been greatly influenced by lessons learned in school of Lincoln's virtues and arduous struggles, his debates with Stephen Douglas, and his "freeing the slaves," it may be painful for us to study him at closer range, lowered from the pedestal on which he is placed in high school civics books. Even as Lincoln's achievements and personal virtues place him among America's heroes, it must still be noted that there is ample evidence that he, too, succumbed to the prevailing disregard of the black plight, considering it a national problem of only secondary concern. Horace Greeley, the eminent editor of the *New York Tribune,* expressed keen disappointment with the policy that Lincoln "seem[ed] to be pursuing with regard to the slaves of the Rebels." In his August 19, 1862 editorial titled "The Prayer of Twenty Millions," Greeley stressed that Lincoln and his generals were "strangely and disastrously amiss" in their habitual disregard of the emancipation provisions of the recently passed Confiscation Act.[10]

Lincoln's response to this criticism is a classic statement of the subordination of the rights of blacks to "higher priorities." Just a few days after the editorial appeared, Lincoln wrote to Greeley saying that, as President, he would support slavery if it would "help to save the Union"; that he would be willing to free all of the slaves if it would "help to save the Union"; or that he would be willing to free some slaves and leave others alone if it would "help to save the Union." For Lincoln as President the major priority was saving the Union, regardless of how harsh the consequences might be to blacks. He summarized his position by saying:

What I do about slavery, and the colored race, I do because I believe it helps to save the Union; and what I forbear, I forbear because I do *not* believe it would help to save the Union. I shall do *less* whenever I shall believe what I am doing hurts the cause, and I shall do *more* whenever I shall believe doing more will help the cause.[11]

In making this reference to Lincoln, I do not disregard his personal abhorrence of slavery, or disparage the significance of the Emancipation Proclamation which he later issued. What I do stress is that egalitarian ideals alone are not enough to protect victims of discrimination unless those ideals are accompanied by affirmative actions. Even for a man as great and benevolent as Lincoln, other national interests took priority over obtaining justice for blacks.

After the Civil War the subordination of justice for blacks to other national concerns continued. Starting with the Hayes-Tilden Compromise of 1877, followed by the withdrawal of federal troops from the South and the death of reconstruction, the problems of uniting the nation, expanding our commercial and industrial systems, and dealing with fluctuating economic cycles seemed more worthy of attention than did granting first class citizenship to blacks. From 1914 to 1918, the national focus was on World War I, a war in which drafted black soldiers fought "to make the world safe for democracy"—in racially segregated units. Gold Star Mothers of black soldiers who fell in battle traveled to France under the aegis of the United States to visit their sons' graves—in government-chartered segregated ships.

In the decades following World War I, the overarching concerns of government were the Depression, World War II, the Cold War, and then the Korean and Viet Nam eras. In all these times of crisis, blacks suffered along with whites; blacks put their lives on the line the same as whites; through their support in the form of direct action or by their taxes, blacks helped overcome these catastrophic dangers to the nation, the same as whites. But blacks did not share proportionately in the rewards of victory over these adversities the same as whites. Blacks were still confined "under the law" to the ghettos—substandard housing, substandard schools, substandard health care facilities, and substandard jobs. To give just one example, black veterans were excluded, by practice and sometimes by law, from purchasing homes in the thousands of suburbs then being built with support from the Federal government through Veterans' Administration and Federal Housing Administration insurance guaranty programs.

A noteworthy exception in this litany of national interests taking priority over the issue of racial justice, was the period from 1954 to 1968. Starting with the leadership of the Supreme Court in the case of *Brown v. Board of Education*[12] and ending with the effective, committed leadership of President Lyndon Johnson, this was indeed a significant era during which equal rights for blacks became one of America's major priorities. The struggle was arduous and marked by violent opposition; however, one could hope that the dream was beginning to be fulfilled.

Where We Are Now and Our Priorities for the Future

The period from 1968 to the present might be called an era of ambiguous priorities. Today, there is a problem of values and priorities in the way in which we treat many of our nation's people. Some might stress that especially in the area of race relations, many dramatic improvements have occurred and certainly much progress has been made. There was a positive thrust for affirmative action and an expansion of broader options for women and blacks and other minorities. Through isolated appointments by the executive, through court decisions such as *Brown v. Board of Education,* and through legislation such as the Civil Rights Acts of 1964, 1965, and 1968, substantial change has been effected and new standards of human and civil rights have been set. Change also has occurred through the private sector. Yet, despite these accomplishments, extraordinary gaps exist and much more remains to be done.

Adding to the problem is the rising of a countervailing force which, in substance, asserts that all our past record of putting race before merit in the market place and in the distribution of rights and privileges of first class citizenship, in the new environment of individual meritocracy, should now be considered irrelevant. But, for meritocratic standards to operate fairly on an individualistic basis requires that all individuals have truly equal opportunities to compete. The lingering legacy of disadvantage from centuries of racism and disparate treatment continues to cast its shadow. We know that genuinely equal opportunity is not a reality for many black Americans. Thus, until that reality has been achieved, to insist upon purely meritocratic standards above all, will be to lengthen that shadow of disadvantage that has darkened much of our past, extending it far into the future.

To understand where we are now and where we are going, another critical factor is the criteria by which one chooses to measure the progress of a society toward a true meritocracy. Those who are devotees of the most publicized media events in sports, politics, and entertainment might get a distorted view of the progress of blacks if they use as their sole index participation of blacks in the National Basketball League or the number of minority athletes in collegiate or professional sports. They might also overassess the progress of the black masses if they count the number of black or minority mayors in major American cities. For those who pay close attention to persons who sing and dance, they might view the applause for Michael Jackson, Prince, and Patti LaBelle as a barometer indicating that blacks as a group are extricating themselves from their disproportionate rates of poverty, unemployment and underemployment. Of course, I recognize and applaud the progress of blacks—whether on the stage, the political arena, the athletic fields, or the federal courts. However, since most Americans—whether black or white—cannot sing and dance like Michael Jackson; do not have the athletic prowess of "Dr. J", Kareem Abdul Jabar, the "Refrigerator Man", or Walter Payton; or the keen intellect of Associate Justice Thurgood Marshall, the lives of most black Americans are seldom in the spotlight of the communications media. Therefore, I submit that there are indices other than the number of blacks in these highly visible areas that must be considered. For me, the data on poverty, unemployment and educational attainment are more relevant in gauging the overall progress of blacks in recent decades. These were the indices used in two recent studies—one by the Children's Defense Fund and the other by the National Urban League—both of which indicate that black progress in recent years has slowed considerably.

In their extraordinary report released in 1985, the Children's Defense Fund describes the overall and comparative status of black and white children in America, the continuing inequality that plagues millions of black children, and the expensive waste in lives and dollars that results from our nation's failure to invest preventatively in all our young—black and white, affluent and poor alike. Using the government's own data, the report concludes that black children are sliding backwards. As evidence, the Children's Defense Fund cites that, "compared to five years ago, black children today are more likely to be born into poverty; lack early prenatal care; have an adolescent or single mother; have an unemployed parent; be unemployed themselves as teenagers; and not go to college after high school graduation.[13]

Children, of course, are not the only victims. It would be misleading to suggest that the disparity in quality of life among children now as compared to the recent past does not also exist throughout the entire black community. In their historic report on *The State of Black America 1985,* the National Urban League analyzed the decade of 1975–1985 to determine whether conditions have improved or grown worse. They concluded:

In virtually every area of life that counts, black people made strong progress in the 1960s, peaked in the 70s, and have been sliding back ever since. Much of this, but not all, is attributable to the shape of the American economy which has gone through some trying times, and is still not out of the woods, as far as black Americans can discern.

One measuring rod for answering the question [of progress] . . . is employment. In 1975, black unemployment was 14.1%, about double that of white unemployment (7.6%). At the end of 1984, black unemployment was 16%, *more than double* that of whites (6.5%). Constituting some 10% of the labor force, blacks account for 20% of the jobless.

The economy is not the only force that continues to operate against blacks. The national will to take positive steps to help set the scales of justice into balance has diminished tremendously over the past ten years, and has been replaced, in large measure, by a feeling that nothing more needs to be done and if blacks are still on the outside looking in, it's probably their own fault.[14]

Black Americans of all ages and abilities are plagued by this backward trend. According to H. Patrick Swygart, vice president of Temple University, so far in this decade the number of black Americans attending college and graduate and professional schools has dropped severely. Swygart notes that "the proportion of Black high school graduates enrolling in colleges and universities has dropped from 34 percent in 1976 to 27 percent in 1983" or "8,000 fewer Blacks were enrolled in colleges in 1983, although there were a half-million more Black high school graduates that year than in 1976." On the graduate level, Swygart's statistics note an even worse trend. "In 1983, the 325 institutions that award doctorates in the United States granted a total of 31,190 doctorates, but only 1,000 of these advanced degrees—less than 3 percent—went to Black students." This is largely a result of their inability to meet the cost of higher education due partly to the lack of government financial aid for higher learning, and partly to the tremendous disparities in income between Black and white families.[15]

As many note the progress that blacks have made in this nation, they are inclined to disregard the greater progress and attainment whites have made during the same period. As an example, the percentage of blacks who had completed four years of college increased dramatically from 1940 to 1975 from two percent to eleven percent. During that same period the percentage of whites had risen from 7 percent to 22 percent. Thus, even as late as 1975, although blacks progressed at a faster rate over a thirty-five year period, the actual proportion of whites completing college over the same period was still twice that for blacks. The heavily lopsided ratios in education, income and other quality-of-life criteria when applied to black children versus white children were graphically illustrated in the Children's Defense Fund study.

Compared to white children, black children are:

twice as likely to
- die in the first year of life
- be born prematurely
- suffer low birthweight
- have mothers who received late or no prenatal care
- be born to a teenage or single-parent family
- see a parent die
- live in substandard housing
- be suspended from school or suffer corporal punishment
- be unemployed as teenagers
- have no parent employed
- live in institutions;

three times as likely to
- be poor
- have their mothers die in childbirth
- live with a parent who has separated
- live in a female-headed family
- be placed in an educable mentally retarded class
- be murdered between five and nine years of age
- be in foster care
- die of known child abuse;

four times as likely to
- live with neither parent and be supervised by a child welfare agency
- be murdered before one year of age or as a teenager
- be incarcerated between 15 and 19 years of age;

five times as likely to
- be dependent on welfare
- become pregnant as teenagers; and

twelve times as likely to
- live with a parent who never married[16]

Nor are elderly blacks exempt from disparate conditions in quality of life due to race. The Urban League Report, *State of Black America 1985*, contains an article by Dr. Jacquelyne Johnson Jackson examining what she calls the "double jeopardy" of aged Black Americans. According to Dr. Jackson, this group lags far behind their white counterparts in income, state of health and overall living standard. For example, the overall life expectancy of white males and females is 71 and 78 years respectively. For black men and women it is 65 and 73 respectively.[17]

As we appraise where are we now and where are we going, I cannot stress too strongly that I am speaking of an America which provides both equal and viable opportunities. I am not urging for the mere elimination of disparities so that blacks and whites will both needlessly and equally suffer. For what does it profit us if all that we achieve is pervasive *integrated* poverty, extensive *integrated* slums, and indiscriminate *integrated* crime.

John E. Jacob closed his extraordinary keynote address at the National Urban League's 1984 Annual Conference with the rhetorical question, "What do black people want?" In response, he asserted:

> We want what white people want—decent jobs, homes and health care, and quality education for our kids so they can grow up in peace and dignity.
>
> We want an open society in which everybody has a chance to make it on their own—a society in which whiteness and wealth confer no special advantages—a society in which black people and poor people are full partners in democracy.
>
> We want a pluralistic society in which everybody can develop to the limits of their human talents—a society that honors the diversity of the multi-colored fabric of America.
>
> We want an integrated society in which race is no longer a barrier and whites and blacks are fully equal, in practice as in law.
>
> We want an America that nurtures its many peoples with respect for the divine spark that dwells within all of us—an America that moves beyond racism to a new era of progress and reconciliation.[18]

Just as we make judgments today of events surrounding the actions and perhaps the hypocrisies of forefathers such as Jefferson and his contemporaries, our generation will someday be evaluated by the high court of history. Future generations will not only question our racial attitudes but will probe deeply into the options we as a nation afforded to the weak, the poor, and the dispossessed. Our generation will not be immune from scholars a century and more hence questioning whether or not we also had distorted priorities. Will these students of history be struck by the irony that in a nation of many fine colleges and universities with high educational standards and achievement, thousands of children receive inadequate public school education? Or will they focus upon the contradiction of a nation that still has pervasive de facto segregation thirty years after its courts declared that state imposed (de jure) segregation would not be tolerated under American law? We have landed a man safely on the moon and several times have sent space shuttles into orbit, but we seem unable to create enough viable jobs for millions of our citizens who seek employment in order to make a better life for themselves. How will the future judge a nation with one of the highest standards of living in the world but also with 25 million persons living below the poverty level in hunger and hopelessness? Centuries from today, we will be judged on whether we were the best that we could have been, and by what distance we missed the mark in our human concerns. Will the verdict be that we have been as insensitive to the plight of black and other poor and powerless Americans as our forefathers were to the basic injustice of slavery? We must not cavalierly opt for profits instead of humanity, as did the slave owners of 200 years ago. This nation's extraordinary bounty affords us the means, even during periods of economic hardship, to rectify our human ills. We must not make economic and social justice contingent upon a "filtering down process" which assumes that the crumbs that fall off the tables of the affluent will be sufficient for those who are hungry, poor or disadvantaged.

As we confront the harsh data on disparities of many kinds, it is obvious that we do not make progress merely by condemning the pathology of disparity. Instead we must focus on systematic prevention or elimination of the causes. Much of the cure will depend on how one views the disease. Will one provide band-aids for sores and open wounds, and medications that only relieve the symptoms? Or can a vaccine be found by which society can immunize itself against the worst ravages of poverty, racism, sexism, and other unfairness in opportunities and results?

From my view, no one has put this problem in better perspective than Dr. James D. McGhee in the Urban League's 1985 report. In his chapter on "The Black Family Today and Tomorrow," he relates the following parable:

> One summer day two men were fishing from a boat in a briskly running stream. Suddenly, they began to see babies in the water floating downstream past the boat struggling and crying and trying to survive. One of the men in the boat quickly jumped into the water and began to catch as many babies as

he could, tossing them into the boat to save them from drowning. Meanwhile, his companion jumped over the other side of the boat and began to swim to shore. Seeing this, the first man shouted "wait! where are you going? Help me," as he continued trying to catch the babies and get them into the boat. The second person kept swimming to shore but paused to respond "you keep trying to save as many as you can, but I'm going upstream to stop that person from throwing them into the water in the first place."[19]

Will we as a nation have the wisdom and the strength to deter those persons who (sometimes even inadvertently) cause the dispossessed and the poor to flounder helplessly against the swift currents of poverty and despair? Will we have the sensitivity to become alarmed about the thousands of premature deaths described by Margaret M. Heckler, Secretary of the United States Department of Health and Human Services, in the Department's momentous study[20] as we have appropriate sorrow for innocent Marines who were killed in Lebanon?

Today, our priorities—not unusually—seem to lie in other directions—with the economy, the Middle East, South America, and the Soviet menace. Where in our nation's hierarchy of priorities will equality of opportunity and more equality in results be placed? In noting these disparities, I am not suggesting that these are problems that the federal and state governments can solve alone. I recognize also that blacks have a critical role in exerting their best and most systematic efforts to decrease the pathology and to motivate the disadvantaged among their own. Every day I see many blacks playing such a leadership role by their example, involvement and encouragement. But at the same time, we must recognize that these disparities and pathologies are of such a substantial extent that, as in the case of most of the poor and disadvantaged, poverty and despair will not disappear unless *all* Americans of good will, including every level of government, are as equally committed to the resolution of these problems as they are to some of the nation's other high priorities.

Our generation, as individuals and through our private and public institutions, must respond to the ambiguities and contradictions in our democratic process. Enlightened Americans must be wise and secure enough not to think that it is either bad taste or unpatriotic to study the frailties of our leaders, past or present. We must focus on their shortcomings just as we note with pride their victories and other noble accomplishments. Stressing the acquiescence and involvement in slavery by many of the most revered and distinguished citizens in our nation's history does not suggest that they did not make profound and extraordinary contributions to the birth of this nation. They were selected to illustrate that individuals as philosophical and reflective as Thomas Jefferson, as eloquent as Patrick Henry, as brave as George Washington, and as humanitarian as Abraham Lincoln, also contributed to the injustice which thousands of innocent human beings suffered. Since even these noble men were part of a system which caused such brutality, we should be aware that by our personal acquiescence, we similarly contribute to injustices which are as destructive of human dignity. As this view of history suggests, in the 1980s, as much as in any era in the past, citizens can and must play a vital role in objectively evaluating and alerting us to our often distorted priorities—even those established by good, well-meaning men and women. We must have the courage to seek the truth and to speak out against practices that fall short of our ideals, so that history will be able to say that our values and our priorities led us to strive valiantly to achieve the kind of world Martin Luther King envisioned when he dreamt:

> I have the audacity to believe that peoples everywhere can have three meals a day for their bodies, education and culture for their minds, and dignity, equality and freedom for their spirits.[21]

Notes

1. *Report of the National Advisory Commission on Civil Disorders* (Washington, D.C.: U.S. Government Printing Office, 1968), 1.
2. See Orlando Patterson, *Slavery and Social Death* (Cambridge, Mass.: Harvard University Press, 1982), vii, where he states, "There is nothing peculiar about the institution of slavery. It has existed from before the dawn of human history right down to the twentieth century, in the most primitive of human societies and in the most civilized."
3. *Virginia Gazette* (Purdie & Dixon), 14 Sept. 1769. (The advertisement first appeared in the preceding issue, 7 Sept., but the text is not available there because of mutilation.)
4. Nathan A. Windley, "Document: Runaway Slave Advertisements of George Washington and Thomas Jefferson," *Journal of Negro History* 53, 4 (Fall 1978): 373–74.
5. See "Taxation No Tyranny" in *The Works of Samuel Johnson* (Oxford: Talboys and Wheeler, 1825), vol. 6, 262.
6. As quoted in Lillian B. Miller, *"The Dye is Now Cast": The Road to American Independence, 1774–1776* (Washington, D.C.: Smithsonian Institution Press, 1975), 3.

7. Thomas Jefferson, *Notes on the State of Virginia* (New York: Harper and Row, 1964), 155–56 (emphasis added).
8. George S. Brooks, *Friend Anthony Benezet* (Philadelphia: University of Pennsylvania Press, 1937), 443 (emphasis added).
9. Paul Jacobs and Saul Landau with Eve Pell, *To Serve the Devil, Volume 1: Natives and Slaves* (New York: Vintage, 1971), 132–33.
10. Henry Steele Commager, ed., *Documents of American History,* eighth edition (New York: Appleton-Century-Crofts, Educational Division, 1968), 414–17.
11. Ibid., 418.
12. 347 US..S 483 (1954).
13. *Black and White Children in America: Key Facts* (Washington, D.C.: Children's Defense Fund, 1985), vii.
14. James D. Williams, ed., *The State of Black America 1985* (National Urban League, Inc., 1985), ii.
15. H. Patrick Swygart,"For Some, College Dream Ended . . . ," *Philadelphia Inquirer,* 12 November 1985, 15A.
16. *Black and White Children in America: Key Facts,* vii.
17. Jacquelyne Johnson Jackson, "Aged Black Americans' Double Jeopardy Reexamined," in *The State of Black America 1985,* 143–83.
18. John E. Jacob, Keynote Address at the 1984 National Urban League Annual Conference, quoted in John E. Jacob, "An Overview of Black America in 1984," in *The State of Black America 1985,* v.
19. James D. McGhee, "The Black Family Today and Tomorrow," in *The State of Black America 1985,* 1.
20. U.S. Department of Health and Human Services, *Report of the Secretary's Task Force on Black & Minority Health,* Margaret M. Heckler, Secretary (Washington, D.C.: U.S. Government Printing Office, 1985).
21. Martin Luther King, Jr., *The Words of Martin Luther King, Jr.,* selected by Coretta Scott King (New York: Newmarket Press, 1964), 25.

Notes on Contributors

James R. Abbott is presently teaching at Franklin and Marshall College, Lancaster, Pennsylvania. His essay is derived from his doctoral dissertation.

Elijah Anderson, author of *A Place on the Corner: A Study of Black Street-Corner Men*, is Professor of Sociology and Associate Director of the Center for Urban Ethnography at the University of Pennsylvania.

Harold J. Bershady teaches sociological theory in the Sociology Department of the University of Pennsylvania, where he has been arguing with and learning from Digby Baltzell for over 25 years. He has published *Ideology and Social Knowledge* and numerous professional papers. He is currently completing a study of the German sociologist-philosopher, Max Scheler. He is the editor of *Social Class and Democratic Leadership*.

Fred Block is Chairman of the Department of Sociology at the University of Pennsylvania. He has written *The Origins of International Economic Disorder* and *Revising State Theory: Essays in Politics and Postindustrialism*, and is co-author of *The Mean Season: The Attack on The Welfare State*. He is currently completing a manuscript on "The Economic Sociology of Postindustrialism." He teaches in the Sociology Department at the University of Pennsylvania.

Laura B. Farmelo is a visiting scholar at Columbia University School of Law (1987–88). She holds a J. D. from the University of Pennsylvania Law School and is a Ph.D. candidate in Sociology at the University of Pennsylvania. She has done extensive research with the Rt. Honorable Judge A. Leon Higginbotham, Jr. on race and American law, and is currently working on a study of law and social change in the Republic of South Africa.

Richard Farnum is a Ph.D. candidate in Sociology at the University of Pennsylvania and Assistant Professor of Sociology at the University of the Arts in Philadelphia. His principal areas of interest are the sociology of education and the sociology of culture.

Frank F. Furstenberg, Jr. is Professor of Sociology and Research Associate in the Population Studies Center at the University of Pennsylvania. His interest in the American family began at Columbia University where he received his Ph.D. in 1967. His most recent books include *Recycling the Family* with Graham Spanier (1984), *The New American Grandparent* with

Andrew J.Cherlin (1986) and *Adolescent Mothers in Later Life* with J. Brooks-Gunn and S. Philip Morgan (1987). He has published numerous articles on teenage sexuality, pregnancy, and childbearing as well as divorce, remarriage, and stepparenting.

The Rt. Honorable A. Leon Higginbotham, Jr., Federal judge on the Third Circuit Court of Appeals, graduated from Antioch College and received his L.L.B. from Yale Law School. He has taught at the Law Schools of the University of Pennsylvania, New York University, Harvard University, Stanford University, Yale University, and the University of Michigan. Judge Higginbotham has received critical acclaim for his book, *In the Matter of Color,* and is currently writing volume two of that series. He has received more that fifty local and national awards, and over thirty honorary degrees. Judge Higginbotham is a life-term trustee of the University of Pennsylvania and an Adjunct Professor in the University's Department of Sociology.

Jerry A. Jacobs is Associate Professor of Sociology at the University of Pennsylvania. His research has focused on social mobility. His book on women's career patterns, *Revolving Doors: Sex Segregation and Women's Careers,* is forthcoming from Stanford University Press. Research in progress includes a study of promotions within a large bureaucracy and a study of the career patterns of physicians.

Samuel Z. Klausner, psychologist and sociologist, is Professor of Sociology at the University of Pennsylvania and an associate in its Energy Management and Policy Program. He has also taught at Columbia University, Union Theological Seminary, The Hebrew University in Jerusalem, Al Mansoura University in Egypt, and Muhammad V University in Morocco. Among his recent books are *Eskimo Capitalists* (with Edward Foulks) and *The Nationalization of the Social Sciences* (with Victor M. Lidz). He recently completed a study of religious, racial, and gender factors affecting executive careers, from which the contribution to this volume is selected.

Victor M. Lidz received his training in sociology at Harvard University from the late Talcott Parsons. Most of his writings have been contributions to the general theory of action. He is one of the editors of *Explorations in General Theory in Social Science* and, with Samuel Z. Klausner, edited *The Nationalization of the Social Sciences.* He was a colleague of E. Digby Baltzall's in the Department of Sociology at the University of Pennsylvania and has also taught at the University of Chicago, St. Joseph's University, and Haverford College.

Samuel H. Preston is Director of the Population Studies Center at the University of Pennsylvania. His principal areas of interest are mortality, marriage and divorce, and mathematical demography. He is a past–president of the Population Association of America.

Michael Zuckerman is Professor of History at the University of Pennsylvania. He recalls with special pleasure the time he coaxed Digby into attending his first Penn-Princeton basketball game.

Index

Abbott, James, 13, 14

Acheson, Dean, 221

Achievement: and privilege, 269ff.; and Puritans, 203; and social esteem, 203, 204; standards of, 4, 7, 12, 18, 69, 72, 162ff.; vs. patronage, 270; represented by Boston, 205; represented by Philadelphia, 205; *see also* Cities; Democracy; Farnum; Lidz; Political parties

Adams, Henry, 275

Adams, John Quincy, 248, 253, 254, 256, 257, 259, 262, 263, 266

Aiken, Michael, x

American Journal of Sociology, 113

Amherst College, 4

Anarchists: *see* Chicago

Anderson, Bernard, 129, 143, 145

Anderson, Elijah, 14, 129, 132, 145, 214

Anderson, Perry, 185, 197

Andover, 3

Anti-Federalists, 243ff.

Arieli, Yehoshua, 272

Ariès, Philippe, 50

Aristocracy, 6; and agrarian style of life, 16, 181, 183; and American political life, 17, 236ff.; and business, 33, 181, 185, 191; and conflict between nobility and monarchy, 184ff.; and rejection of commerce by, 183ff.; and rise of capitalism, 16, 181ff., 190; and the Constitution, 18, 237ff.; consumption patterns of in England, 15, 185ff.; consumption patterns of in France, 15, 191ff.; derogeance among European, 192ff.; education of English, 186; emphasis on display of, 183; "natural," of virtue and talent, 17, 18, 238, 242–244, 259, 260, 267, 268; social condition of, 235; Spanish, 249; status ethic of, 15, 182ff.; *see also* Abbott; Authority; Block; Jacobs;

Leaders; Lidz; Political parties; Status ethics; Tocqueville

Aristotle, 239

Articles of Confederation, 242

Auchincloss, Louis, 4, 19

Authority, 17; and accountability, 217ff.; and adaptability, 218, 220; and authoritarian style, 223ff.; and elites, 216ff.; and persuasion, 17, 227ff.; and upper class, 3–5, 17, 216, 217; aristocratic, 7, 216, 217, 218; as modern problem, 216ff.; charismatic, 218, 225; conservative view of, 216ff.; democratic, 17, 218; informal modes of, 217; legal-rational, 218; post industrial, 17, 223ff., 229; radical view of, 216ff.; representative, 223, 246ff.; traditional, 218; Weber's typology of, 218ff.; *see also* Aristocracy; Block; Leader; Lidz; Political parties

Azarya, Victor, 197

Bailyn, Bernard, 271, 272, 273

Baltimore, 83ff.

Baltzell, E. Digby, ix, x, 1, 2, 3, 4, 5, 6, 7, 8, 9, 10, 12, 15, 17, 18, 19, 33, 34, 69, 70, 71, 87, 88, 90, 91, 93, 103, 120, 147, 178, 201, 204, 213, 214, 216, 219, 220, 221, 235, 245, 271, 272, 273

Banneker, Benjamin, 282

Banning, Lance, 271

Baptists, 40ff.

Barber, Elinor, 192, 194, 197

Barraclough, G., 215

Bauman, Richard, 50

Beard, Charles, 271

Becker, Howard S., 145

Behrens, C. B. A., 192, 197

Bell, Daniel, 196, 198

Bellah, Robert, 51, 271

Benjamin, Walter, 215

Bennis, Warren, 230